Lives Remembered

The Times
Obituaries of 1991

Lives Remembered

THE TIMES OBITUARIES OF 1991

Edited by

David Heaton and John Higgins

Foreword by

Lord Annan

THE BLEWBURY PRESS

Published by The Blewbury Press
Fordata House, Station Road, Pangbourne,
Berkshire, RG8 7AN, England

Cover design by Peter Medcalf

© Times Newspapers Limited, 1991
ISBN 0 9518282 0 7

Typeset by Avocet Typesetters, Bicester, Oxon
Printed in Great Britain by Biddles Ltd, The City Press,
Guildford, Surrey

ACKNOWLEDGEMENTS

The publishers would like to thank the following relatives and organisations for their kind permission to reproduce the photographs in this book.

Mrs Joan Davenport (p. 3), Commander C P Powlett (p. 8), Royal Norwegian Ministry of Foreign Affairs (p. 11), The Devonshire Regiment (p. 16), Atomic Energy Authority (p. 41), Lady Batsford (p. 48), Mr Tim Motion (pp. 54, 55, 144), Mr John Aarvold (p. 58), Viscount De L'Isle (p. 78), Mr Mark Orr (p. 87), Lady St-Clair Ford (p. 89), Torres Wines Ltd (p. 96), Mrs Eleanor Boyle (p. 100), Miss J H H Green (p. 108), W H Smith (p. 120), GRAMMOPHON/Betz (p. 129), The Cinema Museum (p. 183), Mr Jamie Stewart (p. 200), Healey & Baker (p. 210), Mr A Beevor (p. 214), Weidenfeld & Nicolson Limited (p. 223), Mrs Helen Beaumont (p. 232), Racal Electronics plc (p. 234), The Evening Standard (p. 240), Land Rover (p. 244), Rt. Hon. Tony Wedgwood Benn (p. 270), Imperial War Museum (p. 306), The King's Regiment (p. 346).

EDITORS' NOTE

The Obituaries are presented in a chronological order similar to that in which they appeared in *The Times* during 1991.

THE CONTRIBUTORS

The publishers wish to acknowledge their gratitude for the co-operation and guidance of *The Times* team of obituaries writers Peter Davies, Peter Evans and Michael Knipe.

CONTENTS

vii

Contents

FOREWORD
by Lord Annan

During the war a story circulated about a Regimental Sergeant-Major in the Brigade of Guards instructing in stentorian tones the bearer party before a military funeral. "On raising the coffin to the shoulder, let the face assume a melancholy harspect — such as will please the relatives — and the corpse HAS A RIGHT TO EXPECT".

In days gone by in an obituary the corpse could expect to be embalmed in the formal pieties of sepulchral utterance. The voice of criticism was stilled, no breeze of scandal disturbed the air, and before all else the obituarist put the feelings of the bereaved. The sardonic called the formula *De mortuis nil nisi bunkum*. Connoisseurs of obituaries learnt to read between the lines. My college at Cambridge, King's, which was remarkable in printing lengthy obituaries of its graduates, used on occasions certain coded language. "He died suddenly" was a euphemism for suicide. "He died unmarried" well, one could make of that what one wished. "He died in Northampton" could mean that the old Kingsman had lost his marbles before the end and had died in the hospital there for the insane.

Why did the style of obituaries change? Partly because the profile became in the fifties a popular feature first in the Sundays and then in the dailies. The profile made the Great and the Good more human: what was it like to meet this man (rarely this woman) who was in the news? The rules for the profile were simple. No flattery. Show the defects as well as the merits. But don't try to be clever at the subject's expense and score off him. Don't retail malice which the prominent attract like magnets. Accustomed to read such lively accounts of the living, readers expected something more than the inscription on a monumental slab for the dead. They wanted a portrait.

The most startling change in obituaries occurred when the *Independent* was launched. Since it had no file of obituaries stored away, this new quality newspaper encouraged close friends to write much more informally, their exuberance being held in check by the fact that each obit was signed. Yet *The Times*, though it carried a backlog of obits and could not change its style so dramatically, had in fact been altering its style. Friends were made more welcome to add postscripts or corrections. More distinguished foreigners appeared. Fleet Street had always been generous in honouring the memory of its staff, management as well as editors and journalists, but now broadcasters, editors of glossies, fashion queens and designers were remembered. Performers as well as authors and composers, maestros of jazz as well as of great orchestras, pop singers as well as actors or movie stars featured. Great cricketers such as Jack Hobbs or Len Hutton were now joined by the idols of the football terraces and the champions of snooker. The one time darlings of West End matinée audiences were matched by the more familiar figures of television soaps and sitcoms. Occasionally the unsung heroines of the social services found a place. In this volume notorious criminals rub shoulders with Rear Admirals, businessmen and trade unionists begin to outnumber civil servants, and a French Marxist historian is flanked by ballerinas.

The art of the obituarist lies in selecting the telling phrase or event that prints the dead upon the mind for ever. The French pop star Serge Gainsbourg appearing on television "made earthily explicit suggestions to the singer Whitney Houston to the predictable outrage of 17 million viewers, his employers on Channel 2 and Miss Houston herself." Wilfred Hyde White, who after years on the stage made his name as the British Council official in *The Third Man*, "enjoyed working but only, it appeared, if a studio was within easy reach of a racecourse". Appearing aged 75 in the bankruptcy court and upbraided by the Official Receiver for a lifetime of spending money on fast women, fast cars and slow horses, Hyde White offered him a tip but counselled only a small bet. "We don't want to change places, do we?" Sometimes the obituarist achieves his effect through surprise. Elaine Burton struck terror into the hearts of many ministers at question time in the House of Lords so persistent was she, so much the mistress of every pertinent fact, so quick to unmask governmental ineptitude, sloth, indifference and evasion: yet how many of them knew she was junior sprint champion of the world at the age of sixteen?

Some of the most effective obituaries are of those who are all of a piece: like Jean Rook, the great Fleet Street toughie who "would do almost anything for a story" but was a genuine circulation puller. The most admirable are those of difficult complex characters like the brilliant publisher of a new style of children's books. Sebastian Walker was a delightful host. Yet how could his acquaintances have guessed that he was so aggressive in business that his top associates were always leaving? Or there was Laura Riding, for long Robert Graves's companion on Majorca, considered by a minority as the most important woman poet of the century to whom "recognition may well come more easily without her abrasive presence".

Profiles have changed in recent years, and are used to ridicule and expose the failings of the victim. In obituaries the harsh truth is rarely spoken. The death of the Soviet general Boris Pugo, who was a leader in the coup of 1991 to overthrow Gorbachev and shot himself when it failed, "will be regretted by Soviet hard-liners but by few, if any, others". Eyebrows shot up when *The Times* obituary of the ballet dancer and choreographer Robert Helpmann — while doing justice to his genius as a mimic and his flair for the big effect — referred to him as "a homosexual of the proselytising kind who could turn young men on the borderline his way". But some of the old reticences remain. Coral Browne is praised for her versatility, combining every gift in comedy with outstanding performances as Lady Macbeth and Gertrude. An allusion is made to her "robust humour off-stage as renowned as her performance on it": which is one way of saying that her conversation was peppered with four letter words to dazzling effect — some faint hint of which appeared when she played herself in Alan Bennett's television drama *An Englishman Abroad*.

Perhaps some reticence is just as well. Obituaries are not official biographies, still less the biographies of thirty of fifty years later, when skeletons have dropped out of cupboards and the efforts of the dead to hide their secrets are shown to have been in vain. We can do without such sentences as "Gruff in manner though he might be and not one to suffer fools gladly, a heart of gold lay behind his forbidding exterior". But when death strikes, the feelings of those who cherished the dead should be respected, even if the obituarist observes the rule laid down by Leslie Stephen, the first editor of the DNB, "No flowers by request".

SIR ALEC ROSE

Sir Alec Rose, the round-the-world yachtsman, died in hospital on January 12 aged 82. He was born on July 13, 1908.

ALEC Rose, a shy, quietly-spoken green-grocer, captured the public's imagination in 1968 by following in the wake of Sir Francis Chichester, sailing around the world alone in his 36ft ketch-rigged yacht *Lively Lady*, shunning publicity and sponsorship. He was neither the first, nor the fastest, but sailing quietly around the world, minding his own business, he showed that tenacity, a good boat, and careful preparation, not money and publicity, were the key ingredients of success.

Although he had served in the RNVR during the second world war Rose did not

1

take up sailing as a hobby until 1959, when he bought a German lifeboat and converted it. He had begun his working life farming in Canada, returning to England as a haulage contractor before the war.

He called the 27,000 mile voyage "a personal adventure" and had dreamed of completing the circumnavigation since his boyhood days. "I always wanted to sail round Cape Horn. I felt it was the ultimate aim of a man and his ship," he said on his return.

His first attempt in 1966, the same year that Francis Chichester set out for Australia alone, ended in failure. After setting out from his home port of Portsmouth, Rose had to put into Plymouth for repairs. Once back at sea, *Lively Lady* was rammed at night by a ship and then, back in Portsmouth for more repairs, he was forced to abandon the voyage when the boat fell on her side, adding to the damage.

There were many who laughed at his expense but, undaunted, Rose set out from Portsmouth a second time on July 16, 1967, amazed at the thousands who lined the shore to bid him farewell. "I felt rather a fraud having such a wonderful send-off for the second time in a year," he said later. He shunned publicity throughout, telling his wife Dorothy, who stayed at home to run the family greengrocery business in Southsea, that he did not want any of that "Chichester ballyhoo".

After 114 days at sea, *Lively Lady* came close to being dismasted during a Southern Ocean gale when part of her rigging snapped. Aged 59, Rose was forced to climb the wildly swaying mast several times to replace the wires, leaving his thighs raw and bleeding with the effort of clinging to the mast. He finally reached Melbourne on December 17, 1967, after spending 155 days at sea, 52 more than Chichester's time to Australia.

After repairing and repainting his yacht, Rose set sail for Cape Horn, but ran into another storm in the Tasman sea which forced him to put into Bluff on the southern-most tip of New Zealand to await spare parts being flown out from England. Mid-way across the Pacific, he was overcome by fumes while repairing the exhaust pipe and lay unconscious for two hours. Rose finally reached the infamous Cape on April Fool's Day 1968 where he was seen limping around *Lively Lady*'s deck after twisting his knee badly in a fall.

Four months later, 354 days after leaving Portsmouth, Alec Rose returned to a tumultuous welcome from 250,000 people to learn from a naval officer as he stepped ashore that the Queen had given him a knighthood on the advice of the prime minister "for his tenacity, skill and courage".

He returned to run the family green-grocery business until retiring in 1971, but devoted much of his spare time to raising funds for the Royal National Lifeboat Institution. Thanks to Sir Alec's efforts more than £20 million (in today's money values) was raised for the institution in the 22 years since his circum-navigation. He was one of 30 honorary life governors, the highest honour awarded to supporters of the RNLI. In 1969, Sir Alec launched the RNLI's national membership scheme, now titled "Shoreline", which boasts a 200,000 strong membership. In 1973 he led an appeal in Hampshire for an £85,000 Rother Class lifeboat, *Hampshire Rose* (named after the symbol for the county, not Sir Alec) which was launched the following year and remained on station at Walmer, Kent until last year. Eleven years ago, he was also responsible for the launching of a second lifeboat, the 37ft *Shoreline* which cost £150,000 and was stationed at Blyth until being transferred to Arbroath.

After his voyage, Sir Alec was awarded the Blue Water Medal by the Cruising Club of America and the Seamanship Medal by the Royal Cruising Club. He was also given the Freedom of Portsmouth on his triumphant return and made a Freeman of the City of London a year later.

Sir Alec is survived by his second wife Dorothy and four children.

REAR ADMIRAL DUDLEY DAVENPORT

Rear Admiral Dudley Leslie Davenport, former captain of the aircraft carrier Victorious, and later Flag Officer Malta, has died, aged 71. He was born on August 17, 1919.

DUDLEY Davenport's long and distinguished naval career was nearly terminated a few years after it began when the destroyer *Blanche* in which he was serving as a sub lieutenant struck a magnetic mine off Margate shortly after the outbreak of the second world war. He owed his life to the toss of a coin.

The mines had been sown along the Thames estuary the previous night by a flotilla of German destroyers operating under the cover of thick fog. As the unsuspecting British warship, escorting a battle cruiser through the Channel, neared the German minefield early next day, the young Davenport tossed a half crown piece with his fellow officer on the nightwatch to decide which of them would go below first for an early bath.

He won. The other officer died in the explosion which followed minutes later. Davenport, though knocked unconscious by the blast, survived with a hairline fracture of the skull — and a memorable headline in the *Daily Mirror*: "Bloody officer found in bath." Then aged 20 he was already known to the navy as the son of Vice-Admiral R.C. Davenport, who had been brought back from retirement for convoy duties in the trans-Atlantic sea lanes.

When news of the sinking of the *Blanche* came through, a thoughtful officer in the Admiralty sent a signal to the vice-admiral's convoy which was then in the Western Approaches to assure him that his son had survived the disaster. But young Dudley had already won some distinction on his own. Not long after leaving Dartmouth where he was a member of the Hawke term, he was mentioned in despatches when only a midshipman while on security duties off the coast of Palestine.

The sinking of the *Blanche* was, moreover, a dramatic start to what was to be for him an eventful war. After recovering from his injuries he was back at sea in February 1940, this time in the Tribal class destroyer *Mashona*, taking part in the Norwegian campaign and then in the following year in the hunt for the *Bismarck*. While returning from this operation, he escaped with his life for the second time. The Luftwaffe bombed the *Mashona* in the Atlantic, 100 miles to the west of Ireland. More than 40 sailors lost their lives, but Davenport was among the lucky ones to be plucked from the sea by the destroyer's sister ship, the *Somali*. The young officer who hauled him from the sea was Ludovic Kennedy.

After five years of almost continuous action Dudley Davenport was rewarded in 1945 with the command of his own destroyer, the *Holmes*, followed by another destroyer HMS *Porlock Bay*. Like others of his generation who served throughout the war Dudley Davenport learned much from his early experience as a young officer. He took the navy's own staff course in this country, commanded the naval barracks at Chatham and between 1958-60 served on the staff of the Admiral commanding reserves. He did two years in command of the inshore flotilla in the Far East and in 1962 was made director of officer appointments (seaman's branch).

He went to sea again in command of the *Victorious* 1964-7, and in 1967-9, was made Flag Officer Malta.

3

MILES COPELAND

Miles Copeland, former CIA agent, died on January 14 aged 77. He was born on July 16, 1913.

MILES Copeland was a robustly colourful figure, the least secret of former CIA secret agents, who in a best-selling book called *The Game of Nations* and in many articles and broadcast discussions expounded his ideas both about the proper role of covert political action and about the Middle East, where he had been, for several years, very close to Colonel Nasser. A genial bear of a man, he remained almost ostentatiously American, although he enjoyed living mainly in England. Some of his erstwhile colleagues disapproved of such flamboyance, but no-one could question his loyalty or his zeal, any more than his generosity and sociability. Seeking to explain why he had not fitted easily into the Ivy League bureaucracy of the CIA, he once described himself as "an old jazz pianist and riverboat gambler". He was indeed technically qualified for those exotic professions: but, as his record and the width of his acquaintance showed, he was a much more sophisticated operator than he sometimes appeared.

He was born in Birmingham, Alabama, the son of Dr Miles Axe Copeland, who was well known for his work on geriatrics (and himself lived to the age of 97), and Leonora Armstrong Copeland, a school-teacher. He graduated from Ramsay High School and had a quickly discontinued brush with higher education at the University of Alabama; the most useful things he had learned, he would say, were how to play the trumpet and how to calculate the odds at blackjack and poker. He became a trumpeter and arranger for various bands, including those of Ray Noble and Glenn Miller, and was the first white musician to play with Erskine Hawkins's "big band" at the Cotton Club.

In November 1940 he joined the army, having been led by Glenn Miller to believe that an army dance band was about to be formed under Miller's direction. In the event he found himself entertaining the troops only during off-duty hours; his principal duty was to assist the medical corps. After a few months he scored a record grade in the US military IQ test and was transferred to an "intelligence pool" in Washington. A congressman from Alabama introduced him to General "Wild Bill" Donovan, head of the Office of Strategic Services. He was commissioned and assigned to test the security of government installations. In August 1941 he was moved to the American embassy in London as a counter-espionage specialist.

As soon as he arrived in England, he said afterwards, he felt as though he might have lived there in a previous life and determined to make it his home. The following year he married Lorraine Adey, the daughter of a Harley Street neurosurgeon. After D-Day he was sent to France and slipped into Paris ahead of the allied forces in an attempt to make contact with the German commander. When the war ended, he was immediately recalled to Washington, where he joined the Pentagon's "Strategic Services Unit", which was to convert the OSS into the civilian CIA.

In 1947, having been ostensibly seconded to the State Department, he joined the legation in Damascus, where his principal job was to work with the Syrian armed forces, supervising the secret assistance being given by America to the Chief of Staff, Colonel Husni Za'im. His most dramatic adventure was a 22-minute shoot-out with pistols in his own house against intruders who suspected him of being a CIA agent.

Feeling the need to make some money, he resigned from the CIA in 1953 and joined Booz-Allen and Hamilton, management consultants, on whose behalf he undertook the reorganisation of various Egyptian government departments. Gamal Abdel Nasser, who was then deputy prime minister, asked him to become an adviser to the Egyptian general intelligence agency. When Nasser succeeded General Neguib as president, Copeland resigned from Booz-Allen to become personal adviser to Nasser and to the head of the intelligence agency. He had retained an informal connection with the CIA and now acted as liaison officer between the two services. Subsequently, according to one of his favourite stories, he was asked by the CIA to propose a scheme for Nasser's assassination. Regarding the idea as absurd, he discussed possible assassination methods with Nasser himself, and was pleased to report that the security precautions which he and his colleagues had instituted would render any such attempt impracticable.

Rejoining the CIA in 1955, as head of a five-man political action unit, he helped to organise a "games room" in Washington, where international problems could be imaginatively played out. Much of his function, he thought, was to explain Nasser's point of view to the State Department and the White House and to counterbalance the effect of the Jewish lobby. He always insisted that he was not specifically pro-Arab or anti-Israeli, simply pro-American: but, like many foreign service officers whose experience has been principally in Arab countries, he tended not to understand Israel.

Meanwhile the CIA itself was changing, growing larger, more bureaucratic and politicised. He argued against many of the schemes which his unit was supposed to assist. He disapproved of most paramilitary operations, not in the least on moral grounds but because he believed them inherently futile. His concept of political action meant using "agents of influence" within the target country, encouraging factions which were helpful to the United States and discouraging those which were unhelpful; work which must be covert only because, if it were publicly known, it would become ineffective.

The CIA's new policies were not the only aspect which he found uncongenial. He felt himself an outsider among its standard-model functionaries. In May 1957 he retired again, this time permanently, although he considered himself, and was generally accepted as, a "loyal alumnus". He took lucrative commissions as a business consultant, chiefly to oil companies in the Middle East, while at the same time, for example, keeping an eye on Kim Philby in Beirut at the request of James Angleton, the CIA officer most convinced of Philby's guilt.

He wrote two books, *The Game of Nations* and *Without Cloak or Dagger* (in Britain called *The Real Spy World*), expounding his theory of "political action" as a game − or interlocking games, since he distinguished between "the international game", "the domestic game", "the bureaucratic game" and "the personal game". Officially he cleared what he wrote: but it is easy to see why the stuffier members of his trade disapproved of him. When his work for the oil companies dwindled, he acquired other commissions concerning the interplay of politics and business in the Middle East.

His home, however, was always in England. In 1986 he suffered a severe car accident in London, from which he never fully recovered: but he wrote an autobiography, *The Game Player*, published in 1989. "I am," he said, "100 per cent capitalist and imperialist, a believer in Mom, apple pie, baseball, the corner drugstore, and even American style democracy − for us, anyhow, even if I doubt its relevance in many of the alien cultures in which I've worked."

SIR DAVID PIPER

Sir David Towry Piper, CBE, director of the Ashmolean Museum, Oxford, from 1973 to 1985, died aged 72. He was born on July 21, 1918.

BRITAIN has the ability to throw up museum and gallery directors who are articulate and much more broadly steeped in civilisation than is strictly necessary even for the jobs they hold. Sir David Piper illumined the English scene not just as a museum director, for which he was amply qualified, but also as an author of books on London and portraiture and even as a novelist.

Not surprisingly, he never threw off his interest in faces — his books showed his fascination with the way artists saw them — which went with his job as an assistant keeper at the National Portrait Gallery in 1946, then as director, keeper and secretary between 1964-7. His career also took off into the academic world and spanned Oxbridge: as well as becoming director and Marlay curator of the Fitzwilliam Museum in Cambridge, he was elected fellow of Christ's College. He was Slade professor of fine art at Oxford from 1966-7; and Clark lecturer (1977-8) then Rede lecturer (1983) at Cambridge.

His greatest triumph was his direction of the Ashmolean Museum. There had previously been no director of the museum, its direction having been in the hands of whoever was the senior departmental keeper at the time. By 1967 there were four departments that had become accustomed to a degree of independence that was sometimes unruly. To keep the balance, a greater degree of centralisation of the museum was decided upon, and in 1973 Piper was appointed the first director, and elected fellow of Worcester College.

If the four departments were on the look-out for interference in their affairs, they met with none, for he stepped on no toes. Never interfering in detail but always being accessible, he gave the departments free rein to develop their individualities and their diversity. With his firm aesthetic standards, his clear idea of what needed to be done, and his way of getting it done, he directed the museum with self-confidence, unobtrusive strength, subtle diplomacy, and gentle irony. His professional knowledge of the museum world greatly strengthened the Ashmolean, and his cautiously sympathetic attitude to innovation moved it with the times in a changing Oxford.

Something of his personal ideals comes out in *Trial by Battle*, a second world war novel, which chose jungle fighting against the Japanese as the ordeal. Piper's own health suffered when he was captured by the Japanese on the Malaysian Peninsula while serving with the 9th Jat Regiment of the Indian Army.

Alan Mart, his hero or victim, is of a kind once very common in English fiction: quiet, civil, sensitive, questioning but obedient. Evidently from a public school, he has since been to Cambridge, and almost forgotten the necessity to conform and to emulate more sturdy, spontaneous males. Without implying a comparison, Piper went to Clifton College and then to St Catharine's College, Cambridge.

He was very early on fascinated by *The English Face*, the title of a book he produced in 1957 when on the staff of the National Portrait Gallery. Already his scholarship was being directed by an unusually perceptive imagination. He assembled 145 portraits from the beginning of naturalistic portraiture in 1400, to 1900. He said the object was to show how their relationship to the flesh and blood which they represented was controlled — by artistic and sartorial fashions, by the individualities of the sitter and the artist, and how through time that relationship altered. The book indicated his ability to discern subterranean movements that give rise to change, as well as to see it analytically in an historic context.

The faces of London and Oxford were hardly less fascinating to him. In 1964 he wrote *The Companion Guide to London*, which *The Times* said turned out to be a surprisingly rare thing, a book about London that deserved to be read as

literature. "Strangers no less than citizens will find Mr Piper a lively civilised companion as well as guide."

He returned to his subject to write *London* in 1971, which showed that being civilised involves discernment and does not mean acceptance of the merely monumental. He described the tombs and monuments in Westminster Abbey as "the paraphernalia of the illustrious English dead".

His two interests came together in *Artists' London* (1982), which begins with Tudor and Stuart cartographers and leaves the reader wondering with him why the railways did not inspire great art; or why — apart from Ford Madox Brown's *Work* set in Hampstead High Street — London did not appeal to the Pre-Raphaelites. There was no question in his mind about the master: "The moodiest, most haunting visual poetry that has ever been spun out of London was Monet's."

The breadth of his scholarship was again disclosed in the sumptuous *Treasures of Oxford*, a guide to all the art collections in the university and city of Oxford, with an excursion to Blenheim Palace. The survey was illustrated by more than 120 reproductions.

He leaves a widow, Anne, and a son and three daughters.

REAR-ADMIRAL PHILIP POWLETT

Rear-Admiral Philip Powlett, CB, DSO and bar, DSC, DL, wartime destroyer captain, died on January 15 aged 84. He was born on November 13, 1906.

ONE of the most dashing escort captains of his day, Philip Powlett had an active and highly successful war afloat – which was where he best liked to be – much of it in the destroyer *Blankney* which he commanded from early in 1941 to the end of 1942. These were tough years for convoy escorts, a period well before the U-boat menace had been thoroughly mastered, and their commanding officers required nerves of steel. These Powlett possessed in abundance, as well as a thorough mastery of ship handling and a flair for anti-submarine tactics.

Philip Frederick Powlett was born into a naval family. His father was Vice-Admiral F. A. Powlett, whose father, too, had been an admiral. Philip Powlett went to Osborne and Dartmouth, and went to sea as a midshipman in the cruiser *Hawkins*. Between the wars he had a wide variety of sea appointments in ships ranging from sloops to aircraft carriers. By 1939 he had been the first lieutenant of two ships and it was entirely appropriate that he should have got his first command, that of the corvette *Shearwater*, in the very month the second world war broke out. He was immediately employed on convoy duties down the east coast during the phoney war period, but in the aftermath of the Blitzkrieg *Shearwater* was among the ships which were required to go close inshore under the Wehrmacht's guns in two separate operations to sink block ships at

Zeebrugge and Dieppe in an attempt to deny the use of their harbours to the Germans. For his part in these actions Powlett was mentioned in dispatches.

In February 1941 he was given command of the newly-commissioned destroyer escort *Blankney* to begin the two most action-packed years of his war. In May he won his DSC for an action which demonstrated his superb ship-handling skills. While *Blankney* was on escort duty off the east coast of Scotland one of the freighters of the convoy was attacked by German aircraft and set on fire. Soon blazing fiercely, she was in imminent danger of sinking with all hands. Powlett unhesitatingly brought his ship alongside and took off her crew before this happened.

His first DSO came in December 1941 when *Blankney* was based at Gibraltar. Acting in concert with the other escorts, *Blankney* had a hand in the sinking of two U-boats, the second of which, U-434, Powlett rammed after it had been forced to the surface by depth charges. The next 12 months were ones of ceaseless escort duties under heavy air attack as the Royal Navy undertook to keep beleaguered Malta supplied. In June 1942 *Blankney* was involved in the Harpoon convoy to Malta which came under particularly heavy air attack as well as being molested by Italian warships. Four out of the six freighters were sunk before the convoy reached Malta, but the entire convoy might well have been lost had it not been for the skill of Powlett and his fellow escort captains who fought off Italian cruisers and destroyers which tried to close with the convoy. Powlett won his second DSO in these actions and was later awarded the Polish Cross of Valour by a grateful Polish government who appreciated the lengths he had gone to to pick up the survivors of one of their ships which had strayed into a minefield laid by the allies close to Malta.

Powlett had already had experience of Arctic convoys, when *Blankney* was in the escort of PQ-16 in May 1942. After her hectic period in the Mediterranean she found herself back on the Archangel run

in July, in the covering force for PQ-17 of tragic memory. Fearing attack by the German battleship *Tirpitz*, the Admiralty issued and then countermanded orders to both covering force and close escort which led to the convoy being left at the mercy of the U-boats, with catastrophic results. In September *Blankney* escorted two more Russian convoys, PQ-18 and PQ-14.

When his period in command of *Blankney* came to an end Powlett had a spell on the staff of Admiral Cunningham in the Mediterranean where he helped set up a mobile naval defence organisation for North Africa. But he was soon back at sea commanding destroyers, notably *Cassandra*. Immediately after the war he commanded a training cruiser before going for a spell to the operations division at the Admiralty. Among postings in the 1950s were command of the Royal Naval College, Greenwich, and a period as deputy director of naval air organisation and training before two rewarding years commanding the 6th Frigate Squadron. From 1956 to 1958 he was director of the Joint Anti-Submarine School and Senior Naval Officer Northern Ireland. His final appointment was as Flag Officer and Admiral Superintendent, Gibraltar.

He retired in 1962 to a mill house on the river Wensum at Lyng, Near Dereham, Norfolk. He was much involved in the life of the county of which he was made a Deputy Lieutenant in 1974. He was also a member of the Friends of Norwich Cathedral to which he rendered great services. During 15 years as its secretary he oversaw a doubling of its membership, started a youth section, and transformed it into a highly effective body which raised hundreds of thousands of pounds towards the task of re-roofing the cathedral after major repairs had been carried out to the spire. He was also a high steward of the cathedral and a lay reader.

Powlett was twice married, first, in 1935, to Elizabeth Elwell who died in 1987. In 1988 he married Desiree Leyden. She survives him with two sons and a daughter of the first marriage.

KING OLAV V OF NORWAY

King Olav V of Norway, whose reign began on September 21, 1957, died on January 17 in Oslo aged 87. He was born on July 2, 1903.

NORWAY'S King Olav V had strong personal links with Britain. Olav was the son and only child of Princess Maud, the third daughter of King Edward VII. Born in England, he spent two years at Balliol College, Oxford, of which he was later made an honorary fellow. It was in England that, with his father King Haakon, he found refuge in 1940 after Norway had been overrun by the Germans. In Norway he was estimated to be somewhere between 35th and 40th in line of succession to the British throne.

Olav was born at Appleton House, Sandringham, Norfolk, as Prince Alexander Edward Christian Frederick of Denmark. His father, Prince Charles, was the son of Frederick VIII of Denmark and a grandson of Christian IX. In 1905, Norway having decided to break away from Sweden, the Storting (parliament) selected Prince Charles as the first king of a restored monarchy, a move greatly favoured by Edward VII. Prince Charles became Haakon VII. His son was then renamed Olav, after the 11th-century Norwegian king and saint.

After private tuition, Olav was educated at a secondary school in Oslo until he entered the military college in the capital, from which he passed out in 1924. From 1924 to 1926 he was at Balliol, where he studied political economy and international law.

In March 1929 Prince Olav married his cousin, then Swedish Princess Martha, daughter of Prince Charles, Duke of Väastergotland, and his wife, Princess Ingeborg of Denmark, a sister of King Haakon. It would be an exaggeration to say that the marriage smoothed away all the difficulties in the complex relationship between Norway and Sweden, but it was popular in both countries. The wedding was in Oslo cathedral, and apparently the first royal wedding to be broadcast by wireless.

The Prince and Princess had three children, Princess Ragnhild, Princess Astrid and Prince Harald, born in 1930, 1932 and 1937. The heir to the throne and his family lived a somewhat retired life on their estate at Skaugum, 20 miles from Oslo, which had been a wedding present from Baron Wedel Jarlsberg, long Norwegian minister in Paris.

After the German invasion of Norway in April 1940, King Haakon and his son were forced from Oslo with the government and members of the Storting and spent two difficult months driven further and further north, were dive-bombed and often had to shelter in farmhouses or in the forests. The end came after the German breakthrough in France and the British and French decision to abandon Norway. On June 7, Haakon and Olav were evacuated from Tromso in a British cruiser. The government vetoed an offer by the prince to remain in Norway.

During the war Prince Olav played an important part in liaison from Britain with the resistance movements in Norway, in building up the Free Norwegian Forces in Britain and in organising the welfare of the 30,000 Norwegian seamen, who manned that part of the Norwegian merchant navy which had remained at the disposal of the Western allies. He made frequent visits to Norwegian air force pilots in training in Canada. Princess Martha and their children spent the war in Washington, where they had gone in 1940 at President Roosevelt's invitation. The steadfastness of the royal family in exile became the stuff of folk legend in a country that had enjoyed independence for barely 35 years before it was occupied by the Germans.

Prince Olav returned to Oslo on May 13, 1945, five days before the final German capitulation in Norway, in the British cruiser *Apollo* escorted by British and Norwegian naval vessels, and received an enthusiastic welcome in front of the town hall. Until King Haakon's return a few weeks later he acted as regent at the head of a government delegation

and supervised the disarmament of the German forces and the rounding-up of the quislings.

Prince Olav represented Norway at the victory celebrations in London and at the Coronation of Queen Elizabeth in 1953. The celebration of the 25th anniversary of his wedding, in 1954, was clouded by the illness of Princess Martha, who died only a month later.

King Haakon died aged 85 in 1957, after having been in poor health since 1955. Olav was not formally crowned as his father had been, the constitution having been amended to abolish the ceremony. He took the oath of loyalty to the constitution when opening his parliament in January 1958, and then, in June received the blessing of the Norwegian church in Trondheim cathedral, which is dedicated to St Olav.

During the second world war a considerable amount of the Norwegian effort had been based in Scotland. King Olav's wish to thank the Scottish people for the friendship with which his countrymen had been received was gratified in 1962 in a way which went down well in Scotland. His three-day state visit to Edinburgh, where he was the guest of the Queen at the Palace of Holyroodhouse was indeed the first state visit to Scotland's capital for at least 150 years. King Olav received the freedom of Edinburgh, and an honorary LLD from Edinburgh University. He was admitted to the Order of the Thistle as an extra knight.

King Olav, a tall, commanding man, was a keen sportsman. He continued to ski till well past middle life. As a yachtsman, he won Norway's first Olympic Gold Medal at the 1928 games at Amsterdam, sailing his six-metre yacht, *Norna*. In 1953 he captained a Norwegian yacht in an ''old world versus new world race'' off Oyster Bay, Long Island. He was elected honorary president of the International Yacht Racing Union in 1958. At Oxford he represented the university in épée and sabre and, with G. Simpson, won the inter-college sabres. The king was a frequent private visitor to London, where he particularly enjoyed strolling in the streets incognito and going to watch Arsenal.

With his wife dying before he reached the throne, Olav was perhaps exceptionally lonely for a monarch. Many evenings of his widowhood of more than 30 years he spent alone in his private drawing room at the palace, reading or watching television. His father had stipulated the Norwegian monarchy should have only a small court and observe a simple lifestyle. King Olav followed this tradition to a degree which often amazed foreigners.

It was Olav's fate, at it had been that of his grandfather Edward VII, to live long under the shadow of the reigning sovereign, but his relationship with King Haakon was singularly free from strain. From the age of 18 he attended the weekly cabinet meetings and assisted unobtrusively in Haakon's achievement of establishing the monarchy, and justifying and maintaining it, in a country whose national outlook has long been essentially social democratic.

ALFRED HINDS

Alfred Hinds, the former convict who won a place in legal history after winning a libel action against the detective who arrested him, has died in Jersey aged 73. He was born in 1917.

A MASTER of the spectacular, Alfred Hinds ensured himself a place in the folklore of the East End criminal fraternity by escaping three times from prison in the 1950s and representing himself in his numerous court appeals to have a 12-year jail term for his conviction for a furniture store robbery set aside.

Hinds became known to the police in the East End of London as a petty criminal, running up a record of minor offences. He was working as a demolition contractor when he was arrested and charged with taking part in a robbery at Maples in London in which cash and jewellery worth £38,000 were stolen.

Sentenced to 12 years preventive detention in 1953, Hinds continually asserted his innocence. His first escape came two years later when he scaled the walls of Nottingham jail and remained at liberty for eight months. During his time on the run he wrote to newspapers claiming he was innocent. Doubts were expressed in the House of Commons and it was suggested in some quarters that Hinds had been convicted because of his record of minor crimes.

He was recaptured in Dublin but his second escape was even more spectacular than the first. In June 1957 during a High Court appearance he locked up his escorting officer and slipped away. He went to Bristol but was arrested on a plane about to take off for Ireland. Hinds went on a 25-day hunger strike in an attempt to proclaim his innocence, then in 1958 he got out again. He climbed over the walls of Chelmsford jail and escaped to Ireland. He was arrested in Belfast for smuggling cars under the name of Mr Bishop 20 months later. His true identity was not discovered until after he had appeared in court three times and been given a six-months sentence. When they took his fingerprints in jail his real identity was revealed.

He continued his battle to prove he had not taken part in the Maples robbery. After 17 court appearances his luck finally turned in 1964 when, in the High Court, he won a libel case against Mr Herbert Sparks, formerly detective chief superintendent at Scotland Yard and head of its Flying Squad, who had written in a newspaper article that Hinds was guilty of the furniture store raid. In his summing up on that occasion the judge, Mr Justice Edmund Davies, said that Mr Sparks's assertion that Hinds was in fact guilty was not privileged and that he had failed to establish that it was true. Hinds was awarded £1,300 damages.

Hinds continued to protest his innocence even after he had been released in 1964. But his final appeal against his conviction was dismissed in the Court of Criminal Appeal in November 1965. He embarked on a writing and lecturing career and in 1966 published his own account of the events surrounding his case, *Contempt of Court*. Reviewers and readers were struck by its intelligence and liveliness, and equally by its total lack of bitterness about what Hinds felt to have been wrongful imprisonment.

Hinds moved to Jersey where he became a property developer but continued to write and lecture.

ALFRED WAINWRIGHT

Alfred Wainwright, author of seven walking guides to the Lakeland Fells, died on January 19 aged 84. He was born in 1906.

FEW people have done more to make their fellow countrymen more physically aware of a corner of Britain than Alfred (A.W.) Wainwright. His *Pictorial Guides to the Lakeland Fells* sold more than a million copies.

To describe him as best-selling author would be misleading, however. "Best-selling" suggests a commercial slickness that was completely alien to this unassuming northcountryman, striding, pipe in mouth, across the landscape of his beloved Lake District. Nor are the seven Guides conventional books. Every bit of them was the work of his pen – maps, drawings, and accompanying text in his meticulous hand-writing. At first sight, they have an amateurish flavour, reminiscent of those worthy leaflets about the architecture of their churches that vicars write – and the *Guides* were, like worthy little booklets, printed and published by his local newspaper, the *Westmorland Gazette*, in Kendal.

But the craftsmanship and the detail were of a quality that was prized on the one hand by serious fell-walkers, and on the other by the myriad holidaymakers to be seen every year on the easier slopes of the Lake District. The dignified, old-world wording added to their charm. He took Lakeland very seriously indeed, just as many visitors who go there year after year take it seriously. Alfred Wainwright was born in 1906 to a poor family in Blackburn. The story was that he never had a holiday until he was 23, when he went walking around Windermere. He fell in love with the country. A climb up Orrest Head transformed him. He "felt he was some other person". He had qualified in accountancy and quickly contrived to get himself into the borough treasurer's office in Kendal, eventually becoming borough treasurer. Through the 1950s and 60s he watched, not always with approval, as the Lakes became more and more popular. There were so many non-walkers now, he observed.

Yet the *Guides*, which he started to produce at the age of 45, were always tolerant of the ignorance of city-dwellers and Southerners, as here, in his instructions on the ascent of Esk Pike: "The likeliest mistake in bad weather is that a walker may continue along the plain path beyond the shelter and so unwittingly be ascending Scafell Pike when he should be going down to Wasdale . . ."

Wainwright knew when to spell things out. He also knew that Lakeland deserved poetry. "When mist wreathes the summit and clings like smoke in the gullies, when ravens soar above the lonely crags, when snow lies deep and curtains of ice bejewel the gaunt cliffs . . ." That was Great End.

In old age he agreed to spread his authorship geographically, and also to move almost into the coffee-table school of publishing. *Fell-walking with Wainwright* was a best-seller, and so was *Wainwright on the Pennine Way*. He was persuaded, too, to appear on television and radio.

In acquiescing in a higher profile, his motive seemed to be to earn money and publicity, not for himself but for a charity he and his wife had established: his animal rescue organisation.

WALTER TERRY

Walter Frederick Terry, political editor in turn of the Daily Mail, *the* Daily Express *and the* Sun, *died suddenly at his Newhaven home on January 25 aged 66. He was born on August 18, 1924.*

WALTER Terry was one of the outstanding political journalists throughout the Macmillan and Wilson years. His insight and sources made him the equal of such formidable contemporaries as the late David Wood of *The Times* and Derek Marks of the *Daily Express* and at times he led the entire field. His contacts reached up to Cabinet ministers in both Conservative and Labour administrations and at one point during the Wilson premiership they included the prime minister.

His most famous triumph came when he forecast the Macmillan reshuffle in 1962 two days before it was announced. Macmillan sacked one third of his Cabinet in a day and Terry had the news to himself. It is still unknown whether Rab Butler leaked the news to the second Lord Rothermere on the unspoken understanding that it would be passed to Terry or whether Terry received the information directly from Butler. Whatever the route taken by the news it earned Terry the envy of the rest of Fleet Street and the title of Journalist of the Year in the 1963 National Press Awards.

There were other years, too, when Terry had good claim to the title. He forecast that Lord Home would succeed Macmillan as prime minister when his Fleet Street rivals remained committed to Butler or even Hogg; and in 1967 he was ahead again when Wilson devalued the pound. The devaluation story was not obtained from direct information but came as a result of putting together a number of clues. The most significant of these was that Marcia Williams, now Lady Falkender and then personal and political secretary to Harold Wilson, refused to speak to him throughout the pre-devaluation week. Terry concluded that the only explanation for this was that she possessed such important information that she was afraid to have even the slightest of contact in case she should be suspected of being the source of any story he might write.

Terry had good reason to understand when Marcia Williams would not speak to him for at that time they were on the closest possible terms. She was the mother of his two sons born in the late 1960s. For a time it seemed that he might marry her but he became reconciled with his wife and his association with Lady Falkender ceased.

Terry was born in Derbyshire and took what was then the traditional route to Fleet Street by progressing from a local newspaper to a regional evening paper before serving a Manchester apprenticeship to a national daily. In Terry's case he began on the *Glossop Chronicle*, moved to the nearby *Derby Evening Telegraph*, had a spell on the *Nottingham Journal* and was then accepted as a general reporter in the *Daily Mail*'s Manchester office. His potential was recognised and by 1955 he had been moved to London and was already operating in the Commons. In 1959, when Macmillan won his general election, Terry became political editor.

His string of exclusives included the Soviet attempt to ruin Tory MP Commander Anthony Courtney through a sex scandal and Wilson's Vietnam peace initiative — stories almost forgotten now but big news at the time. Prime ministers rose and fell but Terry's contacts on both sides of the House meant that his career was unaffected. As the political editor of the ultra-loyalist Tory *Daily Mail* it might have been thought that he was a Conservative at heart. As Wilson's favourite reporter he might have been accused of Labour's sympathies. The truth is that Terry was neither Tory nor Labour. His private conversations revealed him as deeply cynical about every party and all politicians.

With his private life in disarray Terry was sent to the United States in 1969 as the *Mail*'s Washington correspondent but he soon returned to London as deputy editor. There was a reorganisation when the paper became a tabloid and Terry was re-assigned to his old beat as political editor. In 1973, however, he was made a particularly tempting offer to switch papers and became political editor of the *Daily Express*. The *Express* was not a particularly stable paper in those days and Terry was a victim of changes. By 1975 he had left the paper but was soon picked up by the *Sun* and was promoted to political editor in 1978. This was not a happy move. He never had even the slightest sympathy with the paper's general style and when Kelvin MacKenzie was appointed editor his relations with his office rapidly became much worse. He was fired in 1983. A bad end to a fine career and one which drew protests from his *Sun* colleagues.

Terry was briefly on the payroll of *Today* during its Eddie Shah days but this period was so short that it hardly constituted an association. The fact is that he was never a commanding figure after the early 1970s and the complexities of his private life undoubtedly contributed to his decline.

He was married in 1950 to Mavis Landen, by whom he had a son and a daughter and another son who died in childhood. He is also survived by the two sons of Lady Falkender.

COLONEL "MONTY" WESTROPP

Colonel Lionel Henry Mountefort Westropp, soldier, died on January 26 aged 94. He was born on February 20, 1896.

THE bearing of Monty Westropp in situations of extreme peril when the spirits of many around him were downcast is graphically epitomised in the recollections of the Canadian historian Walter Lord in his book *The Miracle of Dunkirk*: "The long shadow of tradition was now very much in evidence. When Colonel Lionel H. M. Westropp ordered the 8th King's Own Royal Regiment to head down the beach towards the mole he first assembled his officers. He reminded them that they wore the badge of one of the oldest regiments of the line. 'We therefore will represent the regiment as we march down the beach this afternoon. We must not let it down . . .' " As Lord recalls, the battalion set off in perfect step, arms swinging in unison, rifles correctly slung and in immaculate marching order. It was a sight which put fresh heart into the many fearfully battered and demoralised units who witnessed it.

Westropp was already a veteran of war and adversity by the time the second world war broke out. He came from a military family and was educated at Clifton and Sandhurst. In April 1915 he was commissioned into the Devonshire Regiment. A year later he was commanding a company at the Battle of the Somme, all officers senior to him having been killed. Amid scenes of fearful carnage which required men to attack fixed positions heavily defended with wire and machine guns, young officers like Westropp either grew up fast or succumbed to the mental strain of having to send men to their deaths in what Basil Liddell-Hart has called "that human sump-pit". Many brave men cracked but Westropp never flinched from even the most appalling decisions. On one occasion a major in an adjacent unit was fleeing, terrified, to the rear and causing general panic among the soldiers around him. Without hesitation Westropp, then a mere 2nd lieutenant, drew his pistol and brought the officer down. Westropp then called his sergeant major to him, and together they reformed their shaken company and turned their faces towards the enemy in front.

Several days afterwards Westropp was severely wounded in the head and had to be sent to hospital. He spent some months there but was back at the front in time to participate in the Arras offensive of April 1917, yet another of those unequal contests between human flesh and steel and high explosive to which the first world war provides such melancholy testimony. Westropp took part in the fierce fighting which developed around Fresnoy, east of Vimy, in which Canadian and British regiments took the village on

16

May 3, 1917. They were expelled a few days later by German counter-attacks backed by artillery fire which poured 100,000 high explosive and 27,500 gas shells onto allied positions around Fresnoy in 36 hours. Wounded in the leg, Westropp crawled for seven hours through the mud of no man's land, eluding enemy patrols to regain the safety of his own lines. In later years he always felt that the official history of the war had dealt hardly with the failure of British units, including his own, to hold Fresnoy under such fearful odds. The fact is that Arras was an offensive whose laborious (and ostentatious) preparations sacrificed all possibility of surprise and Ludendorff was amply prepared. As the German official account noted at the outset of the battle: "Mountains of shell were piled up in the ammunition dumps, the construction of defences and the organisation of the troops was complete. The enemy could come . . ."

Westropp was never a man to allow even such fearful setbacks to dampen his spirits. On periods out of the front line he knew how to let his hair down. In the rear rest areas he gained a certain notoriety by performing energetic Cossack dances on restaurant tables, accompanied by his Russian girlfriend, Olga.

Between the wars Westropp had six years in India where he was able to indulge himself in his favourite pastimes of tiger and boar shooting and playing polo and rugby. He also won the Khud race, which was competed for by servicemen annually up and down a mountain. Back in England he distinguished himself as an army fencer. From 1933 to 1936 he commanded the anti-gas wing at Winterbourne Gunner and was responsible for writing the British army manual on gas warfare. The subject had acquired a new urgency as British troops in Egypt feared the use of gas by Mussolini, then embarking on his invasion of Abyssinia.

When war came again in 1939 Westropp was was ordered to raise and command a new battalion, the 8th King's Own, which he led as part of the British Expeditionary Force during the Blitzkrieg and through Dunkirk. Later he served in Malta, where during the siege his battalion became known as "Westropp's Own", so complete was his identification with it. While on passage in the cruiser *Manchester* he survived a torpedo attack from an Italian MTB off the coast of Tunisia which killed five of his brother officers. Subsequently he was on the staff for the invasion of Sicily, but he turned down a later offer of staff training, quite correctly believing his metier to be that of regimental soldiering. Indeed, in spite of a sometimes alarming demeanour, he inspired intense loyalty among all ranks under him. His consideration for soldiers and their welfare was legendary. He always placed them above his personal preferment, to the extent during the second world war of defying the high command on their behalf when he thought an order to attack was ill-considered and would have resulted in catastrophic losses.

From 1948 to 1958 Westropp was Colonel of The Devonshire Regiment and in 1956 he was appointed a Deputy Lieutenant of Devon. Above all his attitudes to life were influenced by his having survived the first world war when virtually all his school friends and regimental colleagues perished.

He married in 1937 Muriel Jorgensen. She survives him with their two sons.

JOAN GILBERT

Joan Gilbert, former television interviewer and feature programme presenter, died on January 29 aged 84. She was born on August 11, 1906.

JOAN Gilbert will be remembered with affection by a wartime generation of BBC audiences. She was one of that first generation of television presenters at Alexandra Palace which included Gilbert Harding, McDonald Hobley and Sylvia Peters. She was television personality of the year in 1951.

Born in Cambridge, she spent much of her childhood at a convent school in Sussex. In those years she saw little of her father during his service in India. Early in life she learned to survive on her charm and ability to talk herself into, and out of, difficult situations. All this was good training for live radio and television work where improvisation and spontaneity were essential.

She joined the BBC in 1933 and was first heard on the air interviewing for *In Town Tonight*. In 1938 she transferred to television and worked as a scout and assistant editor for Cecil Madden on *Picture Page*.

Loaned to the Ministry of Information on the outbreak of war, she returned to Overseas Sound Broadcasting in 1940 as presenter of broadcasts to British forces overseas. The first programme of *Hello Gibraltar* was an immediate success. A telegram arrived the day afterwards from 80 military police representing all ranks saying: "Programme smash hit. Everyone wildly excited. Suggest extension immediately." Such was its popularity she flew to Gibraltar in 1943 at the invitation of the governor-general Sir Noel Mason Macfarlane to meet listeners.

She returned to the television service on its re-opening in 1946 as editor-in-charge of *Picture Page*, making her first screen appearance as hostess of the programme, and shared interviewing with Leslie Mitchell. She was in Westminster Abbey to cover the wedding of the then Princess Elizabeth and Lieutenant Philip Mountbatten.

After a long illness in 1950 she gave up editorship, concentrating on television appearances as interviewer and presenter of *Picture Page* and various programmes for women including *Designed for Woman* and *About the House*. Her farewell as a member of the BBC staff was in a special appearance on June 30, 1953. Subsequently she began freelance work, appearing in *Joan Gilbert's Diary* and *About the Home* and writing a weekly magazine column.

Her programmes were designed both to inform and to entertain — her early outside broadcasts broke new ground, taking the cameras and the viewers for the first time into interesting and unusual situations — on the *Queen Mary*, down a coal mine and into a carpet factory. Her evening studio programmes were a model of style and elegance — a full length evening gown being her typical choice.

During those years she enjoyed a wide following for what was described as her unpredictable effervescence. Audiences delighted in her natural enthusiasm, for she refused to be scripted. During one memorable programme, on decorating a Christmas tree, she put her foot in a bucket of whitewash. She invariably insisted on her dachshund, Fitzy, sharing the limelight.

She was unmarried.

JOHN BARDEEN

John Bardeen, American physicist, co-inventor of the transistor and double Nobel prizewinner, died on January 30 aged 82. He was born on May 23, 1908.

TO WIN one Nobel prize is a remarkable distinction; to win two, as John Bardeen did, is to join a tiny elite that can be counted on the fingers of one hand. Only three individuals have won two Nobel prizes for scientific achievement: Marie Curie, John Bardeen, and Frederick Sanger. (Linus Pauling was also awarded the prize twice, but the second, in 1962, recognised his efforts in the cause of peace.)

Bardeen first won the prize in 1956, sharing it with William Shockley and Walter Brattain for the discovery of the transistor. Working together at Bell Telephone Laboratories, the three combined their talents to create one of the most significant inventions of the 20th century: the transistor, a device for amplifying, controlling and generating electrical signals that was small, rugged, and cheap. Its effects in radio, television, computers and a vast range of electronic devices have helped create a new industrial revolution, influencing the way we live profoundly.

To the group Bardeen brought a profound understanding of the way in which quantum mechanics affects the behaviour of solids. Shockley, later better known for his espousal of eugenic theories, led the group working on semiconductor devices, while Brattain added his remarkable experimental talents. Together they produced from a fragment of germanium a device which could duplicate the operations of the electronic valve, at a fraction of the price and with far greater reliability.

Their discovery was made in 1948, but few realised its significance and it was not until 1951 that the first commercial devices were produced. From this simple point-contact transistor is derived the entire range of silicon integrated circuits on which huge industries and entire economies now depend. Few men have lived to see their inventions produce such far-reaching effects.

John Bardeen was born in Madison, Wisconsin, the son of Charles Russell Bardeen. After school he went to the universities of Wisconsin and Princeton before becoming a geophysicist with the firm Gulf Research and Development.

When war came to the United States in 1941 Bardeen became a physicist at the US naval ordnance laboratory, serving there for the duration of hostilities. Afterwards he did not go back immediately to academia but spent the years 1945 to 1951 at the Bell Telephone Laboratory, where his first great discovery was made.

In 1951 Bardeen took up a chair in electrical engineering and physics at the University of Illinois at Urbana, and it was here that he developed a theory to explain the phenomenon of superconductivity. When metals are cooled to temperatures close to absolute zero, they lose all resistance to the passage of an electrical current, a phenomomenon first discovered by Kammerlingh Onnes in 1911.

Once again, Bardeen shared a Nobel Prize for physics with two colleagues, Leon Cooper of Brown university, Rhode Island, and John Schrieffer of the University of Pennsylvania, and the theory that bears their initials, the BCS theory, formed the basis for all subsequent theoretical work on the subject. Bardeen's second Nobel Prize for physics was awarded in 1972.

19

SIR MONTY FINNISTON

Sir Monty Finniston, FRS, former chairman of the British Steel Corporation, died on February 2 aged 78. He was born on August 15, 1912.

HAROLD Montague Finniston was one of Britain's most eminent engineers, who devoted his enormous energy and determination latterly to helping his profession to adapt to the modern world in which the old "smokestack" industries are no longer the country's power base. He began as a metallurgist; was a pioneer of the nuclear energy industry; then, under a Labour government he organised the nationalisation of the steel industry; and in the private sector he held a formidable clutch of directorships over a range of businesses that demonstrated the speed with which he was prepared to assume responsibility.

Never a man who suffered fools gladly, he was not afraid to tell governments of all complexions what he thought of them. And he exercised great influence on the educational and industrial structure through a myriad of public bodies — developing pre-eminently into one of the "great and the good" committee-men. He could never have performed his public role unless he had also had considerable charm to cap his other characteristics, but his rise to prominence was all the more remarkable since he had been unknown to the general public until he was getting on for 60. Before that his work had seldom taken him far from a research laboratory.

Finniston was brought up in Glasgow, where he was educated at three centres of excellence for anyone contemplating a career in engineering: Allan Glen's school, Glasgow university and the technical college which was to become Strathclyde university. He lectured at the college before moving into industry as a metallurgist with Stewart & Lloyds, the steel company.

When war came, Finniston joined the Naval Scientific Service, from which he moved naturally into Britain's nuclear energy programme. From 1948 to 1958 he was chief metallurgist with the Atomic Energy Authority at Harwell, and led the team which produced Britain's first plutonium. He moved back into private industry with C. A. Parsons in 1959. He became a member of the National Research Development Corporation in 1963 and in 1965 got his first real glimpses of the workings of Whitehall as a member of the R & D advisory council at the Ministry of Power.

In 1967 Harold Wilson's government was ready to move towards the mammoth feat of nationalising the steel industry and Finniston joined the planning team. Fourteen autonomous and competitive steel companies were to be merged into the British Steel Corporation. In 1971 (when there was now a Conservative government in power) Finniston became the corporation's chief executive, and in 1973 its chairman. The steel industry he knew, but much of the politics and administrative immensity of the task were new to him. However, he thrived on the cut and thrust of debate and he had boundless zest — he needed little sleep — and expected subordinates to work as hard as he did.

20

His mercurial characteristics irritated his detractors, who existed in high places in Whitehall and in the Labour and Tory parties and who resented, from one standpoint or another, his determination to allow only minimal government interference in the nationalised steel industry. His aim − this was before the deep recession that the industry suffered internationally in the mid-70s − was to produce more steel with fewer employees, using the best technology available. Although an enthusiast for his particular model of nationalisation, he had an almost Victorian faith in the profit discipline.

In 1974 Labour were back in office, and after a spectacular row between Finniston and Tony Benn it was decided that his contract should not be renewed when it expired in 1976. He was knighted in 1975. In 1969 he had been elected a fellow of the Royal Society. When he left the BSC there was no shortage of other jobs for him. The long list of boards he served on at various times included Sears Holdings, GKN, and Cluff Oil. He became a consultant to others.

He served on an almost bewildering variety of industrial, engineering, scientific and educational bodies. Some of them, like the council of the Scottish Business School, represented his west of Scotland background, but most of them were national, and increasingly his voice was recognised internationally too.

Possibly the most important appointment − made by the Labour government in 1977 − was to chair a committee of enquiry into the engineering profession. The Finniston report, when it appeared two years later, turned out to be a major blueprint for the future of British industry. "The regeneration of UK manufacturing competitiveness," it said, "must be given over-riding priority in national policies, with the emphasis on developing market-orientated engineering excellence." Finniston hoped that the committee's findings would counter what he saw as a tendency, in government and among others with influence, to write off manufacturing industry and to imagine that the future lay mainly in the services sector. An Engineering Council was established as a result of the report, although the Conservative government of 1979 was unwilling to agree to the committee's recommendation of establishing a statutory engineering authority.

Never a man to let disappointment colour his judgement, he gave the council every support and encouragement. He also continued to propound his views on the rise of the service sector. In a speech in 1984 he said that the country had to recognise that it was the success of manufactured goods that generated the service industries.

Meanwhile the breadth of Finniston's interests in future patterns of British society was symbolised by his chairmanship of the Policy Studies Institute (formerly PEP). A major survey carried out under his auspices was one on the Metropolitan Police. From 1973-76 he was a member of the NEDC ("Neddy"). A more specialised interest was demonstrated as chairman of the Prison Reform Trust, in which capacity he warned the government in 1987 of the "mayhem" that could be in the offing unless prison conditions were improved.

He was prepared to back views which, however discomfiting they might be to officialdom, were honest, gave new impetus to debate and enlivened it with fresh research. He was frequently given platforms for propagating his views on the human condition when he was invited to deliver public lectures. He became known to a wider public through television where he brought to bear his wide experience and came across as a person of sound, incisive commonsense and an enemy of humbug.

From 1978-88 he was Chancellor of Stirling university and was a member of the council of King's College, London, from 1985 until last year. His honorary doctorates came from his old universities of Glasgow and Strathclyde and from a dozen others.

He married, in 1936, Miriam Singer, who survives him with a son and a daughter.

SIR LAWRENCE GOWING

Sir Lawrence Gowing, CBE, painter, art historian and teacher, died on February 5 aged 72. He was born on April 21, 1918.

OF ALL his abilities, Lawrence Gowing would no doubt have been happiest to be remembered as a painter. He began as a painter, achieved a reputation during the war years (when he was a conscientious objector) and continued to paint up to and beyond his major retrospective at the Serpentine in 1982. But though this was respectfully received, his real talents lay more in art history and especially in conveying to others what he had discovered. He made art come brilliantly alive for the many who studied under him at the Slade and elsewhere, and even more spectacularly for the millions who saw his two BBC television series, *Three Painters*, in 1984 and 1986. His message was that the grandeur of art was a quality of the real world, not some idealised abstraction, and his own impassioned belief compelled a similar belief in others.

Even at the beginning of his career his interests were not limited to painting and talking about painting. After leaving school he had a fashionable yen to become a film-maker. He wrote to W. H. Auden, who was then working for the GPO Film Unit, to ask his advice. Auden replied wryly: "You only want to become a film director because you think it is the art of the future. It isn't. Art is the art of the future." Gowing took this observation to heart; through Auden, coincidentally, he also met William Coldstream, another painter/film-maker who was to be his close friend and colleague throughout his life. If he was dissuaded from trying to communicate through the cinema, he did at least realise that communication was his forte, and soon entered on a lifetime of teaching, achieving the position of professor of fine art at King's College, Newcastle upon Tyne, when he was just 29.

He was a man of strong vanity. He did not take argument well, and many hapless artists and students who got on his wrong side lived to rue the day. On the other hand, his likes were as passionately held as his dislikes. If he sensed real talent in even the most unlikely case he was fierce in its defence, support and propagation. He was also exceptionally able to recognise gifts very different from his own, such as that of the coalminer-artist Nicholas Evans.

He was unstoppable, too, in his advocacy of unfashionable views on the art of the past. His last achievement in this field was the exhibition he organised at the Royal Academy and elsewhere two years ago on the early work of his beloved Cézanne. Almost single-handedly, that brought about a major critical reappraisal.

Coming from a Norfolk farming family of no particular artistic sympathies, Lawrence Gowing was born in Stamford and was educated at Quaker schools, the Downs and Leighton Park.

Within a year of leaving school Gowing had become a precocious member of the circle of Coldstream, Graham Bell, Victor Pasmore and Claude Rogers and had completely assimilated their style of closely observed tonal painting, later nicknamed Euston Road. As a conscientious objector he was able to paint continuously throughout the second world war, and the portraits, landscapes and still-lifes he then painted, vividly observed yet reflecting and even dramatising his admiration for Courbet and Cézanne, are among the more ambitious paintings of the decade. It was at this time that he began to be known as a writer. His *Notes of a Painter* which appeared over a period in John Lehmann's *Penguin New Writing* were fluent, allusive and witty commentaries on every aspect of painting.

Before the war ended Gowing had begun his career as a teacher, working at Camberwell School of Art, where he was soon joined by Pasmore and Coldstream. In 1948 he went to Newcastle upon Tyne; shortly after this it was discovered that he had tuberculosis. While recovering he put the finishing touches to the book that laid the foundations of his reputation as an art historian: *Vermeer* was published in 1952.

In 1953 Gowing was appointed trustee of the Tate Gallery, starting an association that lasted for many years. In 1954 he organised the first of his Cézanne exhibitions, shown at Edinburgh and the Tate. Guided by his painter's judgment of the internal evidence, he challenged the accepted dating of several important works. The furore that this provoked among certain art historians abated when John Rewald produced documents that supported Gowing's dates. In 1959 he left Newcastle to take up a demanding position with the ILEA. Two London art schools, the Regent Street Polytechnic and the Chelsea Polytechnic, were to be amalgamated into a single school. The school that resulted under Gowing's direction became something of a model at a time when art schools all over the country were in the process of re-shaping themselves.

After six years at Chelsea he surprised his colleagues by resigning his trusteeship at the Tate in order to join its staff as keeper of the British collection. In 1966 he arranged the first of several important exhibitions in America. This was his

Turner; Imagination and Reality at the Museum of Modern Art, New York. It was the first time that Turner had been seen in depth by the American public. Gowing's catalogue did not hesitate to present him as a precursor of many of the attitudes current among painters of the New York School. On the heels of his Turner, Gowing organised an exhibition of Matisse for the Museum of Modern Art, ushering in a preoccupation with the great French colourist that lasted for many years and produced a major exhibition at the Hayward Gallery in 1968, a film for the Arts Council and in 1979 the publication of a brilliant monograph.

After two years at the Tate Gowing went to Leeds to become professor of fine art at the university, remaining there until 1975 when he returned to London to take William Coldstream's place as Slade professor at University College. He was at the Slade for ten years, meanwhile continuing public work that included membership of the Arts Council of Great Britain and chairmanship of several of its committees, trusteeship of the British Museum and of the National Portrait Gallery.

Despite his many public obligations, Gowing had continued to paint, often in an experimental vein that took him a long way from the romantic realism of his early work. The most dramatic of these experiments led to a series of figure paintings in which his own body, spreadeagled, naked and covered in paint, was applied to the canvas. These astonishing objects were shown at a retrospective exhibition at the Serpentine Gallery in 1982.

After retiring from the Slade in 1985 Gowing spent a year in Washington as a research fellow at the National Gallery and later accepted a curatorial appointment at the Phillips Collection, commuting between London and Washington until his doctors forbade him to fly.

He was appointed CBE in 1952, elected ARA in 1978 and knighted in 1982.

He is survived by his third wife, Jennifer, and three daughters.

RON PICKERING

Ron Pickering, OBE, BBC sports commentator and athletics coach, died on February 13 aged 60. He had undergone a multiple heart bypass operation just before Christmas and seemed to be on the road to recovery. He was born on May 4, 1930.

TO THE millions who knew him through his television commentaries, Ron Pickering's was the voice which brought an inimitable blend of excitement and knowledge to the BBC's coverage of athletics meetings all over the world. To both armchair viewers at home and competitors at trackside scarcely any gathering of athletes — whether Olympic Games or domestic indoor competition — seemed complete without the informed intelligence and white-hot enthusiasm of Pickering in attendance. Within the sporting world, however, he will be as well remembered as a tireless campaigner against the abuse of drugs in sport, as a first-class coach who was associated with the successes of the Welsh long-jumper Lynn Davies at the very highest levels, and for his altruistic and wise work for Haringey Athletics club, of which he was president.

Ronald James Pickering was born and bred in Hackney. East London was an area with which he was to retain close links all his life, and the energetic support he gave to the scheme to create the London Arena from a vast disused banana warehouse in the Isle of Dogs was characteristic of his concern for sport's social function. After attending Stratford Grammar School he did his national service in the army in the King's Own Regiment where after a modest career as a decathlete he became a useful, if not outstanding, field event athlete. After demobilisation he took a physical education course at Carnegie College of Physical Education, Leeds, and taught for several years at his old school in Stratford and in Wanstead.

He became a protege of England's leading coach, Geoff Dyson, an apprenticeship which gave great impetus to his own coaching career. In 1960, still aged only 30, he was appointed Wales's national athletics coach. This began a particularly fulfilling period in his professional life, which was remarkable for the success of the Welsh long jump champion Lynn Davies, whom Pickering first met and identified as a talent when Davies was still at school. At that point Davies was a triple jumper, but Pickering turned him into a long jumper. The partnership between coach and athlete was crowned by Davies's winning the long jump gold medal for Great Britain at the Olympic Games in Tokyo in 1964, but he also won a gold in the European championships and, for Wales, at the 1966 Commonwealth Games in Kingston, Jamaica. Pickering's inspirational presence and hard work in touring clubs and inculcating enthusiasm at all levels is still remembered in Wales.

In the 1960s Pickering had also begun to be interested in broadcasting, and soon became central to the BBC's coverage of a variety of sports, including gymnastics, volleyball, skiing and ski-jumping, though he will always be most closely associated with athletics, which he first covered at Olympic level for the BBC in Mexico in 1968. Indeed, Ron Pickering and David Coleman, with whom he shared commentary boxes all over the world for 25 years, may almost be said to have created athletics as a television spectacle, and their different, though complementary, styles gave television athletics coverage the shape and "feel" which has come to be the standard of today.

Pickering communicated to viewers not merely a passion for athletics, but as time went on an increasing concern for the advancement of athletes themselves as well as a deep awareness of the perils that lay in wait for them, notably from drugs. On television, at annual conferences of the Central Council for Physical Recreation, at dinners and at any other venue where a few apposite words might be called for Pickering aired his deep concern about the threat drugs represented both to the image of sport and to the health of the participants. Only last Friday he had been seen in a television debate with Ben Johnson's former coach, Charlie Francis, tackling him on these issues.

Yet in spite of his public persona in international sport, Pickering still remained deeply involved with athletics at the grass roots level. As president of the Haringey club he enjoyed involvement with the problems and career prospects of little-known athletes as much as rubbing shoulders with world-class stars. He loved sport for itself, and not merely for its capacity sometimes to transform for the better the lives of those who found fame through it. As he once wrote: "I believe that sport without its ethic of fair play would not have survived 33 weeks let alone 33 centuries." Sport for him meant all sportsmen and not merely the most celebrated ones.

Pickering was appointed OBE for his services to sport in 1986. He was married to Jean Desforges, herself a former European long jump champion and British Olympic captain, and is survived by her, by a daughter Kim and a son, Shaun, who has been a junior international and Welsh record holder at hammer, shot and discus and represented Wales at the Edinburgh Commonwealth Games in 1986.

ROBERT WAGNER

Robert Wagner, mayor of New York from 1954 to 1965, died on February 12, at his Manhattan home aged 80. He was born on April 20, 1910.

ROBERT F. Wagner was the first Democrat to serve three terms as mayor of New York. In modern times only the celebrated Fiorello La Guardia (1934-45) and Ed Koch (1978-89) have served as long. Wagner first won election as the Tammany Hall candidate in 1953, but he subsequently helped to destroy the power of the Democratic party organisation in New York, thus ending the dominance of political machinery in the city's politics.

His 12-year stewardship saw other changes to the city, some of which were not of a positive nature. Many are apt to see the period as the beginning of New York's social ills. Certainly there were race riots, police scandals, school boycotts by blacks and a water shortage during his three terms. The city's budget also more than doubled. In the flight of the Dodgers baseball team to Los Angeles and the departure of the Giants to San Francisco some saw fatal blows to New York's civic self-esteem. Wagner replied by having the Shea stadium built and was in attendance when the New York Mets first played there in 1962.

More importantly he had the building of more than 250 schools to his credit and under him more was spent on teaching, too. He threw his weight behind the construction of 423,000 new dwellings and created a strong municipal fair housing code. In employment, too, he was fair to the underprivileged and immigrants, placing many more Puerto Ricans and blacks in municipal employment. The absence of municipal strikes during his periods of office was a conspicuous result of his policies, and yet this deliberate, ratiocinative figure never seemed to be able to win the hearts of New York's increasing racial minorities. Certainly the race riots which erupted in the summer of 1964 suggested that his administration was running out of steam in its attempt to come to terms with the realities on the city's streets.

Robert Ferdinand Wagner was born in New York of German-Irish descent. His father had arrived in New York from Europe as a boy in 1885. His mother was the daughter of Irish immigrants. He graduated in law at Yale and practised at the bar. In 1937 he was elected to the New York state assembly. He resigned to join the United States Army Air Force when America entered the war in 1941, and after a period serving as an assistant judge advocate at home he went to Britain where he was judge advocate to Eighth Air Force headquarters.

After the war he returned to local government in New York and after various administrative posts in which he was noted for sound rather than spectacular performance (no disadvantage to him at a time when Mayor O'Dwyer's administration was reeling under rumours of scandal) he was elected president of the borough of Manhattan in 1949. He was selected by Tammany Hall to run as Democrat candidate against Mayor Impelliteri in the elections of 1953. Subsequently he was to fall out with the city's Democrat party machine and in 1961, going for for his third term as mayor, was compelled to engage in a primary contest with the Tammany Hall-backed State Comptroller, Arthur Levitt. His victory in this preliminary contest made him independent of Tammany Hall thereafter. Apart from an unsuccessful tilt at the Senate against Jacob Javits in 1956 he won every election he contested.

Nevertheless, in spite of the undoubted achievements of his three terms (which included the pegging of the subway fare to 15 cents, beside other weightier achievements such as the building of the Lincoln Center and free Shakespeare plays in Central Park) he was increasingly seen as a lacklustre figure as the 1960s progressed, with their craving for excitement and charisma in political leaders. Continued public borrowing led to the familiar problems inherited by his successors, while his tendency to appoint long drawn-out commissions of inquiry to investigate every problem confronting the city earned him the reputation of a procrastinator. In July 1964 mob violence, starting in Harlem and spreading across the East River into the Bedford-Stuyvesant area of Brooklyn, shook the city and led to questions about the effectiveness of the police. The riots took place against a trend towards nation-wide ferment in the wake of the enactment of new civil rights legislation, but nevertheless gave the impression that Wagner's administration was losing its grip. His wife died in the same year and he announced he would be retiring to spend more time with his children.

His departure from office went almost unnoticed, but he was not idle for long. From 1968 to 1969 he was US ambassador to Spain and ten years later President Carter made him his personal envoy to the Vatican.

A second marriage, in 1965, to Barbara Joan Kavanagh was dissolved and in 1975 he married Phyllis Fraser Cerf, widow of the publisher Bennett Cerf. She and the two sons of his first marriage survive him.

HIS HONOUR
ROWE HARDING

His Honour Rowe Harding, former circuit judge and Welsh rugby international, died on February 10 aged 89. He was born on September 10, 1901.

BETWEEN 1923 and 1928 Rowe Harding played 17 times for Wales. His first and last caps were against England. He had one further season with Swansea, a club for which he first played when he was only 17, and retired from playing at the age of 28 on being called to the bar by the Inner Temple.

In internationals he played on the winning side only once against the home countries, when he captained Wales against Ireland in 1926. It was a dark period in Welsh rugby history. His speed on the wing – he was a Welsh champion sprinter – and great footballing gifts were not always seen to best advantage in the national team. While at Pembroke

College, Cambridge, he played in four Varsity matches from 1924, captaining the team in 1927. He scored a try in each of his last two appearances. Rowe Harding travelled to South Africa to play three tests for the Lions in 1924.

He was born of a rugby family. His father, Albert, a colliery manager, had established a club, Glais, in the Swansea valley in 1896 to provide facilities and opportunities for the miners and steelmen of the area. Much later, Rowe Harding was himself a founder member and finally president of the Crawshay's Welsh XV, founded "to enable men from all walks of life to take part in a rugby tour", men who might not otherwise be able to afford to travel away for any length of time. Rugby was thought of as a great help in knitting together a tight social fabric in Wales with no class distinctions.

Rowe Harding was chairman and president of Glamorgan County Cricket Club. He sat on numerous committees, councils of institutions and charities in Wales. His was a gentle, quietly influential, contribution. He was a man of many parts, contesting Swansea East as a Liberal National in the general election of 1945. In the general elections of 1950 and 1951 he was parliamentary candidate in the National Liberal and Conservative interest for Gower. On all those occasions he was unsuccessful against Labour. Harding was also chairman of Swansea Porcelain.

His abiding love, though, was rugby football. He was vice-president of the Welsh Rugby Union from 1953 to 1956. He had written in 1929 that as a body it needed business acumen "to guide the destiny of Welsh rugby . . . a task for which some of the sitting members are not fitted either by education or experience . . . A broader, more intelligent outlook is needed and that need will be fulfilled only when the intellectual standard of the Welsh Union is raised." His charm could easily allow him the freedom of such censure and yet not lose the respect of the close community he treasured.

He leaves a widow, Betty, a son and a daughter.

JOHN A. McCONE

John A. McCone, director of the Central Intelligence Agency from 1961 to 1965, died at his home in Pebble Beach, California, on February 14 aged 89. He was born in San Francisco on January 4, 1902.

JOHN A. McCone was regarded by both contemporaries and successors in the field as a man who had been a steadying influence at the helm of American intelligence and security at a particularly trying and sensitive time. Although himself a man of unswervingly Republican sympathies, he served several presidential administrations of both parties. In particular he was instrumental in restoring the badly battered morale of the CIA in the wake of the Bay of Pigs fiasco — the Kennedy administration's failed attempt to overthrow Castro using an invasion force of Cuban exiles — in 1961. He was also at the head of the CIA during one of the most critical episodes for any American president during the post-war period, the Cuban missile crisis which faced John F. Kennedy in 1962. On that occasion McCone's first hunch about the gravity of the threat from the Soviet Union proved to be right, a remarkable piece of perception given that it was not supported by direct intelligence evidence from the CIA itself in the early stages of the crisis.

John Alex McCone was born into a wealthy San Francisco manufacturing family. He moved to the south of California as a child and graduated from Los Angeles High School, taking an engineering degree at Berkeley in 1922. He became an executive of the Consolidated Steel Corporation but left in 1937 to set up on his own, founding a company with Stephen Bechtel. Bechtel-McCone became a leading American construction company, building oil refineries and power stations in the United States, South America and the Middle East.

During the second world war the firm modified B-24 and B-29 bombers at its aircraft modification centre in Alabama. McCone was also president of the California Ship Building Corporation which produced 467 ships for the war effort. His abilities as an organiser of large scale war building created a reputation for McCone as an executive who "got things done". After the war he took over Joshua Hendy Ironworks as president and sole owner, operating tankers and cargo ships in the Pacific. He subsequently sold what had become Hendy International, in 1969.

He was, therefore, already a man of vast experience both in defence and security matters when, in 1947, President Truman appointed him to the Air Policy Commission. In 1948, while serving as a special deputy to secretary of defence, James Forrestal, McCone helped him

28

create the CIA. McCone also served as under secretary of the United States Air Force in 1950-51. Eisenhower, who had long relied on his experience in the defence field, appointed him chairman of the US Atomic Energy Commission in 1958. McCone advocated expansion of international research on the peaceful uses of atomic energy and signed a treaty with Euratom, the European atomic energy community, to provide money and material for European development of nuclear power.

In 1961 McCone replaced Allen Dulles as head of the CIA after the abortive Bay of Pigs invasion in April of that year, which had placed a serious cloud over the intelligence agency. Indeed the agency had barely escaped dismemberment or at the very least the divorce of its intelligence and operations division. McCone broke down the rigid division between operations and analysis that had – incredible as it may seem – actually kept the CIA's analysts ignorant of the operations division's plans to invade Cuba. The intellectual level of meetings between the CIA's intelligence officials and those of other agencies was also markedly improved. McCone worked diligently to rebuild agency morale at all levels and to improve relations with the state department and Congress. This led to greater state department control over the agency, but McCone felt that a small price to pay.

In August 1962 he received reports of a Soviet military build-up in Cuba, which included the installation of anti-aircraft missiles around certain construction sites, and ordered increased intelligence flights over the island. He warned Kennedy that in his judgement the anti-aircraft missiles were being installed to protect what were intended as ballistic missile sites from which the Soviet Union could easily strike at the United States. The president at first dismissed McCone's alarm as that of an over-zealous anti-communist. McCone conceded that his theory was a hunch and admitted that there was, as yet, no photographic evidence to support it. Two months later, however, he was vindicated when U-2 spy plane flights produced clear evidence of the installing of offensive missiles in Cuba. McCone immediately recommended air strikes to incapacitate the missiles before they could become operational. Kennedy rejected the idea, opting instead for the policy of turning back Soviet ships carrying missiles to Cuba and an ultimatum to the Soviet leader, Mr Khrushchev, to remove the threat to America's security. Once Kennedy had decided on the blockade and ultimatum option McCone loyally helped him to carry it out.

After retiring from the CIA in 1965 McCone returned to his various private enterprise interests. He finally retired to Pebble Beach, California in 1979. In the mid-1970s, a senate investigation indicated that during McCone's period of tenure the CIA had carried on illegal surveillance of more than 10,000 US citizens and had tried to assassinate foreign leaders, including Fidel Castro and Patrice Lumumba in Africa. McCone testified before the senate select committee on intelligence in 1975 to the effect that he had never authorised assassination plots and was unaware of any.

A devout Catholic layman, McCone frequently represented the United States by presidential appointment at Vatican ceremonies. He continued to serve as an adviser on Soviet operations in Cuba to many United States presidents, including Jimmy Carter. In 1987 President Reagan awarded him the nation's highest civilian award, the presidential medal of freedom.

McCone was twice married, both his wives predeceasing him.

DAME MARGOT FONTEYN

Dame Margot Fonteyn, ballerina, died on February 21 in Panama City aged 71. She was born at Reigate, Surrey, on May 18, 1919.

MARGOT Fonteyn was one of the great dancers not just of her own time but of all time; her name will live as surely in the history of ballet as those of Taglioni and Pavlova.

She was also one of the rare artists whose names mean as much to the ordinary man and woman as to the devotees of their own particular art. Many dancers have excelled her in virtuosity or in the theatrical intensity they brought to dramatic roles. Fonteyn's special gift was for grasping completely the intention and balance of the dance and the music and bringing them to life for the audience. She never lost the enthusiasm which marked her dancing from childhood, and the ability to communicate her own enjoyment was perhaps the supreme secret of her art.

During the course of an extraordinarily long career she brought that gift to ever wider audiences in many parts of the world where she performed on stage;

millions more saw her on television or in films. Consequently, even more than Anna Pavlova in the early years of this century, Fonteyn awakened a love of dance in untold thousands of spectators.

She was born Margaret Hookham, the child of an English father and a mother half Irish, half Brazilian. She claimed to have inherited her enthusiasm and response to rhythm and music from her mother; and from her father the tenacity and perfectionism to put those qualities to use. From the age of four she attended dancing classes with a local teacher, and continued them in various places abroad where her father's work as an engineer took the family. The liveliness of character dancing attracted her more than the pure classicism which was later to bring her fame.

It was not until she saw Alicia Markova dance *Les Sylphides* during a visit home in 1931 that Peggy Hookham became really ambitious to be a dancer herself. Her father was then working in China and the child was lucky in finding an exceptionally gifted teacher, George Goncharov, in Shanghai. After two years with him she returned to England and studied with Seraphine Astafieva (Markova's teacher) before joining the Vic-Wells Ballet School in 1934. Within a few weeks she was performing with the Vic-Wells Ballet, and before the year was out she had her first solo role as the child in Ninette de Valois's *The Haunted Ballroom*, under an interim version of her stage name, Margot Fontes.

Before her sixteenth birthday Frederick Ashton gave Fonteyn the leading part in a new production of *Rio Grande*, and when Markova left the company soon afterwards, Fonteyn was one of the dancers who shared the ballerina's roles among them. It did not take long for her to emerge as the front runner, and by the time she was twenty Fonteyn had danced the lead in three of the great classics, *Giselle*, *Swan Lake* and *The Sleeping Beauty*, besides creating roles in a series of ballets by Ashton: *Le Baiser de la fée*, *Apparitions*, *Nocturne*, *Les Patineurs*, *A Wedding Bouquet* and *Horoscope*.

30

Fonteyn was fortunate in the colleagues under whose professional influence she found herself at this time. De Valois, directing the young company, had a far-sighted grasp of strategy in repertoire and casting. Ashton, choosing Fonteyn as his new muse in the flush of his youthful creative energy, developed her interpretative gifts and also advised her on how to dress and behave off-stage. She had Robert Helpmann as her most frequent partner, a man with a keen theatrical flair, and the company's music director, Constant Lambert, a man of wide culture, took her particularly under his wing.

The outbreak of war in 1939 brought a more urgent tempo to the company's work. Instead of only two or three performances a week, they began dancing nightly, with matinees besides, to provide entertainment for war workers and troops on leave; long gruelling tours were undertaken between short London seasons. The company was in Holland at the time of the German invasion and escaped with nothing more than what the dancers stood up in. Fonteyn by now was the company's undisputed ballerina, with a consequent demand for her to appear as often as possible. And there were still new roles to add, most notably two by Ashton which extended her range with the passion of *Dante Sonata* and the glitter of *The Wanderer*.

This experience must have helped develop the stamina that made her later career possible, but at the time it did more to consolidate her talent than to advance her artistry. The performances she gave in *The Sleeping Beauty* when the ballet moved to Covent Garden in 1946 seemed impressive at the time but would be only promising by today's standards. Luckily Ashton created in *Symphonic Variations* a work that showed Fonteyn's lyrical gifts to supreme advantage.

A turning point in her career came in 1948 when she went as guest artist to Paris to create the role of Agathe, the cat-woman, in Roland Petit's *Les Demoiselles de la nuit*. The frank admiration of this glamorous young choreographer, and

being treated as a star, seemed to add a new assurance and crispness to everything she did on returning to London. The acclaim she received in New York the next year, opening the Sadler's Wells Ballet's first season there with *The Sleeping Beauty*, completed the transformation into a ballerina of international quality.

Before the American tour, an injury during the first night of Ashton's *Don Juan* had kept her from the stage for several months and prevented her from dancing the premiere of his first three-act ballet, *Cinderella*. When she took over the role later, however, she made it peculiarly her own, showing new qualities of humour and romance.

Fonteyn's career was subsequently interrupted more than once by serious injury or illness, setbacks that might have precipitated early retirement in other dancers. Each time, however, she returned apparently stronger than before, and went on dancing long past the age when a dancer's powers usually decline. In Fonteyn's case the physical loss was compensated by continually developing expressiveness and artistic maturity. The initial impetus to extending her career came, however, when, in her early forties, she first danced with Rudolf Nureyev in 1962. He was, as she remarked, young enough to be her son, but there was such immediate rapport between them, such a chemistry between them on stage and such unanimity of purpose in their preparation that they became a partnership of uniquely satisfying quality. Both learned much from the other, enriching their performances with other partners as well as their joint appearances.

Fonteyn's long career on stage was made easier because her performances had never depended primarily on virtuosity, although in fact her technique was stronger than was often said. It was she who introduced the long sustained balances now expected of Aurora in the Rose Adagio; and when younger dancers took over some of her created roles they revealed unexpected difficulties, probably for lack of her gift of phrasing steps to the music. It can be said that Fonteyn never lacked the technique needed for any role she was cast in.

These covered a wide range. Among the many leading parts created for her with the Royal Ballet were *Scènes de ballet, Daphnis and Chloe, Tiresias, Sylvia, Homage to the Queen, La Féri, Birthday Offering* and *Marguerite and Armand*, all by Ashton; de Valois's *Don Quixote*, Helpmann's *Hamlet*, Petit's *Paradise Lost* and *Pélleas et Mélisande*. As guest elsewhere, John Cranko created *Poème de l'extase* for her in Stuttgart, Martha Graham mounted *Lucifer* for Nureyev and her, and Peter Darrell presented her as a Beardsley seductress in *Scarlet Pastorale* with the Scottish Ballet. She was (against the choreographer's wish but at the insistence of the Royal Ballet's American impresario Sol Hurok) the first Juliet in Kenneth MacMillan's production, and danced also in revivals of Massine's *Three Cornered Hat* with the choreographer, Balanchine's *Ballet Imperial* and *Night Shadow*, Fokine's *Firebird* and *Petrushka*, and Limón's *The Moor's Pavane* among others, also Nureyev's productions of the *Corsair pas de deux, La Bayadère, Raymonda* and the Grand Pas from *Paquita*.

With the Royal Ballet, Fonteyn occupied a position of complete supremacy. It has sometimes been said that her presence held back the advancement of other dancers, but there was never any among her contemporaries or juniors to equal her. By 1959 the demand for seats when she appeared was such that special prices were charged, and in that same year she began to be billed as a guest artist so that she should be free to accept more of the engagements she was offered all over the world. Nevertheless the Royal Ballet remained her base until after Ashton's retirement in 1970, although she also danced with more than 30 other companies and specially assembled groups.

She continued dancing until after her sixtieth birthday, which was marked by Covent Garden with a special gala including a *Salut d'amour* by Ashton which they danced together. Even after that she took on a new role as the leading nymph in Nijinsky's *L'Après-midi d'un faune* during Nureyev's 1979 summer season, and was persuaded by him to dance also two final performances of *Le Spectre de la rose*. Occasionally thereafter she appeared on special occasions but only in roles that required no dancing.

In 1955 Fonteyn married Dr Roberto de Arias, a sweetheart of her girlhood who had meanwhile married and had a family before re-entering her life. Immediately after their wedding he was appointed Panamanian ambassador to the Court of St James's. Fonteyn managed to combine the duties of an ambassador's wife with her already demanding career, and when her husband fell from political favour she supported his attempts to regain power in his own country. This led at one point to her arrest. She also found herself in police custody once after attending a party in the hippie district of Los Angeles. The dignity with which she endured such incidents showed one aspect of her character. Another was revealed by the devotion with which she personally nursed her husband for 25 years until his death after he had been shot and crippled by an associate with a personal grudge.

Two careers, as ballerina and as politician's wife, would have been enough for most women, but Fonteyn also became in 1954 president of the Royal Academy of Dancing and committed herself wholeheartedly to its well being.

In later years, Fonteyn developed a great interest in her husband's farm in Panama, and she continued to live there even after his death with few creature comforts because she had spent most of her money on caring for her husband and then incurred considerable costs having treatment in Texas when she developed cancer.

In spite of her illness she undertook some teaching and coaching, and also visited England each year for the Assembly of the RAD and for the degree ceremony at Durham University, which had elected her chancellor. She wrote and introduced a six-part television series *The Magic of Dance*. This was also the subject of one of several books she wrote; they included an autobiography, a study of Pavlova, and an account of *A Dancer's World*.

Fonteyn was created CBE in 1951 and DBE in 1956. She had honorary degrees from many universities and the Order of the Finnish Lion. A greater tribute however was the affection she inspired all over the world. The purity and musicality of her work won admiration; its liveliness and dedication inspired much warmer and deeper feelings, manifested in a special tribute performance at Covent Garden last May for which Nureyev danced and Placido Domingo sang.

Dame Margot Fonteyn as Ondine

FULKE WALWYN

Fulke Walwyn, National Hunt trainer, died on February 18 aged 80. He was born on November 8, 1910.

IN A career lasting 50 years Fulke Walwyn captured every important jumping race in the calendar. In some he was responsible for the winning horse at least half a dozen times and his final winning tally was 2,188 races won.

He first made his mark in the record books as an amateur rider and had a remarkable Grand National success in 1936. Two fences from home, going easily, the 100-1 outsider, Davy Jones, ridden by Anthony Mildmay, looked a certain winner. But then his reins broke. Meanwhile, Walwyn on Reynoldstown had survived losing not only his whip at Valentine's first time round, but also, more seriously, an iron when his mount blundered on the final circuit. Carrying 12st 2lb and conceding 23 lbs to Davy Jones, the tiring Reynoldstown then had a dozen lengths to make up on his only serious rival. Walwyn, however, with great perseverance and strength from the saddle, ensured that he did so, and, albeit helped by Davy Jones's misfortune, went away to win comfortably.

In 1937 Walwyn turned professional, riding for George Beeby, but a fall and a badly broken arm kept him out of action for much of the season. He had already survived a serious fall and head injuries but in 1938 at Ludlow he had an even worse accident. Unconscious for a month, he was fitted with a metal plate in his head and doctors warned that further injury might prove fatal. Walwyn, heeding the advice, took out a licence to train at Delamere House, Lambourn, in 1939.

Fulke Thomas Tyndall Walwyn was born in Wrexham. His father was a serving officer in the Royal Welch Fusiliers, an outstanding show-jumper and devoted to hunting. Walwyn was in the saddle early, taking part in gymkhanas, show-jumping and hunting and continued to do so at school at Malvern. After Sandhurst he was commissioned into the Ninth Lancers. In 1935, however, in a stuffy matter of regimental etiquette, he was obliged to resign. His "offence" was evening newspaper publicity concerning a court hearing following a fracas in a Soho night-club. Walwyn had appeared as a witness — but for the prosecution.

By the time war was declared, he had achieved 18 winners as a trainer. He was recalled to the colours but his injuries at first prevented active participation and dictated a most unlikely role: in the Military Police. This turned out to have its advantages. He was able to commute between Tidworth and Lambourn where he and his then wife, Diana, continued to run their small establishment. Later he was medically up-graded, rejoined the Ninth Lancers, and served in France. In 1944, Walwyn moved his quarters to Saxon House, Lambourn, where he lived for the rest of his life.

By 1946, with National Hunt racing regaining momentum after the wartime break, he was leading trainer for the first time. In the same year, the late Miss Dorothy Paget sent him some chasers and hurdlers. This was a turning point in his fortunes, though at the time it was not universally seen as such. The eccentric Miss Paget was endowed with limitless money but an equally infinite ruthlessness towards trainers who could not strike the success she craved. Walwyn appeared to be the latest candidate for serving his brief time before joining a lengthy list of summary dismissals by the owner. However, this proved far from being the case and Walwyn eventually earned the reputation of being the man who, at last, had "tamed Dorothy Paget."

It was a successful association. On one afternoon in 1948 Walwyn saddled five Paget winners at Folkestone. He was champion jumps trainer on a further two occasions and gained victories for his mercurial patron on the flat, when he sent out Aldborough to win both the Queen Alexandra Stakes and Doncaster Cup in 1950.

In the early 1960s came some of his best and really great horses: Mandarin, the little chaser, once described as "a non-pareil of courage and toughness," who was owned by Mme Hennessy; Bill Golling's Mill House, winner of the Cheltenham Gold Cup, Hennessy and King George VI Chase, all in 1963; and Team Spirit, another pocket-sized hero owned by an American partnership and carrying the colours of Jack Goodman when, at the fifth attempt at the age of 12, he won the Grand National in 1964.

Although Walwyn himself chose Diamond Edge, dual Whitbread winner in 1979 and 1981, as his "greatest training triumph", many would argue in favour of Mandarin as equally representative of the trainer's skill. He won the first running of the Hennessy in 1957 and the Cheltenham Gold Cup, as well as the King George VI Chase twice. He was three times runner-up in the Whitbread and, with his rider, Fred Winter, was co-star of an epic afternoon at Auteuil in 1962 when capturing the Grand Steeple-chase de Paris despite a broken bridle. Yet his career, like that of Diamond Edge, was beset with injury and setbacks which would have defeated a less-inspired trainer. One of Walwyn's great gifts lay in an almost clairvoyant instinct about, and feeling for, horses which were difficult to keep sound.

In 1973, on the death of Peter Cazalet, Walwyn became trainer to the Queen Mother. This happy association produced a flow of victories in the royal colours, notably with Game Spirit, winner

of 21 races; Isle of Man, another prolific winner; Tammuz, victorious in the 1975 Schweppes Gold Trophy; and, yet another illustration of expertise with older horses possessed of less than perfect legs, the game old campaigner, Special Cargo, winner of three Grand Military Gold Cups, who in the 1984 Whitbread beat his stable-companion, Diamond Edge, into third place.

Among other famous horses were: the Champion Hurdlers, Anzio and Kirrie-muir; The Dikler, winner of a King George VI Chase and a Whitbread, who ran in every Cheltenham Gold Cup between 1970 and 1976, beating Pendil by a short-head in 1973, as well as being runner-up and twice third in other years; and Taxidermist, ridden by John Lawrence (now Lord Oaksey) with a Whitbread and a Hennessy to his credit.

The formidable statistics of Walwyn-trained important winners include the Whitbread Gold Cup, Hennessy Gold Cup, and Grand Military Gold Cup seven times apiece; the King George VI Chase five times; the Cheltenham Gold Cup four times the Scottish Grand National and the Champion Hurdle twice each; and the Grand National once. He was champion jumps trainer five times.

Walwyn was a man who measured his words, but in his gravelly voice spoke from a deep well of equine lore. Training was his life and he had little interest in other pursuits. When he was 60 he said: "I'm getting a bit old, I may give it another year or two before retiring." That was one of his forecasts which happily proved well wide of the mark. He did not give up his licence for another 19 years, retiring at the end of the 1989-90 season and handing over the running of Saxon House to his second wife, Cath, his first wife having died in 1949. Shortly afterwards it was announced that the Kim Muir Memorial Chase — the three-mile race for amateur riders on the opening day of the Cheltenham National Hunt Festival — was to be renamed The Fulke Walwyn Challenge Cup Chase.

He leaves his widow, Cath, and a daughter.

SLIM GAILLARD

Slim Gaillard, jazz musician, died in a London hospital on February 26 aged 75. He was born on January 4, 1916.

SLIM (Bulee) Gaillard first came to prominence in the jazz world in the 1930s when he teamed up with the legendary bassist, Slam Stewart, to form the duo "Slim and Slam". The two had met at Jock's Place in Harlem in 1937 and they scored a hit with "Flat Foot Floogie" in the following year. A long-running series on Radio WNEW brought them national recognition. The hallmark of their routines which led to other big hits like "Tutti Frutti" and "Cement Mixer" was a jive slang, evolved principally by Gaillard, which they called "Vout". This lent a pleasantly incomprehensible quality to their already frenzied act, which drew much of its dynamic quality from Gaillard's versatility as vocalist, pianist, guitarist, and tap-dancer. The vocabulary and idiom of Vout were not confined to music. On one occasion, later enshrined on film and seen in a four-part series about his life on BBC television in 1989, Gaillard was heard expounding a recipe for avocado seed soup to his great friend and admirer, Dizzie Gillespie.

After the war Gaillard's career rather went off the boil in America and he was seen less often in public. But in the 1980s he came to Britain and in London his career took on a new lease of life. In clubs such as the Wag he became the idol of a new generation of admirers and, comparatively late in life, was able to savour the sort of adulation he thought he had left behind in the 1930s.

Much of Bulee Gaillard's life story has a mythical quality about it, but one which entirely fitted his multi-faceted personality. He always said he was born in the Caribbean (though most record books adhere to the more pedestrian origins of Detroit). His father was apparently a German Jew who worked as a steward on cargo boats. His mother was of African descent. His early life, as recounted by himself, had an exotic flavour about it. As he grew up he accompanied his father on his voyages. During one of these, he always claimed, he was left by his father on a quayside in Crete when the boat sailed and effectively orphaned. He wandered the world as a ship's cook. Eventually he ended up in Detroit where he found work with the Ford Motor Company. He was also involved in various illegal activities, such as driving a hearse full of illicit hooch during the Prohibition.

However he did not succumb to a life of crime, and achieved independence for himself by working up a solo variety act which involved playing the guitar, tenor sax and vibes, as well as singing and dancing. These abilities led to his association with Slam Stewart which lasted until 1942 when Gaillard was drafted into the American army air force, where, so the story goes, he was found to have a vastly above average IQ and qualified as a pilot, flying B-25 and B-26 bombers in the Pacific.

After the war he returned to show business. He already had a certain momentum from his pre-war career and from his appearance in several films, such as *Star Spangled Rhythm*, and *Hellzapoppin'*. In addition his good looks earned him the nickname "Dark Gable" and considerable favour with the ladies (he always said he had forgotten how many children he had fathered). Nevertheless his career never really regained its earlier momentum and it was not until he toured the United Kingdom in 1982 that he was to know the pleasing phenomenon of packed houses again. By this time he had again become familar from the television series *Roots — the Next Generation*.

Settling down in Chelsea he became a familiar feature at London clubs and at jazz events and festivals all over Britain. He may not, as a musician, have been one of the great figures of jazz, but his ingenious ability to dramatise his own life and to blur the boundaries between jive and reality makes him one of the endearing originals of its culture.

FELIPE BENAVIDES

Dr Felipe Benavides, Peruvian naturalist, conservationist and diplomat, died in London on February 21 aged 73. He was born on August 7, 1917.

FELIPE Benavides fought many doughty wildlife conservation campaigns but for none is he better remembered than for his stalwart defence of *Lama vicugna*, the vicuña of the Andean plateau. A charming and graceful cameloid ruminant, the vicuña has the misfortune to possess a soft brown wool which is much prized in high quality textile manufacture. The vicuña was the subject of protective regulation at the time of the Incas and successive Peruvian governments had always recognised the animal's economic importance. Nevertheless when Benavides first became interested in the vicuña in the 1950s he was appalled to discover that numbers had dwindled to little more than 5,000 from a population estimated to be one million at the turn of the century. This began a campaign which was in effect to last Benavides for the rest of his life.

The son of Alfredo Benavides a Peruvian ambassador to Britain during the war, and a relative of Oscar Benavides, a former president of Peru, Felipe Benavides began life as a career diplomat.

As a trainee he had been a contemporary of Xavier Perez de Cuellar, present secretary-general of the United Nations. He was at his father's embassy during the interesting period after Peru entered the war on the allied side in 1943. After the war he studied at the London School of Economics under Harold Laski and began a business career in tandem with his diplomatic activities. He represented the construction company George Wimpey in South America and his work in securing contracts for it earned him appointment as honorary OBE in 1963.

In the meantime a thesis on Peruvian imports had already alerted him to the importance of the vicuña. Nevertheless it was the plight of the whale off the coast of Peru which gave him his first wildlife conservation concern. As Peruvian observer to the International Whaling Commission in London he was horrified by the scale of the slaughter worldwide and found that in Peru's case the depredation was the result of a fleet owned by Aristotle Onassis. With characteristic energy he mounted a press campaign which led to a sea chase by the Peruvian navy and the arrest of Onassis's fleet. Onassis was fined $3 million and sold up his whale-catching business.

When he learned of the threat to the

vicuña Benavides began a similarly energetic campaign and his powerful advocacy led to the setting up of reserves, notably at Pampa Galeras, on the Andean *altiplano*, where in little more than ten years from 1967 a herd of 40,000 had been established. This feat earned Benavides the first J. Paul Getty wildlife conservation prize in 1975. But the very success of the experiment brought attendant perils for the vicuña. Claiming that a drought and shortage of grazing would condemn large numbers of the animals to slow starvation a lobby of scientists tried to obtain permission for a cull and the removal of the vicuña from the list of endangered species.

Benavides thwarted the latter threat but with the backing of the World Wildlife Fund for Nature the cull of 7,000 "surplus" vicuñas went ahead. The skins were cured and stored, the meat was sent to Lima supermarkets and Peruvian newspapers carried recipes for vicuña-burgers. The cull severely strained Benavides's relations with the WWF and he resigned his international trusteeship. Meanwhile Benavides's campaign against the cull led to an International Fund for Animal Welfare fact-finding mission to Pampa Galeras which reported that there

was no evidence of drought or over-grazing. Even before that, public outrage had led to a decision from the president of Peru to halt the cull.

Another of Benavides's campaigns was over Paracas, a Peruvian coastal site which is an important staging post for migrating birds. Commercial exploitation of the local shellfish threatened this paradisiac spot with destruction through the construction of a pier, the incessant rumble of heavy trucks and the creation of a shanty town for workers. In spite of the area's being designated a marine national park this was one of Benavides's battles still unresolved at his death.

Like many people of his strong convictions Benavides made many enemies, some of whom, in the case of the vicuña, accused him of using the public's predilection for cute woolly animals to subvert sound husbandry. The WWF felt that the vicuña should pay its way as the price of survival and Peruvian officials called him a "sentimental, egoistical publicity-seeker". He in turn called them "liars and butchers". Certainly no one who saw the television documentary *Benavides!* on Channel 4's *Fragile Earth* series can regret his tireless and eloquent campaign to save an endearing species.

EDWIN LAND

Edwin Herbert Land, the inventor of instant photography and founder of the Polaroid Corporation, died on March 1 aged 81. He was born on May 7, 1909.

POLAROID sunglasses and 60-second photography were just two of the better known achievements through which Edwin Land revolutionised the world of optics in a career during which he amassed over 500 patents. Yet in spite of professorships at Harvard and the Massachusetts Institute of Technology and a string of honorary doctorates, Land was not an academic in the conventional sense and, indeed, never took a first degree from Harvard.

Edwin Herbert Land was born in Bridgeport, Connecticut. His father was a landowner and ran a scrap iron business. Land's first and perhaps most resounding discovery, was the result of an evening stroll down Broadway when he was 17 and a freshman at Harvard. He was struck by the glare from competing theatre and billboard lights and pondered a method of eliminating it. He applied himself with single minded dedication to the challenge, taking time off from his course at Harvard, and at the age of 20, announced his polarising filter. This eventually became the mainstay of the Polaroid Corporation which he set up in 1937 to market his inventions. It was the first of many discoveries in the optical field that eventually embraced work for gun sights and aerial surveillance during the second world war and afterwards. The camera in the U2 spy plane was built utilising his patents. The instant X-ray photograph was another of his achievements.

Land's name is also associated with the system which eventually led to instantaneous dry photographs in colour. As with the polarising lens, Land's inspiration to investigate this possibility led to instant photography being born of an innocent curiosity. In 1941 while he was on holiday with his family in New Mexico, his five-year-old daughter asked him why she could not see immediately the photograph her father had taken of her. His mind set to work. He later recalled: "Within an hour the camera, the film and the physical chemistry became so clear that with a great sense of excitement I hurried to the place where a friend was staying, to describe to him in detail a dry camera which would give a picture immediately after exposure. In my mind it was so real that I spent several hours on the description." Nevertheless it was not until 1948 that the Polaroid system of instant photography was put on sale. Early instant photography meant bulky equipment and the process itself was a messy one. But Land developed the system, refining it over the next 30 years until, in 1972, the SX-70 system provided the first pocket sized instant camera able to deliver dry colour photographs.

Land built the Polaroid Corporation as a business with the same tenacity he applied to developing his scientific discoveries. It was run in accorance with rigid principles, reflecting its founder's conservatism which nevertheless went hand in hand with a sense of fairness. In its early years the company was never allowed to borrow money, choosing instead to finance its own research and product development. Land fostered attitudes of self development in employment, encouraging his workforce to vary their jobs and learn new skills. With giants such as IBM, Polaroid became one of the legends of US business. By 1970 sales had reached half a billion dollars and $1,000 invested in the company in 1938 was worth $3 million. In later years Polaroid instituted suits for infringement of its copyright, notably against Eastman Kodak over its introduction of an instant photography package. The conflict was eventually settled in Polaroid's favour.

Up to the time of his retirement in 1982 when he gave up his active directorship and became honorary chairman, it was always considered that Polaroid's most valuable asset was its founder's knack of coming up with new, practicable ideas. True to his scientific background, he always maintained that financial profit should never be the only criterion for running the business. This led to several failures, most notably Land's persistent attempts from the 1930s onwards to eliminate glare from car headlights. Despite years of research he failed to find a workable, affordable system that could stand bad weather. In the field of photocopying he was beaten by Xerox, whose system was more advanced than his own.

Land was on *Life* magazine's list of the 100 most important Americans of this century and his personal fortune was estimated as being somewhere between $500m and $1,000m. But for a man of his wealth he lived modestly and shunned publicity about his private life. He gave freely to scientific research.

He is survived by his wife, Helen Maislen, whom he married in 1929, and their two daughters.

LORD PENNEY

Lord Penney, OM, KBE, FRS, creator of the British atom bomb, died on March 3 aged 81. He was born on June 24, 1909.

WILLIAM Penney provided the vigorous scientific and administrative leadership in the post-war years which enabled Britain to test and develop both fission and thermonuclear bombs and take its place in the nuclear club. He had already played an important role in the wartime American atomic bomb project and was highly regarded by the Americans. Indeed they had badly wanted him to continue as part of the US team for the Bikini atoll tests of 1946, by which time the British had been excluded by American legislation from partnership in the further development of nuclear bombs and left to work as best they might, in isolation. Throughout the 1950s, when the government's and Penney's conviction that Britain must possess a nuclear deterrent

– and his capacity to create it – led to the British bomb, he remained the British asset coveted above all by the Americans. Undoubtedly the remarkable strides he made towards a British hydrogen bomb were instrumental in restoring the principle of exchange of nuclear technology between the two countries. Penney's gifts as a scientist were intuitive understanding and simplicity of approach and he was good at explaining complex scientific and technical matters to laymen.

William George Penney was the son of W. A. Penney, a sergeant-major in the Royal Army Ordnance Corps. He was educated at Sheerness Technical School, where he showed marked mathematical ability, and from which he gained a scholarship to the Royal College of Science, one of the constituent colleges of the Imperial College of Science and Technology.

Graduating with a brilliant first, he was

41

awarded in 1931 a Commonwealth Fund fellowship and he spent the next two years in the United States at the University of Wisconsin. Thence, with the award of an 1851 Exhibition senior studentship he proceeded to Trinity College, Cambridge, where he carried out theoretical investigations on the structure of metals and the magnetic properties of crystals. In 1936 he was elected to the Stokes studentship at Pembroke College, but in the same year he returned to London as assistant professor of mathematics at Imperial College.

Shortly after the outbreak of war he was on loan to the Ministry of Home Security and the Admiralty to investigate problems connected with the nature and properties of blast waves. It was through this work that in 1944 he came to be sent to Los Alamos to join the British team working on the atomic bomb.

This was the turning point of Penney's career. At Los Alamos his varied abilities received greater scope for development and his qualities of character, which enabled him to lead as well as to work in harmony with others, gained wider recognition. He soon established a high reputation and made many enduring friendships with American scientists. He made blast measurements at the first nuclear explosion in the United States and he was one of the two British observers to accompany the flight when the second atom bomb was dropped on Nagasaki, the other being Group Captain Leonard Cheshire, VC. Penney was also one of the British party at the Bikini tests in 1946, where his reputation was greatly enhanced by his determination of the blast power, using simple equipment, at a time when the United States's more sophisticated gauges failed to operate. For his services to the United States Penney was awarded the US Medal of Freedom (Silver Palm). At home in 1946 Penney was made OBE and appointed chief superintendent of armament research in the Ministry of Supply.

On the failure of the discussions within the Atomic Energy Commission of the United Nations to reach any agreement on control of nuclear weapons, the government decided to build British weapons. The responsibility for the design and development fell to Penney, using plutonium to be made in reactors at Windscale. Penney had to start from scratch without the benefit of US co-operation since the US Atomic Energy Act of 1946 ended the wartime partnership and prohibited the release of any information from the United States. Scientific and engineering teams had to be built up, new technologies developed, and highly specialised facilities constructed at Aldermaston, before the first atomic bomb could be ready for testing. That this was done by October 1952 was a remarkable achievement and confirmed the qualities of character, scientific ability and leadership already recognised in Penney. The test was carried out in the Montebello Islands, off the north-west coast of Australia, and was completely successful. For his distinguished services in this achievement Penney, on his return from Australia, was created KBE.

This development was followed up by Penney and his team at the rapidly expanding establishment at Aldermaston, of which Penney became director in 1953 when, for the first time, it was known publicly as the Atomic Weapons Research Establishment. In 1954, the responsibility for the development of atomic energy was transferred from the Ministry of Supply to a non-departmental body, the United Kingdom Atomic Energy Authority (UKAEA). Penney was appointed a member of the authority with responsibility for the research and development of nuclear weapons. In this he was outstandingly successful. Under his leadership a vigorous programme led to an early test, in May 1957, of the first British hydrogen bomb at Christmas Island in the Pacific Ocean, followed by further tests in 1958.

This achievement had far reaching consequences in that it made possible the bilateral treaty, signed in 1958 between the United States and the United Kingdom for mutual assistance in nuclear defence and the consequential exchange of a range of nuclear information. This ended the total isolation of the British programme. Penney played a leading part in these negotiations as he did in the talks which led, in 1963, to the nuclear test ban treaty forbidding atmospheric nuclear tests. During all these talks Penney's presence and advice were much valued by the British prime minister, Harold Macmillan, in his negotiations with President Kennedy.

Penney's success owed much to his personality and character. In essence he was a friendly, undevious, usually humorous man. Nevertheless he was a shrewd administrator and a good judge of people. The quality which endeared him to his team at Aldermaston was that he treated his scientific staff, of all ranks, as scientific equals. With all the complexities of the phenomena involved in nuclear weapons Penney had also the gift of explaining complicated matters simply and directly to all types of listeners, which was particularly effective in his dealings with the forces and with politicians.

When in 1959 Sir John Cockroft relinquished his post as member of the Authority for Research, with responsibility for Harwell, Penney succeeded him. On a reorganisation of the UKAEA in the spring of 1961, he was made deputy chairman with primary responsibility for scientific and technical co-ordination throughout the authority. He was chairman of the UKAEA from 1964 to 1967. During his later years with the UKAEA Penney presided over many important developments, among them the prototype fast reactor at Dounreay, the diversification of the authority's work into non-nuclear areas and the first nuclear power programme, as well as the drawing up of plans for a second.

In 1967 he left to return to his alma mater as rector of Imperial College of Science and Technology. During turbulent years which saw a great deal of student unrest overseas and in other institutions at home, Penney provided a stable leadership which introduced changes to accommodate the altering circumstances and attitudes. Thanks to a judicious mixture of patience, benign good humour and clear common sense, such problems as a growth in student numbers, increased sophistication of research with its attendant industrial relations problems, the democratisation of the managerial constitution and the increased participation of the students were all confronted with a minimum of disruption. In particular, he extended membership of the board of studies to include students and non-professional staff and created an academic staff assembly. He retired from the rectorship in 1973.

In 1985 Lord Penney gave evidence in London to an Australian royal commission which was investigating the effects of the atomic tests carried out in Australia in the 1950s. In answer to questions about claims of breaches in safety standards, he said that all tests had been conducted in accordance with safety standards and that no information about possible effects on the Australian population had been withheld. He did, however, concede that the technical details of the nuclear weapons had been kept secret from the Australian government since it was the policy of the Australians not to be party to information about nuclear weapons or to become a nuclear state.

Penney was elected fellow of the Royal Society in 1946. He was treasurer of the society for four years from 1956–60, and did much to consolidate its financial positiion. He was created a life peer in 1967 and appointed a member of the Order of Merit in 1969. He received numerous distinctions from academic bodies, being a fellow of Imperial College, London, fellow of Winchester College, and supernumerary fellow of St Catherine's College, Oxford; he was awarded honorary degrees by a number of universities at home and abroad.

He was twice married; first, in 1935, to Adele Minnie Elms, of Queenborough, Kent, by whom he had two sons, and after her death to Eleanor Joan Quennell of Croydon. He is survived by her and by the children of his first marriage.

SERGE GAINSBOURG

Serge Gainsbourg, French pop singer and composer, was found dead in his Paris apartment on March 2 aged 62. He was born on April 2, 1928.

SERGE Gainsbourg is likely to be remembered less for his contribution to French pop music than for the degenerate image he cultivated. As a singer he started out in the mainstream of French popular music as it was in the Sixties and thereafter adapted skilfully to changes in public taste to retain for himself a following among successive generations of pop fans. None of this would have brought him much standing in the international – that is to say largely English-speaking – pop world, without the series of shocking gestures which accompanied the output of songs.

These were presented as the natural fall-out from a dissolute and riotous life but were carefully calculated. Thus the 1969 song "Je t'aime, moi non plus" which made him notorious in Britain through its being ostensibly a recording of an erotic encounter between Gainsbourg and his companion of that time, the British actress Jane Birkin, was, of course, a studio construction with both being passionate on their own in separate booths. But it worked on the fevered

44

imagination of Sixties Britain, the fact that one of the participants was a British girl doubtless adding to its titillating effect on the Anglo-Saxon mentality. Thereafter an attack on the song by the Vatican newspaper, *Osservatore Romano*, and a ban on the song in Italy only doubly ensured it a runaway success in the charts of many countries.

Serge Gainsbourg was born Lucien Ginsburg, the son of a Russian émigré nightclub pianist, Joseph Ginsburg. He was educated at Paris's Lycée Condorcet, from which he was thrown out for indiscipline and at the Ecole nationale supérieure des beaux arts. He started his working life as a pianist and guitarist at the Paris cabaret Milord l'Arsouille in the 1950s. He also began composing and won the grand prix de l'Académie Charles-Cros for his first album, *Du Chant a la une* in 1959. Besides his more fringe writing he also created songs for vocalists such as Petula Clark and Juliette Greco.

In 1960 he began a film career with a part in *Voulez-vous Danser Avec Moi?* and thereafter appeared in a number of features with such characteristic titles as *Erotissimo* (1969) and *Cannabis* (1970). He also composed the scores for a number of films, notably *Les Loups dans la bergerie*, *L'Eau à bouche* and *Le Jardiner d'Argenteuil*.

He met Jane Birkin on the set of the film *Slogan* (1968) which has being directed by Pierre Grimblat. Their relationship lasted 12 years and produced a daughter, Charlotte, who is herself a cinema actress.

Gainsbourg also had a career as an actor and presenter on television where he seldom failed to come up with behaviour calculated to scandalise audiences. On one occasion he was criticised for burning a 500-franc note on a live show. On another − this time the popular family music programme *Champs Elysées* − he made earthily explicit suggestions to the singer Whitney Houston to the predictable outrage of 17 million viewers, his employers at Channel 2 and Miss Houston herself. But such affronts were a carefully calculated part of his broadcasting persona, as was a reggae version of the French national anthem the Marseillaise, which brought threats of violence from right wing groups in France.

Gainsbourg's health suffered badly from his excessive drinking and smoking and he suffered a succession of heart attacks as well as having to have two thirds of his liver surgically removed in 1989.

In recent years he had lived with Caroline von Paulus (better known as the model Bambou), by whom he had a son. A marriage earlier in his life to Françoise Pancrazzi was dissolved.

SIR JOSEPH LOCKWOOD

Sir Joseph Lockwood, chairman of EMI from 1954 to 1974, died on March 6 aged 86. He was born on November 14, 1904.

JOSEPH Lockwood was by profession a miller and when he entered the world of recorded music it was with a fresh eye, but an eye that had been trained in the detail of engineering equipment. It was to prove a potent combination in guiding the development of EMI in the competitive conditions of the 1960s.

Joseph Flawith Lockwood was born in Southwell, Nottinghamshire. His father, also Joseph, was a miller and his mother, Mabel, came from a long line of millers. His father died when Joseph was only six years old. After leaving Newark Grammar School at the age of 16 he joined the family mill, where he trained for three years. But two cousins were earmarked to run the business so he went to study milling in Santiago, Chile.

There Lockwood was made manager of a mill when he was only 20, a position he

46

held for four years. But in 1928 he decided that his future lay back home, where he developed an interest in designing and building mills, and joined Henry Simon, a leading company in that field. He remained with the firm for 26 years. For the first five years he was technical manager at Simon's operations in Paris and Brussels. Then he was made a director of the subsidiary in Buenos Aires, Argentina, chairman of the Australian business and director of the parent company. In 1939 Lockwood wrote the first of two books on the industry, *Provender Milling – the Manufacture of Feeding Stuffs for Livestock*.

During the second world war he was put under the charge of Sir Hartley Shawcross and given the task of organising the protection of factories, docks and other vital installations in the North West Civil Defence region. As the outcome of the war became clear, the government drew on Lockwood's milling expertise, attaching him to the working party planning food supplies for Europe after the war. In 1944 he joined the supreme headquarters of the allied expeditionary force as a civilian officer, to supervise the rehabilitation of devastated flour mills and the revival of the railways.

In 1945 Lockwood returned to Simon and soon wrote his second book, *Flour Milling*, which became a standard work and has been translated into several languages. In 1950 he became chairman and managing director of Simon, and a few months later accepted an invitation to become a director of the National Research Development Corporation, where he was involved until 1967.

That was to prove a fateful appointment, for there he encountered Sir Edward de Stein, the merchant banker. Before long de Stein was asked to find a chairman for EMI, then a loss-making gramophone company. Lockwood found that it was run by directors who had fallen into the trap of indulging their musical whims, rather than finding out what the public wanted to hear. He put these decisions in the hands of a committee which judged proposals on Lockwood's criterion that they had to break even within three years. While EMI maintained its reputation for fine classical music, Lockwood's period of office coincided with the boom in popular music, when EMI signed up the Americans Frank Sinatra, Dean Martin and Paul Anka as well as the biggest prize of all – the Beatles.

Lockwood, who was knighted in 1960, realised the necessity of having a strong US presence and took over Capitol Records, which became America's biggest music company. He also ensured that the company remained at the forefront of technical innovation, which led to the development of the body scanner for medical diagnosis. His engineering interests took him on to the boards of Smiths Industries, Hawker Siddeley, British Domestic Appliances, Beecham Group, Laird Group, and the Industrial Reorganisation Corporation, the Labour government initiative which he chaired from 1969 to 1971.

Although he professed to enjoy the Beatles, his own preference was for classical music. He was particularly fond of Mozart and relished the intimate atmosphere of Glyndebourne. He was a governor of the Royal Ballet School, member of the Arts Council, and chairman of the Young Vic Theatre Company, the South Bank Theatre Board and the Central School of Speech and Drama. From 1971 to 1985 he was also chairman of the Royal Ballet, an appointment in which he took great interest and which gave him much pleasure. He retired as chairman of EMI in 1974, leaving the board five years later.

He never married.

SIR BRIAN BATSFORD

Sir Brian Batsford, painter, chairman of Batsford Books from 1952 to 1974 and Conservative MP for Ealing South from 1958 to 1974, died on March 5 aged 80. He was born Brian Cook on December 18, 1910.

SIR Brian Batsford inhabited diverse worlds in a life which saw him as illustrator, opposition whip in Parliament and chairman of a well-known publishing firm. But it was undoubtedly as Brian Cook, the painter, who provided the eye-catching covers for Batsford's British Heritage series in the 1930s, that he made his most distinctive contribution to his times. And in spite of his other achievements he was content to list himself in *Who's Who* as, simply, "painter".

The son of Arthur Caldwell Cook, he was educated at Repton and joined the production department of B. T. Batsford in 1928. He was a nephew of Harry Batsford, himself of the third generation of proprietors, the first, Bradley Batsford, having founded the business in 1843. Brian Cook began work in the production department but was allowed to take part-time classes at the Central School of Arts and Crafts. His artistic talents were to provide one of the planks of Batsford's salvation in the crisis which struck publishing in the Depression years. Asked to produce a book jacket for *The Villages of England*, he came up with a wrap-round design, a novel feature at that time. His use of flat, bright colours, which, while verging on the garish, had

48

an instantly evocative quality, imparted a striking visual effect to the new series. The design also had the virtue of being printable on rough paper, a perhaps incidental element that was soon to prove a valuable asset.

The crash of 1929 compelled Batsford, along with many other publishers, to reduce its outlay on authors and illustrators, and Brian Cook was designated sole illustrator of a new small format series called British Heritage. In the period before the war he designed over 100 such covers for titles which ranged over such subjects as *English Woodland*, *The Heart of Scotland*, *English Villages and Hamlets* and *The English Country House* and his distinctive Art Deco style became an important influence on how people viewed their rural heritage in an era before colour photography. An accompanying series, The Face of Britain, covered the country geographically and ran on after the war until 1950. The name Brian Cook can also been seen on railway, holiday and travel agency posters of the period and he exhibited in Paris.

Brian Cook's contribution to the visual content of Batsford books ceased when war came. In 1941 he joined the RAF and served in Bomber Command intelligence. After he came out he took the surname Batsford (his mother's maiden name) at his uncle Harry's request in 1946. Thereafter he was much more involved in the affairs of the firm of which he became chairman after his uncle's death in 1952. From then on Brian Cook the painter was well nigh forgotten by the public who perceived only the busy persona of Brian Batsford the publisher and man of affairs.

Politics also interested him. After an unsuccessful tilt at Parliament in a by-election at Chelmsford as a National Government candidate in 1945, he got in as a Conservative for South Ealing at a by-election in April 1958. From 1959 to 1960 he was PPS to the minister of works, and from 1962 to 1964 he was an assistant government whip. But though as a whip he was noted for the quiet persuasiveness of his methods it was through the exercise of his original arts that he made his greatest impact on the House, when he designed the Commons Christmas card in 1962. Depicting a winter scene in Parliament Square, the card sold 100,000 that Christmas.

When the Conservatives went out of office in 1964 Batsford became opposition deputy chief whip, a job he did until 1967. In 1967 he was appointed Conservative parliamentary representative on the Greater London Council, then a new appointment designed to establish co-operation between the party in parliament and the then Conservative-dominated GLC. From 1973 to 1975 he was also chairman of the Royal Society of Arts. In 1974 he retired from parliament and was knighted. He also stood down as chairman of Batsford though he remained president until 1977.

He had continued to paint, but in the 1980s his work gained a new impetus, with two of his paintings being included in an Arts Council exhibition, *Landscape in Britain 1850-1950*, at the Hayward Gallery in 1983. He was suddenly in demand for a range of commercial work ranging from biscuit tin lids for Harrods to Christmas catalogue covers for the National Trust. In 1987 he published the collection *The Britain of Brian Cook* and had a restrospective at the Michael Parkin Gallery.

He was a familiar figure in the beautiful Sussex village of Rye in which he lived until recently at Lamb House, where Henry James had written some of his novels, where E. F. Benson, of *Mapp and Lucia* fame, had been a tenant, and where his brother, A. C. Benson, had written the words of "Land of hope and Glory". For five years from 1978 he was chairman of Rye Conservation Society and had continued as its president.

He leaves his widow, Wendy, and two daughters.

JACK MEYER

Jack Meyer, OBE, founder and first headmaster of Millfield School, died on March 9 aged 85. He was born on March 15, 1905.

ROLLO John Oliver Meyer was bound to make his mark. He was unorthodox, quick to spot where opportunity lay and had unusual flair for teaching and sport. He was not only the founder of one of the most expensive schools in the country but was also a county cricketer who dismissed Bradman. Meyer had ideals; he encouraged princes to pay more for their sons to go to Millfield to subsidise the children of the poor.

Educated at Haileybury and Cambridge, Meyer early gained fame as an all-round games-player rather than as an academic. After a short period teaching, he went to India cotton broking in search of a fortune. At the time it was said that in the first three years of broking you made a loss, in the second three you recouped it and the final three years made your fortune. But the slump came at the wrong time and Meyer left the Bombay business in 1929 after only two years. He made his mark in cricket. In 1931, he moved back into education to coach sons of some of the Indian aristocracy for entry to Oxford and Cambridge. In 1935 he was persuaded to take five of them to England. Millfield was thus established. The five boys were joined by one girl, and the school was co-educational from the start. His wife, Joyce, whom he married in 1931, played a key role. He played holiday cricket for his new county, Somerset, and subsequently captained it.

Millfield was slow to develop at first but entered a period of sudden expansion after the war when many returning ex-servicemen needed an extra fillip to gain university entrance qualifications. At the same time a preparatory department was started. Although the number of pupils increased, the staff to pupil ratio was kept at one to five or six.

Meyer found time to aid the disadvantaged. Dyslexia was then barely acknowledged other than as a euphemism for stupidity or emotional disturbance. In fact, a large proportion of apparently sub-literate children had high IQs, and merely suffered from an eye "defect" which jumbled words. Through his system of eye exercises, and explanations, he found children could often quickly overcome this handicap. In helping them conquer their remaining sense of inferiority, he found that identifying a particular sport in which they could excel and intensively training them in it was a key. This reversed the traditional English concept of the "all-rounder", and as the nurturing of sports prowess progressed it paved the way for an astonishing series of British Olympic medals and other international sporting achievements.

Meyer resigned in 1970 at the demand of the governors of the educational charity he had founded. He exiled himself to Greece, undertaking in return for a modest pension never to discuss his departure publicly. The row caused counter criticism of the governors. Meyer was an avid student of the horseracing form book and trainers' gossip.

The success of Jack Meyer's teaching methods may be judged by the fact that on his retirement he left a thriving Millfield with 1,000 pupils in residence, the parents of whom were prepared to pay the salaries of nearly 200 teachers. He had been appointed OBE in 1967.

His pupils included the Welsh rugby star Gareth Edwards, the swimmer Duncan Goodhew, the athletes David Hemery and Mary Rand, the jockey and trainer Ian Balding and Major Dick Hern, who trained horses for the Queen. Among other pupils were the Kings of Saudi Arabia and Thailand, Sir James Goldsmith, the financier, and Tony Blackburn, the disc jockey.

However, retirement weighed heavily and he attempted to raise capital to start a new international school in Greece, but failing to do so, became head of Campion College in Athens, a day school that had been running for three years. The school had been founded to provide an English-based education for the international community there.

When he took over there were 45 pupils. He started a junior department and kindergarten and by 1977, when he became president for three years, there were over 1,000. In 1980 he founded St Lawrence College, a similar establishment, and was headmaster until he retired through ill-health in 1986.

He was aided in negotiating political minefields by helping the son of one of the Colonels to overcome dyslexia. Finally he was co-founder, rector and director of Byron College, a remedial education centre, for a year. In 1945 he founded and ran until 1971 Edgarley Hall, Glastonbury, which is now a leading preparatory school with over 500 children and is one of the best equipped in the country.

Like so much else that he did, his cricket was based on instinct and imagination. Through his personality, as much as his ability, he was forever trying to manipulate the course of a game. He had the versatility of the natural games-player. Besides being three years in the Cambridge cricket XI, he got a rackets blue and was on the edge of the golf side. When, in 1938, the Gentlemen beat the Players at Lord's for only the second time since 1914, Meyer took the important wickets of Woolley and Edrich.

He found the time to captain Somerset in 1947, while he was still creating Millfield. But his best playing days were over by then. Most of them had been passed in India, where he had taken 28 wickets in only two matches in the Quadrangular Tournament of 1927-28, for the Europeans against the Hindus and the Muhammadans. In 1936, having got back from India, he made 202 not out for Somerset against Lancashire at Taunton. All told he took 412 first-class wickets with anything from leg breaks and googlies to gentle outswingers, and must have written almost as many letters to *The Times* on what should be done about the modern game.

He is survived by his widow and one daughter, another daughter having died as the result of a car accident.

MICHAEL LANGDON

Michael Langdon, CBE, British operatic bass, died on March 12 aged 70. He was born in Wolverhampton on November 12, 1920.

MICHAEL Langdon was one of the best loved artists at Covent Garden in the post-war era. His repertory was huge and eclectic, stretching from Mozart to the most modern scores of the singer's period. He was willing to tackle everything and anything, and give to it his wholehearted commitment. Even so, for many he will be most gratefully remembered for one part, that of Baron Ochs in *Der Rosenkavalier*, which he sang more than a hundred times here and abroad and to which he brought a breadth of humour leavened by a sense of style that

never deserted him even in the most comic roles, such as Varlaam in *Boris Godunov* or the marriage broker Kecal in *The Bartered Bride*, both well observed and highly spiced impersonations.

But comedy was only half the story in Langdon's case. He was very far from being a traditional buffo. Indeed one of his earliest successes was as the Grand Inquisitor in the famous Visconti/Giulini *Don Carlos* in 1958 and not long afterwards he took the three, dark-hued roles of Fafner, Hunding and Hagen in Wagner's *Ring* with equal success. For these he gave his voice greater weight and bite, and assumed a saturnine appearance. He loved to disguise his features in lovingly prepared make-up in order to create a real character. In all, he made more than a thousand appearances at the Royal Opera House to which he added visits to the Vienna State Opera, the Metropolitan Opera, and the Aix Festival, among others.

Langdon studied in Vienna with the baritone Alfred Jerger and later in London with the baritone Otakar Kraus, who helped him launch his Covent Garden career as a principal bass in 1951 after he had spent three years in the chorus. The King in *Aida* was his debut role followed by the Gaoler in *Tosca* (in which later he was a noted Angelotti) and Don Fernando in *Fidelio*. The following season he was already making 81 appearances among which was the role of the First Apprentice in the British premiere of *Wozzeck* under Erich Kleiber. A whole variety of parts followed in the Italian, French and German repertory, not to forget his creation of Mr Ratcliffe in Britten's *Billy Budd* in 1952 and the He-Ancient in Tippett's *The Midsummer Marriage* in 1955.

His first Ochs came in the 1960-61 season after he had returned to Vienna to study the role with Jerger. This was the period of Solti's ascendancy at Covent Garden, and his wish to enhance the careers of British singers was marked by his encouragement of Langdon among others. Langdon's other notable assumptions included Bartolo (Mozart's *The Marriage of Figaro*), Rocco (Beethoven's *Fidelio*), Caspar (Weber's *Der Freischütz*) and Count Waldner (Richard Strauss's *Arabella*) and Bottom (Britten's *A Midsummer Night's Dream*).

Claggart in *Billy Budd*, a role he took at Covent Garden and on television, was one of his later successes. With Scottish Opera he sang Don Pasquale in Donizetti's opera and created the title role in Robin Orr's *Hermiston* at the Edinburgh Festival (1975). During the 1970s he felt that a new regime at the Royal Opera House was trying to phase him out of the picture. It was then that he increased his appearances abroad and in the provinces though his Ochs continued to delight Covent Garden audiences.

In 1977 he announced his retirement, but he reappeared as Colonel Frank in *Die Fledermaus* the following year. In 1979 he became the first director of the National Opera Studio, where his benevolent, helpful reign of seven years was enjoyed by a new generation of singers. He came out of retirement to make further appearances as Colonel Frank in the 1983-4 season at Covent Garden, his farewell to the stage he had so long adorned.

Langdon's genial presence was felt at the Royal Opera House over his long career of 27 years. He was always a fund of good stories about the operatic world, which he told with great relish to whomever would lend an ear. This bluff exterior hid a subtle mind that helped him create his characters on stage.

He can still be heard on Beecham's recording of Haydn's *The Seasons*, as Dr Bartolo in Klemperer's set of *Figaro*, and in the finale of Act II of *Der Rosenkavalier* on Covent Garden's "Twenty-First Anniversary Album". His lively autobiography *Notes from a Low Singer* was published in 1982.

He is survived by his wife and two daughters.

JIMMY McPARTLAND

Jimmy McPartland, jazz musician, died on March 13 aged 83. He was born on March 15, 1907.

JAMES Dugald McPartland was a trumpeter and cornettist, in the legendary tradition of Bix Beiderbecke and a major influence on the early Chicago jazz school. He was the son of a music teacher who started him on the violin at the age of five and on the cornet at 15. He began to take a serious interest in jazz at Austin High School, and his first combo, composed of his brother, two school-mates and other young instrumentalists, was known as the "Austin High School Gang". They performed and began recording in the nervously energetic style that was to become known as Chicago jazz.

At the age of 17 he joined the Wolverines, a famous jazz band of the 1920s which featured Beiderbecke on the cornet. McPartland eventually replaced him when Beiderbecke sought other avenues for his talents. McPartland joined the Ben Pollack orchestra whose graduates included Glenn Miller, Benny Goodman, Jack Teagarden and many others who went on to lead their own organisations.

In 1936 he formed his own jazz group, abandoned it in 1941 and then played briefly with Teagarden before being called up into the US army in 1942. He took part in the Normandy landings and then played in a service show which entertained in north-west Europe in the wake of the invading allied armies. In 1945 in Belgium he met the British pianist Marian Turner then playing in *Bandwagon*, an ENSA show. They married in 1945 and as Marian McPartland she went on to a career in her own right as a broadcaster, performer and jazz pianist. After the war Jimmy McPartland continued to perform with his own groups around New York City and appeared in a television fantasy about jazz musicians called *The Magic Horn*.

His style can be heard in several Brunswick, MGM, Victor and Decca albums while his work with the Wolverines can still be found on the "History of Classic Jazz" series on Riverside. One of his best-known records of the 1950s is *Shades of Bix*, while from the following decade *The Music Man goes Dixieland* is much admired. Though McPartland cannot stand alongside Bix Beiderbecke in terms of the latter's sheer jazz genius, there is much in their tonal approach that is similar and McPartland remains a memorable standard bearer of jazz cornet technique from that great era.

In an interview for his 70th birthday McPartland told a newsagency: "A pro is a pro. Unless you are in the hospital you've got to show up and do the best you can. I want to blow that horn as long as I can possibly play it." McPartland was in fact "blowing that horn" on club dates until into his eighties.

He and his wife divorced in 1970 after 25 years of marriage but remained friends and colleagues over the years, appearing together at the Newport jazz festival in 1978 and at the Nice jazz festival in 1985. By this time Marian McPartland was acknowledged as one of the foremost jazz pianists of her time. They remarried two weeks before his death.

BUD FREEMAN

Bud (Lawrence) Freeman, jazz tenor saxophonist, died in a Chicago nursing home on March 15 aged 84. He was born on April 13, 1906.

LIKE the trumpeter Jimmy McPartland, who died only two days before him, Bud Freeman had his first public performances with the Austin High School Gang, that nursery of Chicago jazzmen, in the 1920s. The Austin High School Gang which had a period as the resident band at the Friar's Inn, modified the New Orleans style of group improvisation to create the distinctive sound of Chicago jazz. During the 1920s Freeman developed a melodious saxophone style and a beauty of tone which was to make him – along with the great Coleman Hawkins, though in a somewhat different manner – one of the most influential players of the instrument, and one of the most distinctive white saxophonists of his era.

Later in the 1920s Freeman joined a band called the Chicagoans, led by the guitarist and banjoist Eddie Condon and the vocalist and kazoo-player Red McKenzie. Freeman stayed with Condon when he formed his celebrated Chicago Rhythm Kings in the 1930s. His recording career began with these bands, a characteristic recording from his early period being "Sugar/Nobody's Sweetheart" with the Chicagoans in 1927. But perhaps his best-known recorded performance is the solo on "The Eel (Home Cooking)" of 1933 which he did with the Rhythm Kings.

From the mid-1930s Freeman was touring with Tommy Dorsey until 1938 when he joined Benny Goodman. This was not a harmonious association. Nine shows a night in which Freeman felt, moreover, that he was not being allocated a fair slice of the solo action by Goodman, soon palled on him and he left to lead the Summa Cum Laude orchestra, an all-star Chicago line-up which in addition to regular hotel work got Freeman a spot in a Broadway musical, *Swingin' the Dream*, based on Shakespeare's *A Midsummer Night's Dream*. The show, which also featured Louis Armstrong, ran only for a few performances, but it was an experience Freeman enjoyed immensely. He was a wryly humorous, many-sided character with the capacity to savour all sorts of experiences.

During the war Freeman served with the US army, leading a service band at Fort St George, and afterwards went freelance, frequently playing with Eddie Condon at his club in New York. A well-groomed – indeed almost immaculate – figure, he stood out incongruously from the ranks of his contemporaries, something which secretly delighted him and to which the title of one of his volumes of memoirs, *You Don't Look Like a Musician*, alludes.

In the 1960s Freeman continued to tour as far afield as Chile and Peru, as well as leading bands in New York and Chicago. He was a member of the Newport Jazz Festival All-stars which regularly opened the festival throughout the 1960s and he joined the World's Greatest Jazz Band when it was formed in 1968. He stayed with the band for six years before coming to Britain in 1974, returning to America in the late 1970s.

Like McPartland, Freeman continued playing into his eighties, still able to produce the strength and beauty of tone of his earlier years and continuing to cut a suave, well-dressed figure of markedly cisatlantic charm.

THE EARL OF CROMER

The Earl of Cromer, KG, GCMG, MBE, PC, governor of the Bank of England, 1961-66, and British ambassador in Washington, 1971-74, died on March 16 aged 72. He was born on July 28, 1918.

LORD Cromer will be best remembered for his confrontations in 1964 and 1965 with Harold Wilson, then prime minister, over the management of the exchange rate in the face of government proposals to implement what were seen as a radical series of socialist public spending measures. In the first weeks of the 1964 Labour government there was a potentially disastrous outflow of foreign exchange reserves in the fight to defend the pound. The prime minister attempted to elevate the issue into a constitutional crisis on the question of "Who runs the country — a newly elected government with a fresh mandate, or international speculators?" On November 11, 1964, the Chancellor of the Exchequer, James Callaghan, announced what amounted to an autumn Budget, increasing social security benefits and pensions, as well as fuel duty and income tax, and introducing capital gains tax and corporation tax. "We were soon to learn that decisions on pensions and taxation were no longer to be regarded, as in the past, as decisions for Parliament alone," Wilson recorded in his memoir *The Labour Government*

1964-70. "The combination of tax increases with increased social security benefits provoked the first of a series of attacks on sterling, by speculators and others, which beset almost every action of

For the next few weeks Lord Cromer, as governor of the Bank of England, became a frequent visitor to No. 10, where he instilled some of the harsh realities of market behaviour into a resentful and at times defiant prime minister. On November 23 Cromer raised the bank rate from 5 per cent to 7 per cent to signal the determination of the authorities to defend the pound. Mr Wilson could not conceal his admiration for Lord Cromer's feat in raising £3 billion of central bank support in an afternoon's telephoning round the world. News of such confidence in the British economy was sufficient to stave off a run on sterling.

What the prime minister did not realise was Cromer's critical contribution in the long and careful preparation which he had made to meet such an emergency. Long before the 1964 crisis, he had made a point of keeping the US Federal Reserve Board fully informed of developments on this side of the Atlantic. By the following July Mr Callaghan was introducing an economic package of strict economic rectitude, postponing the abolition of National Health charges and tightening exchange controls. But the foreign exchange markets were still reacting nervously to the new government's initiatives and that autumn Lord Cromer had to hold a series of dinners for Mr Wilson and Mr Callaghan to meet bankers for the purpose of mutual reassurance. It was an extraordinary episode, in which considerable naivety was displayed on all sides. Thanks to Lord Cromer, many lessons were learned by politicians of all parties and by the City. Nevertheless sterling crises continued to be a feature of economic policy throughout the 1960s and 1970s.

George Rowland Stanley Baring was born into a family with a tradition of high office and public duty. His grandfather, the first Earl of Cromer, made his name in India and as British agent and consul-general in Egypt from 1883 to 1907 set up a modern administration to replace the corrupt autocracy of the Khedive. His father was Lord Chamberlain. Cromer was educated at Eton and Trinity College, Cambridge.

He served in the second world war with the Grenadier Guards and became a lieutenant-colonel. He was mentioned in dispatches and appointed MBE. In 1942 he married Esme Harmsworth, second daughter of the second Viscount Rothermere, proprietor of the *Daily Mail*.

In 1948 Cromer was appointed a managing director of Baring Brothers, the family firm, and became known in merchant banking circles as a courteous and well-informed but shy young man. He succeeded to the earldom on the death of his father in 1953. Cromer's government links were reinforced in 1959 when he became head of the United Kingdom Treasury delegation to, and UK director of, the International Monetary Fund and the International Bank for Reconstruction and Development. He quickly made his mark there, fulfilling banking and social duties with great efficiency and charm.

Cromer returned to London in 1961 and shortly afterwards the prime minister, Harold Macmillan, appointed him governor of the Bank of England on the strength of his international reputation. At 43 he was the youngest governor for 200 years. He soon established his authority. Although he constantly had to deal with people of considerably greater experience, his authority was soon respected and his views rarely questioned. His previous contacts in Whitehall made it easier for him to convey the City's views to those in government, while his clear banking loyalties earned him a strong following in the City. When there was a tricky problem, or unpalatable medicine to be administered, he liked to meet people from the City in the presence of one or two Bank of England experts, while retaining complete command of such meetings.

He objected strongly to any attempt by City institutions to communicate directly with government departments, rather than proceed through Bank of England channels. He liked to accompany the City representatives concerned to meetings with the appropriate minister and civil servants. He then gave full rein to discussion, intervening only when he felt that there was a Bank point of view to be put, or when he considered that some important principle was being disregarded.

The 1964 and 1965 crises showed how robustly he represented the financial community's views to Whitehall. But Harold Wilson took the earliest opportunity to be rid of Cromer. The end of his term of office coincided with the 1966 general election, in which Labour was returned with an increased majority in the House of Commons. He was promptly replaced by Leslie (now Lord) O'Brien.

Cromer's political interventions were not limited to the Labour party. He was a close friend of Edward Heath and was reported to have made plain his preference for Heath over Maudling in the Conservative party leadership contest of 1965. Two years later, he made use of his release from office to attack Harold Wilson's economic policy in a wide-ranging speech. He returned to Baring Brothers in 1966.

Mr Heath rewarded Cromer by making him ambassador to Washington when the Conservatives were returned to power in 1970. There he represented British interests during the difficult period of the Watergate crisis and Richard Nixon's eventual impeachment as president. His particular task was to explain the British government's approach to Europe in Washington. After his return to Britain in 1974 Cromer spoke frequently in the House of Lords on the need for low inflation and a sound currency.

In his later years, he accepted a number of directorships and consultancies for such companies as IBM, Morgan Guaranty Trust, Daily Mail & General Trust, Imperial Group, P&O, Union Carbide, Shell Transport & Trading and Robeco. He retired to Jersey until last year, when he returned to London.

He is survived by his wife and two sons.

SIR CARL AARVOLD

His Honour Sir Carl Aarvold, OBE, TD, DL, Recorder of London, 1964-75, died in hospital on March 17 aged 83. He was born on June 7, 1907.

IN HIS 11 years as recorder Carl Aarvold established himself as London's most colourful and well-liked judge. He had a natural capacity for dispensing justice with unfailing courtesy and humanity and with a complete lack of the irritability and impatience which sometimes afflict incumbents of the bench. He had a deep appreciation of the problems of the inadequate and the disadvantaged. Indeed on his last day in office he celebrated what he called his "feeling of enlarged freedom" by releasing on bail a young man on a violence charge because the accused's son was ill and Aarvold felt he ought to be able to be with him. This was utterly characteristic of Aarvold's unaffected compassion.

He was also a top class sportsman. He played rugby for England at wing three-quarter, winning 16 caps in all, and captaining the national side. He also played several other games to a very high standard.

Carl Douglas Aarvold was born in Durham and educated at Durham School and Emmanuel College, Cambridge, of which he became an honorary fellow on his retirement from the recordership of London. He was called to the bar in 1932, just seven years before the second world war and thus had his legal career interrupted at a crucial stage. He had a distinguished war record and was appointed OBE in 1945.

On resuming at the bar he built up a busy practice in London and on the North Eastern Circuit. He was Recorder of Pontefract for some three years before his first full-time judicial appointment in the City of London in 1954. He was Judge of the Mayor's and City of London Court from 1954 to 1959 and Common Serjeant of the City of London from 1959 to 1964.

Carl Aarvold was tall, handsome and strongly built — possessed of a ready smile and an infectious laugh, when circumstances permitted. As a judge he was an ideal tribunal, fair, understanding, sympathetic and patient but firm in his control of the court and of prisoners guilty of serious offences. In 1972 he was appointed chairman of the committee that recommended a tightening of the system governing the release of psychiatric offenders in the wake of the activities of Graham Young, who had been found guilty of murdering two people after being released from Broadmoor.

As Recorder of London Aarvold had many civic duties, not least the administration of the ever-growing Central Criminal Court at the Old Bailey. He remembered the days of a four-judge Old Bailey and saw it grow to near 20, with numerous new Crown Courts in London as well. There were also many City ceremonies and City occasions to attend and he soon won a reputation as a brilliant speaker at those events. He was in addition the last chairman of the City of London Quarter Sessions before the Crown Court system took over in 1971. Further he was chairman of a number of legal commitees and was nominated to head certain government enquiries.

The Recorder of London has always been an important – and unique – figure in our history. By Aarvold's day it was an onerous position too, calling for long hours and much stamina. In his case stamina was there early, thanks to his prowess at games. Besides his distinguished career as a rugby international (he had also captained Durham County and Blackheath) he was a very good lawn tennis player and a low-handicap golfer. In both games he played competitively and representatively in high class company but he enjoyed most (and was much enjoyed by others in) bar tournaments, where he was a friendly, kindly and generous opponent.

Aarvold was president of the Lawn Tennis Association for nearly 20 years from 1962 to 1981. He was also chairman of the RAC from 1978 to 1981. He received honorary law degrees from Dalhousie and Durham and was elected a bencher of the Inner Temple in 1959.

He married in 1934 Noeline Etrenne Hill of Denton Park, Yorks, and there were three sons of the marriage.

ADMIRAL SIR FREDERICK PARHAM

Admiral Sir Frederick Robertson Parham, GBE, KCB, DSO, died on March 20, aged 90. He was born on January 9, 1901.

FREDERICK Parham commanded the cruiser *Belfast* during the hunting down of the German battleship *Scharnhorst* on Boxing Day 1943 in a second world war naval engagement comparable in drama and importance with the sinking of the *Bismarck* more than two years earlier. *Scharnhorst* was enticed out of a Norwegian fiord northwest of Murmansk, believing it could make mincemeat of an Allied convoy and its three attendant cruisers. In reality the British force was far larger, and included the battleship *Duke of York*. In the chase and action that followed, *Belfast*'s superior radar enabled it to stay in contact with the German ship in spite of appalling weather and visibility.

Frederick Robertson Parham was born at Bath, and, after Osborne and Dartmouth, joined the Fleet as a midshipman in *Malaya* in the early summer of 1917, when the late King George VI was a lieutenant. Towards the end of the first world war, he served in the Dover patrol. He qualified as a gunnery specialist in 1925 and was promoted early to the rank of commander in 1934. He commanded *Shikari* in 1937, and was promoted to captain while commanding one of the powerful new tribal class destroyers *Gurkha* from 1938 to 1940. From 1942 to 1944, he commanded *Belfast*, and for his gallantry, determination and skill in the *Scharnhorst* action was awarded the DSO.

Later in the war, Parham took the *Belfast* close in to the French coast at the time of the landings in Normandy, and fired 4,500 rounds of 6in shells at the enemy. He was mentioned in dispatches for his part in the operations. His last ship command was the new battleship, *Vanguard*, from 1947 to 1949. He was promoted rear-admiral in 1949 and became deputy chief of naval personnel; in 1951 he went out to the Mediterranean as flag officer (flotillas) and second-in-command.

From early in his career, Parham had been marked out as a man of promise; his professional competence, his confidence and his ease of manner all contributed to a series of successful appointments and commands. In 1953, however, a serious illness prevented him from taking up the appointment of Second Sea Lord, which he had accepted. Initially, this was a great disappointment to him; his experience of

naval personnel staff work was extensive, and his interest deep and genuine. However, he accepted the challenge early in 1954 of heading an investigation into the commissioning and manning of the operational Fleet. The pre-war practice of sending ships to foreign stations for two, or more, years entailed a disruption of family life no longer acceptable in post-war social conditions; but the Royal Navy was still required to provide a world-wide deployment of effective, and balanced, forces.

The eventual solution proposed was a compromise, in which most ships would be commissioned for General Service, with periods of deployment alternating between the Home and Foreign Stations, each overseas leg being less than a year.

It is a tribute to Parham's organising abilities and persuasive powers that his proposals were readily accepted by the Commanders-in-Chief, fully endorsed by the Board of Admiralty, promptly acted upon and put into effect within two years.

Although the Foreign Service Commission lapsed in the 1970s, the principles embodied in the General Service Commission still govern the manning of the Fleet, and arguably represent Parham's most outstanding contribution to the Navy.

Parham became Fourth Sea Lord and Chief of Supplies and Transport later in 1954, and from 1955 to 1958 was the Commander-in-Chief, the Nore. He was knighted in 1955, having already been appointed CB and CBE, and in 1959 was appointed GBE.

Parham was not only a distinguished but a popular naval officer. He had a good presence, with strong features, and a confident manner; his strong beliefs gave him an authority that his open nature supported.

In retirement, when he lived at Midhurst, he served on the British Waterways Board from 1963 to 1967. He was twice married, first in 1926 to Kathleen Dobree, who died in 1973, and, in 1978 to Mrs Joan Saunders (née Charig). He is survived by his widow, and by a son.

SIR JOHN KERR

John Robert Kerr, AK, GCMG, GCVO, PC, Governor-General of Australia from 1974 to 1977, died on March 24 aged 76. He was born on September 24, 1914.

SIR John Kerr was the fifth Australian-born governor-general and the most controversial. In November 1975 he created a precedent which caused political turmoil throughout Australia and attracted world-wide attention when he dismissed from office the Whitlam Labour administration before its full term had expired. Kerr had been confronted with a government that was no longer able to govern completely, with a prime minister who would not go to the polls, and with an opposition in the senate which declined to pass the supply (money) bill enabling the Crown to carry on the ordinary services of government.

The governor-general appointed a caretaker Liberal-Country party coalition government to carry on while a national election was organised. When it came the caretaker government, headed by Mr Malcolm Fraser, was overwhelmingly elected. However, the hue and cry which ensued over the legality of the governor-general's actions continued for years. One result was a movement in Australia, Citizens for Democracy, which declared not only in favour of a republican form of government in place of the monarchy but pledged that the office of governor-general should be abolished.

Kerr showed personal courage in the face of a persistent, hostile, and sometimes violent, campaign against him and his office. He said: "Regardless of my personal feelings the constitution is the law and must be obeyed. I acted in accordance with section 64 of the constitution." The irony was that Kerr had Mr Whitlam's backing to become governor-general and that he had been a friend.

He had become a Queen's Counsel in 1953. In 1964 he was president of the Law Council of Australia, and in 1966 he was appointed a judge of the Supreme Court of the Australian Capital Territory. In the same year he became a judge of the Supreme Court of the Northern Territory and in 1972 Chief Justice of New South Wales.

His dismissal of the Whitlam administration remains controversial and divisive. Kerr announced his resignation in July 1977, saying he was stepping down because of the partisan feelings aroused by his dismissal of the Whitlam government. Mr Whitlam described his dismissal as a *coup d'état*.

In February 1978 it was announced that Kerr was to be Australia's ambassador to Unesco, based in Paris. The post was offered by Sir Malcolm Fraser, prime minister, who replaced Gough Whitlam. Kerr accepted the appointment. But three weeks later, on the day he was to have taken up his new position, he stepped down under intense public and political pressure. Mr Whitlam was later to take up the same role.

For a while, Kerr lived in England, where he wrote his version of the Whitlam controversy. In the last 10 years of his life, he became a near-recluse, living in Sydney.

DANIEL MEINERTZHAGEN

Daniel Meinertzhagen, former chairman of Royal Insurance, Lazard Brothers, Mercantile Credit and Alexanders Discount, died on March 22 aged 76. He was born on March 2, 1915.

AS THE senior member of the influential and well-connected Meinertzhagen family, Daniel Meinertzhagen occupied a pivotal position in the City of London during the 1960s and 1970s. During the financial crisis and economic recession of 1974-5, he was head of a leading merchant bank, a major insurance company, one of the biggest finance houses and a pair of investment trusts. All escaped the worst ravages of those years. Yet few outside the City would have heard of him and, even though he was extremely well known to the Bank of England, he was never officially recognised for his contribution during what still ranks as the most difficult period for the financial sector since the second world war.

Daniel's father, Louis, laid the basis for the family's standing in the City through Huth & Co, a family bank in Tokenhouse Yard. Daniel was the eldest of three sons, each of whom was to make his mark in the business world. The youngest, Sir Peter, became general manager of the Commonwealth Development Corporation. The middle brother, Luke, became senior partner of Cazenove & Co, arguably the City's most powerful firm of stockbrokers, which occupies Huth's old office. After Eton and New College, Oxford, Daniel began work at the age of 21 in the gilt-edged department of Lazard Brothers, the merchant bank. In 1940 he married Marguerite, and served during the war with the Royal Air Force Volunteer Reserve, rising to the rank of Wing Commander.

He rejoined Lazard after the war, becoming managing director in 1954. Three years later he was called to give evidence to the tribunal into an alleged leak of a change in bank rate. The tribunal decided that there had been no leak, and all concerned were unreservedly exonerated.

Meinertzhagen was thrust into the forefront of City affairs in 1973, when the then chairman of Lazard, Lord Poole, suffered a stroke and he succeeded to the post. The following year he became chairman of Royal Insurance, a Lazard client, in response to a call for a non-executive chairman. With his other City directorships, he was at the centre of events when the secondary banking crisis broke in 1974 and the stock market plummeted taking the FT index to 146 the following January from a peak of over 500 in 1972. Meinertzhagen's steadying influence played an important part in restoring confidence and fostering recovery. After his retirement from Lazard in 1980 he continued to advise Pearson, Lazard's parent company. In 1981 he became chairman of Alexanders Discount.

An adherent of traditional values in the City, Meinertzhagen is remembered as being a dedicated member of the old school. He could be a hard taskmaster, but was just as capable of getting in touch the next day to smooth matters over. As the pocket calculator began to infiltrate the City, Meinertzhagen used to amaze others with the speed of his mental arithmetic. His great relaxation was gardening when the family lived at Bramshot in Hampshire. He also collected Meissen porcelain.

He is survived by his widow and two sons. One, Peter, is chairman of the stockbrokers Hoare Govett.

ARTHUR MURRAY

Arthur Murray, American teacher of ballroom dancing, has died in Honolulu aged 95. He was born on April 4, 1895.

ARTHUR Murray enjoyed worldwide pre-eminence as a teacher of those staples of the ballroom, the quickstep, the fox-trot, the waltz and the tango, in a career which had begun in the 1920s. He was himself a master of all these steps as well as being a recognised exponent of the rumba and – his favourite – the bossa nova.

Over the years Murray's clients included many of the rich and famous. The Duke of Windsor, Eleanor Roosevelt, Katharine Hepburn and Tallulah Bankhead all beat a path to his studio door, and John D. Rockefeller insisted on private home lessons. From modest beginnings Murray built up a lucrative mail order business and a network of 300 dance studios in the United States, before expanding to Europe and Latin America.

Born Arthur Murray Teichman in New York, he started his business with a dance studio, and his flair for publicity attracted many society figures to it in the 1920s. But it was the expansion into a mail order "footprints" correspondence that made the business really popular and three quarters of a million people were taught to dance by the method. A television show, *Arthur Murray's Dance Party*, made him a household name in the post-war period. Murray sold his interest in the studios in 1952 but continued to manage them until 1964 when he stepped down as president. By that time several millions had learned to dance by the Murray method. He wrote several books.

The organisation was not always above controversy. In 1960 the Federal Trade Commission ordered the Murray studios to stop what were seen as contests and pressurising tactics designed solely to induce people to sign up for lessons. There were also complaints against the organisation from individuals generally women who claimed they had signed up for lessons after being promised that dancing skills would improve their social confidence or make them irresistible to men.

Murray wrote several books, including *How to Become a Good Dancer*, *Let's Dance* and *Arthur Murray's Dance Secrets*. His wife, Kathryn, was both business and dancing partner. They had two daughters.

PARKASH SINGH, VC

Parkash Singh, VC, Punjabi soldier, died on March 23 in London aged 77. He was born in the Punjab on March 31, 1913.

PARKASH Singh won his Victoria Cross for actions on two days in 1943, on both occasions displaying bravery and resource – not to speak of sheer bravado – of a kind which stand out even in the extraordinary annals of the VC. The setting was the Mayu peninsula in Burma, the context a limited offensive planned by Wavell to recover the Arakan coastal region from the Japanese. Parkash was serving as a *havildar* (sergeant) in the 5/8th Punjab Regiment when an advance into the Mayu peninsula began in December 1942. Ahead of the main force a platoon of the 5/8th's universal carriers was sent to reconnoitre the beaches of the peninsula.

The universal, a primitive form of armoured personnel carrier, mounting a single bren gun, provided little enough protection for its crew of four and its armour was not proof against anything heavier than small calibre rounds. When on January 6, 1943, near the Japanese-occupied village of Donbaik a group of the enemy suddenly broke from undergrowth and hurled a salvo of grenades at the lead carrier, Parkash's superior officer, Captain Bert Causey, was immediately hit by a splinter in the face. With blood pouring into his eyes and blinding him, Causey ordered Parkash to take command while his vehicle retired.

Parkash might easily have done the same but he saw that further forward two other carriers had become bogged down in a stream where they were pinned down by heavy fire from a large party of advancing Japanese. Without a second's pause Parkash drove forward to the rescue, shouting at the men in the trapped vehicles to jump and run for it. His bren gunner was wounded but Parkash wrested the weapon from him and, driving with one hand and firing the bren with the other, he charged into the ranks of the astonished Japanese, scattering them and forcing them to run for cover. Not content with this he drove on to their fixed positions causing such consternation that they fled from these also. He then returned to pick up the men from the stranded carriers. As they scrambled aboard, a hail of fire from a fresh Japanese attack broke about their ears, but Parkash embarked all eight men who crouched, shaken, on the floor of the carrier as a torrent of Japanese rifle and machine-gun fire hammered against the casing all the way back to the haven of the British/Indian lines.

On January 19, with an attempt to dislodge the Japanese from Donbaik by frontal assault in progress, the carriers were ordered to advance along the beach and draw the enemy's fire. This futile exercise was greeted by a burst of anti-tank gun fire against which the armour of the carriers was useless. Several were wrecked, including that of Causey, whose driver had both his legs shot off. All their crews were given up for lost as the remaining carriers retreated to their base. But Parkash determined to see if there were any still alive in the burning wrecks on the beach. Dragging his terrified driver out of the trench where the man was cowering, he guided his carrier down the beach which was now being raked by Japanese weapons of small and large calibre. Discovering Causey and his driver in their badly damaged vehicle he elected not to transfer them to his own carrier as they were too badly injured to be moved with safety. In addition they would have been exposed to close range machine gun fire as he tried to lift them from one vehicle to the other. Ignoring Causey's pleas to retreat and save himself, Parkash rigged up a makeshift tow chain, exposing himself to enemy fire as he scuttled between the two vehicles. When he shouted to Causey to put his vehicle in

neutral his superior replied that he was too weak from his wounds to budge the gear lever. Vaulting from one vehicle to the other, Parkash freed the jammed lever and one of the more hair-raising tows in vehicular history took place over rough ground with anti-tank rounds ripping through the hulls of both carriers. For the last hundred yards, in a gesture of admirable bravado, Parkash sat on top of his vehicle, a splendid, beturbanned figure with arms folded, impassively ignoring the Japanese bullets which continued to whistle round his ears. As they came into their own lines one observer said presciently: "There's a fellow winning a VC."

Parkash had been born in Lyallpu in a part of the Punjab which is now in Pakistan, and joined the 8th Punjab Regiment of the Indian Army in 1936. After his Arakan exploits — whose sheer panache was in marked contrast to the dispiriting experiences of most of the 14th Division's units in that disastrous campaign — he trained with the 5/8th Punjab in amphibious warfare, but a projected assault on Malaya and Indonesia was forestalled by the Japanese surrender in August 1945.

In 1946 he returned home to a hero's welcome and a grant of land in his native village. After independence and partition in 1947 it was decided that the 8th Punjab should become a regiment of the new state of Pakistan. But eventually the Sikhs decided that India was really their home and, like others, he gave up his house and land to make the perilous trek over the frontier through bands of brigands and Pathans who several times attacked their camp at night. Eventually they crossed safely to a new life and a new farm which was allotted to Parkash near Jullundur. For the next twenty years he served as an officer in one of the Sikh regiments of the new Indian army, retiring as a major in 1968. He was a frequent visitor to Britain where three of his four daughters settled and had been present at last year's VC and GC reunion in London.

He leaves his widow, Raminder, and all his daughters.

EILEEN JOYCE

Eileen Joyce, CMG, concert pianist, died on March 25 aged 78. She was born in Tasmania on November 21, 1912.

BECAUSE in mid-career she opted for an emphasis on personal popularity, Eileen Joyce's undoubted musicality and virtuosity were for a while overlooked. She was a player of extraordinary skill, at home in Mozart as in Shostakovich and encompassing Chopin, Liszt, Grieg and Rachmaninov along the way, as her many excellent records, recently reissued, reveal. These capabilities had been on display before the war, during which her good looks and charm, allied to her pianistic flair, brought her playing to the attention of a much broader section of the public than generally listened to classical music at that time. At this period she revelled in playing three concertos in a programme, often appearing in a different dress for each. Their glamour attracted some comment at a time when it was unexpected, but she said: "Changing fills in the intervals when I might be biting my nails with nervousness. Would the critics prefer that I should wear black?" She played the piano for Ann Todd in the film *The Seventh Veil* and made a film of an autobiographical nature called *Wherever She Goes*.

Joyce was born of immigrant parents of Spanish and Irish descent. Her mother told her she was born in a tent; her father was a labourer and she was called "Ragged Eilie". They were terribly poor and she first played falteringly on a beer-stained piano from a local pub that was trundled round to her father's house. She was educated at a convent school sitting in the back row reserved for the non-paying pupils. She became well known in Boulder City for her playing and money was collected so that she could go to a larger convent school at Perth.

Her talents were spotted first by the composer Percy Grainger and then by the pianist Backhaus who was touring Australia. They urged that she be sent abroad to study. Grainger was helpful in raising funds so that she could go to the conservatoire in Leipzig. Her teachers there were Max Pauer and the fearfully strict Robert Teichmuller who was responsible for giving her a magnificent technique. After three years at Leipzig she moved to London and continued her studies with Tobias Matthay and Adelina de Lara. Finally she went to work with Schnabel in Berlin.

With such a comprehensive training she astonished the conductor Albert Coates at an audition in 1930. He recommended her to Sir Henry Wood with whom she made a sensational debut that year, playing a Prokofiev concerto. She quickly established an appreciable reputation in recitals and concertos and began a long series of recordings for Parlophone. Her repertoire eventually consisted of more than 70 works, some of which, such as the John Ireland Concerto, were written especially for her.

After her war-time fame she resumed a fairly normal concert career touring all over the world. She could be outspoken publicly, once complaining, in 1957, that there was not one grand piano available for public recitals in three county towns — Winchester, Exeter and Gloucester, home of the Three Choirs Festival. At a musical competition in Geneva she walked out on her fellow judges, complaining of outside influences being brought to bear on the jury. At the Proms in 1958 she gave the first performance in England of Shostakovich's piano concerto, Opus 101.

Her career was hard work. Some of her strong stubby fingers were in 1958 taped to prevent cuts and others had corns. Her hands became weary, her back strained and Harley Street became a second home. Towards the end she was spending more on doctors' bills than she was earning on the concert platform.

In the early 1960s she retired precipitately although in 1967 she was persuaded to reappear to play Rachmaninov's Second Concerto, one of her greatest successes, once more. She was made an honorary Doctor of Music at Cambridge in 1970 and appointed CMG in 1981. Her retirement was spent in Kent, near Chartwell, where she would often entertain friends with her playing.

She was married twice and had a son by her first husband.

RALPH BATES

Ralph Bates, television actor, died of cancer in a London hospital on March 27 aged 51. He was born on February 12, 1940.

RALPH Bates will be associated in audiences' minds with two main television roles, that of George Warleggan, the villainous adversary of the protagonist in BBC 1's *Poldark* and, more recently, as the lovable loser in romance John Lacey in the popular series *Dear John*. The roles could scarcely have been more different. In 29 episodes of *Poldark* Bates was not allowed to smile even once, being under instructions to preserve an icily hostile demeanour throughout.

But he had a gift for comedy, and after a stint in a Ray Cooney farce, the protagonist of *Dear John* was a part which he found highly congenial. With a brand of good looks which could be disarming as well as fiercely formidable (he had been an excellent Hammer horror villain in his younger days) Bates imparted to the role of John Lacey an attractive vulnerability, creating a character who was always destined to be on the losing side in romance and marriage, a man who could be guaranteed to push on doors marked "pull". John Lacey, who in the series joined a singles club after his wife ran off with a physical education teacher, gave Bates a new lease of popularity in a vein which could not have been predicted for the snarling villain of *Poldark* a few years before.

Ralph Bates was born in Bristol. On his mother's side he was descended from Louis Pasteur and at one time held dual nationality – a fact which had its conveniences as well as disadvantages. He retained a love for France and spoke the language fluently, but he also narrowly escaped being called up into the French army.

He read French at Trinity College, Dublin, and after winning a scholarship to Yale Drama School, returned to Ireland to make his stage debut at the Gate Theatre, Dublin, in 1963, in Shaw's *You Never Can Tell*. He went on to a career in rep and in the West End, gaining experience in plays ranging from classics like *Hedda Gabler* through to, more recently, comedies such as *Run For Your Wife*. An effective performance as the murderously insane Roman emperor Caligula in one of the episodes of Granada's series *The Caesars* pointed the way to a profitable period in Hammer horror films in the 1970s, and Bates developed a chilling persona for himself in films such as *The Horror of Frankenstein* and *Lust for a Vampire* (both 1970), *Dr Jekyll and Sister Hyde* (1971) in which he played an evil doctor who inadvertently transforms himself into a seductive brunette, and *Fear in the Night* (1973). He also starred in one of ITV's *Crime of Passion* series in 1972, playing opposite Cyd Hayman in, appropriately, a French murder story, Miss Hayman being the lucky murderess who gets away with shooting her lover, played by Bates, in a *crime passionel*.

It was a natural progression from such roles to *Poldark*, where his dark, stormy George Warleggan made Bates one of television's heart-throbs in the 1970s. In fact he seemed doomed to be type-cast as a screen rogue – if one of undeniable sexual attraction – but the translation in the mid-1980s to the vulnerable anti-hero of *Dear John*, with his drab hair-cut, down-trodden features and the perpetually defeated slouch in his shoulders, indicated a versatility which had much more to give to television drama, had his life not been tragically cut short. Bates certainly had the capacity to inhabit roles with which a mass audience could identify.

His first marriage, to the actress Joanna van Gyseghem, ended in divorce and he married secondly, Virginia Wetherall, herself formerly an actress. She survives him with their two children Daisy, known to television audiences for her role in *Forever Green*, and William, who played his screen son in *Dear John*.

ALFREDO CAMPOLI

Alfredo Campoli, Italian-born British violinist, died on March 27 in Princes Risborough, Buckinghamshire, at the age of 84. He was born in Rome on October 20, 1906.

ALFREDO Campoli was a musician who, like Eileen Joyce who died two days before him, divided his career between the serious and the popular repertory. A player of silvery tone, innate musicianship and technical virtuosity, he loved to play the works of Paganini and charming trifles, as much as he did the works of the classical repertory. But whatever he tackled, he never faltered in his gift of lyrical grace.

He received his musical education entirely from his father who was a violin professor at the Accademia di Santa Cecilia in Rome until the family moved to London when he was six. There he became a child prodigy, appearing in public at the age of 10. Before he was 13 he had already won a number of prizes, and in 1919 received the gold medal of the London Musical Festival for his account of the Mendelssohn Violin Concerto, which continued to be a favourite of his throughout his career and to which he brought a lightness of touch and warmth of tone exactly appropriate to its needs.

At 15 he was already touring the country giving what were then known as Celebrity Recitals, playing a wide variety of pieces. When the slump came in the 1930s he formed his own small orchestra, the Alfredo Campoli Salon Orchestra, to play light music in public and over the radio, an activity which brought him enormous popularity. However he kept his serious career going and was a regular soloist at the Proms.

At the outbreak of war he disbanded his orchestra and gave recitals to the troops in Britain and abroad. After the end of hostilities he resumed his concert career, playing the major concertos with leading orchestras as well as giving solo recitals all over the world. On one occasion an admiring Leningrad audience obliged him to play 11 encores before he was allowed to leave the platform. He also recorded several concertos, discs that have stood the test of time.

He made his US debut at the Carnegie Hall in 1953, and twice toured the USSR. In 1955 he gave the premiere of Bliss's Violin Concerto, which is dedicated to him and which he recorded. During the 1960s he formed a duo with the young pianist Valerie Tryon, and it proved a happy partnership.

In retirement he continued to live happily in his Highgate home, teaching and playing bridge. He played the Dragonetti Stradivarius of 1700, which he was always proud to show to visitors.

He married, in 1942, Joy Burbridge and is survived by her.

MARTHA GRAHAM

Martha Graham, dancer and choreographer, died on April 1 aged 96. She was born in Allegheny, Pennsylvania, on May 11, 1894.

MARTHA Graham was the principal figure in modern dance after Isadora Duncan. Her purpose was — as distinct from the established vocabulary of classical ballet — to discover for each work a range of movement to express its essential mood and intention. With time she found it convenient to codify her own discoveries; this helped spread her influence but also led to many inferior imitations. As an innovator and performer her achievements remain unsurpassed.

The daughter of a physician, she was brought up, the eldest of three sisters, on strict Presbyterian lines. When she was 14 the family moved to Santa Barbara, California, where a different social and physical climate brought her first taste of freedom. At school, seeing a performance by Ruth St Denis awoke an interest in dancing. So when her parents wanted her to attend college she chose the Cumnock School in Los Angeles, which encouraged self-expression equally with learning. She had her first dancing classes there and on graduating in 1916 she enrolled in the Denishawn School of Dance, newly opened in Los Angeles by St Denis and her partner Ted Shawn.

Being overweight and past the usual age for beginning a dance career, Graham had no encouragement at first from her teachers. But Shawn, recognising her temperament in a Spanish dance, used her in a dance pageant, then as a teacher when he had to go on military service. Graham continued teaching and dancing small parts until 1920, when Shawn created for her the title role in *Xochitl*, a dance drama after an old Mexican story. However, St Denis insisted on taking over the role during a season at the London Coliseum in 1922. Disappointment over this and an unhappy emotional attachment led Graham to leave Denishawn the following year. She became principal dancer at the Greenwich Village Follies in New York. After two years she left and supported herself by teaching dance while preparing the first concert of her own works, given at the 48th Street Theatre in April 1926.

During the next few years she evolved a starkly expressive style, but the more individual her work became, the more puzzling spectators found it. Increased prestige came in 1930 when she played the Chosen Maiden in Massine's revival of *The Rite of Spring* at the Philadelphia Academy of Music, the American premiere of Stravinsky's ballet. That year saw her first enduring choreography, *Lamentation*, a solo conveying intense grief. *Primitive Mysteries* (1931) was the first of several dances to which she brought deep religious feeling.

Another recurring theme, her national heritage, entered Graham's work with *American Provincials* (1934) and *Frontier* (1935). The latter was the first work in which she used a decor. As designer she chose a sculptor, Isamu Noguchi — an innovation as influential as her adventurous costuming which presented the body as moving sculpture. Recognition began to come. Mayor La Guardia appointed her to the New York municipal arts committee. She was invited to Berlin for the 1936 Olympics but refused. At Eleanor Roosevelt's invitation she danced at the White House in February 1937.

Public success was consolidated in 1938

with *American Document*, presenting an account of American history in the framework of a minstrel show. For the first time Graham used a narrator and a male soloist, Erick Hawkins; there was also an erotic element new to her work. *Every Soul is a Circus* (1939) introduced a second male dancer, Merce Cunningham, and showed an unfamiliar side of Graham's gifts in the dizzy humour with which she tried to choose between the two men. There followed *El Penitente*, a minor masterpiece inspired by religious fanatics, and a major work based on Emily Dickinson's poems, *Letter to the World*. That, with *Appalachian Spring*, represents the best of Graham's Americana.

Her starting point was, inevitably, the woman's view. *Night Journey* showed the Oedipus story through Jocasta's eyes; *Clytemnestra*, *Phaedra* and *Legend of Judith* were other notable examples. About the same time Graham began a series of joyous pure dance works for her growing company with *Diversion of Angels*. She also converted one of her former solos, *The Triumph of St Joan*, into a group work, *Seraphic Dialogue*, in which four different dancers played Joan as maid, warrior, martyr and saint. One of Graham's best group works, *Acrobat of God*, contained a role for her in which she gave audiences a taste of her wit long after her technique had become eroded with advancing years.

Her company's first European tour was planned for 1950 but Graham hurt her knee on the first night in Paris and the trip, including a London engagement, had to be cancelled. The company eventually gave its first London season in 1954 at the Saville Theatre, to tiny but enthusiastic audiences. Not until 1963, however, did Graham achieve real success in Britain with sold-out seasons in Edinburgh and London.

By then she was almost 70 but her age was a well kept secret and she remained the leading dancer, although increasingly in roles where she could dominate the stage by her presence, leaving the more strenuous parts to others. She stopped

dancing only in 1970, when illness and frailty made it inevitable. For a time her school and company were maintained by her loyal leading dancers while she succumbed to alcoholism, until a young photographer, Ron Protas, helped her overcome this and resume activity. He also put her business affairs on a more secure footing, but unfortunately his protectiveness drove away some long-standing colleagues.

Graham continued to direct her company and make new works for it, besides supervising the revival of old ones, but some of her creative spark had disappeared. She often repeated old formulas, but her most recent creation, *Maple Leaf Rag* (partly a homage to her old mentor Louis Host), was hailed at its premiere in October 1990 for its liveliness and humour.

Acquiring almost the status of a national movement, Graham began to enjoy the support of a fashionable audience at lavish fund-raising galas. She was helped by admirers such as Rudolf Nureyev.

In recent years fashion in modern dance has turned in other directions. Graham's company retained interest as an historic survivor. However, such new leaders as Merce Cunningham and Paul Taylor were among the choreographers who emerged from her dancers even if they mostly reacted against her.

Her influence was as great overseas as in America. In Britain, particularly, the whole modern dance movement which has flourished during the past 25 years arose directly from the enthusiasm caused by her 1963 seasons. The London Contemporary Dance Theatre was founded with her blessing and early help.

Her private life was as tempestuous as her work on stage. In 1948 she married Erick Hawkins but the relationship was never an easy one because he found it difficult to accept her belief in her own superiority. It came to an end after Hawkins had made an ill-judged attempt to salvage the proposed Paris season in 1950 by improvising performances without her.

PAULO MUWANGA

Paulo Muwanga, former vice-president of Uganda, died in Kampala on April 1 aged 67. He was born in 1924.

PAULO Muwanga played a role in virtually every government Uganda has had since gaining independence from Britain in 1962 and had, in a period of self-imposed exile from his country under the Amin regime, run a fish and chip shop in south London. In 1980 he was briefly head of state of Uganda in the chaotic period which followed the overthrow of Idi Amin the year before. In the early part of his career he was associated with progressive spirits who agitated for independence from Britain in the 1960s. But as minister of defence and vice-president of Uganda in Dr Milton Obote's second administration from 1980 to 1985 he was accused before Uganda's human rights commission with abuse of power and gross violations of human rights, including mass murder and torture.

Muwanga joined Uganda's first political party, the Uganda People's Congress (UPC), in the 1950s. When Dr Obote, UPC's founder, became independent Uganda's first prime minister in 1962 Muwanga held various post in his government, notably in the foreign ministry. After Idi Amin's overthrow of Dr Obote in 1971 Muwanga served under the new leader as head of protocol, but in a climate which was rapidly becoming more dangerous for any who had been associated with Obote he was not sorry to become ambassador in Paris in 1971. From there he fled to exile in Tanzania in 1973 and made his way to London in 1975.

For the next two years he ran a fish and chip shop in Caterham before returning to Africa in 1977 to join the group of exiles who were gathering around Dr Obote in Dar es Salaam. As UPC representative he attended the Moshi conference held in Tanzania in 1979 to try to form a common political front among exile groups.

The first post-Amin administration in Uganda, that of Usufu Lule, soon collapsed, as did its successor, led by Godfrey Binaisa. He had found himself at loggerheads with Muwanga, who was working closely with Dr Obote, and in

May 1980 he was removed by a military coup by Muwanga who had the support of the army chief of staff, David Oyite-Ojok.

For several months Muwanga became effectively head of state, as chairman of the military commission of the Ugandan National Liberal Front which ruled the country for several months during the run-up to elections later that year. Muwanga was subsequently accused of trying to establish regulations which would ensure a UPC win (he was afraid that the Democratic party had shaded UPC in the poll). UPC duly came in first and Muwanga handed over power to Dr Obote who became president. Muwanga served as Obote's vice-president from 1980 to 1985 but is generally regarded as the principal author of the reign of terror which characterised the next five years. After the overthrow of the Obote regime numerous witnesses to Uganda's human rights commission attested to killings and tortures, including the mutilation of women, which were authorised by Muwanga. In five years 300,000 civilians were killed and an equal number fled the country, but Muwanga persistently denied any involvement to the hearings of the human rights commission. He had never committed any of his instructions to paper, instead encouraging reprisals against opponents in a series of gnomic traditional proverbs.

In the period following Obote's second overthrow in 1985 Muwanga was briefly prime minister in yet another chaotic period of interim government before the guerrilla leader Yoweri Museveni came out of the bush to take control of Uganda and become president in 1986. Muwanga was arrested and charged with treason. He was released after being found not guilty but was rearrested in 1988, this time to be charged with murder. He had been held in prison until last October when he was acquitted and rehabilitated. Since then his health had not been good; a diabetic, he had also suffered from kidney problems and he died in hospital in Kampala.

GRAHAM GREENE

Graham Greene, OM, CH, novelist, died in Vevey, Switzerland, on April 3 aged 86. He was born on October 2, 1904.

THE reputation of Graham Greene must rest on his serious religious novels, the first to be written in England in this century. But he was versatile and his travel books, short stories, criticism and those lighter novels he called "entertainments" were of high quality. He was an outstanding storyteller; he wrote plays and film-scripts as well as being an excellent film critic; he also contributed to children's literature. No other contemporary British writer enjoyed so high a reputation on the continent of Europe.

Graham Greene, who was related on his mother's side to R. L. Stevenson and, more distantly, to G. J. Whyte Melville, was one of the four sons of Canon Charles Henry Greene; two of his brothers, Raymond Greene, the physician

and climber, and Sir Hugh Carleton Greene, director-general of the BBC from 1960 to 1968, also achieved distinction. Graham Greene, like his brothers, was educated at Berkhamsted School where his father was headmaster. While he was still at school his first short story was published and his first play accepted, but not performed.

He won a history exhibition to Balliol College, Oxford, gaining a second, being more interested in university journalism than in academic work. He was the editor of *Oxford Outlook* and contributed to London as well as Oxford journals. *Babbling April*, a slim volume of poems, was published in Oxford in 1925 but poetry was not his genre and he did not return to it. Strongly influenced in boyhood by Rider Haggard's *King Solomon's Mines*, he developed a lasting interest in Africa and for a time considered going into the Colonial Office. Instead, after an abortive ten days with the British American Tobacco Company, he went to Nottingham where he worked as a sub-editor on the *Nottingham Journal*. There he was instructed in the Roman Catholic faith and was subsequently received into it. Its influence was not apparent in his writing for some time. It took him ten years, he once said, to know enough about Roman Catholics to be able to write about them.

In 1926 Graham Greene came to London, and for three years worked as a sub-editor on *The Times*, where he found the company congenial and the hours, not to mention the disciplines of sub-editing, well suited to the apprenticeship of an aspiring novelist. He married Vivien Dayrell-Browning in 1927 and in 1929 Heinemann accepted and published the third of the novels he had sent them, *The Man Within*. Although he later, and justly, described it as "embarrassingly romantic" *The Man Within* had a great success and was rewarded with a three-book contract. This comparative security proved, significantly, stifling. The next two novels – Greene later omitted them from his list of published works – were barely noticed failures and it was only when his financial affairs reached a pitch of crisis that the thriller or "entertainment", *Stamboul Train* (1932), repeated his first success and he began to be noticed as a writer of originality and power with an especial sensitivity to the world of urban seediness. Of this his interpretation eventually became known as "Greeneland". This country of the imagination extended its boundaries to mid-century Africa, Latin America, the Far East, the Caribbean, Vienna and Brighton Pier.

In the years after *Stamboul Train* other entertainments followed, together with a book of stories, *The Basement Room* (1938) and *Journey Without Maps*, the account of a trip to Liberia, in 1936. Already, distinctive themes were emerging: the betrayal of innocence and trust, especially the innocence of childhood, the lost Eden; obsessive gambling; the tawdry values of the old school tie. To these he added a subject he was to make his own, the problem of sin in a Catholic context, in his novel *Brighton Rock* (1938) with its painful and arresting conclusion. But "I find it very difficult to believe in sin" he once said and insisted that the sense of sin, about which he wrote so powerfully, belonged to his characters and not to himself.

With *The Power and the Glory*, which won the Hawthornden Prize for 1940, Graham Greene became established as a writer of international importance. Here was serious religious fiction being written in England and comparisons were made with such French Catholic novelists as Bernanos and Mauriac. Greene's Mexican whisky priest has passed permanently into literature. Admirable as was much of his subsequent output – notably his later Catholic novels, *The Heart of the Matter* (1948), which bought widespread popular interest, and *A Burnt-Out Case* (1961) – *The Power and the Glory* is his masterpiece.

After *A Burnt-Out Case* his literary talent seemed for a while to lose its sense of direction. There were two more books of short stories; in 1963 the rather fey *A Sense of Reality* seemed to hint at new directions, but these were not developed. In 1967 came *May We Borrow Your Husband?*, bitter but rather lightweight tales of (usually) sexual misery. A longer novel, *The Comedians* (1966), set in Papa Doc's Haiti, contained many excellent things and, though heavy-handed in some of its execution, presaged a return to confidence and form.

Greene then switched course. *Travels With My Aunt* (1969) was a brilliant comedy, the uncomplicated tale of a stuffy bank clerk and the outrageous Aunt Augusta who entices him from his championship dahlias to follow her round the world via Brighton and Istanbul to Paraguay where, his civic virtues hopelessly compromised by spectacular international crime, he prudently becomes engaged to the police chief's daughter. This was an unexpected book from Greene at this stage in his career. But while the nephew and his aunt are little more than figures, the stream of situations which constantly challenge them to action is subtly characteristic of Greene's work as a whole. *Travels With My Aunt* continues as adventurous farce the argument that life can only be savoured to the full by those who accept the need for danger, involvement and risk. It cleared the way for an energetic resumption of these themes in the books that followed it.

"Our interest's on the dangerous edge of things." Greene took Browning's line as the informing text of his autobiographical memoir, *A Sort of Life* (1977), which surprised those who had expected this very private man to offer lengthy revelations of childhood and youth and were offered instead a terse account of poetic escapades from unhappiness at school and their gradual transformation into the adolescent bravura with which the young Greene took on his new (and lifelong) enemy, boredom. As a boy he tried to cut off his leg with a penknife; at Balliol he tried remaining drunk for a whole term. He became a spy in the French-occupied Rhineland. Later in life he took opium from time to time and wrote soberly of the terrible dreams it had given him. If much of the material in *A*

Sort of Life seemed vaguely familiar, that was because there was scarcely a significant episode, experience or setting in his early life Berkhamsted, Nottingham, British American Tobacco which he had not already subsumed in his fiction.

"For a writer," he wrote in his memoir, "success is always temporary. Success is only a delayed failure." A writer is only as good as his last book, the one that really matters. These are the words of the complete professional, and one always had the feeling that Graham Greene could not have stopped writing — or travelling, or using his eyes and ears — even had he wanted to. He followed *A Sort of Life* with *The Honorary Consul* (1973), a novel of guerillas and hostages set on the Argentine/Paraguay border. This was remarkable for its literary grace and readability, its profound sense of paternity (fathers of all kinds haunt its pages) and for its re-creation of a perfect Greene hero, Dr Eduardo Plarr. It was almost as if, as he approached 70, Graham Greene had sat down and written for the pure pleasure of it, the exemplary Graham Greene novel. (One of his more mischievous achievements had once been to win *New Statesman* competitions with pseudonymous parodies of his own style.)

He was to continue to be full of industry over the next 10 years. *Lord Rochester's Monkey* (1974) was a break from fiction to publish a literary biography he had long cherished, that of the seventeenth century poet and rake John Wilmot, Earl of Rochester. But he returned to fiction with *The Human Factor* (1978), a story of treachery in the secret service which appeared timely amid a similar series of actual exposés in British public life. However, for all the fact that such a story was natural Greene territory, many saw in it a falling off of the master's powers, a feeling which was not entirely dispelled by the short *Dr Fischer of Geneva* (1980). *Monsignor Quixote* (1982) transferred Cervantes's hero to modern Spain, made him of the cloth and mounted him in an old car called Rocinante to produce a comedy of light touch. His final novel, *The Captain and the Enemy* (1988) was, again, set in quintessential Greeneland. Contemporary Central America was evoked with the certain grasp of the old hand to produce a tale that was superficially an adventure, but underneath rehearsed the familar themes of innocence, experience and disillusionment.

Greene did a great deal of work outside the field of fiction. He was exceptional in his generation for versatility. For example, no leading creative writer has shown, despite much discouragement, a closer or more lasting interest in the cinema. He was film critic of *The Spectator* from 1935 to 1940 and many of the judgments reprinted in *The Pleasure-Dome* (1972) have stood the tests of time and authenticity well. He took an unfailing delight in figures like Alexander Korda and Orson Welles — plenty of risk, and excitement of a kind, there — and enjoyed "going to the pictures" throughout his life. Many of his books were filmed, sometimes (as with *The Fallen Idol*, a story based on *The Basement Room*) with scripts written by himself; more often, and less fortunately, not. *The Third Man* was an exciting screenplay, filmed with great success by Carol Reed in 1949. None of Greene's other original screenplays was of the same quality, and neither were the few adaptations he made of other people's work.

He had several abortive attempts at playwriting but did not achieve success until 1952 when *The Living Room* opened in Stockholm and was produced in England the following year. This, like his other plays, *The Potting Shed* and *Carving a Statue*, and the farce *The Complaisant Lover* (well worth revival) were notable for their craftsmanship and originality; nevertheless the interpretative vision of his better novels was lacking. Yet another interest was revealed when, in 1966, he produced, with Dorothy Glover, a catalogue of their collection of nineteenth century detective stories in a limited, signed edition. Book-hunting expeditions, particularly in Scotland, were a favourite annual sport.

To meet, Greene was amusing, shy

and, like his brother, Hugh, leaned from a considerable height. He was courteous and kindly, particularly to younger writers, and he was unfailingly alert. Unusually for a writer of his period, he sought no personal publicity. He achieved it briefly as early as 1938, when an article he wrote on Shirley Temple for a satirical journal, *Night and Day*, led to a libel suit whose damages ruined the magazine. In his earlier writing his interest in generally liberal and progressive politics emerged only in the books themselves but youthful membership of the Communist party led, in 1952, to his being refused (and then, as a special exception granted) a visa to visit the United States. He greatly disliked American policy in South-East Asia and satirised it savagely in his novel *The Quiet American* (1955) which was in many ways prophetic of later events. *Our Man in Havana* acquired fortuitous political significance when the Castro coup in Cuba seemed to justify Greene's charges of British intelligence's confusions in the area. "Our man in − ", like "whisky priest" was a phrase Greene added to our language, and his nose for the world's next trouble-spot became so uncannily efficient that dictators were said to turn pale when he set up his typewriter overlooking their capitals.

During the 1950s and 1960s his interest in public affairs increased and he would write to the newspapers on such issues as justice for the Kikuyu in Kenya, support for Dr Castro, and on issues of interest to writers, especially censorship; in 1968 an attempt to divert his Russian royalties to the wives of the imprisoned Sinyavsky and Daniel was, however, unsuccessful. He also wrote an open letter to Malraux, protesting at the Algerian trial of Henri Aleg, author of *La Question* and crossed swords with the Archbishop of Paris who had refused Christian burial to Colette.

But perhaps the most astonishing furore in which he was involved was the campaign of vilification launched on him by a bruised Haitian government after the film version of *The Comedians* − which represented Papa Doc Duvalier's island as a hell of political murder, corruption, voodoo and torture − had produced a dramatic slump in the country's tourist trade. In a publication entitled *Graham Greene Finally Exposed* the Duvalier regime riposted with charges that Greene was a "cretin" and a "pervert". Francois Duvalier even went to the lengths of suing Greene in a French court for ten million francs and won his case but received damages of only one franc. Several years later Greene returned to the attack with a challenge to Duvalier's son and successor Jean-Claude to release named political prisoners as a sign of his good faith. This request was not acceded to.

J'Accuse; the dark side of Nice, echoing Zola, was another dramatic piece of intervention in public matters from Greene, this time in the South of France where he had settled. He castigated local government, police and the judiciary of the resort as venal, corrupt and malevolent. This book was banned by those same authorities and *J'Accuse* cost Greene libel damages of several thousand francs in a French court.

Graham Greene was from 1940 to 1941 literary editor of *The Spectator*, and then went on special wartime service for the Foreign Office to Sierra Leone, which provided suggestive material for *The Heart of the Matter*. He was a director of the publishing firm of Eyre and Spottiswoode from 1944 to 1948, and later of The Bodley Head. He travelled extensively, was in Prague during the communist coup of February 25, 1948, spent some time in Vietnam and visited Israel after the Six Day War.

He was made a Companion of Honour in 1966, and a Chevalier of the Legion of Honour in 1969. In 1986 he was appointed a member of the Order of Merit. In 1970 he had resigned from the American Academy of Arts and Letters as a protest against American involvement in Vietnam. He deplored the American invasion of Panama in 1989; he had been a close friend of President Torrijos (who was killed in a plane crash in 1981) and had an enduring affection for the country.

He had a daughter and a son.

VISCOUNT DE L'ISLE, VC

Viscount De L'Isle, VC, KG, PC, GCMG, GCVO, soldier, businessman, former government minister and governor-general of Australia, 1961-65, died on April 5 aged 81. He was born on May 23, 1909.

VISCOUNT De L'Isle came of a family with a tradition of adventure and involvement in the nation's affairs, but always with the family seat to return to. Penshurst Place, near Tonbridge, dating back 600 years and belonging to the family since 1552, was his retreat and base. It is the subject of one of Ben Jonson's finest poems, which extols the nature of the Jacobean mansion and its relationship to the surrounding community. His many-sided role suited him as a descendent of Sir Philip Sidney, the courtier, poet,

soldier and statesman. "Whither the fates call me," is the family motto.

Educated at Eton and Magdalene College, Cambridge, William Philip Sidney was the 6th baron and a baronet, succeeding his father in 1945. He was created a viscount in 1956. He was commissioned in the supplementary reserve, Grenadier Guards, in 1929 and during the war made his mark as a soldier in a feat of bravery which the regiment remembers with pride. After a variety of postings, he was promoted major and posted to 5th Battalion Grenadier Guards in North Africa as a company commander. In the fierce fighting which followed the allied landings at Anzio, he was awarded the Victoria Cross "for superb courage and utter disregard of danger" near Carroceto.

The action came during February 6-10,

78

1944, which was of critical importance to the Anzio beach-head. The Germans attacked a British division with elements of six different divisions and hand-to-hand local battles were fought. During the night of February 7-8 Major Sidney was commanding a support company of a battalion of the Grenadier Guards. When enemy infantry heavily attacked near his company headquarters he collected the crew of a 3-inch mortar firing near by and led an attack with Tommy guns and hand grenades, driving the enemy out of the gully. He and a handful of men took up their positions on the edge of the gully to beat off the enemy again. They kept most out but some reached a ditch only 20 yards in front, from which they could have outflanked his position.

In full view and completely exposed, he dashed forward to engage the enemy with his Tommy gun at point-blank range, driving them back with dead left behind them. Back again on the edge of the gully, he kept two guardsmen with him and sent the rest back for more ammunition and grenades. The Germans renewed their attack and a grenade bounced off Sidney's face and exploded, wounding him and one guardsman and killing the second man. Single-handed and wounded in the thigh, Sidney kept the enemy at bay until the ammunition party returned five minutes later when once more the Germans were pushed back. Just as he was on his way to a nearby cave to have his wound dressed, the enemy attacked again so he returned to his post and fought for another hour until the left of the battalion was consolidated and the enemy finally driven off. The citation said: "Only then Major Sidney, by that time weak from loss of blood and barely able to walk, allowed his wound to be attended to. . . . There is no doubt that as a result of his action taken in the face of great odds the battalion's position was re-established with vitally far-reaching consequences on the battle as a whole."

Sidney had married in June 1940 Jacqueline Corinne Yvonne Vereker, only daughter of Viscount Gort, VC, himself a Grenadier who was awarded the Victoria Cross in the first world war. It was appropriate therefore that he was decorated with a piece of the Victoria Cross ribbon, cut from Lord Gort's tunic, at the Anzio beach-head on April 2, 1944. He was presented with the Victoria Cross by the King at Buckingham Palace in October that year.

He was transferred to the regular army reserve of officers for parliamentary duties and was returned unopposed as a National Conservative for Chelsea, his birthplace, in 1944. After only a few months in the Commons he succeeded to the barony but he was there long enough to be appointed parliamentary secretary to the Ministry of Pensions in the Conservative caretaker government. His maiden speech, when he moved the address in reply to the King's Speech after only a month in the Commons, was far reaching in its survey of the state of the war, enlivened by personal observation of operations and ringing in its phrases: it indicated a talent which the Commons was so soon to lose.

Maintaining an active interest in the Conservative party, he became in 1948 its joint treasurer. With the return of the Conservatives to power in 1951, he was appointed Secretary of State for Air by Sir Winston Churchill and brought to the job his customary *élan*. He was the first minister to go up in a nightfighter, flying in a Meteor in an exercise over Germany. He was soon up again in a Canberra bomber and took flying lessons himself, always with the instinct of not wishing to be out of the action. When he resigned after four years because Sir Anthony Eden wanted the post to be held by a member of the Commons, Eden wrote to him: "The whole of the air force at home and abroad have come to know of your devotion to the service." He had thrown himself wholeheartedly into the job and had paid particular attention to the conditions under which men in the service were living. In furtherance of this he had toured many parts of the world. In August 1952 he made an 8,000 mile inspection tour of the Middle East RAF establishments. On a visit to Australia he also inspected the weapons research establishments at Salisbury and Woomera.

He was made a viscount when he left the Air Ministry and abbreviated his inherited title name by dropping the "and Dudley" element. Once he had been guest of honour at USAF headquarters at Ruislip, Middlesex, and arrived as Lord De L'Isle and Dudley at the top table to find out that two places had been set for him.

With his war record and go-getting approach, De L'Isle was put forward in 1961 to be governor-general of Australia, an appointment which was welcomed by Mr Menzies, the Australian prime minister, but attacked by the opposition. The Australian Labor party held the view that the governor-general should be an Australian citizen. When the time came for De L'Isle to leave Australia in 1965 Menzies received the news with regret and said the government would have wished, if circumstances had permitted, to extend the appointment so that De L'Isle could continue with the work he had carried out so well.

As with the RAF, De L'Isle believed in involvement. He went into the property business in Australia, buying two properties in northern New South Wales and forming a company. The move was intended to continue the family links with Australia. While he was in Australia he showed himself to be ahead of his time in attacking modern architecture, which much later became a more fashionable pursuit. An honorary fellow of the Royal Australian Institute of Architects, he told 400 architects at the institute's convention: "In every city one sees the same dreary, glass-covered elevated matchboxes stacked up like a row of tombstones, their sky-lines decorated by fuel-oil tanks and lifts."

His business acumen was much sought after and at various times his directorships included the Yorkshire Bank, Schweppes, British Match Corporation, Courage and Barclay, Lloyds Bank and Phoenix Assurance, of which he was chairman from 1966-78. He was also chairman of Palmerston Property Development. He was never afraid to state his views, not least in reply to Tony Benn when De L'Isle attacked the opinion that institutional investors had failed to provide industry with enough capital, an argument that surfaces from time to time. Insurance companies were the custodians of the funds of the general public, he said. De L'Isle was always concerned about the corrosive effects of inflation and with the rights of the individual. This concern took shape with his chairmanship (and later presidency) of the National Association for Freedom, whose charter of 15 basic aims was drafted by Ross McWhirter before his murder in 1975 by the IRA. At that time De L'Isle thought he saw the country travelling towards a drab collectivism and said other threats to freedom included inflation, the growing machinery of government and the extra-parliamentary power of the leaders of organised labour. One of the association's most important breakthroughs came with a ruling of the European Court of Human Rights that it was a violation of human rights to dismiss three men for refusing to join a union. Nevertheless, as a result of some of his views and actions he was regarded in some quarters as an exreme right-winger in his later years.

But he was never without chivalry, even to a wartime enemy. He helped to raise a fund in 1949, to which Winston Churchill subscribed £25, to provide British legal assistance for the defence of Field Marshal von Manstein who was charged with war crimes. De L'Isle's reason was that he considered British counsel necessary to ensure adequate defence. Manstein was sentenced to 18 years' imprisonment, later reduced to 12 years, and he was released for good conduct in May 1953.

Viscount De L'Isle's first wife died in 1962 and he married, secondly, in 1966, Margaret Lady Glanusk, widow of the 3rd Baron Glanusk. She survives him with the son and four daughters of his first marriage. The heir to the title is his son, Major the Hon Philip John Algernon Sidney, MBE.

MAX FRISCH

Max Frisch, Swiss playwright and novelist, died at his home in Zurich on April 4 aged 79. He was born on May 15, 1911.

WITH his contemporary, Friedrich Durrenmatt (who died last December), Max Frisch did much to dispel the image of the Swiss on the international stage as "typical Germans who escaped two world wars" — though this was an aspect of being Swiss which concerned him throughout his creative life and which permeates his work. Thus, in plays such as *Biedermann und die Brandstifter*, known in Britain as *The Fire Raisers* and in the United States as *The Fire Bugs*, the bourgeois protagonist Biedermann is an example of precisely that form of moral flatulence which Frisch deplores among his countrymen. When threatened by an evil in the form of two sinister thugs who are patently arsonists, he is incapable of

summoning the aid which is readily at hand and actually aids and abets the destruction by fire of himself, his household and his city.

This harsh view of an impotent neutrality about unpleasant external threats pointed obvious lessons to be learned from the Nazi takeover of Germany in 1933 and was inspired by Benes's forced acceptance of the communist coup which took over Czechoslovakia in 1948. It was characteristic of a good deal of Frisch's work but he would never have achieved the international reputation he so patently deserved had his preoccupation been only with the Swiss "predicament" as a social and political attitude. At the core of Frisch's work lies something more profound even than a critique of those tendencies which make human beings — as societies — wreak havoc on each other. In his finest works, such as the play

Andorra or the novel Stiller (tr. *I'm Not Stiller*) Frisch raises questions about the nature of human identity itself and whether modern man can do anything to make his humanity prevail against manipulation by external and evil influences. In its exploration of these fundamental issues *Andorra* is unsurpassed by any post-war European drama.

Max Frisch was born in Zurich, the youngest of the three children of Franz Frisch, an architect. He was educated at the Kantonale Realgymnasium in Zurich and then went on to study philology at Zurich University. But his father's premature death forced him to abandon his studies and for the next three years he earned a living as a freelance journalist, writing mainly about sport and travelling throughout Europe, principally in Italy and the Balkans, but also further afield.

In the mid-1930s, however, he went back to study, this time as an architect at Zurich's Technische Hochschule. After getting his diploma in 1941 he practised as an architect and had a good deal of success in obtaining important commissions. His best-known work in this sphere is the design and layout of the Zurich Recreational Park.

During the war Frisch was called up into the Swiss army and was on duty with the frontier forces. This experience tended to confirm him in his view that Switzerland's decision to remain neutral was a matter more of luck than judgment, and that it reflected a lack of commitment rather than a moral statement. Nevertheless Switzerland's neutral position did give him a unique vantage point from which to view the events of a war raging outside its borders.

Frisch had already begun writing. The novel of 1934, *Jürg Reinhart*, was an autobiographghical essay and gave no particular hint of what was to come. During the war Frisch had met Brecht while the latter was in Switzerland and the two had become friends. In 1944 Frisch wrote Santa Cruz, which deals with marriage and freedom, but the influence of Brecht is noticeable in *Als der Krieg zu Ende war* (1949) known in Britain as *When the War was over*. Though *Santa Cruz* is, like its successor *Die chinesiche Mauer* (1947), firmly and unsparingly argued in a way which indicates a qualitiative advance on Frisch's early manner, *Als der Krieg zu Ende war* goes further in using the Brechtian technique of alienation, when the heroine steps outside her role and comments objectively upon her performance in life. Brecht was to be useful to Frisch but never led him into pale pastiche. Brecht appreciated this even while accepting himself as a mentor from the technical point of view: "What Frisch thinks is his own business", he said.

These were followed in 1951 by *Graf Öderland* a twice-revised work which reached England as *Edge of Reason*, a translation of its third version. *Count Oederland* (which is a modern treatment of a German fairy tale), is the story of a little solicitor who, by overthrowing dictatorial power, finds himself exercising it not because he wishes to do so but because everyone believes that the man who overthrows a tyranny must inevitably exercise the power that was the tyrant's. Don Juan, in Frisch's play *Don Juan oder die Liebe der Geometrie* (1953), prefers geometry to women; it is the inescapable pressure of public opinion which makes him a seducer.

Frisch's best-known play, in the English-speaking world at least, is *The Fire Raisers* which appeared in 1957 and was put on in New York as *The Fire Bugs* in 1963. It was written as a radio play, a fact suggested by its spare construction. The Biedermann ("Everyman") of the play knows that fire-raisers are destroying the town in which he lives, but refuses to believe that the villainous, unwanted lodgers who fill his attic with cans of petrol can be in any way involved and suffers for his moral opacity. The play was written with an apparently callous frivolity, which was in harmony with the sceptical spirit of the age, and it did much to establish Frisch's reputation abroad. But a limiting construction tended to be placed on it from a tendency to see it solely in terms of such readily-identifiable targets for moral anger as Nazi Germany or totalitarian communism, and not enough in terms of the problem of what man becomes under certain types of external stimulus.

Andorra (1961) carried the argument about individual identity much further. In the play Andorra is any country, but most specifically a small, mountain-locked one, basking in neutrality. The pettiness and complacency of this society is broken in on when a neighbouring country, which is both powerful and anti-semitic, poses a threat. In these circum-stances the father of the protagonist, Andri, presents his son as a Jew (although he is not) in order to educate his country-men about the fallacy of racialism. But when he tries to enlighten them as to the truth it is too late. Andri has become what he is perceived by others as being, in spite of what he really is. Frisch's characters are fated to be what people think they are although they struggle violently against this destiny until sheer exhaustion recon-ciles them to it.

These cases are expounded with great theatrical skill and (in spite of the dark-ness of their subject) a good deal of wit. Frisch was prepared to allow his charac-ters a fine command of rhetoric and willing to exploit all the necessary theatrical tricks to make his point, and it was, perhaps, as much to this as to his intellectual and moral preoccupations, that his plays owed their success outside the German-speaking world.

The slowing down in the frequency of Frisch's dramatic output after *Count Oederland* was due not to a reduction of his creative energies but to his work as a novelist. His novels, notably *Stiller* (1954), *Homo Faber* (1957) and *Meine Name sei Gantenbein* (1964, tr. *A Wilderness of Mirrors*) were widely translated. *Meine Name sei Gantenbein* pursued Frisch's preoccupation with the nature of human identity perhaps as far as it could be taken. It has never been as popular in English as *I'm Not Stiller*. Its systematic pursuit of its (ultimately unattainable) goal recalls Robert Musil's

A Man without Qualities. The protago-nist's consenting to a "happy" marriage in the knowledge that his wife is deceiving him with other men asks, but cannot answer, the question of where the reality of such a contentment lies in such a situation.

In Britain Frisch's novels did not win a general acclaim comparable to that accorded to his plays. This may well be because they stand in a Teutonic tradition of unremitting intellectual seriousness in which the only way to reality is through densely packed symbolism through which that reality must be filtered before it can be recognised. They do not bring to bear on their invariable subject-matter the biting wit and the intellectual high-spirits which make his plays entirely theatrical treatments of the area of human experi-ence they confront.

Frisch had spent some time in New York after the war and he later lived there for three years. This led to a novel *Montauk* (1975) which was more tradi-tional and therefore more accessible than some of his previous work. Heavily auto-biographical, it was the story of a sixty-year old writer who tries to have a suc-cessful relationship with a woman on Long Island, but finds unhappy memories distracting him from it. Frisch's last substantial work *Man in the Holocene* (1980) was a grim tale, again featuring an elderly man whose sense of personal doom is projected on to external events. After turning 75 Frisch announced that he had ceased to write. Ill-health forced him to stop smoking the pipe which was his constant companion.

As a writer he was a tireless experi-menter and this makes his work either difficult or not always what it seems to be at first sight. But his experimentation was always the search of the right vehicle for the truth he wanted to convey, and not merely a matter of showing himself to be a master of the forms which are sometimes considered to be the *sine que non* of modernity.

Frisch was twice married and divorced and is survived by the three children of his first wife.

SIR DAVID LEAN

Sir David Lean, CBE, film director, died in London on April 16 aged 83. He was born in Croydon on March 25, 1908.

TOWARDS the end of his life David Lean was fond of quoting a piece of advice given him by Noël Coward early in his career. The two men, both master craftsmen and master entertainers, had come together to direct *In Which We Serve*, a film likely to appear a bit jingoistic today but which in 1942 did much to raise patriotic morale in war-buffeted Britain. "Do what pleases you," said Coward, "and if what pleases you does not please the public, then get out of show business."

Lean remembered those words and followed them. He had joined Gaumont British as a tea boy when he was 19. Over

60 years later, when he was well into his eighties, Lean was still obsessed with the cinema and planning the film of *Nostromo* based on Conrad's novel. In the meantime he had pleased himself, despite a tendency to be disparaging about his own work, and he had mightily pleased the public. He had also made a lot of money.

Many critics admired him most for some of his early films, *Brief Encounter* and *Great Expectations*; the public all over the world adored him for the blockbusters which became the Lean hallmark: *The Bridge on the River Kwai*, *Lawrence of Arabia* and, financially the most successful of all, *Dr Zhivago*. He had his setbacks: *Ryan's Daughter* received a critical mauling which wounded him more than he would ever admit, even though it did run for a year at the Empire, Leicester Square. He failed to get his project *Mutiny on the Bounty* to the screen. But Lean was tough enough and carried sufficient weight to bounce back with *A Passage to India* after over a decade of silence.

Lean regarded himself as a story teller, albeit of those invented by others. That was why he so often turned to the great novelists of the nineteenth and twentieth centuries. There were Dickens (*Great Expectations* and *Oliver Twist*), Pasternak (*Doctor Zhivago*) and Forster (*A Passage to India*). Carol Reed, whose best films unrolled their plots with economy and precision, was an early influence, so were the great French directors of the Thirties and Forties such as Carne, Renoir and Duvivier. Lean claimed not to be an intellectual but he gave his scriptwriters a hard time. Christopher Hampton, a mild mannered man, worked for a year on *Nostromo* before he could take it no longer and Lean returned to his old and trusted collaborator, Robert Bolt.

Lean's other obsession was landscape, which played an increasing part as his films became larger and longer. Stories abounded during the filming of *Ryan's Daughter* of camera crews and stars alike being left kicking their heels until just the right cloud formation arrived on the horizon. He explored the world to find precisely the right locations for the next project in hand and this was one of the reasons for his rootlessness. He had his houses, quite recently in London's Docklands and then in the South of France when he despaired of the parsimony and gutlessness of the British film industry. But his natural habitat was much more likely to be a hotel suite in whichever city happened to be catering for his immediate cinematic needs. Off the set Lean's manner was patrician in a way designed to hide a certain shyness and a lack of interest in the small talk and the gossip of the film industry. His nose was aquiline, a boyish lock of hair tended to fall over his brow as he spoke, but his face was dominated by the eyes which fixed on their subject with a steady, almost intimidating gaze. Nothing gave away David Lean's quite modest upbringing among a Quaker family in a London suburb.

He was born in South London and the strict religious observance of his parents, whose good looks he was to inherit, kept him somewhat apart from other children. Cinema-going was not encouraged and the young Lean had to slide secretly away from his Quaker school, at which on his own admission he was an indifferent pupil, to the pictures. An illicit visit to a silent version of *The Hound of the Baskervilles* gave him a taste of the magic the screen could produce and made him determined not to work in the staider profession of accountancy, which is what his parents, now separated, had in mind for him.

From being a tea boy at Gaumont British he progressed to the cutting room, working initially on the newsreels that were part of the diet of cinema programmes in those days. Lean's prowess with the scissors, sharpening such pictures as *Pygmalion*, became known and the technical mastery he was acquiring served him well. Audiences seeing *Great Expectations* (1946) were as terrified as young Pip himself at the sudden cut to Magwitch looming out of the Essex fog.

He worked with Michael Powell on

wartime dramas such as *One of our Aircraft is Missing* before the invitation came from Noël Coward to co-direct *In Which We Serve*. The film helped forge a number of Lean partnerships: he worked several times with its star, John Mills, and was to marry (as his second wife) the actress Kay Walsh, who was also in the cast. Then there was Coward himself. Lean was to work with him on *This Happy Breed*, *Blithe Spirit* and, most importantly of all, *Brief Encounter* with Trevor Howard and Celia Johnson. Some regard the latter as Lean's most perfectly shaped film. Certainly the theme of love in approaching middle age was one that fascinated him and he was to return to it, rather more opulently and less successfully, in 1955 with *Midsummer Madness*, starring Katharine Hepburn and Rossano Brazzi.

During the 1940s and 1950s Lean was highly productive. There were stylish adaptations such as *Oliver Twist* and *Great Expectations*, contemporary subjects including *The Sound Barrier* and one or two films, *Madeleine* and *The Passionate Friends* among them, which have almost disappeared from memory. *Midsummer Madness* marked a turning point: thereafter Lean was to devote himself to epic movies. The gaps between films grew longer and longer as the finance became ever more complex to arrange. Lean the perfectionist became ever more dominant as he demanded the perfect shot and was prepared to spend money and keep everyone waiting while it was achieved.

His reward was world-wide success and plenty of prizes. *The Bridge on the River Kwai* won seven Oscars, including one for Lean himself as best director. *Lawrence of Arabia* equalled that tally, including another for Lean, and no-one seemed to mind too much that it ran for close on four hours. *Doctor Zhivago* was less garlanded, but made MGM more money than any film since *Gone with the Wind*. With *Lawrence* and *Zhivago* Lean owed quite a lot to a young English schoolmaster turned playwright called Robert Bolt. The partnership was to continue in

good times and in those when the going was considerably tougher. Together they had to take the critical savaging sustained by *Ryan's Daughter*. Lean, although he did not say too much in public, was wounded by the reception, not least because the advance publicity, with battalions of journalists descending on Co Kerry where much of the shooting was done, had promised a masterpiece.

Another 14 years were to pass before Lean was to make his next film, *A Passage to India*, based on E. M. Forster's novel. This was a period of disappointment. Lean planned a film on Gandhi, but his rival Richard Attenborough beat him to it. Years were spent on a project to remake *Mutiny on the Bounty*, with Bolt heavily involved as screenwriter despite the fact that he had suffered a severe stroke. But *Bounty* was never to take to the high seas: there were quarrels with the producer, Dino De Laurentiis, over the cost and scope of the film. Its abandonment caused Lean the same disenchantment with the world of movie-making as had the attacks on *Ryan's Daughter*.

His pride was restored by *A Passage to India*. The usual stories, some true and some false, emerged from the locations of wrangles, notably with the temperamental Australian actress, Judy Davis, playing the part of Adela Quested. Any Lean film was news and his first in a decade and a half was something special. When *Passage* was eventually screened there was criticism of the casting of Alec Guinness, but the consensus was that Lean had lost none of his skill as a storyteller and none of his eye for a landscape with which to embroider it.

He had hinted that this would be his last film but as he turned 80 he was already embroiled in Conrad's *Nostromo*, searching out locations in Mexico and mocking the studios for lining up "reserve" directors in case his health failed him.

There is confusion about the number of his marriages, but he is known with certainty to have been married five times and leaves his widow, Sandra.

SIR ALAN ORR

Sir Alan Orr, PC, OBE, a Lord Justice of Appeal from 1971 to 1980, died on April 3 aged 80. He was born on February 21, 1911.

ALAN Orr was a quiet unassuming judge of exceptional quality. His career reminds us that good judges do not need, and are often better without, a charismatic public personality. In court he listened, he perceived truth with a quick and accurate mind and he knew the law: the result was findings of fact based on a detailed and perceptive understanding of the evidence, with the law applied accurately and lucidly. Not many appeals against an Orr judgment succeeded. Few outside the legal profession and the business community knew of him: he did justice consistently − and that is not news.

Alan Stewart Orr was born in Scotland. He made the journey south and, like so many other fine Scotsmen, enriched England with his talent. His gifted mind soon showed itself. From Fettes he went to Edinburgh University where he obtained a first in classics. He was then, like other brilliant Scots, drawn to Oxford by the magnetic influence of Balliol, where he took a first in law.

He was called to the English Bar in 1936 with a certificate of honour gained in his bar examinations. In the war he served in the equipment branch of the Royal Air Force reaching the rank of wing commander and being appointed OBE. He was a Harmsworth scholar of the Middle Temple.

After the war he returned to the bar where he at once established himself in practice. As a junior barrister he displayed his talent at its best. Lucky was the leader who had Alan Orr as his junior. His grasp of fact and law and his speed in analysing the complexities of a case were invaluable to the many silks with whom he was briefed. And he never sought the limelight − a mercy which many leaders thankfully recognised and which, of course, greatly strengthened the teamwork which cases of complexity demand of the lawyers engaged. His practice was largely in London but he did work on circuit, becoming Recorder of New Windsor in 1958 and deputy-chairman for a time of Oxford court of sessions. For a few months before his elevation to the bench he was Recorder of Oxford.

He made his name at the bar by his service as junior counsel to the Inland Revenue from 1957 to 1963 when he took silk. Tax, with its complexities of facts, figures and law was the sort of challenge he liked and met with ease. Tax being the universal scourge that it is, he needed to dig deep in many fields of the law. He was well fitted to do so. But he was more than merely competent. He was also well aware of the need to be fair to the tax payer. Judges knew they could rely on him and his opponents had the same confidence. There were few more trusted "tax devils" than Alan Orr.

He was appointed a High Court judge in 1965. Some thought it strange of the Lord Chancellor to have appointed him to the Probate, Divorce and Admiralty Division where he had seldom appeared as a barrister. But that was the way things were managed those days. In fact, to such a fine lawyer with wide experience and a mastery of a difficult field of the law, learning the intricacies of divorce law presented no problems. He proved to be an excellent and understanding divorce judge.

In 1971, he was appointed to the Court of Appeal where he served with distinction until he retired through ill-health in 1980. He had been struck by a vehicle as he was leaving the High Court in May the previous year and had sustained head injuries and a broken leg.

In his private life he was a delight. A devoted husband and father, he found time to help his wife, Molly, who died in 1986, bring up four fine sons. Law and his family occupied his life: but he did manage some rather strange golf every now and then with his friends. His contribution to English law may remain unsung: but he was a judge of talent and character who seldom made a mistake. He did justice quietly, effectively, and consistently well.

His four sons all survive him.

CAPT. SIR AUBREY ST CLAIR-FORD

Captain Sir Aubrey St Clair-Ford, Bt, DSO, whose ship rescued Lord Louis Mountbatten during the second world war and who later commanded the cruiser HMS Belfast, *died on April 8 aged 87. He was born on February 29, 1904.*

NEXT month sees the 50th anniversary of one of the most hazardous rescue operations of the war when nearly 300 British sailors were plucked from the embattled seas around Crete under continuous attack from the Luftwaffe. Those saved included the commander of the 5th Destroyer Flotilla, Captain Lord Louis Mountbatten. The man to whose daring and skill they owed their lives was Aubrey St Clair-Ford.

In late May 1941 Mountbatten led his own ship *Kelly*, together with its sister vessel *Kashmir*, on a mission to bombard an airfield in north Crete. As they withdrew at 30 knots next day they were dive-bombed by two squadrons of avenging Stukas. *Kashmir* was sunk within minutes and *Kelly* was hit and capsized shortly afterwards.

St Clair-Ford, in command of *Kipling*, had stayed behind while the destroyer was undergoing urgent maintenance. Alerted by the sound of gunfire over the horizon, *Kipling* steamed at full speed towards the scene where, during the next three hours, the captain and his crew displayed great qualities of seamanship and courage, jinking and dodging more than 80 bombs from the Stukas while at the same time picking up survivors.

Damaged by a collision with the drifting half-submerged *Kelly* the overladen *Kipling* ran out of food and fuel as it limped back to its home port of

Alexandria. But the operation not only won the DSO for St Clair-Ford but also the admiration of Mountbatten, who later described him as a "brave, brilliant and highly competent officer".

The rescue was, however, only the first and most celebrated in a sequence of actions in which St Clair-Ford won distinction during the early years of the war. Shortly before Christmas 1941 he won a bar to his DSO when *Kipling* sank a marauding U-boat while on convoy escort duties off the north African coast. Next March he was mentioned in dispatches during the second battle of Sirte when a small British force under Rear-Admiral Philip Vian successfully protected a convoy bound for Malta from a larger force of Italian warships.

Two months later he was mentioned in dispatches again, though this time in rather more disastrous circumstances, when *Kipling* was one of three British ships sunk by the Luftwaffe in the Mediterranean.

The man who was known to his sailors as "Strawberry" (inspired partly by his Christian name and partly by his ruddy complexion) was a product of Osborne and Dartmouth naval colleges, having entered the Royal Navy in 1917. Two of his brothers also became naval officers while the third, Major-General Sir Peter St Clair-Ford, died two years ago.

After the loss of *Kipling*, Aubrey, who was to succeed to the baronetcy in 1948, served ashore and was later hand-picked by Mountbatten to serve on his combined operations staff. He moved to the Pacific before the end of the war.

After 1945 he commanded first the Royal Navy electrical school HMS *Collingwood* then the Royal Naval air station HMS *Sea Eagle* in Northern Ireland before returning to sea in command of the cruiser *Belfast* in 1950. He took the *Belfast* to the Korean war where its support of allied land forces won him two more mentions in dispatches and led to his being appointed an officer of the United States Legion of Merit. He retired in 1955 as Commodore of the Royal Naval air station at Lee-on-Solent and moved into private industry.

For the last five years members of his crew in *Kipling* have assembled at his home in Fordingbridge, Hampshire, for an annual reunion. Pride of place was given to the silver tankard, donated to the ship by the Kipling Society, which was always used by St Clair-Ford on his bridge and was rescued by a sailor after the destroyer went down.

He leaves a widow, Anne, whom he married in 1945, a daughter and a son — who succeeds to the 198-year-old baronetcy.

MICHAEL PERTWEE

Michael Pertwee, playwright and screen-writer, died on April 17 aged 74. He was born on April 24, 1916.

MICHAEL Pertwee began his life as a dramatist with a series of crackling stage farces of that irresistible kind which never fails to bring a smile to the face of even the most unreconstructed misanthrope. Subsequently he carried his comic gifts into radio and television, where he was closely involved in the birth and writing of the BBC's first television soap opera for adults, *The Grove Family*. He did a good deal of work for films and wrote some taut stage thrillers too. But the dramatic terrain he naturally inhabited was that of the farce, represented at its best by such vintage fare as *Don't Just

Lie There, Say Something! (1971) which ran in London for over 600 performances at the Garrick before translating to the cinema screen as a movie of the same title.

Pertwee was born in London into a theatrical family. His father, Roland, was a playwright, novelist and short story writer. His younger brother, Jon, was to become well-known, as a comic actor, not least among devotees of the radio serial *The Navy Lark*, for his performance as the quite impossible Chief Petty Officer Pertwee aboard that zaniest of Her Majesty's ships, HMS *Troutbridge* – and of course to a generation of children as television's Dr Who. The Pertwees' mother left their father when they were still quite small and they were largely brought up by a grandmother until their father married again. Michael Pertwee was educated at Sherborne School and in France. He began work as a journalist at the age of 17 but he had already sold his first short story the year before.

In 1938 he gave up journalism to go into films. He had by that time already sold his first stage play, a thriller called *Death on the Table*, which was put on in London and New York in 1938. In those days of more chaste humour its jokes were adjudged a trifle robust for family audiences by some theatre critics and drew the attention of the censor. The headlines which accompanied this, "Censor Swoops on New Play" and so on, garnered some notoriety for its young author which did him no harm. Even in the thriller genre it was the jokes which were predominant, pointing the way to Pertwee's likely development.

The outbreak of war gave a temporary check to a career which had started so promisingly. Pertwee joined army intelligence and became a major; he was also mentioned in dispatches for his work. But these experiences did not quench his creative spark for long. Indeed the inherent absurdity of so much of service routine provided a rich vein of humorous incident (as his brother found when turning his own war experience in the RNVR to good account in *The Navy Lark*). Radio drama was consuming plenty of material in the war years and from 1941 Michael Pertwee wrote a number of scripts for the BBC.

After the war he embarked on the series of West End farces − many starring Brian Rix and some co-authored with his father − which established his style. Characteristic among his earlier essays was *It's Different For Men* (co-authored with Brenda and Monja Danischewsky, 1955), a familiar tale of a discarded wife who surprises her wayward husband by finding a newly seductive persona. To its stock situations of sexual confusion Pertwee brought an irrepressible liveliness. From the early 1950s onwards he also wrote for television, one of his early assignments being *The Grove Family* which was first transmitted on April 2, 1954. The audience for the series, on which Pertwee worked with his father, leaped to nine million in the first year and it was to claim the energies of the father and son writing team for the next three years before they were forced to withdraw from the fray from sheer inventive exhaustion.

From the late 1940s Michael Pertwee wrote screenplays, beginning in 1948 with *Silent Dust* (from his and his father's play of that title) and including *The Naked Truth* (1957), a frenzied black farce featuring Peter Sellers, Terry-Thomas and Dennis Price, and (co-written with Melvin Frank) *A Funny Thing Happened on the Way to the Forum* (1966) with music and lyrics by Stephen Sondheim.

Pertwee, who was three times married, leaves his widow, Maya, their son and daughter, and a daughter from a previous marriage.

STEVE MARRIOTT

Steve Marriott, singer and guitarist, died on April 20, aged 44. He was born in Bow, London, on January 30, 1947.

AS THE singer and co-songwriter of the Small Faces, Steve Marriott contributed a good deal to English pop music in the Sixties, with a string of hits including "All or Nothing", "Itchycoo Park" and "Lazy Sunday".

He began in showbusiness at the age of 12 as a child actor, playing among other roles the Artful Dodger in the London stage production of Lionel Bart's *Oliver!* When he was 16 he released his first solo single, "Give Her my Regards", and later formed his first group, Steve Marriott's Moments.

With drummer Kenney Jones and bassist Ronnie Lane he founded the Small Faces in the summer of 1965. They got into the charts with their first single, "Watcha Gonna Do About It", an amphetamined reworking of an old Solomon Burke riff which was notable for Marriott's vocal performance, a high-pitched white-soul shout that combined raucous enthusiasm with an ability to hit the right note.

As an embodiment of Carnaby Street chic and the emergent mod culture, the Small Faces had their moment but enjoyed a limited shelf life. Despite the success of their final album, *Ogden's Nut Gone Flake*, a No 1 in 1968, they never fully made the transition from being a singles to an albums act.

The group disbanded in 1969 and Marriott formed Humble Pie together with guitarist Peter Frampton, bassist Greg Ridley and drummer Jerry Shirley. They enjoyed five years of success but then faded and split up in 1975.

Marriott reformed the Small Faces in 1976 and Humble Pie in 1980, but to no avail. A man prone to mishaps, he crushed his fingers in a Chicago hotel door in 1981 and was ill with an ulcer in Dallas. A rumbustious character who lived life to the hilt, he responded with phlegmatic cheer to these shifts of fortune.

By the end of the Eighties he could be found in considerably reduced circumstances playing the London pub circuit with his last band, Packet Of Three. It was testament to his great spirit that even at the Putney Half Moon he always performed as if he was on stage in a major auditorium.

He leaves his widow, Toni.

WILLI BOSKOVSKY

Willi Boskovsky, Austrian violinist and conductor, died on April 21 in Visp, Switzerland, aged 81. He was born on June 16, 1909.

WILLI Boskovsky became for the post-war generation the very epitome of the Viennese waltz. In the famous new year concerts from Vienna, which were broadcast abroad and recorded, he brought to the music of Johann Strauss an authentic touch, at once lilting and buoyant. The geniality of Vienna could be seen in his face and was carried through to his hands, which seemed to waft the music into new existence every time he was on the podium. Players obviously enjoyed his presence there as they played whole-heartedly for him.

He studied violin and theory at the Vienna Music Academy from the age of nine, and won the Kreisler prize there when only 17. He joined the Vienna Philharmonic Orchestra in 1932 and was made one of its leaders as early as 1939. In 1937 he founded the Boskovsky Trio. Ten years later it expanded to the Vienna Quartet, which itself quickly became the noted Vienna Octet. He led the Octet until 1958 during which time he travelled and recorded frequently with great success.

Boskovsky first conducted the New Year's Day Concert in 1954 and continued to do so for more than 25 years, giving it an unbuttoned, relaxed, warm quality all his own. His violin career ran concurrently with his conducting duties until 1971 when he decided to retire from the Vienna Philharmonic.

Boskovsky was renowned for his recordings of Johann Strauss, of other members of the Strauss family, of their predecessor Lanner, and of Lehar. In the 1960s he recorded all Mozart's dance music with the Vienna Mozart Ensemble, which consisted of leading members of the Vienna Philharmonic. He once said that he really learned about Mozart from playing all the violin concertos under Bruno Walter before the war.

He also made excellent sets of several operettas, among them Strauss's *Die Fledermaus*, Zeller's *Der Vogelhändler* and Lehar's *Paganini*, but it was in the waltzes of Strauss that he most excelled and a selection of Strauss numbers on record made the long-playing Top Twenty in 1969. He was very much at home in the recording studio to which he brought a spontaneity not always achieved by more eminent conductors. He seldom strayed from his beloved Austria, but his records of Brahms's *Hungarian Dances* and Dvořák's *Slavonic Dances* proved that he could trip lightly, too, in rhythms other than the waltz.

DON SIEGEL

Don Siegel, American film director, died at his home in California on April 20 aged 78. He was born in 1912.

DON Siegel is best known for the crime thrillers and science fiction films like *Invasion of the Body Snatchers* (1956) and *Dirty Harry* (1971) which were such popular successes. But he had begun his directing life in a very different vein with two shorts, the nativity allegory *Star in the Night* and the very different *Hitler Lives*, both of which won Oscars in 1945. In retrospect the gulf between such films and the later box office hits is seen to be less great than might be imagined. Nothing Siegel did was ever less than craftsmanlike and he brought his own brand of thoughtfulness even to films which appeared merely riproaring or to be revelling in violence.

Siegel had learned his craftsmanship in Hollywood in the days of the great studios and he was to treasure that apprenticeship as long as he lived. Born in Chicago, he had studied in London at the Royal Academy of Dramatic Art before returning to the United States where he got a job in Hollywood in the stock shot library at Warner Bros. He became an assistant editor and then worked in the insert department which shot any scene the director found too boring. His next formative experience came with his appointment as head of the montage department, creating the sequences which in those days were often used to indicate the passage of time in the film's story. Siegel's montages were seen in many of the studios' biggest titles and the work he did on *Casablanca* (1942) earned him the rare compliment of a credit.

Grateful though he was for the experience he gleaned from it, Hollywood and its procedures irked him and when, in 1944, he got his chance to direct himself his first thought was how he might most infuriate Jack L. Warner, the executive producer. As a Jewish born atheist he hit upon the idea of a contemporary retelling of the nativity story, *Star in the Night*. The result, in which a Mexican couple, José and the pregnant Maria, arrive at a motel just in the nick of time, does not wear well today, but it won Siegel an Oscar, thus totally failing in its intended aim of irritating Warner. Its successor, *Hitler Lives*, a compilation film, had the same success.

Siegel moved into thriller territory in 1946 with *The Verdict*, from Israel Zangwill's Victorian murder mystery novel, *The Big Bow Mystery*. It was the first of a series of B pictures on which he increasingly stamped a personal style. By *Riot in Cell Block Eleven* (1954) he had emerged as a thoughtful film maker, able to operate within a low budget, in a picture which made an eloquent plea for prison reform. The *Invasion of the Body Snatchers* (1956), another low budget sortie, is a science-fiction classic with its subtle unravelling of the story of the takeover of a small American town by aliens. It remains an object lesson in the art of making science-fiction convincing without the visual trappings which are available to the contemporary director.

These gifts of economy continued to be seen in films like *Baby Face Nelson* and *The Killers*, the first feature film to be made for television. Siegel went on to direct a number of television pilots in the 1950s and 1960s.

Siegel had now graduated to big budget pictures and in *Coogan's Bluff* (1968) he directed Clint Eastwood in a story of an Arizona sheriff employing western police methods on the streets of New York — an effectively-done story which inspired the television series *McCloud*. Roles were reversed for *Play Misty for Me* (1971), in which Siegel played a barman in Eastwood's movie of a disc jockey pursued by a homicidal female fan. Siegel directed Eastwood again in *Dirty Harry* (1971) a violent cop movie which became a cult and spawned numerous progeny. Eastwood also appeared in *Escape from Alcatraz* (1979), a terse, brooding film which purportedly told the story of an actual breakout from San Francisco's

island fortress prison almost 20 years before. In the meantime Siegel had directed a distinguished line-up of stars, John Wayne, Lauren Bacall and James Stewart in *The Shootist* (1976) which brought thoughtfulness and poignancy to an unusual, late flowering example of the Western genre.

He is survived by his wife, Carol, by a son and by four adopted children.

MIGUEL TORRES

Miguel Torres, Catalan wine maker, died on May 15 aged 82 in Barcelona. He was born at Vilafranca del Penedes on February 3, 1909.

FEW vintners achieve the distinction of making their own name better known than that of the area in which their grapes grow. Miguel Torres was one of them.

The labels with the Torres stamp and the characteristic heavy, black gothic lettering are familiar throughout the world, from restaurants in New York to the shelves of duty-free shops in east European airports. But only a portion of those who draw the corks from his bottles are likely to identify the Penedes region of northern Spain, where his vineyards are.

From the start Miguel Torres had energy and ambition. He was an astute marketing man and he learned how to impress his brand names on the minds of the wine-drinking public. He also knew how to back up this expertise with a reliable and drinkable product. Torres was one of the first men to push Spanish wine, as opposed to sherry, through national frontiers and to make his label into an international one.

At first it was difficult. Torres found himself at the head of the family firm when he was 23 in 1932. The Spanish Civil War was just round the corner and during its course the winery was commandeered by the Republicans, which was not at all to the taste of the autocratic Torres although he was said to have been treated well. A bomb intended for the railway station at Vilafranca hit the Torres' vats instead and wine stained the streets of the town red.

With the Franco regime in power Miguel Torres began to rebuild. He even visited America during the war to sell his wines and immediately hostilities were over he crossed the Pyrenees with a car full of samples to sell his bottles to a thirsty Europe. This was bold at a time when Spain was very cut off from her European neighbours.

Torres began by buying in wine, blending it and selling it under his brand names. The most famous of the reds was Sangredetoro, Bull's Blood, which caused a little difficulty in the British market because there was a quite heavily promoted Hungarian red of the same name. It was later promoted to Gran Sangredetoro. Torres had a small black plastic bull hanging from the capsule of each bottle, but some wine merchants finding it a bit naff were said to remove it discreetly before wrapping up the bottles for their better class of customer. The most popular of the whites remains the Vina Sol and in Britain Torres now sells slightly more white wine than red.

Torres then decided to buy vineyards and eventually owned some 900 hectares in the Penedes region. Spurred on by his son, Miguel Jr, a trained oenologist, modern methods of vinification learnt in France were introduced. Torres too started planting French grape varieties: the sauvignon and chardonnay were used to give more subtlety to the whites and the cabernet sauvignon to lighten the reds. Bottles were produced for the top end of the market, the most famous of which is probably the Gran Coronas Black Label retailing now at not far short of £20. The Torres operation began in some ways to resemble that of Robert Mondavi in California: a very solid base of modestly priced wines supporting the production of those aimed at the top of the market.

Under the guidance of Miguel Torres the Penedes region began to rival – some might say outstrip – its major competitor, Rioja. But he was not content to stay at home. Major properties were acquired in Chile and then in America's Sonoma Valley. Sales of the Spanish produced wine are reckoned to run at about 17 million bottles a year with a further seven million of brandy.

His son, Miguel, seems likely now to take control of the family firm.

JACK "KID" BERG

Jack "Kid" Berg, world junior welter-weight boxing champion, 1930-31, and British lightweight champion, 1934-36, died on April 22 aged 81. He was born in London on June 28, 1909.

JACK "Kid" Berg was statistically the most successful world boxing champion Britain ever produced and perhaps the most ferocious British fighter to step into the prize-ring. Nick-named "Yiddle" and known as the "Whitechapel Windmill" because of his all-action style, Berg won the world junior welterweight (now known as light welterweight) championship from Mushy Callahan of New York in 1930 and successfully defended the title a record nine times before losing in 1931 to Tony Canzoneri, an American whom Berg had beaten a year previously. Berg held the British lightweight title from 1934 to 1936. He won 157 of his 192 fights, drew nine and suffered 26 defeats. Despite his success, his achievements were never fully recognised by the British press or boxing establishment during his heyday. This was partly because he was regarded as an unspectacular performer in British rings before his sudden departure to America in 1928.

It was also because the junior welterweight division was not recognised in Britain at that time. Indeed, at the ringside at Berg's world title-winning effort against Callahan at the Royal Albert Hall, Lord Lonsdale protested that there was no such title as junior welterweight and argued that the fight should not have been accorded championship status. But Berg struck a chord with the British public, who warmed to his perpetual motion style. In spite of his lack of a big punch, he overwhelmed opponents with the sheer volume of his attacks.

The progress of Berg's American campaign was followed avidly in Britain. Hundreds would congregate outside the boxer's family home in Romford Street, East London, to hear his father read out the telegram carrying news of his son's latest fight.

When Berg returned briefly to London during his championship reign, police had to be called to restore order at Victoria Station as thousands turned out to greet the conquering hero, lining the streets as the champion returned to Whitechapel via the West End at the head of a 20-car motorcade.

Berg was born Judah Bergman above a fish shop in Christian Street, Stepney, then a notoriously deprived area of the East End. He was the son of Jewish immigrants from Odessa and the arrival of the young Bergman into the world was greeted with more than customary excitement because he was born with a caul, a second skin covering the head which was believed to instil a sixth sense in its owner. Although the caul was stolen while Berg was still a baby, he always maintained that it had given him luck for life. Luck was perhaps the only luxury available at that time to the immigrant Jewish population, many of whom had left Eastern Europe believing themselves en route to America but found themselves instead facing grinding poverty and open hostility from the gentile gangs of London's East End.

It was not surprising that boxing found willing devotees in second generation Jewish boys such as Berg, in spite of the disapproval of the Jewish establishment. Gyms flourished and fight halls such as the Judean Club, Wonderland and Premierland proliferated in the Jewish quarter between Cable Street and Whitechapel Road.

It was at the Judean Club, in the year of Berg's birth, that Ted "Kid" Lewis, Berg's idol, made his debut. Lewis, born Gershon Mendelhoff, became welterweight champion of the world and was to be instrumental in launching Berg's career. For it was while fending off unwanted admirers of Lewis's lefthand drive American car outside Premierland in 1924 that Berg came to the attention of the hall's promoters, who signed him up.

Berg's fistic journey had begun, and soon it took him across the Atlantic, where he teamed up with the great American trainer, Ray Arcel, a venerable fight figure who was still working the corner of world champions in the 1970s.

Together Berg and Arcel plotted Berg's greatest victory: a 10-round points decision over the legendary Cuban, "Kid" Chocolate, in June 1930. Chocolate was unbeaten in over 100 bouts before meeting Berg, and a crowd of over 40,000 turned out at the Polo Grounds in Harlem for the fight.

Berg's triumph was the sporting sensation of the year. But the following year, after his nine successful defences of the junior welterweight title, he challenged Tony Canzoneri for the world lightweight title. He had already fought and beaten Canzoneri in a non-title fight but this time was stopped in three rounds. Canzoneri claimed both titles, which Berg disputed, but when they met again five months later Canzoneri won a narrow points victory.

Three years later Berg won the British lightweight title by stopping Harry Mizler in ten rounds in 1934. He then went to South Africa in a vain bid to win the Empire lightweight crown and subsequently lost his British title in Liverpool when he was stopped in nine rounds by Jimmy Walsh in 1936.

Outside the ring Berg lived up to his billing as "the champ". From his base off Broadway, where he took a hotel suite a floor below that of Mae West, Berg would make regular forays to the nightspots of Harlem. In spite of prohibition there were more speakeasies than there had ever been bars and Berg found a home in this illicit but fashionable New York milieu as he had never done in London. He was often in the company of Walter Winchell, the columnist, or at his own reserved table at the Cotton Club in Harlem, an establishment which was owned by another friend of Berg and Arcel's, Owney Madden, the so-called "Duke of the West Side".

Although his last bout was not until 1945 and in 1941, aged 33, he beat the up and coming Eric Boon, Berg was never again to scale the heights of his victory over "Kid" Chocolate but he remained an irrepressible personality, finding work as a stuntman and bit-part actor in Hollywood, falling off innumerable horses and even diving to a memorable screen death from the lifeboats of the Titanic. Berg treasured his souvenirs from film making and, at the age of 80, could be seen striding through Soho in bootlace tie, Cuban heels and Al Capone hat.

In 1988, some 60 years after his championship reign, Berg, living in retirement in Southend with his second wife, Morya, returned to New York to find the Polo Grounds pulled down, Harlem dilapidated and the night clubs gone. This saddened him, but not for long, for Berg was an incorrigible realist always on the lookout for a new source of excitement. Approached by a gang of youths in Harlem, he told them he was an ex-boxer. "Oh yeah," one gang member said. "How many knockouts?" "Quite a few," said Berg. "Want me to try it?"

He leaves his widow, Morya and his daughter, Stephanie.

ANDREW BOYLE

Andrew Boyle, author and broadcaster, died on April 22 aged 71. He was born in Dundee on May 27, 1919.

ANDREW Philip More Boyle was a pioneer of modern current affairs radio journalism and capped a substantial output as a biographer with an investigation into the treason of the Soviet agents, Burgess, Maclean and Philby, that led to the public unmasking of Anthony Blunt, the Queen's former art adviser, as a traitor.

Although personally convinced of Blunt's complicity in the Burgess, Maclean, Philby conspiracy, Boyle could not prove it and so referred to him in *The Climate of Treason*, when it was first published in 1979, only as "Maurice". Nevertheless his revelations in the book led to questions in the House of Commons concerning Blunt's activities. These resulted in Margaret Thatcher disclosing in a Commons statement on November 15, 1979 that 15 years earlier, after being guaranteed immunity from prosecution, Blunt had confessed that while he was a Cambridge University don in the 1930s he had been a recruiting agent for the Soviet Union. Immediately after the prime minister's revelations, Buckingham Palace announced that Blunt had been stripped of his knighthood and Boyle began a speedy rewrite of his book.

It was widely acknowledged that it was Boyle's dogged and meticulous research that had brought the Blunt scandal into the open. He had stumbled upon Blunt's involvement three years earlier while visiting Cambridge during the early stages of his research for his book. He had later asked Goronwy Rees, a friend of Guy Burgess, who it was that Burgess had named when he had admitted in 1936 that he had been a Comintern agent since his Cambridge days. Boyle wrote later: "Goronwy whispered in my ear the two words: 'Anthony Blunt'." Boyle established that Blunt had operated hand in glove with Burgess, unobtrusively turning the proceedings of The Apostles, a secret society of the cultural elite at the university, into a progressive Marxist cell.

Boyle's first experience of the world of spying came during the second world war. After escaping in 1940 from France where he had been a university student and spending two years in the RAFVR, he served in military intelligence in the Far East from 1944 to 1955. After the war his enthusiasm for broadcasting led him to join the BBC as a scriptwriter/producer rather than becoming press attaché at the British High Commission in India which would have given him twice the salary. At the BBC he became assistant editor of the current affairs programme *Radio Newsreel* and deliberately stayed with radio rather than moving into television

In 1965 with William Hardcastle, a former Fleet Street newspaper editor, as anchor man, Boyle created a new style radio news formula with *The World At One* which was broadcast on what was then the Home Service. Until that time radio news had consisted of mostly anonymous announcers reading out news agency reports. With Boyle as producer *The World at One* introduced a sense of urgency, created its own stories rather than simply following up those published in the national newspapers and with presenters such as Ludovic Kennedy, Christopher Chataway, Rene Cutforth and Leonard Parkin quickly earned a reputation as the brightest and best informed lunchtime news bulletins and comment programme. It spearheaded a revival in the fortunes of radio news and soon attracted four million listeners. *The World At One* also attracted complaints of bias from various politicians but Boyle rode them out.

After five years producing *The World at One* and other similar current affairs programmes, including *The World This Weekend* and *PM*, Boyle became head of news and current affairs at BBC Scotland. He confessed to a love-hate relationship with the BBC and from 1976 began concentrating on his parallel career as a biographer. This had begun in 1955 with the publication of *No Passing Glory*, his account of the life of Group Captain Leonard Cheshire VC which was followed in 1962 by a biography of Lord Trenchard, the first Marshal of the Royal Air Force. In 1967 Boyle wrote a life of Montagu Norman, governor of the Bank

of England from 1920 to 1944, which was credited with shedding much new light on Britain's financial and economic affairs between the wars. This was followed by a biography of Lord Reith, the creator and first director general of the BBC. A fifth biography, of Brendan Bracken, the politician and journalist, won the Whitebread award for biography in 1974, a prize which led Boyle to win a test case against the Inland Revenue which attempted to claim tax on the £1,000 prize money.

Andrew Boyle was born in Scotland, although only because his mother insisted on returning to her home town from England for the birth of each of her children. As an author and broadcaster he developed the ability to assess what made people tick and a thorough understanding of how Westminster and Whitehall operated. He was also adept at inferring the nuances in what people did not say. He listed as a favourite recreation watching bad football matches from public terraces, especially at Fulham. Before his death he was working on another book dealing with espionage which was expected to centre on the career of Sir Dick White who was director general of MI5 from 1953 to 1956 and head of MI6 until 1969. This prompted reports of alarm in Whitehall and predictions that there would be attempts to suppress publication.

This was familiar territory for Boyle. His exposé of such a highly placed traitor as Blunt took considerable courage because of the possibilities of pressures from within the establishment and the danger of encountering expensive libel proceedings. He said later that he pitied Blunt but wished the traitor had expressed more sense of shame. Boyle maintained that in addition to Blunt his research had uncovered as many as 25 possible traitors working for British intelligence. Some of them were eminent people but, he said, it was up to the government to name them.

He leaves his widow, Eleanor, and a son and daughter from a previous marriage.

PAUL BRICKHILL

Paul Brickhill, Australian writer, died in Sydney on April 23 aged 74. He was born in Melbourne on December 20, 1916.

PAUL Brickhill was one of the best and most successful of the writers who satisfied the public craving for heroic stories of the war which was such a feature of the 1940s and 1950s. Indeed his three best-known books, *The Great Escape* (1951), *The Dam Busters* (1951) and *Reach for the Sky* (1954), may almost be said to constitute an anthology of the cardinal points of wartime heroism as it was received by the generation of schoolboys who grew up in the post-war period. The second world war was one in which the flyers had had the most glamorous role; the scientists had also performed in a manner which presented a deeply satisfying picture of British technical ingenuity backing up the courage of the fighting men. Thus Brickhill's *The Dam Busters*, with its story of Barnes Wallis's unique bouncing bombs breaching the Ruhr dams thanks to the skill and daring of Wing Commander Guy Gibson and the pilots of 617 squadron, endowed a single air raid with a mythological status it has never lost. *Reach for the Sky* made its protagonist, the legless Group Captain Douglas Bader, quite simply the war's most famous fighter pilot, while at the same time setting before the young a quite extraordinary story of courage triumphing over adversity. In a Brickhill book courage and a refusal to succumb to life's disappointments were emphasised. Stupidity and obtuseness, whether they were exhibited by the enemy or by officialdom at home, were obstacles merely to be surmounted. Obstructiveness on the home front was not dwelt on as having had an eroding effect on the war effort, as tended to happen in the more acerbic style of war book which came into vogue from the 1960s onwards. That said, Brickhill was a good writer who had the technical knowledge as an ex-fighter pilot himself to make his accounts convincing and the perceptiveness to breathe life into his war heroes. He set a standard in the telling of popular war stories which has never been surpassed.

Paul Chester Jerome Brickhill was born in Melbourne but brought up in Sydney. He was educated at North Sydney High School and Sydney University where he graduated in the 1930s. In the years before the war he worked as a journalist on the Sydney *Sun* among other papers. In 1940 he joined the Royal Australian Air Force, learned to fly and got his wings as a fighter pilot. He was posted to the European war theatre and served in the United Kingdom and the Middle East. He was as much of a dare-devil as any of the heroes he was later to write about and on one occasion he was court-martialled (though acquitted) for "low and dangerous flying" after "beating up" a Bournemouth pub in his Spitfire.

During the North African campaign his aircraft was shot down over Tunisia in 1943. Wounded, he managed to bale out and on landing was captured by the

102

Germans. He spent the rest of the war in captivity in Stalag Luft III in Silesia where he was involved in organising escapes. This first hand experience later gave *The Great Escape* its authenticity.

After his release he went back to newspapers and spent the years 1945-47 travelling as a foreign correspondent in Europe and the USA. But he wanted to write books and his first, *Escape to Danger*, written in collaboration with Conrad Norton, appeared in 1946. A description of the experiences of a number of pilots who had had to bale out of their aircraft in wartime, it was praised for its authenticity. Its reception persuaded Brickhill to abandon journalism. This instinct was confirmed by the financial rewards garnered by his next book, *The Great Escape*. It was the story of the breakout by 78 RAF officers from Stalag Luft III on March 24, 1944, which Brickhill had helped organise but which ended tragically when 50 of the escapees were shot on Hitler's orders. It was not actually made into a film until 1963 when it provided a vehicle for a host of screen stars such as Steve McQueen, Richard Attenborough and Charles Bronson but the book was a huge success. Brickhill followed it almost immediately with *The Dam Busters*. This told not just the story of the famous raid on the Möhne, Eder and Sorpe dams of May 15-16, 1943, but continued the story of 617 squadron and its unique precision bombing missions, which included finally dispatching the battleship *Tirpitz* in a Norwegian Fjord, until the war's end. It was a thoughtful as well as enthralling book and Barnes Wallis emerged from its pages as a hero in his own way to rank alongside such men as Gibson and Leonard Cheshire. A

film of the same title (1954), using Guy Gibson's book *Enemy Coast Ahead* as well as Brickhill as source material, with a script by R. C. Sherriff and featuring a sensitive performance by Michael Redgrave as Barnes Wallis, is a war classic.

The Dam Busters is Brickhill's best (in the sense of being his most truthful) book but as a commercial success it was exceeded by *Reach for the Sky*, which came after *Escape or Die* (1952), a series of stories of RAF escapes with an introduction by H. E. Bates. In its telling of the story of a young RAF pilot who lost both legs during an aerobatic stunt he undertook "for a dare", *Reach for the Sky* did not mince words over the demonic ego of one of the war's legendary figures. In Brickhill's apparent admiration of Bader's enthusiasm for the "big wing" tactics which could have lost the war, the book inadvertently does less than justice to that patient and wise commander, Hugh Dowding. But as a tale of Bader's dogged refusal to acknowledge the odds against his achieving anything – much less commanding a fighter squadron – the account compels wonder even while it patently asks for hero worship. It is still in print. The film of 1956 starred Kenneth More, perhaps too "nice" a man to give a totally convincing portrayal of the ferocious fighter ace. But it was a box office hit and contains some memorable scenes.

These books and the films they spawned made Brickhill's fortune and he published little more afterwards apart from *The Deadline* (1962). He had married Margaret Olive Slater in 1950. The marriage, of which there was a son and a daughter, was dissolved in 1964.

REAR-ADMIRAL
ROYER DICK

Rear-Admiral Royer Dick, CB, CBE, DSC, chief of staff to the Flag Officer, Western Europe, 1948-50, and standing group liaison officer, North Atlantic Council, 1952-55, died on April 23 aged 93. He was born on October 14, 1897.

ROYER Dick had a career afloat and in action which took him from the first battle of the Falklands in 1914 to command of the cruiser *Belfast* at the end of the second world war. In between he had been a midshipman at Jutland and had fought the Bolsheviks in the White Sea and the Italians off Cape Matapan.

Royer Mylius Dick was born into a family with interesting French connections: his mother had been brought up in France; his aunt wrote the popular song "Because". He grew up speaking fluent French, a fact that was later to be professionally useful to him and much valued by a succession of superiors in a navy where linguistic skills were not rife.

He joined the navy in 1910. At the outbreak of war he was serving in the cruiser *Carnarvon* which was part of Admiral Sturdee's squadron sent to put an end to the commerce-raiding activities of Admiral von Spee in the southern oceans. As such he was present at the battle of the Falklands on December 8, 1914, in which Sturdee's ships pursued and sank *Scharnhorst*, *Nürnberg*, *Leipzig* and *Gneisenau*, thus avenging the British naval defeat at Coronel the month before and eliminating von Spee's threat to British merchant shipping in the outer seas. From 1915 he served in the battleship *Barham* in the Grand Fleet and was present at the battle of Jutland in the following year.

Dick won his DSC during the British-American attempt to encompass the destruction of Bolshevik rule in the nascent Soviet Union through landings on the shores of the White Sea in 1918. He was commanding the gunboat *Razlyff* on the Dvina river when a number of barges and other boats seemed likely to fall into enemy hands. Pressing forward under heavy fire from the banks of the river, Dick rescued these craft and brought them and their crews to safety.

In 1920 he specialised in signals. Among his jobs between the wars were a period as a French interpreter and two ship commands, those of the destroyers *Dainty* and *Basilisk*. When war broke out again in 1939 he was at the plans division of the Admiralty but he soon went to the Mediterranean where he had two periods on the staff of Admiral Cunningham.

Dick's knowledge of French eased Cunningham's problems of communication during the numerous and often delicate contacts with the French. It was particularly useful to Cunningham when he came to negotiate the surrender of French warships at Alexandria after the fall of France to prevent them from ending up in German hands. The tragic events of Mers-el-Kebir at the other end of the Mediterranean, where British ships had had to fire on their French counterparts, were avoided. The French Admiral Godfroy was persuaded to immobilise a battleship and four cruisers without conflict. Cunningham's success owed much to Dick's knowledge of the French psychology.

In March 1941 he was present at the battle of Matapan which ended the Italian naval threat in the Mediterranean and he was later involved in planning many of the naval and amphibious operations in the North African and Italian theatre. Cunningham was later to speak very highly of Dick in his autobiography, *A Sailor's Odyssey*.

Later on in the war the Americans also developed a high regard for Dick's abilities and he was made an officer of the Legion of Merit in 1943. He took part in the Sicilian landings that year and after the Italian capitulation countersigned the Italian armistice as the representative of the British commander-in-chief.

He had by this time been promoted to commodore but he dropped back in rank to captain to take command of HMS *Belfast* in 1944. He took her out to the Far East where, in 1945, she was one of the first allied warships to enter Shanghai when 4,000 British internees were released from detention camps there.

Among his post-war appointments was chief of staff to the Flag Officer Western Europe, another job in which his French was useful as his chief was the French Admiral Jaujard. After a spell as Flag Officer Training Squadron in 1951-52 he was back to Western alliance service in 1952 when he was appointed standing group liaison officer to the North Atlantic Council.

He retired in 1955 but was active in the St John Ambulance Brigade for many years and was its commander-in-chief from 1962 to 1967. He was also chairman of the Royal United Service Institution from 1965 to 1967.

He was twice married, first, in 1928, to Agnes Mary Harben and second, in 1955, to Vera, widow of Colonel Bertram Pott. She predeceased him, as did the children of his first marriage, one of whom was killed in action.

LIEUT-COLONEL
JOHN CODRINGTON

Lieutenant-Colonel John Codrington, soldier and spymaster, died on April 25 aged 92. He was born in London on October 28, 1898.

JOHN Codrington was a soldier, spymaster, world traveller and professional gardener; also, at various times, a policeman, a fireman, a brewer's drayman and the fixer for a film company. He fought in the first world war, helped escapers from Occupied Europe in the second and was equally at home in the best clubs and the lowest dives both in his native London and in the remotest parts of the globe.

The Codringtons are an old Gloucestershire family, one of whose forebears carried Henry V's standard at Agincourt. John Alfred Codrington was the youngest son of Lt-General Sir Alfred Codrington. He was educated at Harrow, Sandhurst, Oxford, and Strasbourg. On May 1, 1917, he joined his father's regiment, the Coldstream Guards, with whom he served in France and Germany.

After the war, though still in the army,

106

he went up to Christ Church, Oxford, under a special scheme for servicemen, to obtain an abbreviated degree in modern languages – French and, later, Greek. In 1920 Codrington became ADC to General Sir Thomas Bridges in the British Military Mission at Smyrna, and then liaison officer with the Greek Army in Asia Minor. He was awarded the Greek Military Cross. Subsequently he was appointed interpreter to the committee of allied generals in Constantinople afterwards moving to Beirut as liaison officer with the French Forces of the Levant. His knowledge of French *argot*, which might have enabled him to pass as a Frenchman, had been acquired, he used to say, in the working-class bars of Paris.

He secured a unique attachment in 1930 to the French Foreign Legion and the 2nd Spahis in North Africa. Codrington was officially invited to represent the British Army at the centenary of the Foreign Legion in 1931 at Sidi-Sel-Abbès.

After serving with his regiment in the Sudan and Egypt, he went to India as ADC to the Commander-in-Chief, Sir Philip Chetwode. Horticulture having been an interest since childhood he helped in designing, very ingeniously, the residency gardens. He travelled back through Russia to England and rejoined his regiment but in 1936 left the army and was recruited to MI6. He worked in London, Paris and Vienna. After the war began, he spent his evenings, based at Chelsea police station, as Special Constable 169 before being recalled to the army, with the rank of lieutenant-colonel, to serve as Assistant Chief-of-Staff to Lord Gort, the Governor of Gibraltar: but he was, in reality, still with MI6. To those responsibilities he added work for MI9, dealing with escape and evasion, and liaison with the French Secret Intelligence Services in Algiers.

Returning to England in 1944, he was posted away from MI6 to the administration of Occupied Territories. While waiting to go abroad he worked as a labourer for Watney's brewery, first in the malt loft and then on the delivery vans. He was finally demobilised on VE

Day, but then acted for a while as personal assistant to General Urquhart, Director of the Territorial Army.

The job he took in 1947 was perhaps the most surprising of his career. He found himself in a totally unfamiliar, delightfully crazy atmosphere, working for Sir Alexander Korda at London Films, arranging transport and accommodation and, when the need arose, the co-operation of the Household Cavalry. As though he needed extra occupation, he joined the Auxiliary Fire Service as a fireman based in Clapham; in which capacity he fought many spectacular and hazardous conflagrations.

In 1956 he left London Films for BOAC, where his principal duty was, on behalf of the chairman, to welcome or see off important persons at Heathrow. This job was axed in 1960, whereupon he turned his hobby into gainful employment, becoming – and continuing to be for the rest of his life – a professional garden designer. He offered his clients water-colour sketches of the garden before, and as it would look after, his ministrations. Among his more exotic assignments were the public gardens at Timbuktu; a place which he said was well worth visiting at full moon, when the shadows were black on the silver sand and there was no sound in the unmotorised streets.

The fees he charged for horticultural advice were deliberately modest, but enough to finance incessant travel. In his late 80s, and after turning 90, he went to New Zealand and Australia, found a ship to take him through the Straits of Magellan, visited Easter Island, Mexico and Hawaii, Egypt, Korea and the Falklands. Everywhere he travelled, he filled his sketch-books (a series running back to the battlefield of the Somme) and still enjoyed slipping away to pubs and bars. In London he frequented the Garrick, Pratt's and the Beefsteak. Innumerable friends, far younger than he, would say he was among the most remarkable men they had ever met.

In 1936 he married Primrose Harley. They were divorced in 1942.

BRIGADIER
SEBERT GREEN

Brigadier Sebert John Hely "Jimmy" Green, DSO, MBE, soldier, died on May 3 aged 84. He was born on November 17, 1906.

"JIMMY" Green's life could have filled an issue of *Boys' Own*. He did indeed feature in *Blackwood's Magazine* when, single-handed, he fought off a mob of vengeful tribesmen with his sword after being ambushed on the northwest Indian frontier. As a "Piffer" — a member of the Punjab Infantry Frontier Force Rifles — he slew Persian guerrillas, Chinese head-hunters and Japanese jungle-trained troops and was decorated in Italy and Burma. But his most celebrated exploit was on November 25, 1928, when he led a relief column to Miranshah Fort to rescue, among others, T. E. Lawrence, then serving as Aircraftman Shaw in the Royal Air Force. Jangi Khan had laid siege to the fort in the belief that "Shaw" had been posted there as a British spy. In fact Lawrence was toiling as a humble fitter, looking after the garrison's single aircraft. But his presence made the incident world famous.

The young subaltern who could thus claim to have saved the life of Lawrence of Arabia was born in Bermuda into a family of both military and ecclesiastical distinction. "Jimmy" himself was the youngest son of Major-General S. F. St D. Green and, after Cheltenham College and Sandhurst, enlisted in the Indian

Army in 1927. He joined the 6th Royal (Scinde) battalion of the 13th Frontier Force Rifles and served on the northwest frontier between 1928 and 1936.

He was then posted to the Burma Military Police and subsequently to the Burma Frontier Force. He commanded columns in operations against Chinese bandits and head-hunters in unmapped territory on the Hunan border for the League of Nations' Boundary Commission. When called to rejoin his regiment in southern India in 1939 (for service in Eritrea) he walked with one servant through the Yoma mountains from the upper reaches of the Chindwin river where he had been conducting operations against human sacrifice tribes. He then fought the Italians in Africa under Brigadier Slim (as he then was) until 1941. He was brigade major at Moulmein with the 2nd Burma brigade when the Japanese struck in 1942. In its subsequent retreat across Burma only 400 of the brigade's 5,800 men got out and, of these, 300 had to be hospitalised. Green, whose knowledge of Burmese proved invaluable, was appointed MBE for gallantry and the march was later described by Compton Mackenzie in *Eastern Epic* as one of the great withdrawals of the war. He then served as second-in-command of his regiment in the Persian mountains, fighting pro-Nazi tribesmen.

He took over the command of his regiment in December 1943, by which time it was fighting in Italy with the 8th Indian division. By coincidence it was exactly 100 years since his great uncle, General Sir George Green, had helped found the regiment. He stayed with it throughout the successful battles at the Gustav, Gothic and Hitler lines. The battalion won more decorations for gallantry than any other in the Indian Army and he was awarded an immediate DSO at the Gari river crossing in the Cassino battle for capturing the division's objective of Pignataro − thus opening up the Liri valley and outflanking Monte Cassino. One of his men won the VC.

In 1947 he was made assistant adjutant-general at Delhi and in the same year raised an independent brigade group at Gurgaon to deal with increasing civil unrest arising from the partitioning of India. One night his brigade found 250 villages ablaze and every man, woman and child in them slaughtered. He retired in 1948 following Indian independence.

He retired to St Lawrence, Isle of Wight, where his mother's family had been the first lords of the manor. He became a county councillor in 1954 and a South Wight borough councillor after the local government reorganisation in 1973. He was prominent in the island's civil defence and diocesan affairs and read the lesson in the church built by his forebears.

He is survived by his wife Eileen and their daughter Jacqueline.

BERNIE WINTERS

Bernie Winters, comedian, died on May 4 aged 58. He was born on September 6, 1932.

BERNIE Winters first achieved fame in a comedy double act with his brother Michael which followed in a long line of such acts epitomised after the second world war by Jewell and Warriss and more recently by Morecambe and Wise. Mike and Bernie Winters bridged the gap between the music hall era and the new audiences which sprang up around the stars of popular music, becoming nationally known as resident comedians on the 1950s BBC television pop music show *Six-Five Special*.

They purveyed a boisterous, unsubtle form of humour with the emphasis on knockabout rather than verbal wit. Mike was the straight man, while Bernie, wearing clothes several sizes too large, played the idiot, a gormless twit with a toothy leer. The pair reached their peak on television in the 1960s and early 1970s. But they never gained the critical or popular acclaim of Morecambe and Wise and in 1978, after thirty years, they split up amid some acrimony.

Mike became a businessman in Florida and Bernie continued in showbusiness, starring in his own television shows and appearing regularly on panel games. He was often joined by a new "partner", an 11-stone St Bernard dog called Schnorbitz

110

and established himself as one of Britain's most popular performers.

Winters, whose real name was Weinstein, was born into a Jewish family in Islington, north London. Leaving school at 15 he worked as a salesman, while appearing by night as a stand-up comic in dance halls. After a spell in the Merchant Navy Bernie was the first of the two brothers to enter showbusiness fulltime but had little success until he teamed up with Michael in 1949. Their father was the driving force in the brothers becoming a comedy double act and it was for his sake that they overcame their temperamental differences and delayed the breakup of their act until after his death in 1978.

The Winters worked the variety halls with another comedian, Jack Farr, in an act called the Three Loose Screws, but then branched out on their own. Their radio performances included programmes such as *Variety Parade*. In 1956 their big opportunity came when they appeared on stage on the same bill as Tommy Steele and began forging their popularity with the younger generation that was to lead to the residency on *Six-Five Special*.

They later had several series on ITV and appeared regularly in pantomimes and summer shows. But their success was precarious and at one stage they came close to emigrating to Australia until a televison show, *Big Night Out*, revived their careers.

In spite of their popularity and extensive television work their material was often not regarded as particularly original and their strength lay more in their presentation and comic timing. Bernie Winters, as the funny man, had a charming way of saying the most outrageous things with apparent innocence. In 1966 and 1971 they attempted to break out of their comedy double act and move into situation comedy but without success. Although Bernie Winters' public image

was of a carefree softy, he admitted to having a short temper and was the worrier of the duo. After the act split up, he was immediately successful with his own television series which reached the top ten.

In 1981, he made his debut as an actor, giving an excellent portrayal of Bud Flanagan in *Bud 'n' Ches*, a television play about Flanagan and Allen. He was partnered by Leslie Crowther and two years later they played the same roles in a West End stage production, *Underneath the Arches*, taking over from Roy Hudd and Christopher Timothy. During the 1980s Winters hosted *Make Me Laugh*, in which members of the public had to keep a straight face while they were told jokes. He also compered *Whose Baby?*, a show featuring parents or children of famous people, and became a familiar face on *Give Us a Clue*, *Punchlines* and *Blankety Blank*.

Winters first fell ill with cancer in February last year but continued to work although he almost collapsed on stage at a birthday gala for the Queen Mother. After an operation in which much of his stomach was removed, he returned to the stage playing Widow Twankey in a six week run of *Aladdin* at Basildon, Essex, appearing in up to three shows a day.

In spite of his illness Winters continued to smoke 20 cigarettes a day. For much of his career he was actively involved in charity work with the Water Rats, the showbusiness charity, and playing football with the TV All Stars soccer team. His partnership with Schnorbitz led him to become president of the St Bernard Dog Association.

He and his brother ended a 17 year rift with a reconciliation in 1985.

Bernie Winters is survived by Sigrid (Siggi) Heine, a German-born former dancer, whom he married in 1958 and their son, Raymond.

JERZY KOSINSKI

Jerzy Nikodem Kosinski, the American writer and sociologist of Polish birth, died by suicide in New York on May 4 aged 57. He was born in Lodz on June 14, 1933.

JERZY Kosinski is most famous for his novel *Being There* (1971), which was made into a successful film by Hal Ashby in 1979 with Peter Sellers as the illiterate gardener who becomes a celebrity on the basis of the banal cliches he has learned from watching junk television.

Kosinski was born a Pole but emigrated to America where he worked at scraping ships, truck-driving, cleaning bars and nightclub photography before entering Columbia University on a Ford Foundation fellowship as a graduate student in 1958 and obtaining his PhD. He had taught himself English for this purpose: by listening to the radio, watching television and by translating Shakespeare and Poe into Polish and Russian, "memorising whole pages of the original text". This had a profoundly liberating effect on him, regenerating in him "all that was flabby and moribund" — "in English I was not afraid to be myself, to speak freely — there was no party to police me, no censorship, no capital socialist collectivity to punish me."

Kosinski's parents were Russian Jews who left their country in 1918. His father was a university professor, his mother a concert pianist. He was educated at the University of Lodz, and by 1955 was the Polish equivalent of an American associate professor of the Polish Academy of Science in Warsaw. His subjects were history and political science; he specialised in collective behaviour.

Kosinski's academic career in America was spectacularly successful: at Columbia until 1964, he moved on to the New School for Social Research in New York (1962-5), and then became a fellow of the Centre for Advanced Studies at Wesleyan University (1968-9). In the following year he was visiting lecturer in English prose at Princeton.

In order not to jeopardise this more than promising career ("to prevent myself becoming involved in controversies which might have led to the interruption of my academic work") he used the name Joseph Novak on the title-page of two impressive but also deeply depressing sets of case-studies of collective behaviour, *The Future Is Ours, Comrade: Conversations with Russians* (1960) and *No Third Path* (1962). These are essentially studies in how the Russian mind works, or worked then. In Poland he had already published two orthodox studies with the Scientific Society of Lodz: there is no doubt that those represented to him exactly what he wanted to escape.

His sociological studies completed, Kosinski began to work on his first novel, *The Painted Bird*, published in 1965. Characteristically, he wrote it 15 times before its text even began to satisfy him. He would go through all 12 volumes of the Oxford English Dictionary almost over-obsessively searching for the right word. Its protagonist, called simply "The Boy," who is separated from his parents and brutalised by everyone he encounters, learns that survival depends not at all on kindness or facing God, but, on the contrary, on hatred and the pursuit of vengeance. *The Painted Bird* was almost rapturously well received, and was awarded the French Prix de Meilleur Livre Etranger in 1966.

Steps (1968), its more openly experimental successor, is even more negative, consisting of what one critic called "small, deceptively plain, exploding capsules" describing incidents of disturbing cruelty, usually sexual. Its skill was universally recognised, but some readers worried for Kosinski's mental health. After the perhaps superfluous *Notes of the Author on 'The Painted Bird' 1965* (1965), Kosinski published *The Art of the Self: Essays à Propos "Steps"* (1968); in this he tried to explain its technique as designed to awaken the reader to his own guilt, a sort of self-analysis kit; but the process was far too violent for it to succeed in this therapeutic respect.

At this point Kosinski produced the work by which he is likely to be judged, the comparatively relaxed gentle parable *Being There*. Its protagonist is a retarded gardener called Chance whose Eden is shattered when his employer dies. His trivial, TV-inspired remarks and ignorant silences are misinterpreted as profundity by the "silent majority" and by the president himself, and he ends up a likely vice-presidential candidate. *Being There* represented the height of Kosinski's achievement, and later works, such as *The Devil Tree* (1973, revised 1981) and *Passion Play* (1979) began to fall victim to a destructive and sometimes narcissistic negativity. Kosinski never in any sense descended to the degraded and degrading depths of the so-called "horror" genre, being quite incapable of such puerility. But *Blind Date* (1977), in particular, which was loosely based on the Manson killings, is so relentlessly horrible that, in Keats' famous phrase, its "disagreeables" entirely fail to evaporate, and it disturbed many of its readers. Perhaps having been a guest at the party after which Sharon Tate was tortured and murdered by Manson and his crazy gang was simply too much for him.

Kosinski remained devoted to humanitarian causes. He was president of American PEN (1973-5), and director of the International League for the Rights of Man.

In 1962 he married Mary Hayward Weir, daughter of the steel magnate Ernest Weir. She died in 1968. He later made another marriage, and his wife survives him.

WILFRID HYDE WHITE

Wilfrid Hyde White, actor, died in Los Angeles on May 6 aged 87. He was born in Gloucestershire on May 12, 1903.

WITH his slightly roguish, debonair charm, Wilfrid Hyde White established himself in both Britain and America as the quintessential urbane Englishman. Although not a great actor, he was capable of adding an effective element of menace to this affable presence when the need arose.

His career reached its peak in 1964 when he played Colonel Pickering in *My Fair Lady*. He may not have originated the stage role of the retired Indian army officer in the Lerner and Loewe musical, but when he chided Rex Harrison on screen for his treatment of the poor, misused Liza Doolittle, the polish and breeding showed.

He played similar military gentlemen with suave professionalism in the Danny Kaye film *On the Double* and on numerous other occasions, not least in the 1959 *Carry On Nurse*. He was equally adept at playing parsons and conmen. He was both in *Two Way Stretch* in 1961. Playing a parson was not inappropriate

for a man born the son of a canon of Gloucester cathedral.

Success came largely with middle age. By nature an elegant and sophisticated man of the world, Hyde White carried this image into the theatre and on to the screen where his unfailing imperturbability and unruffled acceptance of every eventuality made him an ideal choice for light comedy of the drawing room school. He looked what women, from young girls to matrons, liked to call distinguished. Indeed from his forties onwards his somewhat gaunt look and the silky white hair made him the perfect elderly gentleman.

Wilfrid Hyde White was born in Bourton-on-the-Water — before the tourists came, a sleepy beauty spot in the Cotswolds — where his father was vicar. He was educated at Marlborough where he first made up his mind to be an actor. It was not an occupation which his parents thought remotely suitable for the son of a clergyman and they decided that the best way of talking him out of his plans was to send him to see an uncle, the actor J. Fisher White. The young Hyde White was so taken, however, with the old actor's country cottage, chauffeur driven limousine and beautiful young mistress that he decided that was just the life he wanted. "Ho, ho, I thought," was how he remembered his immediate reaction. It was an expression which fitted as well into his natural conversation as into any script and he used it frequently in both. He studied for the stage at the Royal Academy of Dramatic Art where he revealed no outstanding talent and made his first professional appearance in the summer of 1922 at the age of 19 playing the part of Maitland in *Tons of Money* in a production at Ryde in the Isle of Wight.

Three years later he made his London debut at the Queen's Theatre playing a juror in *Beggar on Horseback*. He became a journeyman actor going from production to production without any notable success. It was the same story with the film career which he began somewhat inauspiciously in 1936 with a minor part in Alexander Korda's *Rembrandt*. But in 1949 he played a worthy British cultural official in *The Third Man* and he was finally noticed.

There were bigger stage roles for him in the early 1950s. He appeared with Sir Laurence Olivier's company in *Caesar and Cleopatra* and in *Antony and Cleopatra*. One of the best of his performances was in the 1955 production of *The Reluctant Debutante* in which he played Jimmy Broadbent. When he repeated it on Broadway he was nominated for a Tony Award in 1956 but he did not play it in the film – ironically Rex Harrison had beaten him to that. There were other smallish roles which he somehow succeeded in making appear bigger, like that of the headmaster in *The Browning Version* and in pictures like *The Million Pound Note*, *North West Frontier*, *Crookson Anonymous* and the now cult Peter Sellers film *Two Way Stretch* in which he played "Soapy" Stephens.

He first went to Hollywood in 1959 to appear in the film, *Let's Make Love*, with Marilyn Monroe. As with David Niven, Hyde White's urbane Englishness was much appreciated and other Hollywood films followed. In the 1960s came *My Fair Lady*. He continued to appear on the stage for some years. In 1971 he was in James Bridie's posthumous *Meeting at Night*; and in 1972 he took over the Marquess of Candover in William Douglas-Home's *The Jockey Club Stakes*, a part that suited him precisely and which he repeated in New York earning a second nomination for a Tony Award. Back in London in 1976 he appeared in *The Pleasure of Your Company* and later in Douglas-Home's *Rolls Hyphen Royce*.

He always gave the impression – one which he seemed to cultivate – of never taking life too seriously. He enjoyed working, but only, it appears, if a studio was within easy distance of a racecourse – preferably Goodwood. But Goodwood was merely part of the good life, which he craved. "I've only been interested in material things," he once said.

"Racehorses, Rolls Royces, mistresses in Paris, London and New York." A suite at the Savoy, a chance to share a whisky and soda with a visiting journalist whom he invariably addressed as "my dear fella" – and he appeared a happy man. But even the consummate Englishman succumbed to the lure of Hollywood after the Pickering role in *My Fair Lady*. He lived in Los Angeles for the rest of his life, at first the apparent successor of such former elder statesmen of the British colony there like C. Aubrey Smith and Boris Karloff.

But the number of parts diminished, while his high-spending life-style continued. In 1979, aged 75, he was declared bankrupt because he owed the Inland Revenue £12,000 but he later cleared the debt. Even in the bankruptcy court his style never left him, however. When the Official Receiver made a barbed reference to his predeliction for betting on the horses, Hyde White responded by naming a winner at Ascot adding: "Of course, dear fellow, only have a small bet. We don't want to have to change places do we?"

Following his bankruptcy, his personal circumstances worsened when his second wife, the actress Ethel Drew, whom he had met while working on *The Reluctant Debutante* and who was 30 years his junior, left him after 22 years of marriage.

His career enjoyed a revival with the success of an American television comedy series called *The Associates* dealing with the chaotic affairs of a New York law firm in which he incongruously played an American lawyer. His last acting roles were on television – in *Damien Leper Priest* in 1980 and in *The Toy* in 1982.

In recent years he was virtually bedridden, living in a rented bungalow. The resources accumulated over the years having dwindled to virtually nothing, his former *joie-de-vivre* had largely disappeared. He said he hated California but could not afford to leave it.

He had one son by his first wife, Blanche Pope Aitken, whom he married in 1927, and two children by Ethel Drew.

RUDOLF SERKIN

Rudolf Serkin, the American pianist of Austrian birth, died in Vermont on May 8 aged 88. He was born at Eger in Bohemia on March 28, 1903.

RUDOLF Serkin was one of the leading exponents of the Austro-German classics this century. He played Bach, Mozart, Beethoven and Brahms with the unvarnished strength and probing articulation that totally eschewed extraneous show — apart from the involuntary grunts and occasional clattering of his heels that became his trademark. A masterful interpreter of concertos, he was equally adept in chamber music, which he loved to play with his colleagues and friends. Above all he was one of the most profound of 20th century pianists, on the level of Schnabel. He often sacrificed merely beautiful tone in pursuit of musical truth as he saw and heard it. He could box the compass of tone between the delicacy of touch needed in Mozart and the leonine exploits called for in Brahms's D minor Concerto, in which he was supreme. An inveterate investigator of less familiar repertory, he championed the concertos of Mendelssohn and Max Reger, the piano music of Dvořák and the neglected Burleske of Richard Strauss.

He was the son of a none-too-successful singer and a businessman, who were determined that the young boy, showing his talent when he was only four, should have a chance to develop it. So the whole family moved from Bohemia to Vienna with that end in mind. Serkin studied at the Vienna Music Academy with Richard Robert for piano and Marx and Schoenberg for composition. Indeed he averred that Schoenberg and the whole avant-garde milieu in Vienna at that time exerted a deep influence on his upbringing. His debut came in 1915 at a concert with the Vienna Symphony Orchestra.

The next great influence on Serkin was the violinist Adolf Busch. A chance meeting with him in Berlin led to a duo partnership of many years standing. They played the Sonata of Busoni (another seminal influence on the pianist) to the ailing composer who said that Serkin's style was too clean and transparent – he should dirty it a bit. Serkin took due note of the advice. Busch and Serkin recorded sonatas together before the war and also the fifth *Brandenburg* Concerto, in which Serkin's playing is truly phenomenal. At this period Serkin was also indebted to Schnabel and to Sir Donald Tovey, the musicologist, who widened the young pianist's horizons. In 1926, with darkening political clouds in Germany, he

and Busch moved to Basle, where Serkin married the violinist's daughter Irene. From then until the war he divided his time between Switzerland and the United States, where his reputation was quickly established after his debut with the New York Philharmonic under Toscanini in 1936. He made his home in Philadelphia in 1939 and taught at the piano department of the Curtis Institute there, becoming its director in 1969. In 1950 Busch founded the Marlboro Festival and after his death in 1952 Serkin took over its direction. It was and is a small but distinctive gathering at which young musicians learn about chamber music from hearing the great ones play in various combinations.

Although he confessed he hated recording, he leaves behind a considerable legacy of performances, many of them just re-issued on CD by Sony Classical, successor to American Columbia. His readings, in the company of such luminaries as Szell (the two Brahms Concertos – superb), Bernstein (the Beethoven Concertos), Ormandy, Casals (a regular at Marlboro) and the Budapest Quartet, have stood the test of time. So, even more, have his pre-war records, not least the Brahms Piano Quintet with the Busch Quartet. In more recent times he partnered Abbado and the LSO in Mozart Concertos on record following memorable concerts of the same works at the Barbican (Serkin always enjoyed his visits to Britain for the innate musicianship of players here). But perhaps his most notable legacy is his recordings of sonatas by Beethoven and Schubert in which he seemed to commune personally with each composer in turn.

His various qualities of sincerity, intelligence, technical strength and soul made him a paragon amongst pianists, one to whom innumerable younger players looked up with reverence – as did his admiring audiences. His son Peter is also a noted pianist.

JIANG QING

Jiang Qing, widow of Mao Tse-tung and a former member of the politburo of the Chinese Communist party, committed suicide in her Peking residence on May 14 aged 77. She was born in 1914.

JIANG Qing was a woman of immense ambition who finally lost in her struggle for power in the turbulent life of revolutionary China. She aimed to win mass appeal but genuine admiration eluded her. She sought political authority but so used it as to antagonise all those on whom she depended for support.

As an actress in Shanghai in the 1930s; as an important political figure by virtue of her marriage to Mao Tse-tung; as leader of the group — later to be condemned as the "Gang of Four" — which wielded such power during the cultural revolution; as the reformer of Chinese drama in order to dress it in true revolutionary style and, in the last dramatic month after her husband's death in September 1976, as an aspirant for the Communist party chairmanship — in all these her ambition outran her judgment and her personal ability. Her subsequent trial showed her to be indomitable, dignified and convinced to the last of her own rectitude.

But the popular verdict went against her as did that of the judges. Politically she was a faithful follower of Mao but

did not share his spartan tastes or his dedication to the revolutionary's simple life. She was exigent and luxury-loving, an enemy of Western culture while entranced by Hollywood films, and she was a woman who hankered after the world of fashion while appearing in the drab garments of political uniformity. Yet she could appear to outsiders as a woman of intense magnetism and charm. Nevertheless her vindictiveness made her many enemies in China once she began openly to pursue a political career.

Born Luan Shumeng in Shandong province, she was brought up by grandparents after her father's early death. A spell with a travelling troupe when she was 14 led to two years as a border at a drama academy.

In Jinan, the provincial capital, she met and married a film critic with whom she went to Shanghai. But the marriage soon broke up and she lived for a time with a film director.

She went to Chongqing (Chungking), the nationalist capital, after the Japanese invasion and made a film there. In 1938 she abandoned the nationalist side for the communists, travelling to Yanan to sit at the feet of Mao Tse-tung and ask eager questions after his political lectures. He was equally attracted and soon they were living together. Mao's existing wife, He Zechen, was in Yanan but they had separated. Jiang nevertheless insisted on marriage. Mao's wife and colleagues opposed this but in the end acquiesced on the understanding that Jiang would have no political role.

Publicly Jiang made no appearance for many years, even after Mao promulgated the People's Republic of China in Beijing in 1949, and she became "first lady". She was active behind the scenes in support of Mao's view that literature and the arts should serve politics first and foremost. Thus she was directly involved in 1955 in the campaign against the writer Hu Feng, a one-time communist sympathiser who opposed the Maoist strait-jacket and demanded freedom for the creative artist.

When she did move back into her old world in Shanghai in 1963 cultural reform was again her objective, supported by a local party boss who was fiercely pro-Mao and hostile to the liberal wing of the party. The base which Jiang Qing built in Shanghai served in 1965 to launch the cultural revolution on its assault on the intellectual stronghold of Peking. Jiang Qing now emerged quite openly into public life as deputy leader of Mao's personally appointed Cultural Revolution group and as cultural adviser to the army which also became active in support of the Cultural Revolution. For a time she enjoyed a brief partnership with Lin Biao, the general whose ambitions were also pinned on Mao's victory in the mounting upheaval.

Together with her Shanghai colleagues, Zhang Qunqiao and Yao Wenyuan, Jiang Qing emerged as a member of a "shadow" politburo during the Cultural Revolution. The power this gave her enabled her to throw out of public life all the cultural figures with whom she had differed 30 years earlier in Shanghai. She ran her own private Red Guard groups and was able to pursue her own vendettas, not least by cruelly persecuting and maltreating Wang Kuangmei, wife of the president of the republic and Mao's one-time deputy, Liu Shaoqi, whom Jiang saw as her rival in public life.

At the ninth party congress in 1969 Jiang's new political status was duly confirmed. Thenceforward her role as leader of the political faction active in support of the continuing ideals of the Cultural Revolution rose as Mao declined in senility. They had ceased to live together as husband and wife by 1973 but continued to collaborate and make use of each other in the intensifying political struggles.

In the mid-1970s Jiang Qing's reformed drama held the stage in China. *Taking the Bandits' Stronghold*, *The Red Detachment of Women*, *The White Tiger Regiment* and a few other operas, plays or ballets, all dealing with warfare, in which spotless communist heroes vanquished evil, revisionist, bourgeois reactionaries, were attended by dragooned and usually bored audiences.

These were the standard fare in place of the traditional historical and mythological subjects which were now rejected as being feudal.

The 10th party congress in 1973 brought Jiang to the pinnacle of power. Her protege, Wang Hongwen, the labour leader from Shanghai, was promoted by Mao directly to a senior vice-chairmanship, making him third in the hierarchy after Mao himself and Premier Chou En-lai. Jiang Qing's "Gang of Four", which included Wang Hongwen, Zhang Qunqiao and Yao Wenyuan, now dominated the pro-Maoist cause and were able to attract many respectful followers (Hua Guofeng among them.)

The death of Mao Tse-tung in September 1976 altered these fair prospects with startling suddenness. Any hopes of the party leadership were dashed when both Hua Guofeng, the new prime minister, and Wang Dongxing, commander of Mao's personal security unit, turned their backs on her only three weeks after her husband's death, in October 1976. With other members of the "Gang of Four" Jiang Qing was arrested and accused of treason. At her trial, which did not take place until 1980-81 she and the other members of the gang were blamed for the excesses of the cultural revolution. Jiang stoutly defended herself, repeating that she had merely followed Mao's orders as an obedient wife. At one point during the hearing she told her judges: "I was Chairman Mao's dog. If he said bite someone, I bit him." This forceful — though somewhat implausible — plea failed to convince the judges and she was condemned to death in January 1981.

Her sentence was commuted to one of life imprisonment in 1983 as Deng Xiaoping, by then the new power in China, had no wish to make a martyr of her. She remained in custody until 1984 since when she had been allowed to receive medical treatment and live at home.

She had one daughter, Li Na, by Mao and brought up another born to He Zechen — who was duly rehabilitated when Deng came to power in the 1980s.

SIR CHARLES TROUGHTON

Sir Charles Troughton, CBE, MC, former chairman of W. H. Smith & Son (Holdings) Ltd and president of the British Council, died on May 13 aged 74. He was born on August 27, 1916.

CHARLES Troughton was a business-man who loved poetry. Though he had no conceit about it — that would have been alien to him — those who knew him well realised that if he wanted to, he could out-quote them with his extraodinarily retentive memory for verse, as he could most people. His own approach was self

deprecating. "I haven't got an ear, and I haven't got an eye," he said. His life did not entirely bear that out, since he was concerned about design, as his career showed, and verse is nothing if it cannot be read aloud. Yet his most enduring legacy comes from his encouragement of people. He liked picking someone good at something and nurturing that talent. The sense of reward that people felt as a result endeared him to them.

He became chairman of the British Council in 1977 after a long and dis-tinguished career as a director of W. H. Smith, culminating in the chairmanship

120

of the company. His success as cultural ambassador — enhanced by the active support of his wife Gillean — was so marked from the outset that he was persuaded to continue his chairmanship of the British Council until the end of 1984 when he became president. He then also brought his considerable energies and influence to the cause of English literature by taking on the chairmanship of the National Book League, using all his charm and arts of quiet diplomacy at a time when British authors, publishers and booksellers faced especially grave problems, not least cuts in spending and the threatened imposition of VAT on books.

"Dick" Troughton, as he was known, was a man of many parts and wide interests, both business and cultural. Educated at Haileybury and Trinity, Cambridge, where he took an honours degree in history, he was in the Territorial Army for many years, the Oxford & Bucks Light Infantry, and won his MC in France in 1940. Taken prisoner at Dunkirk, he spent the rest of the war in captivity. During that period he contrived to study law, and took a first in the Bar finals by correspondence. He recalled later how a stolid German academic made sure that he sat properly at a desk with a clock timing him, then sent the papers back via the Red Cross and Switzerland. His time in captivity must also have meant reliance on the reflective nature that goes with an appreciation of poetry.

He became a partner in W. H. Smith in 1948, chairman of the operating board in 1969, and chairman of the Holdings Board in 1972 — the first ever non-Smith chairman. He had been encouraged to join the company in 1946 by Lord Hambleden, the chairman, who had known him as a boy. Under Troughton, the company was rationalised, little shops went on generous terms to managers who with their families could live off their trade. Bigger shops were developed in larger centres. But the emphasis remained on the written word and standards were maintained; what W. H. Smith would display became a test for overt morality.

Troughton backed his views with money. His literary and cultural interests were exemplified by his special interest in two projects of patronage sponsored by W. H. Smith. One was Poets in School, a scheme organised in collaboration with the Poetry Society under which two poets visited a school on several occasions and on the final evening the pupils and staff would put on a show when the best poems were read and prizes given. The other project which he backed enthusiastically was the W. H. Smith annual literary award. Troughton saw poetry as the one art form in which the English excelled. He was almost alone among businessmen in giving moral and financial support to the poetry movement in Britain at a difficult time.

As chairman of the British Council Dick Troughton represented British culture with his own mixture of humour and dignity across the world. The council's job is to build and maintain closer relations for Britain with countries abroad in the fields of culture, education and technology. Because of changes before he arrived, he found the council in some disarray, but working with Sir John Burgh, director general, he re-established morale and, at a time of funding difficulty, he got on well with Mrs Thatcher, who said she was always interested in speaking with someone who had a well presented case.

At various times he held directorships of Barclays Bank, Whitbread, Equity & Law Life, Electrical & General Investment Company, Times Newspapers Holdings (of which he was an independent national director), and Wm Collins and Sons (where he became deputy chairman). Between 1975 and 1979 he was on the Design Council and the council of the Royal College of Art, and was appointed a governor of the London School of Economics in 1975. He was for 20 years a civilian member of the NAAFI Board of Management, and served a term as chairman of the British Kidney Patient Investment Trust.

He leaves his widow, three sons and a daughter.

RAJIV GANDHI

Rajiv Gandhi, prime minister of India from 1984 to 1989, was killed in a bomb explosion at Sriperumbudur, Tamil Nadu, southern India on May 21 aged 46. He was born in Bombay on August 20, 1944.

WHEN Rajiv Gandhi became India's prime minister in 1984 at the age of 40 after the assassination of his mother and predecessor in that office, Mrs Indira Gandhi, he did so in circumstances which seemed to promise great things. He was swept to power on a massive wave of sympathy. His very lack of political experience was seen as no disadvantage in a country where the machinations of Congress party politics and the personal power of his mother had already once been rejected by the electorate, in 1977. In India and in the outside world it almost appeared that the death in an air crash in 1980 of his brother Sanjay, a man both powerful as his mother's right-hand man and disliked for his ruthless manipulation of that power for personal ends, was in fact a stroke of benign fate, in that it compelled Rajiv to give up his sequestered life and enter politics.

He came into the political arena as a man entirely free of the taints attaching to either his mother or his brother. At the time of his accession to the leadership of the government of the world's largest democracy four years later nothing had happened to alter the public perception of him as a modest, courteous, well-meaning man, determined to put his country's good before personal ambition and to heal the wounds caused by factional fighting, poverty, disease and corruption. His other main aim, to cleanse and revive his party, the Congress, which had long been India's central political institution, was also applauded and this went hand in hand with a determination to apply the techniques of modern business management to the untidy politics of this most complex of nations. In the election which followed his accession to power Gandhi achieved the most overwhelming victory ever to be registered by a leader in the history of the subcontinent. The Congress (I) party took 410 of the 508 seats in the Lok Sabha (lower house of the Indian parliament) and appeared to have been given a whole-hearted mandate for reform. His personal popularity was reflected in his being known throughout India purely by his first name.

These good omens came to nothing in five years of political, economic and moral failure, which led to a catastrophic electoral defeat in 1989, the second heaviest in the history of the Congress party. At the end of that time the name of Rajiv was as heartily reviled as it had previously been adored. Most tellingly, corruption, which he had pledged himself to banishing, stalked the political stage as nakedly as ever. The Bofors scandal, in which suspect "commissions" had been paid to secure a contract to supply guns to the Indian army, had shaken his administration deeply. The relations between India's different races and religions were as unharmonious as ever. Finally in the election campaign which unseated him he was seen by members of his own party to be a ditherer who had not acquired even the rudiments of political judgment. Allegations of vote-rigging in his own Uttar Pradesh constituency merely set the seal on a wretched five years of incompetent and morally ambivalent administration. Perhaps to restore political and economic stability was a task beyond the powers of any one man in a country which often seems to verge on the ungovernable. At any rate the electorate had latterly seemed prepared to forgive Gandhi's failures and his Congress party was thought likely to capture a majority of seats in the Lok Sabha in the current general election, even if not to win outright.

Rajiv Gandhi was the son of Indira Gandhi, herself the daughter of Jawaharlal Nehru, who was to become India's first prime minister, and Feroze Gandhi, a businessman. Both were activists in the movement for Indian independence and, although it took a long time for Rajiv to assume his own place in the famous Indian dynasty he was aware of his historic family from an early age. As a babe-in-arms he had been taken to visit his maternal grandfather in a British prison. As a child he had met Mahatma Gandhi. But it was a westernised, cosmopolitan family. The marriage of his Oxford-educated parents had cut across barriers not only of caste but of religion as well — his mother being a Hindu and a Brahmin and his father a Parsee. Before he went to school he was looked after by a Danish governess who was a strict disciplinarian.

In his very early years Rajiv Gandhi's family moved into the palatial official residence of Jawaharlal Nehru, by then prime minister, so that Indira Gandhi could serve as her widowed father's hostess. For more than a decade the boy had fleeting encounters there with world statesmen. On one such occasion, when the Dalai Lama went missing from a reception in his honour, he was discovered playing in the garden with Rajiv Gandhi and his younger brother Sanjay.

Gandhi attended the elite Doon School, in Dehra Dun, which was run on British public school lines. It was there that he met many of the men who formed his inner circle of advisers when he later entered politics. In 1961 his interest in engineering took him to Imperial College, London, and the following year to Trinity College, Cambridge, where his grandfather had studied. He lived on a tight student budget and found work during the holidays in Britain in a deep freeze factory, in a bakery, as a fruit picker and as an ice-cream salesman. He left Cambridge before taking a degree but in his time there he began to develop a serious interest in flying. He also met Sonia Maino, an Italian student reading English, who in 1964 became his wife.

After his return to India he concentrated on flying and in 1967 joined the staff of the state-owned domestic airline. For 13 years he flew propeller-driven aircraft and developed a reputation as a reliable, rather reticent man. Throughout that period he lived quietly with his family in the residence of his mother who for most of that time was India's prime minister.

In 1974-75, when Indira Gandhi's political difficulties mounted, Gandhi occasionally appeared on public platforms with his mother. But unlike his younger brother Sanjay, who became the second most powerful figure in India during the state of emergency that extended from mid-1975 to early 1977, he remained aloof from politics and concentrated on his flying. He continued to do so during the difficult period between his mother's heavy election defeat in February 1977 and her return to power at the general election in the first week of 1980. Later that year Gandhi qualified to fly jet aircraft, a prospect that he regarded with delight. But when his politically active brother was killed while flying a small aeroplane in June 1980 Mrs Gandhi appealed to her elder son to enter public life, as her confidant and political heir.

He did so wtih great reluctance, though acknowledging finally: "The way I look at it, Mummy has to be helped somehow." In May 1981 he was elected to parliament from his brother's former constituency, Amethi. Within a few months he was made one of the five general secretaries of the All-India Congress committee and his influence behind the scenes was immense.

When asked to choose a project on which to gain political experience, he elected to oversee the Asian Games which took place in Delhi in December 1982. This proved a success although at vast cost to the taxpayer. Gandhi supervised the planning and construction of stadia and athletes' housing, and the day-to-day events during the games. That experience and his years as a pilot convinced him of the value of technology and what he deemed the scientific techniques of modern business management, developed in the corporations and business schools of the West. He also had great faith in market forces to regenerate India's economy which had stagnated mainly, in his view, as a result of its large, underproductive state sector.

When his mother was shot by members of her Sikh bodyguard on October 31, 1984, Rajiv Gandhi was in West Bengal. He immediately flew back to the capital and was sworn in as prime minister late that evening when President Giani Zail Singh returned, having cut short a visit to South Yemen. Undoubtedly his accession to power brought to the helm of the government of India a man genuinely anxious to cut through the bizarre and often corrupt ways of the ruling Indian elite and the country's suffocating bureaucracy. As prime minister he was guided by his faith in modern management and market forces and by the knowledge that his Congress-Indira party was severely torn by factionalism and populated by corrupt and criminal elements, many of whom had joined in his brother's day. In an attempt to cleanse the party he excluded many sitting MPs whom he regarded as dubious from the candidate list at the general election in late December 1984, which was called in the immediate aftermath of his mother's murder. At that election, his opponent in his own constituency was his brother's widow, Maneka Gandhi, who wished to be her husband's political heir.

On his becoming prime minister Gandhi moved swiftly in an attempt to heal the wounds which had been the cause of the dramatic manner of his coming to office and which continued to suppurate. An outbreak of violence directed against the Sikh community threatened to tear the very fabric of the country apart and as the death toll mounted to almost 3,000 he was after four days of seeming political paralysis to order the army on to the streets. Nevertheless he did not shrink from announcing the due general election which he might easily have found an excuse for postponing and with the huge mandate for action he received he was able to press on with other parts of his programme which were designed to soothe away some of the racial and political hatreds for which his mother's actions had been responsible.

He released from jail the more moderate leaders of the Sikh community whom his mother had imprisoned in 1984 after she had sent the army into the Golden Temple at Amritsar, the Sikh religion's holiest shrine. This led in July 1985 to the Punjab accord which was to grant to Punjab the exclusive use of Chandigarh, until then the joint capital of Punjab and neighbouring Hariyana. But this pleased no one. The moderate Sikh signatory of the treaty, Sant Harchand Singh Longowal, was murdered a few weeks later by Sikh extremists who regarded the whole agreement as a betrayal of the Sikh aspiration for a separate state, while the Hindu population of Hariyana saw the agreement as yet another instance of central government pandering to the already over-indulged Sikhs. Congress party fears over the alienation of the Hindus of Hariyana and the consequences for the party's future electoral fortunes led to repeated post-ponement of the the Chandigarh decision. The Punjab continued to be a problem for Gandhi. Violence broke out again in 1988 leaving 1,500 dead and Gandhi was himself compelled to use paramilitary forces to dislodge Sikhs who had again occupied the Golden Temple.

But there were other successes. In Assam Gandhi reached agreement with the leaders of an agitation which had troubled the state for years and left thousands dead, though here, too, there was criticism by his own party of a solution in the state which brought a non-Congress government to power. There was a similar settlement with the leaders of an armed insurgency in the north-eastern territory of Mizoram. Here, also, in spite of the annoyance it caused his own party, Gandhi passed the responsibility for dealing with the area's problems on to an elected government of the indigenous inhabitants. These critics found vindication as the prime minister's party lost a string of state elections in the years following his landslide of 1984. His political judgment was repeatedly called into question by party regulars and he found himself frequently reshuffling his cabinet. A particularly damaging quarrel was that with Zail Singh who as the president appointed by Mrs Gandhi had repaid her faith in him by moving so swiftly to swear in her son as prime minister after her death.

Politically the single largest blow to Gandhi's reputation was the Bofors scandal which clouded the second half of his period in office. It emerged that large "commissions" had been paid by the Swedish arms manufacturer in connection with a contract for weapons for the Indian army. It was never established that any of the money had come Gandhi's own way but he clouded the atmosphere by seeming reluctant to prosecute inquiries into the matter. He was accused of lying in parliament amid suspicions that he was protecting others who had taken bribes. As speculation mounted he ignored calls to resign but the whole episode fatally damaged the reputation of his administration.

In foreign policy Rajiv Gandhi initially gave rise to hopes in the West that he might alter his country's traditional preference for the Soviet Union. His interest in technology and the market encouraged a view that he would find a natural ally in the United States and his first ventures overseas seemed to confirm this view. In visits to both the United States and Britain during his first months in office he was warmly, if uncritically,

welcomed. But it soon became apparent that his position as chairman of the non-aligned movement was incompatible with close links with the West, of which he did in fact become increasingly critical, and Indian relations with the Soviet Union were not changed. The attack by United States aircraft on Libya in 1986 took place while the non-aligned foreign ministers were meeting in Libya and caused deep outrage.

Closer to home, one of Gandhi's major misadventures was over his decision to send the Indian army to support the Tamil minority in neighbouring Sri Lanka against the Sinhalese majority. Over 50,000 Indian troops eventually found themselves embroiled with the militant Tamil Tigers who feared any Indian-inspired settlement with the moderates. In a not unfamilar outcome the Indian army found itself embroiled with a section of those it had gone to protect and after a savage and fruitless campaign was finally withdrawn, six months after Gandhi's removal from power, in 1990.

The general election of 1989 saw Gandhi at the nadir of his influence. It was an unsavoury campaign even by the standards of Indian elections and violence was rife. Insecure even in his own constituency Gandhi is thought to have sanctioned the organisation of vote-rigging. None of this saved the Congress from one of its most resounding defeats at the hands of the electorate. As prime minister Rajiv Gandhi had never really overcome an aloofness (which amounted really to nothing more than a wish to be again the private person he had been before his brother's death) which made his relations with the press and other politicians frequently difficult. Latterly, in opposition, he had been making much greater efforts to develop a more accessible public persona, breaking free from his motorcade and mingling with crowds. At his death he was certainly more popular with the Indian public than he had been at any time since his year-long "honeymoon" of 1984-5.

He is survived by his wife, Sonia, a son, Rahul, and a daughter, Priyanka.

ERIC HEFFER

Eric Heffer, Labour MP for the Walton Division of Liverpool since 1964, died on May 27 aged 69. He was born on January 12, 1922.

WHEN Eric Heffer was eight years old he organised a strike of his fellow choir-boys. It proved an appropriate prelude to a life which combined lasting faith in his church with dogged belief in left-wing socialism. To many he appeared prickly and vindictive but this was never a view accepted by his friends. Julian Critchley, the Conservative MP who was his long-term pair in the Commons, once summed him up: "His nature is as good as his fuse is short."

Undoubtedly Heffer was a mass of contradictions. He was a High Anglican who never severed his connections with Marxism, an internationalist who came to detest the Common Market and a political interventionist with a lifelong mistrust of centralisation. He affected to despise Labour intellectuals but he was much better read than most MPs, building up a personal library of more than 12,000 books. His often bullying manner masked a kind and even sentimental nature.

The most famous memory he leaves is of a great hulk of a man, lips pursed and face scowling, stalking from the platform at Labour's 1985 conference in protest at Neil Kinnock's attack on the Militant Tendency in Liverpool. It was one of Kinnock's most successful speeches but to Heffer it was a betrayal of Liverpool, his adopted city and power-base, as well as an obvious attempt to rid the party of the Trotskyists with whom Heffer had more than a passing association.

There was also a suspicion that Heffer's fury was not only with Kinnock's words but with Kinnock himself, the man who had trounced Heffer in the 1983 leadership contest and who had pointedly failed to recognise Heffer's talents afterwards. It was certainly resentment at Kinnock and the way in which he was moving the party to the right which prompted Heffer's announcement in 1989 that he would not be seeking re-election to the Commons and giving this reason: "I find myself increasingly out of step with the way the Labour party is going."

It was not the first time he had found himself out of step. His career was a continuous story of belligerent protest, of resignations from parties and rejections of office, of consistent courage and frequent pig-headedness.

He was born in Hertford of a father who was a socialist boot and shoe repairer and a mother who progressed from scullery-maid to cooking in the big houses around the town. He attended a Church of England school and went to church three times each Sunday. His Christian faith never failed, even when he was in the Communist party. It was not a soft childhood but it was a happy one, marred only by his failure to get into Hertford Grammar School, a fact which in itself is a criticism of the education system of the 1930s.

He was apprenticed as a carpenter and joiner. Years later he was reported to have said: "Like Jesus I was a carpenter." In fact, this was an invention of another Labour MP but it was widely believed to be Heffer's own phrase – which gives a clue to his not unlikeable vanity, one of his characteristics. By the time he was 16 he had joined both the Labour party and the woodworkers' union. He stayed in the union but he was soon out of the Labour party, joining the Communist party and retaining membership through his wartime services in the RAF and beyond.

By 1948 however, he had left the Communists after leading an unofficial carpenters' strike and had rejoined the Labour party – but not for long. In 1954 he helped to start the semi-syndicalist Socialist Workers' Federation but this soon failed and by 1956 he was back in the long-suffering Labour party. This time it was for good.

Once he had settled down in the party his progress was rapid. He became president of Liverpool Trades Council in 1959 and a year later he was elected to the city council. From there it was a natural progression to a parliamentary candidacy and he was duly selected for Walton, which he captured from the Conservatives in 1964. He increased his majority at election after election until it reached 23,253 in 1987. The Labour leadership may not have liked him but Liverpool loved him.

In the House he pursued an orthodox left-wing line during the first two Wilson governments – against the Vietnam war, against the prices and income policy, against trade union reform. He also began a persistent Parliamentary campaign against hare coursing, introducing bills regularly over a period of 20 years up to 1989.

Wilson, always anxious to neuter his critics with offers of office, wanted to make him Parliamentary Secretary for Technology in 1967 but he refused. This was just as well because within months Heffer was engaged in a long battle against Barbara Castle's plan for reforming the unions and his resignation then would have been inevitable.

After Labour's defeat in 1970 Heffer did go on to the front bench as a spokesman for industrial relations but as a result of disagreements with Reg Prentice, the shadow minister who later became a Tory MP, he resigned his first post under Wilson in 1972. This followed close on another resignation – this time from the RSPCA because it refused to rebuke Princess Anne for fox-hunting.

With Labour back in office he was appointed minister for state at the Department of Industry in 1974 but after little more than a year he had returned to the back benches. This time he had not resigned but was sacked after falling out with Wilson after an anti-EEC speech. He was never to be in government again.

The Labour party was fond of Heffer but not fond enough to risk him as a front-line figure. He suffered two bruising defeats when he stood for key positions. In 1983 he opposed Kinnock and Roy Hattersley, the two front runners for the leadership, but came a bad third with only 6.3 per cent of the votes. Five years later he ran for the deputy leadership and it was the same story. Hattersley was the easy winner against John Prescott with Heffer trailing in third with just over 9 per cent.

In his remaining years he became increasingly frustrated as it became obvious that the majority of the party considered his grass-roots socialism outdated. His support for Militant did not help his popularity with successive leaders either. His 1985 pro-Militant Conference walk-out was only part of the problem. When he was on the national executive he fought off any action against Militant as early as 1980 and in the following year he opposed an enquiry into this Trotskyist organisation. By 1982 he was opposing Militant expulsions and in 1984, as conference chairman, he was widely criticised for calling a disproportionate number of Liverpool speakers with Trotskyist tendencies. He was always fearful of being accused of deserting his left-wing roots but his critics said,

possibly unfairly, that he was even more fearful of seeing Militants take his Walton seat away from him.

But despite his far-left record he was an instinctive opponent of authoritarianism. He was an active supporter of the illegal trades unions in the Soviet Union years before the Gorbachev reforms, and one reason why he left the Communist party was his reaction against Stalinist centralism. His verdict on his one-time leader: "Stalin was one of the greatest villains who ever lived." He was the first MP to attack the Soviet Union for the invasion of Afghanistan and backed Lech Walesa and the Solidarity movement in Poland years before this was fashionable in Britain.

Heffer fought cancer with the same courage he had shown throughout his political life. He wrote letters from his bed in Westminster Hospital to newspapers, protesting about what he regarded as the new right-wing policies of his party. During the final stages of his illness, he persisted writing his memoirs and completing a shorter work on Christianity. During his last appearance at the House John Major, newly appointed as prime minister, walked across the floor of the chamber to salute his courage. When he became too ill to leave London members of Liverpool city council came to the Speaker's house to present him with the freedom of the city. And when he was too ill even to leave his room the annual Houghton Prize for services to animal welfare – recognising his long campaign against hare coursing – was presented to him at his home.

The central figure in his life was his wife, Doris. They met during the war while he was in the RAF and lecturing in uniform to the Young Communists in her home city of Liverpool. She followed him out of the Communist party, into the Labour party, out of the Labour party and back again, acted as his secretary, adviser and beloved friend, and was responsible for securing his base in postwar Liverpool. He was large, she was tiny but their childless marriage was one of the most successful unions in modern politics.

WILHELM KEMPFF

Wilhelm Kempff, German pianist, died on May 23 aged 95. He was born at Juterbog on November 25, 1895.

WILHELM Kempff was one of the most thoughtful and rewarding interpreters of the Austro-German pianists of his generation, but his skills extended into other areas: he was a renowned player of, among others, Chopin and Liszt. He was also in demand as a chamber-music pianist, and at various periods of his long career teamed up with many noted string players to tackle sonatas for two instruments and the piano quartet and quintet repertory. Before the war he and the violinist Georg Kulenkampff were a noted duo — "I was the impulsive player, he was the classical, thoughtful one", he once said. Menuhin and Fournier were among his partners after Kulenkampff's early death.

Kempff came from a family of church musicians and began his studies with his father, after which, at the age of only nine, he entered the Berlin Academy of Music, working with Robert Kahn on composition and Heinrich Barth on the piano. After further studies, in philosophy and the history of music, he began his career by touring as pianist and organist with the Berlin Cathedral Choir. He recalled as a youth hearing Busoni play his own music, meeting Sibelius, and hearing — from the fifth row of the balcony of the Berlin Hofoper Caruso (in 1912) singing Don José.

His debut recital in the Berlin Singakademie in 1915 was a foretaste of what was to come. The young pianist tackled a programme that included two of the most formidable works, technically and intellectually, in the pianist's repertory — Beethoven's "Hammerklavier" Sonata and Brahms's Paganini Variations. He was immediately acknowledged as a player of enormous promise and the recital led to his first appearance with the Berlin Philharmonic in 1918.

From then until the outbreak of the second world war he established himself securely on the international scene with tours all over the Continent, South America and Japan — but not to Britain. His debut here was delayed until 1951, when he was immediately acknowledged as a player of formidable stature. From then on he was a regular visitor both in recital and concertos. He gave many performances of the complete cycle of Beethoven's piano sonatas, preferring to tackle them chronologically because that gave a biography of the composer in musical terms. "In Opus 110 you can almost hear the composer's bodily pains near the end of his life," Kempff averred.

He recorded for Deutsche Grammophon over a period of almost 60 years, broken only by a spell just after the war with Decca with whom he made a number of discs that have become collector's items. Back with DG, he recorded the complete sonatas of Beethoven (twice over), the Beethoven concertos, all the sonatas of Schubert, the Beethoven violin sonatas (with Menuhin) and his cello sonatas (with Fournier). Many of these sets are considered classics and have reappeared on CD.

Kempff's playing was notable for its lyrical, almost improvisatory nature, yet in spite of this apparent spontaneity of approach, his readings were controlled by a sharp-edged intellect. He concentrated on a singing legato, clarity of texture, and a natural fluidity where tempo was concerned. He always avoided any harshness of tone, preferring to impress by beauty and intellect rather than by bombarding the ear with decibels. In spite of his emphasis on the German classics he had loved Chopin from his student days and often quoted Furtwangler's dictum to those who were shocked at him playing a composer some considered inferior: "A pianist who doesn't love Chopin is no pianist." Kempff felt that playing Chopin and Liszt kept him from becoming too academic in his music-making although he deliberately eschewed Liszt's more showy pieces.

Kempff was also an eminent teacher, before the war at the Music Academy in Stuttgart and at summer courses in Potsdam. From 1957 he directed courses on Beethoven at Positano. He also composed two symphonies, a violin concerto, chamber music, song, ballet scores, and no fewer than four operas, all alas, forgotten. They are in a tonal vein as he abhorred most of the modern "advances" in composition. He also edited the piano works of Schumann, another composer Kempff interpreted with great discernment.

His wife died five years ago. He is survived by seven children.

BRIGADIER PETER THWAITES

Brigadier Peter Thwaites, soldier, sportsman, playwright and chairman of the Hurlingham Polo Association, died on May 23 aged 64. He was born at Ambleside, Westmorland, on July 30, 1926.

PETER Thwaites had a career of remarkable variety and versatility which included experience of military operations all over the world, particularly in the Middle East where he held senior commands in the forces of Muscat and Oman. This went hand in hand with a career as a West End playwright and he was, in addition, at the time of his death chairman of the Hurlingham Polo Association, the ruling body of the game.

Peter Trevenan Thwaites was educated at Rugby and commissioned into the Grenadier Guards in November 1944. He began a period of service with the 1st, 2nd and 4th battalions of his regiment. Following his stint as a platoon commander with the British Army of the Rhine he went on to serve in a distin-

guished series of regimental and staff appointments in Egypt; the British Cameroons; British Guiana; Malaya, where he was brigade major to the 2nd Federal Infantry Brigade from 1959 to 1961; Muscat, where he commanded the Muscat Regiment of the Sultan's armed forces, 1967-70; and Singapore where he had a senior appointment on the staff and was a governor of the Singapore International School, 1971-73. He had also been a member of Sir William Penney's scientific party to the United Kingdom atomic bomb trials in south Australia in 1956.

A graduate of both the Staff College and the Joint Services Staff College, he was promoted brigadier in 1975 and in that rank took up his last British Army appointment, as head of the Ministry of Defence logistic survey team to Saudi Arabia in 1976. He retired from the army in 1977 and was appointed chairman of the joint staff of the Sultan of Oman's armed forces in that year. He made a considerable contribution to the operational efficiency of Oman's defence capacity during a period of service which lasted until his final retirement in 1981. His decorations in that time included the

Sultan's Bravery Medal, the Special Commendation and the Distinguished Service Medal for gallantry.

Meanwhile Thwaites, a man of fecund and lively imagination and narrative power, enjoyed marked success as a playwright and a number of his pieces had West End runs. Plays produced under his signature included *Love or Money* (with Charles Ross, 1958), *Master of None* (1960), *Roger's Last Stand*, starring Roy Kinnear and Leslie Phillips at the Duke of York's (1976), *Caught in the Act* which starred Martin Jarvis and Judy Geeson at the Garrick (with Charles Ross, 1981) and *Relative Strangers* (1984).

In his youth he was also a keen amateur jockey and game shot and was not only captain of his regimental polo team but also represented other teams wherever he served in the army. That experience, coupled with his affable and humorous personality and his reputation as a capable administrator, prompted the Hurlingham Polo Association, of which Viscount Cowdray was then vice-chairman, to invite him to take on the post of chairman in 1982; he held it until his death.

With the banning of Argentinians from the British game following the Falklands conflict and the decision to allow their return in 1988, the last decade had been a difficult one for the Hurlingham Polo Association. But it was one in which, too, the game in Britain expanded enormously, showing a vigorous mushrooming of new clubs and several hundred new names on the handicap lists. In these vicissitudes, despite painful and increasing illness over recent years, Thwaites quickly gained a name for great managerial flair, quiet diplomacy and firm and impartial decision-making.

Peter Thwaites married first, in 1950, Ellen Theresa, daughter of William J. King, an American. The marriage was dissolved and he married secondly, in 1974, Mrs Jacqueline Inchbald (née Bromley) who survives him. There were two sons and two daughters by the first marriage.

BRIGADIER LORNE CAMPBELL OF AIRDS, VC

Brigadier Lorne Campbell of Airds, VC, DSO and Bar, OBE, TD, died on May 25 aged 88. He was born on July 22, 1902.

LORNE Campbell of Airds was a fighting solder whose courageous leadership in the second world war brought new honour and fame to the Argyll and Sutherland Highlanders, a fact reflected in the VC and the two DSOs he won in some of the major campaigns of the war.

In the 1940 retreat across France, in 1942 at El Alamein and in the following year at Wadi Akarit this Territorial army officer matched his wits and skill against German army units in vastly differing circumstances but each time with gallantry of the highest order. Himself the nephew of a VC — the Vice-Admiral Gordon Campbell who fought in Q-ships in the first world war — Lorne Campbell remained the most modest of men. Fiercely proud of what he believed in, and relishing the honour, for a territorial

officer, of having temporary command of his division in Italy, in later life he modestly declined to join the VC and GC holders' association, to become deputy chief scout, or to seek election as an MP. For himself he had no ambition.

His father, the late Colonel Maxwell Campbell of Airds, served through the first world war as a captain in the 8th Battalion the Argyll and Sutherland Highlanders and became its honorary colonel in 1929. Lorne Campbell achieved the same honour 25 years later.

Lorne Maclaine Campbell of Airds was educated at Dulwich College, where he was captain of school in 1920-21 (his father and famous uncle were also there in their day). A Postmaster at Merton College, Oxford, he missed a rugby Blue through injury but was anchorman for the Oxford tug-o'-war team.

He joined the 8th Battalion Argyll and Sutherland Highlanders in 1921 under his father's command and by 1939 was second-in-command. Sent to France with them as part of the 51st (Highland) Division, he won his DSO during the Blitzkrieg and British withdrawal.

Campbell was ordered to find the battalion's two leading companies and regrouped the remnant in a new defensive position as Rommel's armoured division poured along the coast road. Campbell intended to support the British counter-attack by cutting across the enemy van but it became depressingly clear that there would be no counter-attack. Saved from the German tanks by the onset of night, Campbell took his men for two breathless days across France without the loss of a single one. His remnants joined "Arkforce" and got out of France via Le Havre, thus escaping the fate of the remainder of the 51st (Highland) Division which was captured at St Valery. Morale during their uncomfortable hours at Le Havre was transformed by a personal signal to Lorne Campbell: "The Royal Navy will see the Argylls safely off tonight", signed by the naval liaison officer, his brother Alan (a third brother was an officer in the RAF).

When the new Highland Division was

formed Lorne Campbell commanded the 7th/10th Battalion Argyll and Sutherland Highlanders in North Africa and won the bar to his DSO at Alamein. Before he could officially receive it he had won his VC.

The action for which he earned this occurred on April 6, 1943, when he led his battalion in its crucial task of breaking through a minefield and anti-tank ditch to form a bridgehead for the division at Wadi Akarit. For the first time the Eighth Army was operating without the benefit of moonlight and the battalion had a difficult approach at an angle to the line of advance. This was successful, with 600 prisoners taken, and next day Campbell personally led an operation to correct the alignment of the gap in the anti-tank ditch with the cleared lane for vehicles. Under heavy fire he retrieved the gap but by late afternoon enemy tanks were counter-attacking. Exposed in full view of the enemy, he rallied his men, reorganised the position of a forward company which had been forced to give ground and, although painfully wounded in the neck, stood in the open to direct the fight under close fire from German infantry. Both the official narrative and *The Times* assessment by its military correspondent showed that the Argylls held their position till night fell and after; and that but for Campbell's actions the bridgehead would have been lost. "In such cases," *The Times* commented, "the whole issue of a battle may hang upon the action of one man . . ."

The arrival of a territorial brigadier — Lorne Campbell — in charge of 13 Brigade was at first viewed with suspicion but he took the brigade through Sicily, Anzio and much of Italy and, in the GOC's absence for several weeks, commanded the famous 5th Division.

In 1944 he went to the British army staff in Washington until the war ended and he won the US Legion of Merit. Later, in Germany, he led an official mission which studied the chances of establishing scouting there as an antidote to the ideals of the Hitler Youth.

He returned to his career in the family firm of wine shippers in the City and became a leading figure in the trade. Though less of an expert on wine itself than his father had been he followed him in the rare distinction of being made a liveryman *honoris causa* of the Vintners' Company and was later its Master. He had much to do with setting up the qualification for "Master of Wine" and served on committees selecting wine for the royal cellar and for government hospitality. On his retirement he was appointed OBE.

After living in Amersham, like his father, he returned to Scotland. He was much admired both as an after-dinner speaker and in his duties as senior steward of the Argyllshire Gathering. His great loves were fishing, gardening, the Scout movement in younger days (though he declined high office in it later on) and his regiment; one of his ancestors had commanded a company in the 98th (later 91st) Argyllshire Highlanders when they were raised.

In 1935 he married Muriel Campbell of Auchendarroch, daughter of Alastair Magnus Campbell of Auchendarroch. She died in 1950. They had two sons.

CORAL BROWNE

Coral Browne, stage, film and television actress, died in Los Angeles on May 29 aged 77. She was born in Melbourne on July 23, 1913.

CORAL Browne was one of the wittiest actresses of her generation on-stage and an equally striking personality off it. As a classical actress she had power and authority while her sheer stylishness and her commanding personality lifted many a commercial piece well above its natural level. In the theatre her talent was often shown in a single inflection or a charged pause that might have brought immediate triumph in the kind of sophisticated revue popular during the 1940s and 1950s.

One of her great qualities was her special chamelion gift. Tall, poised and elegant, she was totally at home in those light-comedy parts that look so simple from the front but that need the craft of a consummate technician who at the same time really relishes the task in hand. Coral Browne could go straight from this sort of thing to the power and menace needed for Goneril, Regan or Lady Macbeth and return to the insubstantial comic ethos in a way bewildering to those who liked to see their players adhering to at least certain notions of type. Her Lady Macbeth for the Old Vic (1956) is regarded as one of the finest accounts of the role in modern times, while in the following year she had a scarcely less memorable success in Shakespearian comedy, also for the Old Vic, with her Helena in *A Midsummer Night's Dream*, creating of the role a soulful, questing creature bewildered by the complexity of life and love.

Her robust humour off-stage was as renowned as her performance on it and tales about her public utterances — generally true in spirit even when short on strict fact — abounded. One such piece of lore concerned her and Vincent Price's purchase of a bed in the days before their wedding. Miss Browne was then in her sixties and her future spouse a couple of years older. Having made their selection, the couple were informed by the salesman of the London department store that delivery would take three months. Miss Brown is alleged to have fixed him with an imperious glare: "Just look at us" she demanded, "D'you think we've got that long?"

Coral Edith Browne was born the daughter of Leslie Brown, a restaurateur (her own name acquired its terminal 'e' for stage purposes). She was educated at Claremont Ladies' College, Melbourne, and later studied painting. But she had first gone on the stage when she was 17 and she subsequently played through a teasing medley of parts — though at that stage no Shakespeare — that spoke for much of her future. Already as a young actress she embraced farce, social comedy, Ibsen's Hedda, Shaw's Orinthia (*The Apple Cart*) and Barrie's Mrs Dearth.

During the autumn of 1934, among several Australian migrants to the English theatre in this period, she arrived in London (as an understudy) but she had to wait for real recognition until her Maggie Cutler in *The Man Who Came to Dinner* (1941) and a confident Mrs Cheyney in the Savoy revival of *The Last of Mrs Cheyney* (1944) with Jack Buchanan. More of the sort of part she grew to play with such assurance followed: Maugham's Lady Frederick (1946), one of Lonsdale's quartet in *Canaries Sometimes Sing* (1947), and — with Buchanan, a perfect stage companion – Boss Trent in Alan Melville's *Castle in the Air* during its career at two theatres.

Being the artist she was, she then needed change. She got it in the hardest way by going to the Old Vic as a straight, strong Emilia to Douglas Campbell's Othello (1951) and as Regan (1952) in an unlucky *King Lear*; the revival had been designed for Wolfit but he had left the company. Soon she was back in the West End for a forgettable comedy, *Affairs of State*, which nevertheless lasted 18 months. It was not long, however, after other trivialities, before she returned to the classics, first, in New York as the suffering Zabina in Tyrone Guthrie's production of *Tamburlaine the Great* – his direction always appealed to her. Then, in 1956 at the Old Vic, a theatre she always loved, came her celebrated Lady Macbeth, a role she also took on tour in America. By this point she seemed to have become a confirmed Shakespearian. To come were Gertrude – to John Neville's Hamlet – her enchanting Helena in *A Midsummer Night's Dream* and Goneril, all at the Old Vic. She was Gertrude again with the Stratford company for its visit to the Soviet Union in December 1958 to Michael Redgrave's Hamlet.

But this was actually to be her last Shakespearian venture. In the West End such pieces as *The Pleasure of his Company*, *Bonne Soupe* and *The Right Honourable Gentleman* came and went after substantial runs without adding noticeably to her reputation. But there were other roles in which she did star such as the resolutely dramatic Mrs Erlynne ("I feel a passion awakening within me that I never felt before") in Wilde's *Lady Windermere's Fan*, Shaw's Mrs Warren for the National Theatre company at the Old Vic (1970) – her first Shaw since her early days in Melbourne – and two difficult parts in Anouilh revivals, Emily in *The Waltz of the Toreadors* (1975) and the Countess in *Ardèle*.

She had entered films in 1935 and though the cinema always came second to her stage career she made pictures, on and off, for the next 50 years. They ranged from a George Formby comedy, *Let George Do It!* (1940) through the Anna Neagle romances, *Piccadilly Incident* and *The Courtneys of Curzon Street* and *Auntie Mame*, filmed in Hollywood in 1958, to *The Roman Spring of Mrs Stone* (1961).

Her most publicised appearance came in 1969 in *The Killing of Sister George*, where she played the television executive who fires Sister George from the serial which has been her working life (and steals her young and attractive girl friend at the same time). Her explicit lesbian scene with Susannah York, playing the young girl friend, was highly controversial in the climate of the times, causing a furore which detracted from a recognition of the quality of her chillingly effective performance as the one character in the story who gets exactly what she wants. Among her later films were *The Ruling Class* (1972) from the stage play by Peter Barnes and *Theatre of Blood* (1973), a hilarious horror comedy which starred Vincent Price playing a splendidly hammy Shakespearian actor who revenges himself on those theatre critics.

In 1983 she had a triumph on television, playing herself in Alan Bennett's drama *An Englishman Abroad*. It was based on a bizarre meeting in Moscow with the spy Guy Burgess during her visit with the Old Vic's *Hamlet* in the 1950s. Burgess (played in the BBC film by Alan Bates) burst into her dressing room one night, invited her to dinner and asked her to have clothes made for him by a London tailor. In 1986 she was Mrs Alice Hargreaves in the *Dreamchild*, playing an octogenarian dragon of inimitably English breed, in a film which portrayed a visit to New York by the old lady who had once been the model for Lewis Carroll's Alice.

Her first husband was the actor, and later agent, Philip Pearman, who died in 1964. She married Vincent Price in 1974. She had met him for the first time during the making of *Theatre of Blood*, "in a graveyard, of course", she always claimed.

SIR ANGUS WILSON

Sir Angus Wilson, CBE, novelist, short story writer and professor of English literature at the University of East Anglia from 1966 to 1978, died on May 31 in a nursing home at Bury St Edmunds, Suffolk, aged 77. He was born on August 11, 1913.

UNFAMILIAR though the judgment had come to seem in his latter years, Sir Angus Wilson was the nearest that Great Britain came in the post-war period to producing a major practitioner of fiction. His reputation had faded of late, undoubtedly in part because he had been stricken with disease and consequently inactive for a period of time lengthy enough to have taken him out of the public eye. But that his work, and especially his earliest work – in which he tried to revive the "traditional" novel – will be looked at again with critical seriousness is not open to doubt. Indeed the process of putting his work before the public, so that a revalu-

ation can be made, has already begun. A number of his novels are due to be reissued in Penguin. Two of the best known of them, *Anglo-Saxon Attitudes* and *The Middle Age of Mrs Eliot*, are to be made into films. Meanwhile, his critical books are still gratefully read and his brilliant lectures are still remembered by those lucky enough to have heard them.

Angus Frank Johnstone Wilson was born at Bexhill-on-Sea, East Sussex. His childhood was not a happy one; he gave an incomparable, brief account of it in the *Spectator* essay that deserves reprinting, "Bexhill and After", in 1958. His parents, a shiftless Scot and the daughter of a South African jeweller, were already middle-aged at the time of his birth and he had five much older brothers. There was a reasonable private income but Wilson senior liked to gamble, putting the family into a position of genteel poverty – as well as compelling it to move hurriedly from place to place. Wilson early knew the full meaning of "doing a flit".

Both parents were given to histrionics, a trait he inherited and put to good use. He was educated at a series of prep schools, and then at Westminster School, where was known as "the mad boy" and "the boy with hair" because of his (often wilfully) eccentric behaviour and ostentatiously scruffy appearance. He drew freely and skilfully upon all these boyhood experiences in his fiction. By 1932, when he went up to Merton College, Oxford, to read history, his mother had died – and he had discovered, too, that he had been much more attched to her than he had realised.

He took a good degree, thought of but renounced the notion of taking up acting as a career, drifted from job to job (including one helping his elder brother run a restaurant) and finally landed up (1936) in the British Museum's Department of Printed Books. He mixed quite easily and built up a reputation as a mimic and buffoon; but he felt uneasy because he found himself unable to come to terms with his homosexuality. He could obtain nothing lasting from the affairs he had, which, in his earlier days, at least, tended to land him in damaging emotional involvements.

In 1942 Wilson went to the Foreign Office at which he was engaged on secret work until 1946, when he returned to the British Museum. Here he was given the immediate task of replacing some of the 300,000 books destroyed in the Blitz. He had been suffering from semi-crippling attacks of nervous anxiety for some years when, in November 1946, he took to writing short stories at the weekends — which he spent in the country — as a partial cure. His friend the painter Robin Ironside showed some of these to Cyril Connolly, editor of the prestigious *Horizon*, and Connolly started to print them.

The British short story was then, as it usually has been, in the doldrums. Publishers of collections seldom broke even and they were regarded as a drug on the market. But Fred Warburg's hunch about *The Wrong Set* (1949) proved correct: this collection looked likely to institute a renaissance of the form. That did not happen; but these stories have lasted and no representative anthology of the form, whether national or international, could properly be complete without at least one. They were for the most part beautifully judged satires on pretentious people, but were never lacking in depth or compassion. Some critics have even felt that Wilson never bettered them and that the short form suited him best.

Wilson will be partly judged on this work, which was unique in its mixture of sharp, accurate social observation and presentation of character in depth. It is likely, too, that he will be found to have produced his finest work in the decade after the publication of his second collection of stories, Such *Darling Dodos* (1950). His superb critical book *Emile Zola* (1952), thoroughly revised in 1965, was followed by his two major novels, *Anglo-Saxon Attitudes* (1956) and *The Middle Age of Mrs Eliot* (1958). He left the British Museum Reading Room, where he had been deputy superintendent

since 1949, in 1955 in order to devote himself to full-time writing.

Hemlock and After (1952) had been his first novel. Moving and humane, it dealt with the predicament of a married homosexual novelist, Bernard Sands. This was certainly in the liberal tradition of E. M. Forster (Wilson tended to be irritatedly disingenuous when trying to shrug off this powerful influence, which he nonetheless admitted had been crucial), and, even if its seams are a bit obtrusive, it remains in retrospect a mature and deeply felt work. But its two successors, novels of altogether larger canvas, are superior. They are important not least because they embody a deliberate intent to emulate the values and the techniques of the traditional novel as it had emerged from the hands of George Eliot. Whether such a revival was possible or not, or whether (as Gore Vidal continues to insist) the novel is dead, and was dead then, is clearly still a matter for debate; but *Anglo-Saxon Attitudes* and *The Middle Age of Mrs Eliot* are undoubtedly a factor in that debate. At present not in fashion, they live on in the work of such novelists as A. S. Byatt and they are, at the least, impressive if not monumental. They may well represent the most valiant, intelligent and able effort yet made in English fiction in the second part of this century to revive the tradition.

Wilson's novels from *The Old Men at the Zoo* (1961) onwards have not been judged as wholly successful although they were often welcomed by reviewers at the time of their issue. As he himself stated, he tried to become an experimental (the word he used) novelist, experimenting in particular with pastiche and animal — and plant — imagery. He felt that critics had missed out on the modernistic elements in such novels as *Late Call* (1964), "failing to see innumerable jokes, alienations, pastiches and other non-traditional techniques." The truth may be, however, that although these later novels are very distinguished in parts they fail because they fall between the two stools of a possibly over-self-conscious desire to be regarded as "modern" and natural abilities of a more traditional sort. Critics were often embarrassed by the "non-traditional" elements in his later works, such as *Setting the World on Fire* (1980), where there is a sense of strain.

Wilson's chief energies increasingly went into his role as critic and lecturer. In 1963 he became a very successful lecturer at the University of East Anglia and he was made professor in 1966. He had been Ewing lecturer at the University of California at Los Angeles (1960) and from then on held a series of distinguished American appointments as visiting lecturer or professor (at such universities as those of Georgia, Chicago and Johns Hopkins). He was also Leslie Stephen lecturer at Cambridge (1962-3).

He was an immense success, his lectures being models of dramatic and enthusiastic lucidity, and he was as great a success on the many campuses he visited. His acting abilities, perhaps frustrated earlier in life, came to the fore in his shrewd and robust attacks on the theorists (F. R. Leavis was a *bête noire*) whom he reckoned to have tried to ruin literature with abstractions and ignorance of human nature. Underneath what sometimes seemed – especially when he was exhausted – petulance, there always lay in Angus Wilson the humanity and kindliness of the old-fashioned liberal. He could be petty and vain, as well as too evidently exhibitionistic; but his realisation of his lapses was an altogether rarer quality which always shone through, even in the later and possibly less satisfactory novels. He was disappointed that these were not more enthusiastically received, yet perpetually consoled by the triumph of his role at East Anglia and elsewhere. Besides the lecturing success of his professorship at East Anglia there was the MA in creative writing which he started with Malcolm Bradbury, a course which attracted students who are now well-known novelists in their own right, such as Ian McEwan and Kazuo Ishiguro.

As a playwright Wilson aimed, and just missed, with *The Mulberry Bush*, which had a production in London in 1956, and with several television plays that did not quite come off. In literary criticism he was much more assured, adding to the work of Zola books on Dickens (1970) and Kipling (1977). The latter, a sympathetic biography, was certainly the most sophisticated book on its subject, and it broke – although discreetly – the taboo on speculation about the ambiguous nature of Kipling's sexuality. Some of his best criticism is usefully collected in *Diversity and Depth in Fiction* (1953).

Towards the start of his literary career Wilson met Tony Garrett, the man who was his companion until the end and who nursed him in his decline with such devotion. To Garrett it fell to look after his friend when he became stricken with the encephalitis which led progressively to the impairment of his mental faculties and the loss of his ability to speak. This tragedy, combined with the relative poverty in which Wilson found himself, clouded his latter years. In 1985 he decided to live abroad permanently and bought a house in the South of France. But his illness gained ground on him and he had to spend some time in a nursing home at Nîmes. Latterly, with health and memory deteriorated to a fundamental extent, he entered a nursing home at Bury St Edmunds where he suffered his fatal stroke.

Wilson had himself been a member from 1966 of the committee of the Royal Literary Fund – that body which has saved so many writers from disaster and destitution. The fund helped him in those last years, when royalties from his work had dwindled, granting him a pension to supplement his meagre earnings. The University of East Anglia also raised several thousand pounds for its emeritus professor.

Angus Wilson was a man who thoroughly deserved the many honours he received (FRSL, 1958; CBE, 1968; CLit, 1972; a knighthood, 1980; and numerous honorary doctorates from universities here and abroad). His reputation cannot but increase from this point onwards; he is indisputably a part of the history of the development of the English literature he loved so much.

FARNHAM MAXWELL

Farnham "Freddie" Maxwell, trainer of the winner of the Ascot Gold Cup three times in the 1960s, died on June 2 aged 85. He was born on June 6, 1905.

PANDOFELL in 1961 and Fighting Charlie in 1965 and 1966 were Freddie Maxwell's Gold Cup winners and there was drama connected with both of them. Pandofell, a 100-8 outsider, won unchallenged by five lengths, putting to rout a considerable French invading force which included Puissant Chef, the previous season's Prix de l'Arc de Triomphe winner and odds-on favourite.

The following month, Pandofell was due to appear again at Ascot but was found to have been doped and thus missed the Goodwood Cup. Happily he recovered in time to add the Doncaster Cup to his laurels but the doping had almost certainly deprived him and Maxwell of the stayer's Triple Crown.

Lester Piggott rode Pandofell and, also, in the first of his Gold Cup victories partnered Fighting Charlie, bred and owned by Lady Mairi Bury, youngest daughter of the seventh Marquess of Londonderry. But the following season he chose to ride Aegean Blue instead. On the Sunday before the Royal Meeting it had been discovered that Fighting Charlie had badly swollen forelegs. The Lambourn vet, Frank Mahon, saved the day. He had the horse strapped up in harness, gave him electrical treatment and applications of clay and camphor. Fighting Charlie went to post sound. But the drama was not yet over.

Greville Starkey had taken over as his jockey and they went smoothly into the lead half a mile out. Then, beginning to feel his legs, Fighting Charlie swerved and almost ran out. It took all of Starkey's persuasion to get him going and in the end they not only made up for lost ground but passed the post a handsome eight lengths clear to a hero's reception.

William Farnham Maxwell was born in Ireland at Birr, Co Offaly. No one ever used his christened forenames, however: he was always known as Freddie or Maxie. He joined the stable of Aubrey Hastings at Wroughton in 1923 and rode winners on the flat then over the jumps. Before the war, in which he served in the RAF, he had returned to Ireland to train and on demobilisation resumed briefly at Wiseton, near Retford, before joining Evan Williams as assistant at Kingsclere.

On Williams's retirement in 1953 Maxwell once again set up on his own, at Blewbury, with about 13 horses. Five years later he moved to Lambourn where he remained.

One of Maxwell's great skills was in the art of placing his horses, Young Christopher, as a two-year-old in 1963, providing a perfect example with seven victories in a row. Then in 1964 he won the Jersey Stakes at Royal Ascot and was runner-up in the Irish Two Thousand Guineas. Other notable successes were with Horse Radish (Northumberland Plate), Alto Volante (Yorkshire Cup), Merry Madcap (July Cup) and with the outstanding two-year-old filly of 1970, Cawston's Pride, unbeaten in eight races and officially rated only 2lbs inferior to the subsequent champion Mill Reef.

Maxwell, a quiet and eminently likeable man, retired in 1977. He leaves a widow, Norah, and a daughter.

CHRISTOPHER SERPELL

Christopher Serpell, OBE, BBC foreign correspondent, died on June 3 aged 80. He was born on July 1, 1910.

CHRISTOPHER Serpell was one of the BBC's pioneer foreign correspondents and later its diplomatic editor. His dispatches from Paris, Rome and Washington were always elegantly written and often very funny. He was one of the great broadcasting journalists.

Towards the end of the second world war the BBCs new director-general, William Haley, who had started his journalistic life on *The Times* and was due to return as its editor, decided to form a post-war corps of BBC foreign corres-

pondents. One of his guiding principles was that a BBC correspondent based abroad must have "a status not less than the best of his colleagues, such as those on *The Times*." It was not surprising that several of the first appointments should have been from the ranks of the paper.

Thomas Barman, the first BBC diplomatic correspondent, had held a similar post in Printing House Square; Thomas Cadett, formerly *The Times* correspondent in Paris, returned there at the end of the war as BBC correspondent. He was briefly joined by Christopher Serpell, who was on his way to establishing the BBC's bureau in Rome.

Serpell was a Yorkshireman who joined

the editorial staff of the *Yorkshire Post* in 1934 after reading Greats at Merton College, Oxford. He moved to London the following year and then had eight years on *The Times* as a sub-editor handling home news, the Court page, letters to the Editor, obituaries and foreign news. His war service was with the Naval Intelligence Staff at the Admiralty. He began contributing radio talks on naval aspects of war and also spoke frequently in schools current affairs programmes under the pseudonym of Christopher Searle.

The BBC recruited him in July 1946, gave him training in radio news and a short spell with Thomas Cadett in Paris and then moved him to Rome. Italy was not at that time making a great deal of international news. But Serpell's broadcasts found prominent places in such programmes as *Radio Newsreel* because he always managed to make them so interesting. He had a great liking for Italians and had a sharp eye for the drolleries of life in post-war Rome. He spoke excellent Italian and had a very good microphone manner.

At the end of 1953 Serpell was transferred to Washington as the BBC's chief correspondent. He covered the Eisenhower years, including the heyday and downfall of Senator Joseph McCarthy, and the strain on the special relationship imposed by the Anglo-French military action over Suez on the eve of Eisenhower's second presidential election.

The Washington experience of superpower politics stood Serpell in good stead when the responsibility of a growing family of three girls and a boy brought him back to Britain in 1960. He held a variety of posts in the BBC's news division, all connected with foreign news, and he became the editor of *News Extra* an early television precursor of *Newsnight*. He worked first as the assistant and eventually as the successor to his friend and former colleague Thomas Barman, the BBC's diplomatic editor.

Serpell was as adept in Westminster as he had been in Rome and Washington at collecting the threads of international news and weaving them into a clearly presentable pattern. He covered innumerable conferences and summit meetings. The day after he retired, at the end of 1972, he was appointed OBE. But Serpell's broadcasting career was not over. For many years he contributed wise and penetrating analyses of international developments to the BBC's World Service.

In his later years Christopher Serpell took a great interest in the history of old London and in 1977 with his wife, Jean, he wrote a traveller's guide to Elba and the Tuscan archipelago which was translated into German. Jean Serpell died in 1985. He is survived by his son and three daughters.

EVA LE GALLIENNE

Eva Le Gallienne, actress and theatre director, died in Connecticut on June 3 aged 92. She was born in London on January 11, 1899.

EVA Le Gallienne was, with Lynn Fontanne (also London-born) and Katharine Cornell and Helen Hayes, a member of that quartet of powerful American actresses who between the wars and often on long regional tours of the USA began to take charge of what had hitherto been a male-dominated industry. The high priestess of classical drama in America, Le Gallienne always believed that the classics should be as readily available to the public in a theatre as they were on library shelves.

Her father was the British poet Richard Le Gallienne, and her mother the Danish writer and journalist Julie Norregaard. Eva was educated first at the College Sevinge in France and then at RADA,

before making her stage debut on 21 July, 1914 as a page in *Monna Vanna* at the Queens Theatre. Thereafter, apart from one or two domestic alliances with equally powerful women, her life was totally devoted to acting, teaching, writing and a succession of Yorkshire terriers.

She moved to New York in 1915, made her Broadway debut that year in *Mrs Botany's Daughters* and by 1917 was already on a long tour of California in *Mr Lazarus* and *Rio Grande*. Back in New York a year later, she joined the Ethel Barrymore company for *The Duchess of France* and *The Off Chance*, but it was not until 1921 that she made her name as Julie in *Liliom* (the play that was later to become Rodgers and Hammerstein's *Carousel*) in a performance which several critics described as "perfection".

Two years later, again on Broadway, she achieved a similar success as Princess Alexandra in Molnar's *The Swan* (the role which later marked Grace Kelly's final screen appearance), but despite such triumphs Le Gallienne was already restless within the commercial constraints of contemporary Broadway. Her ambition was to form her own classical company, and to spread the word, of those who (like her) had seen Eleanora Duse on stage, that there was a more natural and realistic way to appear before an audience than the mix of sentimentality and bravado which then passed for stardom along the Great White Way.

By 1925 she had her wish: the Eva Le Gallienne Company opened in a series of special matinees of *The Master Builder* of which *The New York Times* wrote: "Miss Le Gallienne reveals every facet of Hilda Wangel: her entrance, knapsack in place, dressed in muddy tramping togs, was bold in the extreme. Sparing of gesture, she created a vibrant illusion of strength, directness and eerie perception."

Le Gallienne then toured Europe, where she found audiences more receptive to her often revolutionary artistry and was able to make a pilgrimage to see Duse, before returning to America and the realisation that her truest and best audiences often lay far outside New York.

With the missionary zeal that was to be found in this country in the contemporary career of Sybil Thorndike, Le Gallienne formed several of her own companies and troupes, specialising in Ibsen and Shakespeare off-Broadway and on the road.

In 1927 she returned to Broadway itself in *Cradle Song*, went on to Hedda Gabler and Varya in *The Cherry Orchard* before directing and starring in a revival of Peter Pan which for many critics improved on the American original of Maude Adams. In the following year she played Juliet, Masha in *The Seagull* and Anna Karenina before going on to *Camille* in 1931. This was the performance which first unleashed on her the loathing of the powerful critic George Jean Nathan ("this is the first Camille I have ever seen die of catarrh"), a loathing which was to pursue her over the next twenty years and lead, some felt, to her semi-retirement from the stage and decision to concentrate on teaching after the war. On one occasion Nathan accused her of "trying to soar like an eagle, equipped only with the wings of a cuckoo" but there is some evidence that his loathing was as much to do with Le Gallienne's butch manner and offstage sexuality as with her undeniably remarkable talents as producer and star.

Through most of the 1930s, Le Gallienne ran her own Civic Repertory Company on 14th Street, a classical repertory company for which she fought long and hard through the worst of the Depression but which finally foundered on the familiar rocks of a cash crisis: it had regularly been losing a hundred thousand dollars a year while collecting some of the best reviews in the history of New York theatre.

Returning to Broadway in 1935 Le Gallienne premiered *L'Aiglon* and revived her Hedda before settling into a programme of classical tours which was to last well into the war. In 1937 she returned to New York for a celebrated female Hamlet, and two years later was still playing Juliet. In 1941 she produced and directed Eugene O'Neill's *Ah Wilderness* before joining Margaret Webster and Cheryl Crawford in the foundation of the American Repertory Theatre, yet another attempt to get the classics to the masses and this one thwarted by strong union objections to the rates of pay.

Undaunted, Le Gallienne formed a theatrical academy for students, paying for it by stints on Broadway as the White Queen in *Alice in Wonderland* and tours of Emlyn Williams' *The Corn is Green*. In October 1957 she starred with Irene Worth in Tyrone Guthrie's famous production of *Mary Stuart* ("thin, pale, fastidious, with a small voice that can express great emotion," thought *The New York Times*, "Miss Le Gallienne gives a big performance within a small compass").

Throughout her sixties, Le Gallienne continued to tour America in *Mary Stuart*, *The Cherry Orchard* and *Elizabeth the Queen*. Nathan delivered his last attack on her in *Ghosts* ("she is so cold that one expects a frosty mist to issue from her mouth") but she enjoyed considerable success with the National Repertory Company and began making the occasional film and television appearances, notably as Gertrude to an early Richard Burton *Hamlet* and as Mrs Dudgeon in the Olivier-Burt Lancaster *Devil's Disciple* (1959).

By now her stage appearances were more infrequent, but she was on Broadway again in 1968 for Ionesco's *Exit the King* and in 1970 played the Countess in *All's Well*, as well as directing, in Connecticut, her own translation of *The Cherry Orchard*. Her last appearances included *The Royal Family* (Broadway 1975 with Rosemary Harris) and the 1980 film of *Resurrection* with Ellen Burstyn and Sam Shepard.

In 1964 she won a special Tony award for services to the theatre: she also wrote a biography of Eleanora Duse, several Hans Christian Andersen translations and two autobiographies.

STAN GETZ

Stan Getz, jazz saxophonist, died on June 6 aged 64. He was born on February 2, 1927.

WITH the death of Stan Getz, jazz has lost a towering saxophonist whose lyrical style won a following which spanned all generations and extended beyond the confines of jazz itself. Although he spawned few imitators and was by no means a radical innovator, he possessed one of the most distinctive sounds on the tenor saxophone — a langurous shimmering tone. This was ideally suited to ballads but Getz had a prodigious tech-

nique, much admired by fellow musicians, and could be dazzling on uptempo numbers where his speed of thought and dexterity of performance gave him an edge over many rivals. His often poetic and understated eloquence followed in the style first developed by Lester Young and in an era dominated by more abrasive, not to say bombastic, players he represented the traditional virtues of melody and phrasing.

Getz was born in Philadelphia, the son of Russian Jewish parents who shortened the family name from Gayetzsky. His father worked variously as a tailor and printer and had emigrated to America via London's Whitechapel. Getz grew up in the Bronx and when he was 13 his father bought him first a bass, then a bassoon. He subsequently took up the alto saxophone before switchng to tenor. His headmaster recommended him for a scholarship at the Juilliard Academy of Music but in his mid-teens he quit his studies and turned professional. Benefiting from the shortage of musicians in America because of the second world war, he joined the band of Jack Teagarden, the jazz trombonist, in his mid-teens touring and making his recording debut at the age of 16. He then spent a year with the Stan Kenton Orchestra and in 1947, when Woody Herman reformed his band — as the so-called "Second Herd" — Getz won a place in the reeds section. Alongside such saxophonists as Zoot Sims, Al Cohn and Serge Chaloff he became part of the celebrated "Four Brothers" team. Getz attracted immediate attention with his solo on the Ralph Burns tune "Early Autumn." Such was his impact that by 1949 he was able to leave Herman to form the first of his small groups. As the years went by Getz was often regarded as a precursor of "cool" jazz — the West Coast-based response to the frenetic tempo of bebop — but he was too much of an indivdualist to be neatly bracketed in any one school of playing. Moreover, albums such as *Getz at Storyville* showed that his style was growing more, not less muscular. Other successful records from this period included *Getz & J.J* —

recorded with trombonist J.J. Johnson. Getz also performed with Norman Granz's touring showcase "Jazz At The Philharmonic", where he more than justified his nickname "The Steamer". His popularity, however, was increasingly undermined by personal problems and drug addiction and he was involved in an abortive hold-up at a drug-store in Seattle that led to a six month jail sentence. Writing from prison in 1954, Getz explained that after failing to convince the pharmacy assistant that he had a gun, "I left the store and went to my hotel. When I was in my room I decided to call the store and apologise. In doing so, the call was traced and my incarceration followed."

He was featured in the film, *The Benny Goodman Story* in 1956 but, disillusioned with the American jazz scene and struggling to combat his drug problem, Getz departed for Europe in 1958, settling in Copenhagen. He was not to return to America until 1961 when he cut one of his most satisfying albums, *Focus*, graced by string arrangements by the composer Eddie Sauter. His public profile soared the following year when he and the guitarist Charlie Byrd latched on to the bossa nova craze. With its hit theme "Desafinada", jazz samba was an instant commercial success. Getz followed it up with the album, *Getz-Gilberto*, a collaboration with the guitarist Joao Gilberto and Antonio Carlos Jobim, the composer of "Desafinado". This session produced the evergreen "The Girl From Ipanema", with impromptu English vocals added by Gilberto's wife, Astrud. With a huge commercial triumph on his hands, Getz was assured of the kind of financial security which is out of reach for most jazz musicians. To his credit he continued to play Latin pieces only sparingly. Many critics noted, moreover, that his use of the bossa nova helped improve his sound, adding an extra degree of dynamism. He continued to play "straight" jazz throughout the 1960s, always showing a keen eye for young players; Gary Burton and Chick Corea were among those given exposure.

As a musician steeped in melodic invention, he took little interest in the avant-garde and fusion explosion, and from 1969 to 1972 he went into semi-retirement in Europe. Late in 1971 he met Chick Corea in London and commissioned him to write a series of original compositions for a new group he planned to organise. The group made its debut in January the following year at the Rainbow Grill in New York. Shortly afterwards it recorded its first album although this was not released until 1975 under the title *Captain Marvel*. The personnel included Corea on piano and Stanley Clarke on bass, Tony Williams on drums and Airto Moreira on percussion. *Captain Marvel* heralded his return to the forefront of the American jazz scene and the group remained together with Hank Jones later replacing Corea. But the 1970s were, by and large, an unproductive decade for Getz in which the tenor player struggled to come to terms with electric instrumentation. "There was a good deal of pressure to keep up to date," he later explained, somewhat dryly. "It really felt alien to me. After all, I've spent my life trying to make acoustic sounds."

By the 1980s he had returned to a traditional line-up. With the cushion of his 1960s royalties, he was able to minimise his touring. Nevertheless he remained on form with the albums *Poetry* — 1983 duets with pianist Albert Dailey — and *Voyage*, recorded with his quartet in 1986. In 1988 he underwent surgery when a growth was detected behind his heart and removed. It was malignant but Getz fought the disease with determination and homeopathic therapy. When he appeared at the Festival Hall shortly afterwards, he still seemed frail, but the sumptuous tenor sound was indisputably intact. Unusually for a leading soloist, he left behind little in the way of compositional work. However, as artist-in-residence at Stanford University from the mid-1980s onwards, he ensured that his instinctive approach to improvisation would be passed onto a younger generation. He was married twice and leaves five children.

VERCORS

Vercors (Jean Bruller), French writer, died in Paris on June 10 aged 89. He was born on February 26, 1902.

JEAN Bruller had a successful career before the war as an illustrator and engraver and, as Vercors, his wartime pseudonym, continued as an author after it. But it is his novel *Le Silence de la mer* and his clandestine wartime publishing activities which have given him his place in French literary history and a name of honour amongst his countrymen.

Jean Marcel Bruller was born in Paris where he was educated at the École alsacienne before taking a diploma as an electrical engineer. From 1925 to 1939 he worked as an artist and engraver. When war broke out he was called up into the French army. In June 1940 he was wounded while with his unit in a small village in the Alpine Vercors range (later,

also, to give its name to one of the most active resistance groups, the maquis du Vercors). There he waited, gloomily, for the collapse of the French army and the surrender of his country to the invading Germans.

Before the war he had been a pacifist. Indeed, until the German entry into Prague he had always been convinced that somehow the better side of the German nature would prevail against Nazism. The betrayal of Czechoslovakia and French cowardice and complicity in that moral defeat had shaken him deeply. Now, returning to Paris after the surrender, he saw anew, at close quarters, the pusillanimous behaviour of some French politicians and the rush to climb on to the collaborators' bandwagon, in those early days of occupation when the invaders were still behaving in a conciliatory manner towards the conquered. Besides

146

shame at the national humiliation he felt deep disgust and disillusionment.

He was also a brave and resourceful man and was determined to demonstrate to the world outside that not all France was prostrating itself in cynical defeatism. Nevertheless to make a stand for intellectual honesty required great caution. While working unostentatiously as a carpenter in a village outside Paris, he sounded out friends as to the possibility of publishing. Chameleon-like, Jean Bruller became several personages at once: the writer Vercors, the publisher Desvignes and the printer and binder Drieu. The last pseudonym commented with pleasant malice on the activities of Drieu La Rochelle who was then editing the *Nouvelle Revue Française* under benevolent German patronage. As Desvignes Bruller was co-founder of the now-celebrated Éditions de Minuit which kept French intellectual life going in the hours of humiliation with its editions of poets like Louis Aragon and Paul Eluard, men who had rejected the blandishments of the Vichy regime and the benefits of collaboration.

But Éditions de Minuit's first and most famous production was Vercors's *Le Silence de la mer* which was printed in 1941 on a clandestine press in the heart of Paris. A brief but eloquent study of the relationship between a young (and "good") German officer and a French household, and of silent but obdurate resistance to the enemy, *Le Silence de la mer* became one of the key texts of wartime heroism. Its effect on the oppressed French spirit was electrifying and at a time when the allied cause seemed to be faltering in all the theatres of war translations of the book were eagerly read in Britain and the United States. Curiosity as to its author's identity reached fever pitch with celebrated names such as Francois Mauriac, André Gide and Aragon being pressed forward as candidates. The fact that it portrayed a German in a sympathetic light only increased its value (and, incidently, its effectiveness as a clarion call to resistance), lifting it well above the level of propaganda. Resistance to the Nazi menace was shown to be the fundamental battle for decency itself, a struggle which never ends even when wars are over.

In *La Bataille du silence* (1967, published as *The Battle of Silence* in Britain in 1968, a year in which liberties were again being crushed on the streets of Prague and held up to stern examination in the *événements* of Paris) Vercors recalled, in undemonstrative and self-effacing fashion, the difficulties under which Éditions de Minuit had laboured. As more texts were published and the operation grew larger, more people had of necessity to be let into the secret. But it was always a perilous business, tiptoeing under the watchful eye of the Gestapo. *The Battle of Silence* also vividly described daily life in Paris as the civilised mask of the occupiers came off and the brutalities of the regime became clear in their naked hideousness.

Besides being brave Vercors was a naturally modest man. He did not need the fame that came his way in the hour of liberation. As he foresaw, a new generation of literary and political placemen came on the scene and he was content to bow out. He did not mind. He had had his hour. Though he continued to write prolifically he never did anything quite like *La Silence* again, though his *Sylva* of 1962, the story of the "taming" of a vixen by her English squire husband, is a frolic of great charm. Some of his works, which included essays, plays and translations as well as further fiction, were translated by his second wife, Rita Barisse. He was also muh in demand as a lecturer and as such he travelled all over the world. Among his other achievements he evolved a highly effective method of reproducing paintings. It was characteristic of him to be able to engross himself in such an exercise of practical ingenuity. He never sought the mantle of a great author. His wartime experiences had taught him one, profound truth, that the battle against evil is never over: "I knew that in a sense the Nazis would remain victorious; because of them mankind would know that it had aged."

BERTICE READING

Bertice Reading, singer, died in London on June 8 aged 58. She was born in Chester, Pennsylvania.

WITH her exuberant personality and rotund shape Bertice Reading was a black American singer of the blues who found her greatest professional success on this side of the Atlantic and settled here. She appeared in musicals, straight plays, nightclubs, jazz festivals, on television and in one-woman shows, and critics described her voice, variously, as being like a velvet foghorn or "dripping molasses".

The popular press took great delight in her 18-stone weight, her love of champagne and her complex private life which included four marriages – to a Swiss impresario, a Belgian airline executive, an English aristocrat and finally to an astrologer less than half her age. Bertice Reading took this in her stride. She delighted in being both fat and funny and her personality and life-style were undoubtedly of the larger than life variety.

She first came to London in the 1950s as singer with the Lionel Hampton band and stayed on to join the cast of the musical review, *Jazz Train*. She was seen in this show by Princess Margaret and invited to Windsor Castle to perform in front of the Queen.

In the ensuing years she broadened her range, appearing at the Royal Court and on Broadway in Tony Richardson's productions of *Requiem for a Nun* and William Faulkner's *Sanctuary* and, in 1981, in a National Theatre production of Shakespeare's *Measure for Measure*. In 1959 she was nominated for a Tony award for best supporting actress for her performance in *Requiem for a Nun*.

She had perhaps her greatest success starring in a stage revival of *South Pacific* in 1988 playing Bloody Mary, a role she seemed born to perform. She said that after consulting the original James Michener short story, *Fo Dolla*, she had ignored the more insipid portrayal of the character in the Hollywood film version and performed the role as a gutsy earth mother.

Bertice Reading was born into a black, Catholic family in Pennsylvania, the only daughter of a hospital therapist, and according to her own account, began her career at the age of three dancing with the celebrated tap-dancer, Bill "Bojangles" Robinson. She later won a talent contest in which the prize was a week's engagement with the Lionel Hampton Orchestra. When Ernestine Anderson, the band's regular vocalist, broke her arm, Reading replaced her and travelled with the muscians to Europe.

After *Jazz Train* she appeared at the Royal Court in *Member of the Wedding* and then, in 1958, in *Valmouth* for which Sandy Wilson wrote her the role of Mrs Yaj. She also appeared in *Simply Heavenly*. For a while she lived in Paris and Geneva and in 1987 appeared for three months at the Folies Bergere singing while perched on a tightrope.

She performed in four one-women shows at the London fringe theatre, the King's Head, two of which transferred to the West End. Her screen roles included appearances in *Little Shop of Horrors* and *The Moon in the Gutter*. She was rehearsing for a new musical, *Notre Dame*, based on the Victor Hugo story *The Hunchback of Notre Dame*, when she suffered a stroke.

BILL PONSFORD

Bill Ponsford, Australian Test batsman of the 1930s, died in Kyneton, Victoria, aged 90. He was born at North Fitzroy, Melbourne, on October 19, 1900.

THE oldest surviving Test cricketer, William Harold Ponsford was also the only man to pass 400 twice. Only illness, which affected him on one tour to England, and the bowling of Larwood in the notorious "bodyline" series of 1932-3 ever notably unsettled him. He followed a first century for Victoria in 1922 with a maiden hundred against England at Melbourne in the next season, but on his first visit to England in 1926 his form suffered from ill-health.

By the following winter he had recovered and averaged 130 for Victoria, scoring hundreds in five successive matches. In England in 1934 he averaged 55 in Tests with a century at the Oval, but he far surpassed this on his last tour in 1934. With scores of 181 at Leeds and 266 at the Oval his average in the Tests was 94 and his aggregate for the summer 1,784.

Yet although he made over 2,000 runs in international cricket, his record is memorable chiefly for the other immense scores and partnerships standing to his name. With his preliminary shuffling movements forward and back he was not a graceful or elegant batsman, but in spite of an unorthodox uplift of the bat (which was said to have been the heaviest in use for a hundred years) he was very hard to dismiss and when he was once set the bowlers might well have been excused for giving up hope. Few have ever wielded a bat that looked so broad. Larwood, almost alone, exploited a weakness on the leg stump.

Among his finest performances were his 429 in Tasmania in 1923 and his 437 against Queensland in 1927, both made at Melbourne. Ponsford was associated with Woodfull in many big opening partnerships, 375 against New South Wales being their highest, though before this he had shared 456 with E. R. Mayne. In 1934 he had stands of 451 and 388 with Bradman at the Oval and Leeds.

He was often said to be the only player who could share in an enterprise with Bradman as an equal. There was something of the Bradman machine about his batting even if he lacked the Don's genius.

He retired in 1934, having scored 13,819 runs in first-clas cricket at an average of 65.18 including 47 centuries.

149

CLAUDIO ARRAU

Claudio Arrau, pianist, died on June 9 in Austria aged 88. He was born in Chile on February 6, 1903.

CLAUDIO Arrau was not only universally acclaimed as among the most penetrating interpreters of his time, but also through his teacher, Martin Krause, a pupil of Liszt, as one of the last surviving depositaries of 19th century tradition. Total involvement in whatever he undertook, coupled with a predilection for unhurried tempo, gave his playing an exceptional expressive intensity and breadth, obliterating all awareness of the technical means by which his ends were achieved. Yet nobody will quickly forget the unique fullness and depth of his sonority (emanating from a belief that weight should come from the entire upper part of the body) or the rich liquidity of his cantabile (achieved by artful fingering rather than reliance on the pedal) which stemmed from his love of the human voice. He once admitted that singing a passage often gave him the clue to phrasing.

For two decades Arrau refused to play in his native Chile in protest first against the Marxist government of President Salvador Allende and then against the right-wing dictatorship of General Augusto Pinochet. He eventually returned in triumph in 1981.

He continued to undertake rare and much-awaited performances during his eighties. Although his technical prowess may no longer have been quite what it was, his interpretations grew ever deeper and more mature. He last played in public in 1989.

His earliest tuition came from his mother who was widowed when Arrau was only one year old. Having made a debut at five in his birthplace, Chillán, Arrau moved to Santiago for lessons with Bindo Paoli. He won a government scholarship to study in Berlin after a concert he gave at the age of seven in Santiago which was attended by the then president, Pedro Montt. He was eventually introduced to Krause at the Stern Conservatory, who recognised what he subsequently described as "the greatest piano talent since Liszt". Krause watched over every aspect of Arrau's education and personal well-being like a father while judiciously presenting him to the German public at large. A Berlin recital in 1914 came first, and a Dresden performance of Liszt's A major concerto under Nikisch, the celebrated Hungarian conductor, the year after. Arrau won the Liszt Prize among others in 1919 and 1920 when he also made a successful London debut with Bach's *Goldberg Variations*.

But after Krause's untimely death in 1918 Arrau went through an acute crisis of emotional, artistic and financial insecurity, which, intensified by a calamitous American reception in 1923-4, lasted until his meeting with the Jungian psychoanalyst, Dr Hubert Abrahamsohn, who remained a friend and counsellor for life. With confidence restored, Arrau joined the staff of the Stern Conservatory in 1926 and in 1927 won the Geneva Competition (with Arthur Rubinstein among the judges) while steadily widening his vision by immersion in the teeming cultural and social activity of Berlin in the 1930s.

Shortly before his marriage in 1937 to Ruth Schneider, a soprano, he played

Bach's keyboard works complete in Berlin, following this feat with cycles of Mozart, Weber, Schubert and Beethoven. Mexico City was the first to hear all 32 Beethoven sonatas from him, in 1938. Leaving Germany by a circuitous route in 1940 to settle in America, he gave a recital in New York's Carnegie Hall in February 1941 that provided the turning point in his career. By the 1950s he had the world, including Britain, at his feet, and, until a slight slackening in his last decade, regularly carried out an international schedule of around 130 concerts each year.

A man of wide interests (including dancing, gardening and dogs) and unlimited intellectual and philosophical curiosity and resource, Arrau, an avid reader in many languages, was no believer in musical specialisation. Chopin, Liszt, Debussy, Ravel and Schoenberg, to mention only a few favourites, found as regular a place in his programmes as the German classics (though he gave up playing Bach on the piano after hearing Landowska's harpsichord). It was nevertheless to music of intellectual and visionary grandeur that his temperament, more searchingly Germanic than spontaneously Latin, was most closely attuned, not least to Beethoven's, whose 32 sonatas emerged in a scrupulously annotated Urtext edition of his own in 1978. During the bicentennial celebrations of 1970 he also gave a memorable series of master classes in Bonn on Beethoven.

Arrau was very much at home in the recording studios. He had already made a name for himself in this field with some much-treasured performances in the era of 78rpm records and he continued to visit the studios right into the 1980s, when he embarked on yet another exploration of the Beethoven sonatas, ever his first priority. Throughout his recording career, he worked congenially with all the major conductors, most recently with Giulini, Haitink, and Colin Davis. His approach to the major concerto repertory is reflected in his austere, Olympian readings on record. Nobody achieved more cogently a combination of classical intellect with intuitive, intimate musicianship. If this sometimes meant spontaneity was excluded, it was a price well worth paying for the thoughtfulness of his interpretations.

Sir Neville Cardus once said that Arrau had his "intellect in his fingers", a nice conceit that certainly describes the special quality that separated Arrau from his contemporaries. When he was at the keyboard, you felt palpably the player's mind was dominating all he did. Much of the strength of his style lay in the importance he gave to the left hand, Arrau never being an interpreter who relied mainly on melodic line to delight his audience.

Arrau was aeons away from the popularising influence in classical music abroad today, although that never prevented him talking at length to the press or on radio about his philosophical, laid-back approach to his art and to life. Indeed he was usually keener to talk to a visitor about the latest play or painting he had seen or book he had read than reiterating his well-known views on his own playing. He also could discourse, in his quietly-spoken way, variously on Etruscan art, Proust, Goethe or Turner and always have something valuable to tell his listener.

His interest in psychology was lifelong. As he once commented: "You have to be in touch with your subconscious to stay creative" – and in touch he stayed throughout a very long, productive and satisfying career.

Arrau is survived by two children, Carmen and Christopher.

VISCOUNT ST DAVIDS

Viscount St Davids, 2nd Viscount, died in London on June 10 aged 74. He was born on February 19, 1917.

JESTYN Reginald Austen Plantagenet Philipps, the second Viscount St Davids, became publicly conspicuous in his younger days mainly because of his unlikely pursuits, his marital mishaps and his remarkably ancient lineage. However, he was also a leading inland water mariner and the founder and patron of a floating youth club in premises styled like a pirate's castle which have become a landmark on the Regent's Canal near London Zoo.

St Davids was educated at Eton and Trinity College, Cambridge, married three times, divorced twice and his diverse career included being a mate in a sailing barge, a sergeant in the army, a naval petty officer and a lieutenant in the Royal Naval Volunteer Reserve.

His father was a successful businessman who really did know Lloyd George and received from him the family viscountcy. St Davids senior was already a 13th baronet; the head of a family of great antiquity in south Wales which was descended from a 12th century crusader. He had been one of the founders of the British Electric Traction Company which, as BET, became one of the City's biggest money-spinners. St Davids junior appeared to inherit little of his father's business acumen, however. At various times he devised a new sailor's knot and promoted a boat in the design of a coracle, which goes back to the time of the ancient Britons, but at the age of 37 he was forced to sell Roch Castle, his family home in Pembrokeshire, and went bankrupt when his company providing canal barge pleasure trips on the Regent's Canal foundered.

Two years later he became known as the vanishing viscount when he disappeared after leaving his home – and his second wife – apparently to buy a newspaper but instead sailed to West Africa as a deckhand on a merchant ship.

St Davids succeeded to the viscountcy in 1938. In the House of Lords he was joined later by his mother who, as the holder of the baronies of Strange of Knokin, Hungerford and De Moleyns, became the first peeress to sit in the chamber in her own right following the Peerage Act of 1963. Unlike his father who was a Liberal, St Davids accepted the Labour whip. Over the years he spoke out on various, often off-beat, issues: opposing restrictions on immigration, the sale of fireworks to minors and questioning the legal status of the American Hallowe'en practice of "trick or treating". He made little impact politically, however. Indeed, when Jeremy Thorpe, the leader of the Liberal Party, disclosed during the 1974 general election that a peer, whom he did not name, had defected from the Labour Party the political sensation lasted only until it emerged that the peer in question was St Davids. Because of his obscurity Mr Thorpe was generally considered to have

produced not a rabbit but a political mouse and Harold Wilson summed up the Liberal blunder caustically saying: "It seems to me a case of Bertie Wooster rides again with a script partly written from *The Pallisers* by Trollope." In vain did St Davids respond that as far as he knew Bertie Wooster had never been a socialist while he had been one all his political life. A decade or so later, however, he described himself as a convert to Thatcherism – because he was a radical and she was the most radical person around.

Friends and acquaintances enjoyed St Davids's amiable eccentricities – he said the best use he had for *The Times*, after reading it, was to use it to build mountains and embankments for his model railway – and he was clearly happiest when on the water. He lived for a time on a motor yacht called *Tortoise* moored at Paddington Basin, on the Grand Union Canal, and later in a house alongside the Regent's Canal. He promoted enthusiastically the introduction of electric motors to provide a silent, nonpolluting source of power for inland waterway boats. To children in Camden Town he was known as Pegleg or the Pirate King because he founded the Pirate club which gave them the opportunity to muck about in boats. An accident in his youth had give him a crooked back which together with his 6ft 2ins frame, lopsided smile and missing teeth added to his piratical presence. Having enjoyed the water all his life it gave him great pleasure to introduce city children to boating. Sipping sherry as he watched the boats go by, he would reminisce about chartering yachts and diving for shells in the Caribbean, and the time he broke his spine on a Basque cargo boat during the Spanish civil war.

His first marriage was in 1938 to Doreen Guinness by whom he had a son and four daughters. The marriage was dissolved in 1954. In the same year he married Elizabeth Woolf. That marriage was dissolved in 1959 when he married Marjorie Harris. He is survived by his wife and children.

DAME PEGGY ASHCROFT

Dame Peggy Ashcroft, DBE, actress, died on 14 June 1991 aged 83. She was born on December 22, 1907.

SINCE the death of Edith Evans, Peggy Ashcroft had held the undisputed place of first lady of the English stage. Her performances were among the Shakespearian peaks of the past 60 years, but she is no less vividly remembered for her work in the modern repertory and for the television and film roles that won her a huge audience during her final decade. She also had a larger vision of the theatre than can be conveyed by summarising her acting career.

From her girlhood reading of Stanis-

lavsky she was, from the start, an actress in search of a company. She briefly glimpsed her goal during the 1930s and finally achieved it after the war with the foundation of the English Stage Company, the Royal Shakespeare Company and the National Theatre. To each she gave wholehearted support at a crucial time in its fortunes. What they gained from her was not only the services of a great classical star but a moral force which was as visible in her performances as it was in her personal life. She was seen as an embodiment of British integrity, a factor that was turned against her by such critics as James Agate and Kenneth Tynan who persisted in regarding her as

154

a class-bound home counties lady who had no business to be essaying Cleopatra or the Duchess of Malfi. In fact these parts were fully within her range and if one point emerges from the roll-call of her most successful performances it is that there was no such thing as a typical Ashcroft role.

What did set her apart from actors who simply disappear into whatever they are playing was the presence of a central moral intelligence authorising whatever imaginative leap the character demanded. When she became the first establishment actress to play Brecht, or when she first hurled a four-letter word at a West End audience, she left a landmark behind. To recount her life is to tell the story of the English theatrical renaissance.

Edith Margaret Emily Ashcroft was born in Croydon, the second child of a land-agent father and a Danish-German mother — herself an amateur actress who had taken lessons from the poetic speech pioneer Elsie Fogerty, at whose Central School of Speech and Drama the 16-year-old Peggy Ashcroft enrolled on leaving Woodford School. "I learned very little about acting there," she later declared, being as resistant as her fellow student Laurence Olivier to the school's stress on the Voice Beautiful. Her theatrical education began with her reading of Stanislavsky's *My Life in Art* and her discovery of his emigre compatriot Theodore Komisarjevsky who was then revolutionising the English stage from his tiny theatre in Barnes. She made her professional debut in 1926, playing opposite Ralph Richardson in a Birmingham Repertory revival of Barrie's *Dear Brutus* after which — except for illness or personal choice — she was seldom out of work.

In the early years, like any newcomer, she took what was going, though even then she was more at home in London's adventurous little theatres than in the commercial machine. Critics of the time were struck by her freedom from any kind of stage trickery and by the transparent honesty which remained one of her sovereign qualities. One conspicuous

early event was her 1930 performance of Desdemona to Paul Robeson's Othello, which also marked her political awakening (a star in the Savoy Theatre, Robeson was unwelcome upstairs in the hotel). The turning point came not on the professional stage but in the 1932 OUDS production of *Romeo and Juliet* which brought her into contact with undergraduate George Devine and his guest director, John Gielgud, her two closest allies over the next 25 years.

The alliance was delayed by her marriage to Komisarjevsky and a season with the Old Vic where she piled up a succession of Shakespearian leads at breakneck speed under the direction of Harcourt Williams. By then a member of the unofficial "family" that grew up in the Motleys' Studio (Gielgud's designers), hatching theatrical revolution over endless cups of tea, she came into her own as Gielgud's leading actress when he embarked on the untried adventure of setting up a classical company in the West End. Beginning as Juliet in the legendary 1935 New Theatre production, she returned for Gielgud's subsequent seasons at the Queen's and the Haymarket, playing Nina in Komisarjevsky's *The Seagull*, Irina in Michel Saint-Denis's *Three Sisters*, and the Duchess of Malfi (then a controversial novelty) for George Rylands: productions that left an indelible mark on theatrical memory. True to her company loyalties, she also joined in Saint-Denis's ill-fated 1938 Phoenix season before the "family" was dispersed by the war.

Had Gielgud's companies not kept breaking up, she would gladly have stayed inside them. As it was, she rebuilt her career at the Stratford Memorial Theatre (under Anthony Quayle) and in the West End. She often undertook parts with severe misgivings but then turned them to triumph: as with the alcoholic wife in Robert Morley's *Edward, My Son*, the victim-turned-avenger in *The Heiress*, and (originally her prime *bête noire*) the suicidal Hester Collyer in Rattigan's *The Deep Blue Sea*.

The pattern of her career underwent its

second great change in the 1950s with the dawning of the age of subsidy. First she resumed her alliance with Devine in the 1954 *Hedda Gabler* and when Devine launched the English Stage Company two years later, Ashcroft − at the height of her commercial success in Enid Bagnold's *The Chalk Garden* − forsook the Haymarket for the wilderness of Sloane Square to double as Shen Te/Shui Ta in his production of Brecht's *The Good Woman of Setzuan*. The ESC, however, did not maintain a permanent troupe so, although she subsequently joined Devine in revivals of Chekhov and Ibsen, her main allegiance went to Peter Hall's newly-formed Royal Shakespeare Company. She began by reclaiming two shrews, Kate and Paulina in *A War of the Roses*, in which (then in her late fifties) she began as a young girl and aged into a demonic septuagenarian in *Richard III*. This was a woman, Philip Hope-Wallace wrote, "kept alive by sheer passion of inner hate". With Hall, she also became an incomparable advocate of Pinter, Albee, and (when Hall moved on to the National Theatre) Beckett. Just as she had championed the young Peter Hall at the start of the RSC, so she supported his younger successor, Trevor Nunn, with whom she achieved her crowning stage performance as the Countess of Rousillon in the 1981 *All's Well That Ends Well*, in which she lent something Chekhovian to Shakespearian comedy.

Nunn once made the point that actors achieve greatness only in old age when "life has tested them and they've come through." This was clearly true of Ashcroft, both on stage and in her final creative breakthrough on film. Three times married, CND supporter, and veteran campaigner against social injustice (so much so that when she was created DBE in 1956 Hugh Beaumont nicknamed her "the Red Dame"), she was not short of living experience. In her youth an epitome of the intelligent *ingénue*, in middle-age a radical actress exploring the desperation of women of violently contrasted classes and cultures, she finally took on a quality in which

acting became wisdom. Nunn again: "You simply lose yourself in the largeness of her spirit." In her film and television work she was able to take the spectator straight to the heart of character. One of her most remarkable small screen roles was Barbie Batchelor in Paul Scott's *The Jewel in the Crown* (1984), where she showed the development of character from robust decency to ferocious despair with minimal reliance on external effects. This performance won her a BAFTA award. She had acted in films from *The Wandering Jew* of 1933 and had a role in Hitchcock's *The Thirty-Nine Steps* of 1935. But she picked her film parts. She had a success as the Mother Superior in *The Nun's Story* (1958) and won an Oscar as the best supporting actress for her portrayal of Mrs Moore in David Lean's film version of E. M. Forster's *A Passage to India* (1984). At 81, in 1989, she shared the best actress award, the Coppa Volpi Prize, with Geraldine James at the Venice Film Festival for her performance in Sir Peter Hall's film *She's Been Away*. It was a remarkable achievement for an actress who had made her debut 60 years before. Her most recent public appearance was at the Olivier Awards in London in April when she was given a special award to mark her life's service to the theatre.

Her work was always hard to describe. She herself called it a process of arriving at psychological truth by means of tonal accuracy. Externally it was made up of innumerable small details of gesture and facial expression; but what she was clearly mattered more than what she did, with the result that any attempt to express it in words was liable to turn into gush. Colleagues habitually summed her up by contrasts: "English containment and wild passion", "fearlessness and vulnerability", "ferocity and tenderness." Anthony Quayle put it more simply: "She's a crusader, she's *Pilgrim's Progress* to the end."

Besides Komisarjevsky, she was married to Sir Rupert Hart-Davis and to Jeremy Hutchinson (now Lord Hutchinson of Lullington), by whom she leaves a son and a daughter.

LORD MILES

Lord Miles, CBE, actor, director and founder of the Mermaid Theatre, died on June 14 aged 83. He was born on September 27, 1907.

BERNARD Miles was one of the most individual figures on the English stage, creator of the Mermaid Theatre and an actor and director who in a crisis never lost his confidence. This gallant assurance sustained him during many testing periods when the Mermaid, and all that it meant to him, was endangered. He was a complete theatre man having been during his early years designer, stage carpenter, property-master and scenic artist. He was a racy character actor and a loyal company member but was happiest when he was alone with his impersonation of a gnarled countryman in an old hat and reprehensible corduroys, speaking in a broad Chiltern accent − the kind of voice

a clod of loam might use if it were given tongue. During such performances he stood behind a cart-wheel that became his inseparable companion on the variety stage. Off-stage he was renowned for never wearing a collar and tie and once had to borrow one from a Royal Marine usher to get past Black Rod into the House of Lords.

Although he was to become one of only a handful of actor-peers and appeared in Greek tragedy, he could never lay claim to the peaks of stage performance. But some of his roles linger in the mind, notably his magnificent, sinister Iago to the Othello of Frederick Valk. Doubtless he wanted to do too many things. In middle and later life he was profoundly engaged with what had always been his dream, the administration of his own theatre, the first for 350 years in the City of London. He never stopped working for it. Ever ready to talk, explain, argue, coax, he was a splendid salesman and, against all odds, contrived to establish the Mermaid in what had been a derelict, bombed warehouse at Blackfriars. Thereafter, administration, acting, direction, invention – he was prolific in new ideas – filled all his days.

He was not invariably an easy colleague, for when he had decided to do a thing, he did it. His resolution – some might call it obstinacy – could imperil work on which his heart was set. Basically generous, he could be ruthless on the Mermaid's behalf. He made lasting friendships; but paradoxically for all his daily gregariousness he remained a man alone, fortunate in the constant understanding of his wife, Josephine.

Bernard Miles loved the history of the English theatre about which he wrote, talked, and anthologised with a fluency and vigour natural to him. He had collected a fine library, most of it sold when the Mermaid needed funds; and he had a curious, detailed knowledge of the stage over four centuries or so. Especially he loved the late Elizabethan and Jacobean theatre: his insistence that audiences would agree led to some Mermaid disappointments.

Bernard James Miles was born at Uxbridge, the son of Edwin James Miles and his wife, Barbara. He was brought up in a Baptist household. From his father, a market gardener, he learned a love of country life and lore and from both his parents (his mother was a Scottish cook) an understanding of the virtues of effort and hard work. He was educated at Uxbridge County School and Pembroke College, Oxford. After university he started work as a schoolmaster. But he did not stick at it for long.

In 1930 he made a stage debut as the second messenger in Baliol Holloway's revival of *Richard III*. Later he spent several years using his skills – actor to carpenter – in a number of repertory companies. He found a London name in *Late Joys* at the Players' during 1938-9 and particularly in three Herbert Farjeon revues, first at the Little (1939) and, early in the war, in the two productions of

Diversion (Wyndham's). During 1941 he toured as Iago with the Old Vic company and acted the part uncannily at the New Theatre in July 1942. A couple of months later he directed *Men In Shadow* (Vaudeville) and that December followed John Mills in the leading part.

His work for the Old Vic at the New (1947-8) moved between the Inquisitor (*Saint Joan*) and Christopher Sly. These were almost his last stage parts except a consistent music-hall run as his old countryman – obviously a poacher in a useful way of business – before the Mermaid was born as an Elizabethan-style playhouse in the garden of his home at St John's Wood. There during 1951 he was Caliban in *The Tempest* and persuaded Kirsten Flagstad, Edith Coates and Maggie Teyte to sing in Purcell's *Dido and Aeneas*. Next year he was Macbeth – the cast used something thought to approximate to Jacobean pronunciation. And in 1953 he presented four plays when the Mermaid stage and tiring-house were reconstructed at the Royal Exchange in the City.

Determined now to have a permanent Mermaid, he spent six years toiling and talking for it. Constructed in a converted warehouse at Puddle Dock, practically on the site of the old Blackfriars Theatre, it opened in May 1959 with *Lock Up Your Daughters*, Miles's musical version of Fielding's *Rape Upon Rape*. That Christmas he was Long John Silver in his own adaptation of *Treasure Island*, a production and a role which was to become a great favourite, especially with children as a Christmas show. It was revived repeatedly at the Mermaid over the years and Miles also played the role at the New London Theatre and had toured in it as far afield as Canada.

Sometimes he carried the Long John Silver swashbuckling persona over into his off-stage dealings, as on one occasion when he "kidnapped" the governor of the Bank of England, taking him for a short boat journey on the Thames during the course of which he relieved him of a cheque for £25 to help the Mermaid cause. This piece of buccaneering allowed him to say thereafter that the Mermaid was "supported by the Bank of England".

The rest of the story is one of courageous devotion to an ideal. Companies at the Mermaid might sometimes be competent rather than outstanding but Miles let nothing obscure his favourite plays, particularly the Jacobeans and those of Bernard Shaw. Though he could cast himself wrongly – as John Gabriel Borkman or Oedipus – he took such richly fruitful chances as Ezra in *All In Good Time* (1963), Brecht's Schweik in *Schweik in the Second World War* (1963) and a Falstaff played with immense relish in both parts of *Henry IV* (1970). The Mermaid's extraordinary list could vary between the Greek tragedies and Pinero's *Dandy Dick* besides innumerable Sunday night programmes; there was also the thriving Molecule Club which explained the wonders of science to a young audience. Administering, directing, acting, Miles was unwearied in spite of moments when the adventure seemed to falter. (It was saved at one point by the lease of the theatre for a long run of *Hadrian VIII*.) During the 1970s it staged a pair of acclaimed song-anthologies, *Cowardly Custard* and *Side by Side with Sondheim*.

Because of elaborate reconstruction around it the Mermaid was doomed to a long closure. But Miles's enthusiasm and sheer hard work got a new and enlarged building, with an impressively deep stage, to open on the site in the summer of 1981. Unfortunately the production with which it reopened, a musical version of the 17th century play *Eastward Ho!*, proved to be a financial disaster and lost £80,000. Over the next two years the theatre ran up a deficit of £650,000 which impelled its trustees to order its sale. Miles stood down as artistic director.

He and his wife, the actress Josephine Wilson, who was his unstinting partner at the Mermaid, had sunk almost all their own money into the theatre and in 1989 were forced to move from their four-bedroomed house in Canonbury, north London, to a flat. Following his wife's death in 1990 Miles lived in a Middlesex nursing home, suffering from the effects of a badly broken leg, reportedly with only his state pension as an income and, so it seemed for a while, forgotten at the Mermaid. However, when reports were published of his financial circumstances the theatre's new management staged a gala benefit in his honour in March this year. This was attended by Lord Miles, by then confined to a wheelchair and suffering from a degree of deafness, but able to enjoy the tributes which were paid to him.

Bernard Miles had a long film career, beginning (1932) in *Channel Crossing* and going on to such films as *Quiet Wedding* (1940) and the splendid Noël Coward-directed flag-waving vehicle *In Which We Serve* (1942). Playing alongside a galaxy of British stars including Coward himself, John Mills, Celia Johnson, Richard Attenborough and Michael Wilding, Miles carved out a niche in the film for himself as one of the members of the crew of a destroyer which has been torpedoed. Later films included *Moby Dick* (1956), *The Smallest Show on Earth* (1957) and *Heavens Above* (1963). He was co-author and co-director and played the lead in *Tawny Pipit* (1944), a gentle comedy about the disruption to the life of a sleepy wartime village caused by the arrival of two rare birds to nest in a local meadow. He was also known to television audiences, not least for the catch phrases he popularised – "It looks good, it tastes good and by golly it does you good" – in an advertisement for Mackeson's stout and "Go to work on an egg," for the Egg Marketing Board. His Long John Silver was also seen on the small screen in a BBC serial version of *Treasure Island* in the 1950s. His books were: *The British Theatre* (1947), *God's Brainwave* (1972), *Favourite Tales from Shakespeare* (1976) and (edited with the late J. C. Trewin) *Curtain Calls* (1981).

Miles was created CBE in 1953, knighted in 1969 and made a life peer in 1979 as Lord Miles, of Blackfriars in the City of London.

He is survived by a son and a daughter.

VLADIMIR PETROV

Vladimir Petrov, a former Soviet spy who defected to Australia, died on June 14 in hospital, aged 84, after 37 years in hiding. He was born on February 15, 1907.

VLADIMIR Petrov was a Soviet spy at the height of the cold war whose revelations during his debriefing after defection provided independent confirmation from behind the Iron Curtain that Burgess and Maclean had been recruited by the Soviets while still at Cambridge. But in spite of this clue Anthony Blunt, who helped to enmesh them and later served in the Security Service, was not uncovered; and his spying career did not end until 1964.

Burgess and Maclean were to prove to be a major source of information for the Soviets. Petrov disclosed during his debriefing that the volume of espionage traffic coming out of London from Bur-

160

gess and Maclean was so enormous that radio cipher clerks at the Soviet Embassy were kept busy coding for sometimes 12 hours a day.

There remains controversy over the exact extent of the Petrov revelations. Mr Ron Richards, the former deputy director of the Australian Security Intelligence Organisation, was quoted as saying that their defection resulted in more than 600 Soviet agents in Europe and Australia being identified. But Mr Gareth Evans, Australia's Foreign Minister, said yesterday he did not know of any.

Petrov and his wife Evdokia were both identified as senior KGB agents and he arrived in Canberra in February 1951, nominally as consul. He came into the old espionage service before it became known as the KGB. The Australian Security Intelligence Organisation within months used one of their own men, Michael Bialoguski, to contact him. Petrov's cover was blown anyway because the West's intelligence services had his career on file. Bialoguski, a Polish refugee used to acting as a communist sympathiser, seized on Petrov's grievance with the Russian ambassador, whose wife had quarrelled with Mrs Petrov.

Petrov was said to have become alarmed at the possibility of recall to Moscow, fearing arrest and banishment to a labour camp. Australian intelligence had a tape recording of him arranging for completion of the purchase of a farm in Australia and defection.

Petrov had kept the defection plan secret from his wife, since she, too, was in the KGB, but did not tell this to the Australians. When the Russians realised he had disappeared she was kept under guard at the Embassy. Australians surged forward in protest as the Russians drove her under guard to Sydney airport to be escorted on the first stage of a flight back to Moscow. When she told the crew she wanted to stay in Australia, the captain alerted Darwin and police came aboard. They disarmed the two Soviet guards who were carrying Walther automatics.

The defection was a shot in the arm for Australia's anti-communist prime minister Mr Robert Menzies on the eve of a general election. When he set up a Royal Commission into the affair, accusations of witch-hunting came from the Labor Party.

Petrov disclosed that he had been instructed by the Soviets to set up a fifth column in Australia in case of war. He was instructed to recruit agents with access to intelligence and counter-intelligence work. Interception and unmasking of enemy agents in Russia was also part of the plan.

One of the more intriguing revelations by Petrov, in view of later developments, was his claim in *The People* of September 18, 1955, that Burgess and Maclean had been recruited by the Soviets before they had graduated from Cambridge. Philby, who for the time being kept his cover, took refuge in the fact that if that was all Petrov knew he could survive the immediate attentions of MI5.

Petrov, chief at Canberra of the Soviet spy network, got news of the Burgess and Maclean secrets from his assistant, Kislytsin. Kislytsin had been stationed in London where he was in personal touch with the two diplomats and afterwards worked in the department in Moscow handling the Burgess and Maclean operation. The British Foreign Office following *The People* story was forced in 1955 to publish a White Paper on the affair but there was no mention in it of any suspicion attaching to Philby, who had also been at Cambridge in the early 1930s. In Washington, where Philby had served in the SIS to liaise with American intelligence, the FBI director J. Edgar Hoover was reportedly furious and appalled that Philby had apparently been exonerated and is believed to have leaked information to the *New York Sunday News* which for the first time published on October 23, 1955 that Philby was the Third Man. Philby's name, after more than a year, was now in the open, but he still managed to survive, so far unscathed. Nevertheless Petrov in a small but important way had helped set in motion moves which would eventually make the Philby scandal public.

SEBASTIAN WALKER

Sebastian Walker, children's book publisher, died on June 16, aged 48. He was born on December 11, 1942.

ON THE surface at least "Sebby" Walker was like a character from the children's books he published so effectively − a Mr Munificence who launched a company which produced joyful collections of baby books, toddlers tales and kids capers. Children delighted in their brightness; parents approved of their literacy. Authors flocked to him because he paid them the largest advances. And he pampered his staff, first by providing them with elegant office space and free lunches; then by establishing a company nursery; and eventually by giving them, together with his authors and illustrators, 51 per cent of his company.

Some outsiders complained that many of his books concentrated more on style than substance, providing remarkably few words alongside the extravagant illustrations; and others of his petulance

in his professional relationships. But it was a fairy-tale approach to publishing which paid off. At a time of take-overs and amalgamations in the trade Sebastian Walker successfully established his company as the only major independent specialist in children's books. Walker Books won four of the five major awards for children's titles in 1989 and now produces 300 titles a year with an annual turnover of about £25 million. "Crumbs," Sebby would say. Although a childless bachelor he had an instinctive appreciation of what would appeal to the young as well as an exceedingly astute marketing technique. He was much given to the use of childish language and on his 40th birthday his staff gave him an illustrated ABC: "A is for Absolutely! B is for Boardbook, C is for Crumbs," etc.

Sebastian Walker was born into a family which owned a prosperous engineering company and was educated at Rugby − where Salman Rushdie was a contemporary − and at New College, Oxford, where he read French. He worked for a time in the family business, only turning to book publishing in 1970 when he became a representative in the Cape-Chatto & Windus consortium. He quickly rose to European sales manager but left in 1975 to join Marshall Cavendish and to begin the development of his special avocation by starting that company's children's imprint. He returned to Chatto two years later as a director with particular responsibility for children's books and in 1980 really launched on his career with the establishment of his own company, operating initially from his spare bedroom.

There were several reasons for its success. Walker worked – almost obsessively – hard to build his company. He was an unashamed and highly persuasive pirate of other publishers' outstanding authors. He was also an able and aggressive marketeer with original ideas. While dining in the company of Lady Sainsbury – the wife of the supermarket magnate – in 1985 he suggested selling children's books in Sainsbury stores with the result that today nearly three million Walker books a year ride to cash-counters in supermarket trollies alongside cornflakes and fish-fingers. (He boasted that some of his books were cheaper than a tin of baked beans and even more nourishing.)

But above all he gave to children's authors and illustrators in the early 1980s more generous terms, a remarkable sense of commitment to them and their work, and a communicated conviction that children's books were of major significance in the publishing world. It was this that enabled him to develop a list of remarkable strength. His titles ranged from the baby board books of Helen Oxenbury through to powerful and disturbing teenage novels such as *Why Weeps the Brogan* by Hugh Scott, which won the Whitbread Children's prize, and his stable of authors includes such names as Shirley Hughes, Quentin Blake, Nicola Bayley, Martin Handford and Jill Murphy. He was also concerned to give excellent facilities to designers. Nor did his authors and illustrators need to fear

that, overnight after a dramatic deal or coup, they might find themselves working for some strange, huge conglomerate: growing success brought Walker good offers from many sources – Pearson and Simon and Schuster among them – but he was resolute in refusal. He was a crusader in the cause of protecting authors and their works from exploitation at the hands of avaricious multi-national conglomerates and in the cause of protecting children from exploitation. Four-year-olds, he said, were on the threshold of literacy so he eschewed television tie-ins and cassettes in his catalogue.

In 1990 Walker's unprecedented step of signing over 51 per cent of his company to a discretionary trust – he and two associates were the trustees – astonished the publishing world. It was no mere advertising stunt: in March the trust paid £1,000 each to 104 of his authors and illustrators.

All this suggests an entirely amiable and benevolent character. This image was supported by Walker's skilful use of publicity: he enjoyed giving interviews in which – with some relish – he represented himself as a jolly, jokey, likeable chap who produced and purveyed books for kids. In fact his character was far more complex.

In spite of the amenities of its splendid premises in Vauxhall Walk, with its nursery facilities for the children of female employees, Walker Books was not the happiest of ships. Julia MacRae, the doyenne of children's book editors, was one of a number who left the company after lively rows and the earlier departure of Kate Mortimer – brought in from the Rothschild think-tank as chief executive – was acrimonious. Walker worked immensely hard and expected everyone else to do likewise; he had strong opinions and did not welcome dissenters. Indeed, although he led a very full business and social life and had a host of acquaintances, he was essentially a very private, complicated and probably not very happy man, with few really close and easy friends.

JEAN ARTHUR

Jean Arthur, American film and stage actress, died at her home in Carmel, California, on June 19. Reference books are at loggerheads about her age which may have been anywhere between 82 and 90.

THE film career of Jean Arthur began in the silent era in the early Twenties after a spell modelling and playing small parts on the Broadway stage. It was a long and somewhat weary apprenticeship which threatened to submerge her as yet another, predictably pretty, ingénue. In desperation she even returned briefly to the Broadway stage. But the advent of sound films transformed her prospects. Suddenly she was able to demonstrate that she was much more than a tailor-made doll. Petite, and with an inimitable, half squeaky, half husky voice which seemed to go perfectly with her diminutive figure and pert bearing, she brought intelligence and wit to a series of the crazy social comedies which had their heyday in the Thirties and Forties.

It was not a long career. Apart from a few footnote performances it was virtually over by *Shane* (1953), a film which gave her a very different sort of role as the hard-working wife of an honest John homesteader in the pioneering West. But it was a career with its own kind of integrity. Jean Arthur never willingly lent herself to the second rate, once she had established herself in the kind of roles she played better than anyone else.

Her screen debut was in 1923, playing a small role in John Ford's *Cameo Kirby*. At this stage she was just one among many young starlets on the Fox lot, appearing in a string of two-reel comedies and at the end of her year's contract she made numerous other comedies and small Westerns for other companies. Their titles give some idea of their weight and content: *Biff Bang Buddy*, *Travellin' Fast*, *Tearin Loose*, *Thundering Through*, &c.

Her first leading role was in *The Poor Nut* (1927) opposite Jack Mulhall. Thereafter things improved professionally speaking. She had her first important part as Richard Dix's leading lady in *Warming Up* (1928) and a number of films for Paramount followed, among them *The Sins of the Fathers* (1928), *The Mysterious Dr Fu Manchu* (1929) and *The Return of Dr Fu Manchu* (1930). But she found none of this particularly satisfying from a personal point of view and in 1932 she left films briefly to go back to Broadway. If she did not make a great success of it she nevertheless demonstrated that she was more than just a pretty face. When she returned to Hollywood it was to encounter changes which worked very much in her favour.

The arrival of sound film revealed to Hollywood that as well as an attractive presence she had an agreeably husky voice and a piquant personality. It was only a matter of time before someone should have the idea of featuring her in one of the fast-moving, whacky comedies of the period. Her real break came in 1935 when she appeared in John Ford's *The Whole Town's Talking*, opposite Edward G. Robinson who played a gangster with a penchant for posing as his double, a meek little clerk. This was a great hit with the public. In the following year her performance in *Mr Deeds Goes to Town*, as a hard-nosed reporter eventually succumbing to the innocent charms of

Gary Cooper, who played a small town poet who arrives in New York with more money than street sense, gave her one of her biggest successes.

This was the first of three famous films in which she appeared under the direction of Frank Capra. She was an ideal Capra heroine, tough yet warm, sensible and practical, yet capable of encompassing the most extravagant ideals and translating them into practical terms. Before continuing her collaboration with Capra, however, she appeared in two other films of some interest, the spectacular de Mille Western *The Plainsman* (1936) and Borzage's *History is Made at Night* (1937), a glossy romance culminating in a sea-disaster based on the sinking of the Titanic.

In her two other Capra films, *You Can't Take It With You* (1938) and *Mr Smith Goes to Washington* (1939), she was partnered by James Stewart. Her forthright style in streetwise roles found a perfect foil in his hesitant and oblique approach. Both films were characteristic Capra mixtures of good-natured comedy and easy sentiment, negotiated with consummate ease by the two principals. In the latter, particularly, as a cynical political aide who nevertheless falls in love with Stewart's politically naive senator, out to expose corruption in high places even if it costs him his career, she was in her element. The film was sheer delight as an uninhibitedly honest look at America by itself. Not surprisingly, the conservative Senator Joseph P. Kennedy pronounced: "I feel that to show the film in foreign countries will do inestimable harm to American prestige all over the world." The world, to this day, has not agreed.

Only Angels have Wings (1939), a typically tough Howard Hawks movie, was not her natural territory, but she held her own against Cary Grant and Rita Hayworth in a tale of romance among cargo plane pilots which never quite came off. During the war Jean Arthur made fewer films than before, but among them were two of the best comedies of the Forties, both directed by George Stevens,

in which she had another chance to show her excellent timing and engaging screen personality. The first was *The Talk of the Town* (1942), with Cary Grant, an unusual blend of comedy and drama in which she played a girl in love with both a murder suspect and his lawyer. In *The More the Merrier* (1943) she played a girl who allows two men to share her apartment in a sprightly romantic comedy. The performance won her her only Oscar nomination.

Her relationship with Hollywood had never been a cordial one, in spite of her success there, and on the day her contract with Columbia ended she skipped round the studio whooping with delight. After the war she returned to private life for much of the time (she was at this time married to the producer Frank Ross), making only occasional appearances in films or on the stage. Her only films of this period were Billy Wilder's bright satirical comedy about life in occupied Berlin, *A Foreign Affair* (1948), and George Steven's classic Western *Shane* (1953) in which she gave a vivid performance in a role which did not call on her characteristic comic gifts. On stage she appeared with great success in *Peter Pan* on Broadway (1955), with Boris Karloff as Captain Hook, and rather less successfully as *St Joan*. Thereafter her appearances were fitful. A television series *The Jean Arthur Show* in the Sixties was not a great success; in the Seventies she returned briefly to the stage opposite Henry Fonda in a play, *The First Monday in October*, but then gave up the role.

Jean Arthur carved out a special place for herself even among the gallery of talented comediennes who were available in Hollywood during the Thirties. If she was not so much at home in the climate of post-war Hollywood and found few suitable comedy roles, this was a considerable loss to the cinema.

She was twice married, firstly, to a photographer, Julian Anker, secondly, to the producer Frank Ross. There were no children of either marriage, both of which ended in divorce.

SIR ISAAC WOLFSON

Sir Isaac Wolfson, 1st Bt, FRS, business-man, philanthropist and creator of the Wolfson Foundation, died on June 20 in Rehovot, Israel, aged 93. He was born on September 17, 1897.

BY TRANSFERRING shares worth £6 million from his company, Great Universal Stores, to a philanthropic foundation in 1955, Isaac Wolfson became Britain's biggest private benefactor since Nuffield. The foundation, whose primary purpose was the advancement of health education and youth activities in Britain and the Commonwealth, helped to establish new colleges at both Oxford and Cambridge and in its first 13 years had disbursed more than £13 million. Wolfson made similarly generous endowments in Israel. All this resulted from the entrepreneurial flair of a man who left Queen's Park school in Glasgow at 15. Isaac Wolfson built up GUS into the largest mail-order business in Europe. He became at one point Britain's biggest retail trader with more than 2,000 shops and accumulated more than 250 companies and it was said, even in the 1950s, that a quarter of the population were his customers.

Wolfson was the son of a Russian Jewish immigrant who settled in Glasgow and worked as a cabinet-maker. On leaving school he at first helped in his father's small furniture workshop for five shillings a week and then went on the road canvassing for orders. The key moment in the advancement of his business appears to have come almost by chance when he encountered the head of a mail order company while selling clocks and mirrors at a stall in Manchester's exhibition hall in 1926. The businessman was impressed by his commercial talent and took him on as a buyer. The firm concerned – Universal Stores – carried on a style of business known as "club trading." It advertised for agents who formed clubs into which the members paid a shilling a week or more. When the subscriptions totted up to £1, the members chose goods from the company catalogue.

The company was renamed Great Universal Stores in 1930, and it is primarily on the impressive growth of GUS that Wolfson's fame and personal fortune came to be built. The early expansion resulted from a series of mostly private deals made during and immediately after the second world war. By the late 1950s, after a series of dramatic takeover operations, he had control of two per cent of the country's shoe shops, five per cent of the furniture business and an important stake in fashion stores, clothing factories, an embryonic supermarket chain, a house-building company and a travel agency.

GUS is still the fifth most valuable retail undertaking in Britain. With a stock market value of £3 billion and profits of more than £400 million a year, it ranks behind only Marks & Spencer and the three largest food supermarket groups. For many years GUS has eschewed expansion into fashionable new business developments or takeover bids to the extent that it is now seen in the City as dull, though extremely solid. Sir Isaac's creation, of which he remained honorary life president, is still by far the biggest mail order group in Britain, with more than a third of that market under several brands, has a large finance business and owns Burberrys and Scotch House stores.

Arising from the work of his foundation, and especially dear to Wolfson's heart, was the establishment of the two Wolfson colleges for post-graduate studies, particularly in science and medicine, at Oxford and Cambridge respectively. In the launching of the first he was closely involved and he played a determining role in finalising the gift from the foundation to the college in 1966. The financial support for Wolfson College, Oxford, came jointly from the Wolfson and the Ford foundations. Delighted with the success of this ambitious educational project, and not least by the impressiveness of the building and the property site – in this area he was an expert – Wolfson remarked in his foundation speech that, although Isaac was a patriarch, Isaiah (Isaiah Berlin was the first Wolfson College president) was a prophet.

Wolfson also took a keen interest in the financing (on which formal agreement was reached in 1972) and opening (by the Queen and the Duke of Edinburgh) of Wolfson College, Cambridge, in 1977. Those present on the occasion recall the genial family atmosphere induced by the presence of a deeply committed Wolfson and his wife, Edith.

Wolfson was a short stocky man who neither drank nor smoked and lived without ostentation. He was understandably gratified by the recognition given to him for his benevolence and those to whom he wrote would notice the string of honorary degrees proudly revealed after his name at the top of his writing-paper. But to most people, he was known chiefly as a shrewd and powerful businessman and his achievements were especially indentified with the period in the 1950s when, along with several other highly individualistic businessmen, he made his mark on British economic history by a rapid-fire series of carefully-planned take-over bids which left him the controller of a large commerical empire and affected the lives of millions at home and at work.

He was appointed merchandise controller of GUS in 1932, and became a joint managing director a few months later, having bought a majority share in the business. In 1946, he also became chairman of GUS and he remained sole chairman until 1986.

In business activities, Wolfson early showed the qualities of drive, exuberence and daring that characterised his operations all his life. As with so many successful entrepreneurs he appreciated the changing demands of his, initially, mostly working and lower middle class customers, and he had an instinctive insight into the possibilities opened up for efficient profitable selling as their living standards improved. He understood that one of the best ways of making money was to lend it and his contemporaries noted that he never insisted on cash payments. During the 1930s, Wolfson also showed his realisation of the need to widen the trading base of GUS – too dependent on the vagaries of mail order – by buying new companies both in the mail order and "tallyman" business, the most important acquisition being that of Alexander Sloan in 1938. During the war years, Wolfson planned ahead for when there would be a resurgence of demand for consumer goods and was helped on the way by the financial weaknesses of many family businesses during the decade 1940-50. His first sortie was into the furniture trade, in 1943, when he bought the privately controlled firm, Jays and Campbells, which owned nearly 200 shops. A series of comparatively modest take-overs – several rebuffed – followed and then, in the 1950s, Wolfson set in train a continuous almost brutal process of business expansion through financial bids.

In these operations, to retain effective family control of GUS itself and to avoid paying cash for new acquisitions, Wolfson made extensive use of a class of share – the "A" Ordinary, without voting rights – which proved very attractive to investors, largely because of the brilliant financial progress of GUS, but which eventually incurred sharp criticism. The first "A" shares were issued in 1952. Thereafter, following acquisitions for cash of several companies, "A" shares were used partially in the take-over of

Town Tailors (owning about 150 Weaver to Wearer shops), Jones and Higgins (after a notable financial tussle), the furnishing group, Oetzmanns, and Waring and Gillow, the big London store. At the same time, in response to hire-purchase restrictions nationally imposed in 1955, Wolfson shifted the emphasis in many of his stores from furniture to a wider range of products. The following year his sustained policy of diversification took a decisive turn with the entry of GUS into the shoe business, when "A" shares and cash were successfully offered for A & W Flateau and the Greenless group, with its 300 or so retail shops.

The acquisition − by agreement with existing boards or direct offers to shareholders − of companies such as Morrisons (Holdings), the Houndsditch Warehouse wholesale group and the outfitters Hope Brothers, in the late 1950s, consolidated the stronghold of GUS on important sectors of British wholesale and retail trade: primarily, furniture, clothing, fabrics, and footwear, although GUS also bought its way into hotels, travel and building supplies.

One of Wolfson's and GUS's most characteristic expansion moves came in the summer of 1968, when a £12.5 million share and cash bid was made for the Times Furnishing-Willerby group. The bid was agreed with the controlling Jacobs family. It added to the GUS empire in men's wear (Neville Reed, John Temple, Hector Power, etc) about 100 additional shops, and to the furnishing chain owned by GUS (already Britain's largest) over 70 new outlets. By the mid-1980s GUS had grown into a somewhat lethargic looking giant, with most of its profits coming from mail order (about 50 per cent), finance (about 29 per cent) and shops and exports.

As early as 1963, when Wolfson joined the board of City Centre Properties, after making a substantial investment in that company, his personal domination of GUS was modified by extensive management re-organisation and he increasingly found time for outside interests. Nonetheless GUS continued to be identified with the name of Isaac Wolfson till his death, even after he had gone to live in Israel and, in 1986, stepped down as joint chairman of the group. It was felt that his influence was largely responsible for the refusal of the board to enfranchise non-voting shareholders and for its lack-lustre though financially solid performance in the early 1980s.

The company was criticised for lack of initiative in the High Street and over-reliance on its cash holdings. In 1986 important management and operational changes were signalled when GUS reached an agreement on business credit with Harris Queensway whose chairman, Sir Philip Harris, joined the board. Subsequently when Wolfson became life president and his son Leonard (Lord) Wolfson joint chairman and managing director, it seemed as if the group was preparing for a thorough re-appraisal of its business strategy.

Wolfson was a sharp and wily business operator in his youth and middle age, an abstemious and religious man, generally affable in his private relationships and an eager art collector besides being a prodigiously generous benefactor of good causes. Many of Wolfson's charitable acts went unrecorded. He tended to fight shy of publicity but in his middle years his interest in Jewry brought him to public attention, notably on the occasion when he played a leading part in the controversy over the appointment, in 1964, of a new minister to the New West End Synagogue. Visiting Israel in 1968, for the Jerusalem Economic Conference, he showed great enthusiasm and imagination in proposing the formation of a strong business consortium to give more thrust to industrial development, both in Israel and where practical in Arab countries.

Wolfson was founder fellow, Wolfson College, Oxford, honorary fellow of the Weizmann Institute of Science, Israel, and a Freeman of the City of Glasgow, to cite just a few of the many honours and dignities conferred on him.

In 1926, Wolfson married Edith Specterman, who died in 1981, and he is survived by his heir, Lord Wolfson.

CYNTHIA LONGFIELD

Cynthia E. Longfield, entomologist, died at Cloyne, Co Cork, aged 94. She was born on August 16, 1896.

CYNTHIA Longfield was an outstanding authority on dragonflies and an intrepid traveller. In 1924, she joined the St George scientific expedition to the Pacific. The expedition, to Coiba, Cocos Island, the Galapagos, the Marquesas, the Tuamotu Archipelago and Tahiti, was a forerunner of many others which she made to remote parts of the world. She travelled much in Africa, including the Congo and Angola.

With her tidy, good clothes and plucked eyebrows, she looked as if she was about to open a rather smart village fete, but her real self would be revealed by such remarks as: "I find machetes so useful in the jungle, don't you?" Once when searching for dragonflies in the Chaco, a largely unexplored and disputed region, she met the Paraguayan army on its way to invade Bolivia. She surprised the Bolivians by telling them what was in store for them. Cynthia Longfield's adventurous travelling led to important scientific results.

The journeys were followed by months of painstaking study at the Natural History Museum, London, where she was an honorary associate. Her work led to the description of new species and the publication of papers which give a deeper understanding of the taxonomy of dragonflies, notably of difficult genera such as *Orthetrum* and *Ceriagrion*.

While working at the museum, she was always willing to drop what she was doing and help other students of dragonflies. She was characteristically generous. She would guide them through the intricacies of taxonomy and give sound practical advice. She had a great influence on those young research workers on dragonflies whom she encouraged. She also enabled a much wider public to delight in these ancient and beautiful creatures and, in so doing, laid a firm base for conservation work.

Her book, *The Dragonflies of the Britih Isles*, which was published in 1937, was the first popular book on the order. It led to an increasing correspondence with observers throughout the United Kingdom and Ireland and enabled her to record the distribution of British dragonflies far more accurately than had been done before. In 1960, she shared the authorship of *Dragonflies* in the New Naturalist Series with two of her younger colleagues. It was particularly fitting that later she was made the first honorary member of the British Dragonfly Society.

Cynthia Longfield was a much valued member of the council of the Royal Entomological Society of London, and was for a time its vice-president. As a wartime firefighter, she on one occasion probably saved the museum, where she worked, from destruction.

GERALD PRIESTLAND

Gerald Priestland, broadcaster and writer, died on June 20 aged 64. He was born on February 26, 1927.

GERALD Priestland, who had an eventful career as a foreign correspondent before becoming the BBC's religious affairs correspondent, liked to tell how he came closest to losing his life as a reporter when covering the papal elections in 1978. He and a colleague were tottering dinnerwards through the alleyways near Rome's Pantheon after imbibing too well from a bottle of Scotch when they found themselve blocking the path of an impatient motorist. Reluctantly making way for the vehicle, Priestland gave it a hearty thump as it passed causing the car to squeal to a halt and four men to leap out drawing pistols. As it became clear they were a mobile anti-terrorist squad on the prowl for subversives, Priestland flung his hands up shouting: "Don't shoot, don't shoot! I'm only a poor drunken English journalist, the religious affairs correspondent of the BBC!"

The anecdote captured the irreverent manner in which Priestland brought the earthy style of the worldy hack to the more ethereal realm of religious affairs reporting. To some he was a pompous bore and his down to earth style upset the more straight-laced religious adherents (as on the occasion he said that the blood of

Christ was not really his cup of tea). But in the main he had considerable success in bringing religion to a mass audience. *Priestland's Progress*, a series of 13 Radio Four religious programmes broadcast in 1981 which he described as a plain man's guide to religious faith, was heard by millions and attracted a postbag of 20,000 letters, an unprecedented response for a religious programme. The book of the series was a best-seller and the same year listeners to BBC Radio Four's early morning *Today* programme voted him ahead of the Pope and second only to the Prince of Wales as their man of the year. Priestland's irreverence was astutely applied. He believed passionately in the need to awaken the latent interest in religion of the man in the street and he used his expertise as a reporter in doing so.

In spite of his BBC training he did not believe his job to be that of a mere reporter providing neutral facts. He was a committed Christian, he said, and as such an interpretive correspondent dealing with metaphysical affairs which could not be measured in the way economic and political correspondents could more dispassionately measure money or votes. People in Britain, he maintained, were fundamentally religious but because of neglect of their spiritual concerns by the media, the failure of the Church and the education system, many thought religion was "old fashioned, a bit loony and something to be ashamed of." His approach was to question everything and to "get religion out of the Gothic arches of the past."

He castigated the Church of England in 1986 over its handling of the dispute surrounding acceptance of women priests which he said seemed to the general public to be ludicrous and almost beyond comprehension. At a time when the nation was being corroded by atheism, materialism and armchair humanism, the Church of England was fiddling while Canterbury burned, he said. The shame was that it was the Christians who were doing the fiddling.

Gerald Francis Priestland was born in Berkhamsted, Hertfordshire, and educated at Charterhouse and New College, Oxford, before joining the BBC where he stayed for 32 years. His first job in 1949 was as a trainee sub-editor where he began by punctuating the weather forecast. After five years he became a foreign correspondent first in India and Pakistan (1954-58) before moving to Washington (1958-61) and then Beirut (1961-65). He went back to Washington as chief correspondent from 1965 until the summer of 1969, most notably interviewing Martin Luther King shortly before the civil righs leader's assassination in 1968. On his return to Broadcasting House he devised and presented Radio Four's *Newsdesk* programme from 1970 to 1974 and remained a presenter on both radio and television until 1976.

He did not become a committed Christian until 1976 — the year before he was appointed Religious Affairs Correspondent — when he became a Quaker. Reporters are usually regarded as a hard-bitten ungodly lot so it was an unexpected conversion. Priestland's turning point was a nervous breakdown which he attributed to the violence he had seen while covering the Vietnam war and race riots in America. He recovered from his state of depression with the help of psychiatric treatment during which he said he became aware of the love of God and the reality of forgiveness. He became a Quaker partly because of his friendship with Gerard Hoffnung and found it the ideal base from which to operate because nobody felt threatened by it.

Priestland left the BBC in 1982 and concentrated on writing books. Among these were: *Who Needs the Church?* (1983); *Priestland Right and Wrong* (1983); *The Case Against God* (1984); *For All the Saints* (1985); an autobiography, *Something Understood* (1986) and *The Unquiet Suitcase* (1988). Earlier books included: *America: The Changing Nation* (1968) and *The Future of Violence* (1976).

Priestland died in hospital after suffering a stroke while returning from a shopping trip. He is survived by his wife, Sylvia, two daughters and two sons.

RUSSELL HINZE

Russell Hinze, Australian politician, died on June 29 aged 72. He was born on June 19, 1919.

ALTHOUGH he remained a Queensland state politician, the moral and physical phenomenon of Russ Hinze loomed larger to most Australians than any federal leader of the past 20 years. Outrageous, hilarious, and the key minister in the Queensland National government of Sir Johannes Bjelke-Petersen, in America he might have been an invention of Tennessee Williams. Russell James Hinze's hulking 22-stone frame, richly blasphemous tongue, extreme right-wing prejudices, and personal fortunes, made in areas over which he held ministerial portfolios, embodied the classic image of an old-time outback politician. He ended up as Bjelke-Petersen's "Minister for Everything".

Hinze died of pneumonia while facing criminal charges for allegedly receiving A$1.4m in corrupt payments while a state minister. He claimed his long battle

172

against cancer prevented him from appearing in court, athough this did not stop him watching his horses at the race track and chatting with his gambling cronies almost to the end.

The current Labor government of Queensland refused him a state funeral but offered to pay the expenses, which his widow Fay promptly donated to charity. His prosecution followed the Fitzgerald Royal Commission which alleged years of corrupt government under the former National party premier, Sir Joh Bjelke-Petersen. But even among some of his enemies there was a curious affection for Hinze, the man who said cattle duffers (rustlers) should be "shot and questioned later", rapists should be castrated and capital punishment should be reinstated, using the firing squad. Among his supporters, he was considered a mischievous saint.

He was worth an estimated A$10-15m when he died in a private hospital on Queensland's garish high-rise holiday strip called "the Gold Coast", the region he helped create, and which helped make his fortune. Born in Brisbane, he left school at 12 to work with his father, a farmer and logger. After a tough upbringing in the Depression, he said he learnt mathematics and letter-writing as secretary of the local cricket club, becoming a local councillor and then the state MP for South Coast in 1966. The outspoken back-bencher was made minister for local government and main roads in 1974 — earning him the soubriquet the "Colossus of Roads". Hinze ignored the clamour of protests over a perceived conflict of interests when he almost immediately started to dig up his dairy farm for gravel to supply his state road building projects. He maintained the same stance of innocence as allegations of corruption from opposition politicians and the media escalated as he acquired further portfolios including that of the police. Of his qualifications for this Hinze laughed: "I've got big feet, no brains and I'm 21 stone."

A young traffic policeman who stopped the new minister's car was told by Hinze: "Right son, where would you prefer to go, Birdsville or Bedourie?" — two of the most isolated spots in the Australian interior. Aborigines were "drop-outs, hangers-on and agitators"; Hinze's attempt to have "dull bludgers", or cheats, identified with neck chains and tattoos was rejected. His fame spread to Britain in the mid-1980s where the *Sun* newspaper called him "supergut" after he was pictured in Queensland's inaugural Beer Belly Championships, laughing and exposing his vast, naked torso.

But behind the humour were growing reports of his involvement with Queensland's "white shoe" brigade of property developers during the state's tourist boom. Hinze was forced to resign from the Queensland parliament in May 1988. The following November he was questioned for eight days by the Fitzgerald Royal Commission about loans and payments totalling A$1.14m from developers. He denied all charges, saying the money was borrowed from friends and always paid back.

In December 1989 Hinze was remanded on bail at Brisbane Magistrates Court on charges of corruptly receiving A$520,000 from developers. Last December Australian property developer George Herscu was jailed for bribing Hinze. Hinze maintained his innocence to the end, saying: "I've been sentenced by the Lord."

Of Queensland's notorious electoral gerrymander, which kept the National party in power for so long, Hinze once said: "I told the premier (Bjelke-Petersen), If you want the boundaries rigged, let me do it and we'll stay in office forever. If you don't, people will say you are stupid." His only disappointment was not becoming premier. Hinze said: "I'm just a bit unlucky that I struck Joh Petersen. He's so bloody healthy." Bjelke-Petersen, who was forced to resign as premier in 1987 after 19 years in office, also faces criminal charges arising from the Queensland corruption enquiry.

Besides his widow, Fay, he leaves three sons and three daughters by a previous marriage.

LEE REMICK

Lee Remick, American actress, died of cancer on July 2 in Los Angeles aged 55. She was born on December 14, 1935.

A NATURAL beauty, with blonde hair and striking blue eyes, Lee Remick was an intelligent and versatile performer. As the years went by she matured marvellously without ever seeming to age. Imperceptibly the innocent blue-eyed young girl of her early films took on the deeper nuances of her latter roles. She became an adept at expressing the apprehension of a woman who has lived life and knows the cause of fear. Though she had a lovely face that could melt hearts, it was the eyes that were her most striking characteristic. They could express sheer delight or – and even more effectively – combine with nervously sloping eyebrows and an ever so slightly puckered brow, to send a frisson of apprehension to the back of the cinema. It was a face and a capacity to express emotion which lent distinction even to such shameless shockers as the *Omen* series of films with their crude assault on the senses. When harnessed to a role of real quality the face

became a mask concealing depths of complexity and feeling. Her range became much wider than her early roles might have suggested it would be. Beginning as a pretty sex symbol she soon rebelled against what could have been the fatal typecasting which is so useful to Hollywood film-makers and to which, apparently, American film audiences do not violently object. She was to take in her stride an alcoholic in *Days of Wine and Roses*, a mental wreck in *The Women's Room*, an introverted pianist in *The Competition*, a nymphomaniac in *The Detective* and a rape victim in a remake of *The Letter*.

Lee Remick was very much an intuitive actress although she claimed in later life that she had never meant to become one. But at school she had loved reciting poems "the long ones" she always said, which to the chagrin of her classmates she never had any trouble learning. She was in fact blessed with a freak memory which was to stand her in good stead in her later career. There was no film script which she could not commit to memory after three readings. Few needed even that much attention.

She was born in Boston, Massachusetts, where her father was a department store owner and her mother an actress, Patricia Remick. Her parents divorced when she was a child and her mother took her to New York when she was seven. There she trained as a dancer, taking ballet lessons as a child and later studying modern dance, and made her first stage appearance in summer stock when she was 17. While attending finishing school in Manhattan she was spotted by an agent and given a part in a Broadway play, *Be Your Age*. She went on to appear in several musicals, including stock company productions of *Brigadoon*, *Show Boat* and *Oklahoma!*

During the 1950s she took part in more than 40 shows for television. She was launched into films by the director, Elia Kazan, who spotted her in a television show, and with fine performances in *Anatomy of a Murder* and *Days of Wine and Roses* quickly established herself as one of Hollywood's leading stars.

She made her film debut in Kazan's *A Face in the Crowd* in 1957. Her small part as a nubile drum majorette attracted immediate attention and she soon went on to bigger things: the Southern temptress of William Faulkner's *The Long Hot Summer* and the alleged rape victim in *Anatomy of a Murder*, provocatively removing her glasses and letting down her hair during the trial.

Kazan directed her again in *Wild River*, as a widow comforted by Montgomery Clift. This time the sexuality was kept cleverly in check and it was a subtle performance. Even better was her portrayal as Jack Lemmon's alcoholic wife in *Days of Wine and Roses*, a painful study in disintegration which brought her an Oscar nomination.

She was excellent as the calming wife of Steve McQueen's paroled convict in a neglected film, *Baby the Rain Must Fall*, and in 1966 she spent a year on Broadway playing the blind woman in Frederick Knott's thriller, *Wait Until Dark*, directed by Arthur Penn.

Back in the cinema, she enjoyed herself as one of Rod Steiger's intended murder victims in the black comedy, *No Way to Treat a Lady* and was sexually provocative again as Frank Sinatra's nymphomaniac wife in *The Detective*. At the end of the 1960s she came to Britain to make *A Severed Head*, from Iris Murdoch's novel, and Joe Orton's *Loot*, providing a rich comic performance as the doll-like nurse. In 1970 she married William (Kip) Gowans, a British assistant film director, and for the next 12 years they made their home in London. During the 1970s her films included Edward Albee's *A Delicate Balance* and *The Omen*, in which she played the distraught mother of the anti-Christ child. The best of her later film roles was the capricious baroness seeking a husband in Boston in James Ivory's *The Europeans*.

By now she was turning increasingly to television. She had made an impressive BBC debut in 1972, playing the frustrated Southern spinster in Tennessee Williams's *Summer and Smoke* and three years later she enjoyed a big popular success, and won a BAFTA award, as Winston Churchill's American mother in *Jennie*.

She played General Eisenhower's British chauffeur and secret lover, Kay Summersby, in *Ike* and among other television series were *Wheels* and *Mistral's Daughter*. In 1987 she returned to the BBC to star opposite Dirk Bogarde in *The Vision*, an apocalyptic look at television in the satellite age. In 1976 she made her British stage debut as Cherie, the good-hearted tart, in the first London production of William Inge's *Bus Stop* at the Phoenix Theatre.

Lee Remick had been a close friend of Jill Ireland, British actress and wife of Charles Bronson, who died of cancer in May 1990. After her friend's death Lee Remick became a spokeswoman for victims of cancer and helped raise money for research into the disease.

Her first marriage, to the American television director, Bill Colleran, was dissolved in 1968. There were two children.

SIR BERNARD WALEY-COHEN

Sir Bernard Nathaniel Waley-Cohen, Bt, Lord Mayor of London in 1960, died on July 3 aged 77. He was born on May 29, 1914.

SIR Bernard Waley-Cohen was a leading banker, industrialist and farmer whose services to the City of London reached their apogee when he was elected Lord Mayor in 1960. At the age of 46, he was the second youngest Lord Mayor to be appointed this century and followed in the footsteps of an ancestor in holding the office.

He was born in London, the elder son of Sir Robert Waley-Cohen, KBE, and Alice Violet, daughter of Henry Edward Beddington. Sir Robert, who died in 1952, was an oil industry pioneer and Shell's first managing director. He rose to become the leading lay figure in Anglo/Jewry and his children were reared in the dual tradition of service to country and community.

In 1927 Bernard Waley-Cohen entered Britannia Royal Naval College, Dartmouth. To his great disappointment, after more than half-way through the course, his eyesight was adjudged to be below the exacting standards required. He had to leave Dartmouth and went to Clifton College, Bristol, his father's alma

mater, where he became head of Polack's, the Jewish House founded by his great uncle, Lionel Cohen. As his father before him, he subsequently served on the college council and governing body, retiring after a 30-year stint. From Clifton he went to Magdalene College, Cambridge, where he read modern history and helped to found the undergraduate newspaper, *Varsity Weekly*.

His career in the City started immediately he came down from Cambridge in 1936 as a fledgling in Lloyd's underwriting "box". After three years he was elected a Lloyd's underwriting member. He became a liveryman of the Clothworkers' Company, of which his father was master in 1944.

In 1937 he joined the Honourable Artillery Company but the following year, as the result of a riding accident, he lost the use of his right eye and was discharged. During the second world war, he served respectively as an executive officer attached to the Port of London Emergency Service, recruiting officer and commander of the Exmoor patrol of the Home Guard and, from 1940 to 1947, as principal at the Ministry of Fuel and Power, where he was concerned with building up emergency stocks of coal at strategic positions throughout the United Kingdom.

Returning after the war to the world of finance and commerce, he became a director of the Palestine Corporation, founded in 1922 by a group of leading figures in the City to foster the economic development of the territory. From 1947 to 1954 he served as vice-chairman of the corporation and its Union Bank of Israel.

City administration began to claim an increasing amount of his time and energy. The family connection with the City spanned six generations, extending back to Waley-Cohen's great-great-great grandfather, Levi Barent Cohen, who had left his native Holland to establish himself in the City as early as 1778.

Following his appointment in 1949 as one of HM Lieutenants for the City of London, he was elected the same year as an alderman for the Portsoken Ward and six years later was elected sheriff. In a speech on his election to the shrievalty, he proudly alluded to his long family connection with the City, remarking that one of his forebears, Sir David Salomons, had taken office as sheriff 120 years previously. Sir David, a doughty fighter for religious emanicpation, became the first Jewish Lord Mayor of London in 1855. Sir Bernard — he had been created KBE in 1957 — followed his illustrious ancestor in becoming the seventh Jew to be elected Lord Mayor in 1960. On his election as the City's first citizen, he spoke of himself as "a proud Englishman of the Jewish faith" with a strong family attachment. In office he was punctilious in upholding the City's traditions and he carried out his duties with great zeal and application. At the same time he did not neglect his work for the Jewish community as vice-president of the United Synagogue (Anglo-Jewry's premier religious body) as treasurer of the Jewish Welfare Board and at the helm of several philanthropic and cultural societies.

Outside the City and his business interests he devoted much of his time to the furtherance of education. Apart from his close connection with Clifton College, he was chairman of University College London, from 1971 to 1980.

His term of office as Lord Mayor was particularly memorable in that it included a 30,000 mile two-month tour of Australia, New Zealand and several Far East countries. The tour, undertaken during the summer recess to avoid interference with civic duties, proved to be a remarkable exercise in fraternal goodwill, cementing ties between the City of London and the administrations of the countries visited.

A month or so before the Australian tour, the Lord Mayor had paid an official visit to Holland, in the course of which he was received by the Mayor of Amersfoort in the local town hall, once the residence of an ancestor who had settled in the town as a tobacco dealer in 1690 and had founded a synagogue there.

Another memorable occasion was when Waley-Cohen gave a Guildhall banquet for President Bourguiba of Tunisia, affording the opportunity for a demonstration of inter-faith goodwill between Muslims, Christians and Jews. The only problem was the form of grace at the meal which each representative of the monotheistic religions would find appropriate. It was amicably solved when the Lord Mayor's chaplain recited a theocentric grace with which all could concur.

On the completion of his term of office as Lord Mayor, Waley-Cohen was elevated to a baronetcy. Relinquishing office did not imply a diminution of public work and in 1971 he was appointed a commissioner and deputy chairman of the Public Works Loan Commission.

Apart from his civic and business interests, Waley-Cohen loved nothing more than to repair to his estate on Exmoor. He was an enthusiastic countryman who took great pride in owning one of the largest herds of pedigree Devon cattle in the country, which won golden opinions and many prizes at local shows.

As chairman of the Devon and Somerset Staghounds, he became embroiled in a fierce controversy with anti-bloodsport organisations, which led to an acrimonious newspaper correspondence. In his younger days he had taken part in point-to-point riding, from which he retired in 1952 after winning the Devon and Somerset Hunt Cup. Shooting was another of his hobbies. In temperament Waley-Cohen displayed an affable gentility, overlaying a bustling, business-like proficiency. Heavily built and bespectacled, his strong physique matched a strong character. He had played rugby for the Harlequins 'A' team and enjoyed country rambling. In 1934, for a wager, a good dinner, he climbed Mont Blanc without any prior mountaineering experience.

In 1943 he married Joyce Constance Ina, only daughter of the first Baron Nathan of Churt. They had two sons and two daughters.

SIR GODFREY NICHOLSON

Sir Godfrey Nicholson, 1st Bt, former Conservative MP, died on July 14 aged 89. He was born on December 9, 1901.

GODFREY Nicholson had a career as a Conservative MP that started in the era of Stanley Baldwin and Ramsay Mac-Donald and ended in that of Harold Wilson and Edward Heath. He was an individualistic backbencher who always put his principles before the demands of the Whips.

Frequently he found himself speaking in ringing phrases – all the more telling because he had a mild, self-effacing parliamentary style – on behalf of the liberal wing of his party. At the time of Rhodesia's unilateral declaration of independence, for instance, he came out unexpectedly with a denunciation of Ian Smith's "police state". He had the satisfaction of seeing one of his daughters, Emma Nicholson MP, rise to an influential position in the Conservative hierarchy. Another daughter, Rose, is married to Sir Richard Luce, Conservative MP for Shoreham.

Godfrey Nicholson was educated at Winchester and Christ Church, Oxford. People meeting him casually might well have marked him down as an academic

(he was a fellow of the Society of Antiquaries). In fact, by profession he was a distiller, chairman for a time of the family firm. At the age of 30, in the 1931 general election – which was a debacle for Labour – he won the mining seat of Morpeth for the Conservatives. His defeat of "Ebby" Edwards was one of the sensations of the election. As MP for Morpeth he put through Parliament an important measure on workmen's compensation for miners. But, predictably, he lost the seat at the next General Election in 1935.

Nicholson returned to the House in 1937 at a by-election at Farnham, which he represented for nearly thirty years. One of his early concerns was the Government of India Bill, and later he went to India as a member of a parliamentary delegation at the time of independence. During the war he served in the Royal Fusiliers and the Commandos.

Back in the House he never achieved ministerial office but the real and growing respect with which he was held was eventually marked by his election in 1961 to one of the most important posts open to a backbencher: chairman of the estimates committee. In 1958 he was made a baronet.

When Rhodesia, in the time of the Wilson government, unilaterally declared independence, the orthodox Conservative line was to condemn Ian Smith's action but to try to deal with him sympathetically. Nicholson, who had been watching the evolution of the Commonwealth to self-government since the time of the India Bill, had no sympathy with Smith. To deal with him, he told the House, was appeasement, "and appeasement has never won a race yet: it is a bad horse, bred by good intentions out of paralysis of will."

After retiring as an MP in 1966 he attracted political attention again in 1975 by writing a characteristically worded article for *The Times* when Conservative MPs were about to hold the election which led to Mrs Thatcher being chosen as party leader. Nicholson's theme was that what was needed in the next leader was another Stanley Baldwin who would "bind together all classes of our people in an effort to make life in this country better in every sense of the word."

His extra-political interests included the chairmanship of the Friends of Friendless Churches. From 1973 to 1981 he was president of the British Association of Parascending Clubs. He himself made a parachute descent at the age of 60 – "just for fun," he said: "not enough things are done for fun these days."

He married, in 1936, Lady Katharine Constance Lindsay, a daughter of the 27th Earl of Crawford. She died in 1972. He leaves four daughters.

GABY SCHREIBER

Gaby Schreiber, consultant designer, died in London on July 3. She was born in Austria in the early 1920s but was secretive about her exact age.

WITH her work for BOAC, designing the interiors of a series of prestigious passenger jets from the Comet IV to the VC10, Gaby Schreiber established herself as one of Britain's leading post-war interior designers. Another high profile commission came when she was one of five men and three women asked by Cunard to create the interior decor of the QE2 transatlantic liner which, in 1965, was set to be a showpiece of "modern" British industrial and shipping eminence.

An elegant and dynamic brunette who headed her own team of 20 specialists, Schreiber played an influential role in setting the design standards of the 1960s. Gaby Schreiber & Associates were adept at combining their concept of style and taste with required standards of functionality in designs for supermarkets, high street stores, office blocks and factories at a time when the significance of industrial design was little appreciated in Britain. Her operations were based on "versatility not specialism" and she emphasised that her group handled what she called "total design projects, from tea-cups to buildings."

When she was appointed interior design consultant for the BOAC fleets in 1957 one of the airline's senior executives remarked that until then the airline's interior styling had looked as though it had been thought up overnight. Schreiber's task was not only to stamp a distinctive style on the passenger cabins by specifying the colour of the upholstery and tablewear. Her group undertook the shaping of the interior walls and bulkheads, ventilation grilles, lighting, air-conditioning and luggage-racks while taking into account the particular problems of fire-proofing, weight, durability and maintenance.

Gaby Schreiber was a fellow of the Chartered Society of Designers and served for two years on the Council of Industrial Design (now the Design Council), during which time she was twice on the Duke of Edinburgh's selection panel for his prize for elegant design. In her firm, which she formed in 1943, she gathered around her a talented team who crried out a number of important projects. Perhaps the most notable of these were the designing of interiors of the Comet IV, the DC7C and the Britannia.

There was much controversy over the design of the interior of the QE2. Cunard had appointed a team composed largely of interior decorators under Lady Brocklebank, the wife of the Cunard chairman, but also including interior designers James Gardner, Dennis Lennon and Gaby Schreiber. This caused strong criticism and the Board of Trade referred the matter to the Council of Industrial Design who were unable to persuade the Cunard board that there was a difference between an interior decorator and an interior designer and that it was the latter

which was needed in this case.

In the end, on a change of chairmanship of the Cunard company, Lady Brocklebank and several interior decorators resigned and James Gardner was charged with the exterior design of the QE2 in conjunction with the naval architect of the company and Dennis Lennon was put in overall charge of the interior design. He divided the work between himself, Schreiber and several others.

Gaby Schreiber was half Austrian, part German and a little French. She was born in Vienna, the daughter of Peter Wolff, and she studied art and stage design in Vienna, Florence, Berlin and Paris before she came to England not long before the war. She was already married to Leopold Schreiber.

At first she went to work at Lord Antrim's furniture factory at Glenham. During the war she designed plastic eating utensils for the forces and also developed factory-made army huts. After the war she extended her activities to designing more elaborate kitchen and household equipment. Mass production interested her. She saw it as a means of creating luxurious conditions for the public at large and was an early advocate of applying good standards of taste to products sold in chain stores. Schreiber was a successful and efficient businesswoman in an area in which, at that time, it was not easy for a woman to succeed. At the same time she retained her femininity. She dressed at Balmain, spoke four languages and had many friends, who enjoyed her generous hospitality in her beautiful flat in which were displayed a collection of works of art and craft including, at one time, works by Constantine Guy, Marino Marini, Van Gogh, Picasso and Matisse.

She married secondly, in 1953, William Fishbein. Both marriages were dissolved and there were no children.

LORD VIVIAN

Lord Vivian, impresario, died on June 24 aged 85. He was born on March 4, 1906.

IN AN incident which was one of the minor scandals of the time and still evokes something of its flavour, Lord Vivian was shot in the stomach in 1954 by his mistress, Mavis Wheeler. She was the former wife of Sir Mortimer Wheeler, the archaeologist and broadcaster, mistress of the painter Augustus John and sister-in-law of Neville Chamberlain. With a peer and an elegant blonde socialite as its central characters, the shooting drama, captured the newspaper headlines. Although the couple remained devoted to each other, Lord Vivian almost died from his wound and his mistress stood trial for attempted murder.

She was acquitted of that charge but sentenced to six months imprisonment for maliciously wounding him. Appearing in another court on a drinking charge that same year Vivian had caused some hilarity by saying his occupation was "a peer of the realm." That, said the magistrate, was a description, not an occupation. In fact, Anthony Crespigny Claud Vivian, the 5th Baron, had had a varied career before being caught up in the notoriety of the shooting incident. The son of a former Gaiety Girl, he was educated at Eton, worked as a farm labourer in Canada, later helped in the theatre, and became a publicity manager in San Francisco.

On his return to London he was a theatrical and dance-band agent before enlisting in the ranks of the Royal Artillery at the outbreak of the second world war. After being invalided out in 1940 and succeeding to his title, he went into partnership with the legendary impresario C. B. Cochran who was then 74. Their first joint production was Sir Alan Herbert's light opera *Bless the Bride* with music by Vivian Ellis, which ran for two-and-a-half years; but two other joint productions failed. After Cochran's death, Vivian continued mounting West End productions, including a musical revival, *The Two Bouquets*, but without recapturing his earlier success. After the shooting incident he recovered his health but lost control of Cochran Productions. He later had a career in catering, and in 1967, 27 years after succeeding to his title, he made his maiden speech in the House of Lords. Lady Vivian died in 1985.

The couple had two sons and a daughter and Brigadier Nicholas Crespigny Laurence Vivian succeeds to the peerage.

MICHAEL LANDON

Michael Landon, American actor, writer and director, died on July 1 of cancer aged 54. He was born on October 31, 1936.

MICHAEL Landon starred in three long-running television series which spanned three decades. The most popular of them was the 1960s western, *Bonanza*, in which he played the wild, trigger-happy Little Joe, the youngest son of the Cartwright family. Blessed with boyish good looks and an affable screen presence, he followed this with *Little House On The Prairie*, playing the father of the Ingalls family who battled against wolves, Indians and bush fires in the 19th century mid-west. Then came *Highway to Heaven* in which he played an angel.

All three productions were specifically designed to be family entertainments. Landon said he was attracted to what was described as ''uplifting'' television because of his own unhappy childhood.

Having initially been simply an actor, he began writing scripts while in the *Bonanza* cast in 1963. On one occasion when the regular script was late arriving he spent a weekend writing an episode involving the Cartwright brothers being mistaken for bank robbers. Its success led to him writing and then directing other episodes. He later wrote and directed various television films and was also the writer and director of most of the episodes of *Little House on the Prairie*. In 1976 he wrote, directed and acted in *The Loneliest Runner*, a television film based on his own childhood traumas.

Bonanza was a phenomenally successful television series, running for 14 years from 1959 to 1973. During this time it topped the viewing ratings for seven consecutive years in America and was transmitted in 86 other countries with an estimated weekly viewing figure of 400 million. The *Prairie* series ran for eight years from 1974 and *Highway to Heaven* for six from 1984. Landon was scheduled to begin work on a new series when his illness was diagnosed.

Landon was born Eugene Maurice Orowitz in Collingswood, New Jersey. His Roman Catholic mother and Jewish father had fought frequently, he said, and his mother had often threatened suicide. His schooling was also troubled. He had a poor academic record, was frequently involved in fights and recalled being subjected to anti-Semitic taunts. On the strength of his prowess as a javelin thrower he won a place at the University of Southern California. After tearing a ligament he dropped out of college but eventually went to the acting school run by the Warner Bros film studio. Landon was in a number of television productions before his film debut in *I Was a Teenage Werewolf*.

In contrast with his sweet-natured roles on screen Landon had a tempestuous reputation in both his professional and private lives. He was accused of arrogance and of alienating some colleagues with his film-set demands and for a time he was dependent on tranquillisers, taking more than 120 a week. However, his talent was much admired by his bosses at NBC television. Landon admitted to having a fierce temper and losing it frequently both at the studios and with his family.

He was married three times, fathered six children and adopted three more.

THORLEY WALTERS

Thorley Walters, character actor, died on July 6 aged 78. He was born in Devon on May 12, 1913.

THORLEY Walters appeared in well over 80 films, beginning in 1934, but became known throughout the world through his roles in the Hammer Horror films — *Frankenstein Created Woman*; *Vampire Circus*; *Dracula, Prince of Darkness* and *Frankenstein Must be Destroyed*. With a shock of white hair and moustache, Walters played alongside Peter Cushing or Christopher Lee in scenes that moved from elaborate laboratories to ruined gothic castles.

Walters suffered a major stroke three years ago from which, sadly, he only partly recovered. Gavin Millar had a cameo role especially written for him in John Le Carré's *Murder of Quality*, which was shot last year. He arrived at Shepperton studios escorted by a nurse. This was to be his last role, although he was seen recently on television in the repeat of Le Carré's *Tinker, Tailor, Soldier, Spy*.

Walters's father was a canon at Exeter Cathedral. He wnt to school at Monkton Coombe, near Bath, where he first took an interest in the theatre, visiting cinemas and the Theatre Royal, Bath, whenever he could. He enjoyed dressing up and was often found acting in front of his school friends.

Upon leaving school his father gave him the choice of the stage or the church. Walters took the former. He impressed Lilian Baylis at the London Old Vic and during the 1933 season began to play small parts alongside Flora Robson, Charles Laughton, Marius Goring and James Mason, Athene Seyler and Desmond Walter-Ellis. The latter two remained close friends throughout his life.

One of his first films, for British Fox, was *Once in a New Moon* (1934) followed by *The Love Test* and *Lucky Star*, but he continued with his stage work and joined the Manchester Rep for a successful season. One of his early triumphs in the West End was at the Theatre Royal, in *Mary Goes to Sea* with Marie Tempest.

Just before the war he began to write and appear in comedy sketches and was spotted by Cicely Courtneidge and Jack Hulbert. This was to lead to a career in musical comedies including five musicals with the comedienne. These included the lead in *Gay's the Word*, written by Ivor Novello. A life-long friendship with the director Roy Boulting was to lead to many film roles with the Boulting Brothers: *Private's Progress*, *Brothers-in-Law* and *Carlton-Browne of the FO* were the most successful.

He first appeared on television before the war and by the time of his death had played over three hundred roles on the small screen.

HOWARD NEMEROV

Howard Nemerov, poet laureate of the United States from 1988 to 1990, died of cancer at his home in St Louis, Missouri, on July 5 aged 71. He was born in New York on March 1, 1920.

BESIDES being one of the most distinctive poetic voices of his generation in his own country, Howard Nemerov was also an accomplished and intelligent novelist and a perceptive critic. He had retired as a professor at Washington University, St Louis, only last year. Any of these activities might, taken singly, have amounted to a career of distinction. But it is his poetry which gives him his particular place in contemporary American letters.

In a period in American poetry which produced figures more spectacular, more memorable in their manner of living — and dying — than himself the life and work of Howard Nemerov provided a focus of lucid urbanity which often recalled the poets of an older generation. The rage of Sexton and Plath, the hysteria of Lowell or the verbal high jinks of the Beats are missing from Nemerov. So, too, are their not infrequent explosions of emotional power. Nemerov always kept his undoubted potentialities under civilised restraint. There were dangers in this. His poems, relatively conservative and formalist with their adherence to rhyme and metre and a vocabulary drawn from wide reading in the world's literatures, are manifestly those of an academic. Yet they do not smell of the study. Though he settled in academia — and served it well

– Nemerov was very far from being a man of cloistered life (he flew as a fighter pilot in the second world war). His restraint as a writer consisted rather of a determination not to let the horrors of existence overwhelm his poetic matter, as they had done the matter – and the lives of – Sexton, Plath and Lowell.

Howard Nemerov was born into a Jewish family. His father, David Russek Nemerov, was owner and chairman of Russek's Fifth Avenue, a clothing retailer. One of his sisters was the photographer Diana Arbus who committed suicide in 1971. Nemerov went to school in the Bronx and afterwards took a degree at Harvard. After graduating he decided not to join the family business. War had come – to Britain and her dominions if not to the United States – and he volunteered for the Royal Canadian Air Force in which he trained as a fighter pilot. Coming to Britain with an RCAF squadron, he flew 57 missions before America entered the war and in 1942 he transferred to the United States Army Air Force. With the US 8th Air Force he flew fighter-bomber sorties until the end of the war.

Surprisingly little of this experience with its potent ingredients of drama and conflict found its way immediately into his subsequent output of poetry. Returning home after the war, he embarked on an outwardly unruffled academic career, teaching English at a number of colleges and universities and spending the year 1962 as writer in residence at Hollins College, Virginia, before going to Washington University, St Louis, in 1969 as Fannie Hurst professor of creative literature. He was subsequently appointed as Edward Mallinckrodt distinguished university professor at the university, retiring in 1990 but continuing as distinguished poet in residence.

From the later 1940s onwards successive volumes of verse revealed a poet of considerable potential in a manner which was at a conscious remove from the headier verse of more "exciting" practitioners of the period. Sometimes, when

he lapsed into passages of somewhat measured, old-fashioned sounding verse which appeared to be the slave of, rather than the reason for, his use of rhyme and metre, it appeared he was having difficulty finding the right manner to match his generally philosophical thought. Nemerov's strengths (and weaknesses) are summed up in his *Collected Poems* of 1977. These proclaim him, whatever their occasional shortcomings, a poet of stature.

Nemerov can also be considered in his own right as a novelist, and not merely as a poet who wrote the odd novel. His first, *Federigo, or the Power of Love* (1954), is also his best known. With the *Doppelgänger* theme which was to become his characteristic it observes Greenwich village life with sardonic wit and detachment. *The Homecoming Game* (1957), a novel about a college campus crisis arising out of a professor's bold decision to fail the football team's star in his history exams, was made into a film, *Tall Story*, in 1960. Though it starred Jane Fonda and Anthony Perkins the film version did little justice to the complexities of Nemerov's original. *Journal of the Fictive Life* (1965) defied classification as either novel or autobiography. It was, refreshingly, *not* a novel about writing a novel; considered either as fiction or as a series of personal sketches it was replete with the kind of reflection and speculation so dear to Nemerov's mental make-up. These qualities were often displayed in his criticism, never better than in *Figures of Thought: Speculations on the Meaning of Poetry and other Essays* which appeared in 1978.

Nemerov was awarded the Pulitzer prize for poetry in 1978 and the National Medal of Arts in 1987. He held the poet laureateship of the United States – though honorific, a prestigious and salaried position – for two years from 1988. He was the third occupant of the post which was created by Congress only in 1985.

Nemerov leaves his widow, Margaret, and three sons.

FRANK RIZZO

Frank Rizzo, former mayor of Phila-delphia, died on July 16 aged 70. He was born on October 23, 1920.

IN THE racially and politically charged atmosphere of America in the early 1970s – when race-riots and anti-war protests were daily events and crime was the third urban preoccupation – Frank Rizzo seemed like the answer to a prayer to the working class whites of Philadelphia. He rose from street cop to mayor of what was then America's fourth largest city and came to personify the tough city leader who offered ruthless authority to a people suspicious of the trendy radical-chic liberalism of the political mainstream.

Rizzo pledged, during one of his election campaigns, to run a law-and-order administration that would make "Attilla the Hun look like a faggot". In spite of excesses which became inter-nationally notorious, he held office from 1971 to 1979, nominally as a Democrat although he supported Richard Nixon's presidential candidacy; his reign ended in the mire of corruption scandals but he was campaigning to regain the mayor's office – this time as a Republican – when he died of a heart attack.

Frank Rizzo was a burly figure, 6ft 2ins tall and 17 stone. He was renowned for attending a formal function in a dress suit with a truncheon stuck in his cummerbund.

The eldest son of an Italian immigrant who was also a policeman, he dropped out of high school, served in the navy before joining the police at the age of 22. As a young cop in the 1940s, using only his fists, he put four hold-up men who resisted arrest into hospital. Later he led a series of well-publicised raids on illegal bars and homosexual meeting places.

At the end of the 1960s, when he was police commissioner, he earned his reputation for dealing severely with race-rioters and anti-war protesters. During one raid, on the offices of the Black Panthers, the militant black political movement, the occupants were ushered into the street, stood against a wall, ordered to strip naked and photographed. Liberals were appalled but not his supporters who said that under his police stewardship Philadelphia had a lower crime rate and fewer disturbances than most American cities and that he had kept the lid on an explosive racial situation. Critics argued that Philadelphia's crime rate was low before and that he simply aggravated the city's racial problems.

Soon after he was elected to his second four-year term of office, things began to turn sour for the mayor. First the city newspapers exposed the existence of a secret police detachment, answerable only to Rizzo, whose duty was to compile his enemies list.

The mayor was soon being accused of concocting phoney budgets, allowing mob violence to intimidate the press and closing the only municipal hospital; he also failed a lie-detector test which he agreed to take in an effort to rebut allegations of making a secret political deal.

Undeterred by these difficulties Rizzo attempted unsuccessfully to have the city charter changed so that he could serve a third successive term. In 1983 he lost the Democratic primary. Four years later he switched parties and won the Republican primary but failed to regain the mayoral office.

He is survived by his wife and two children.

PETER KANE

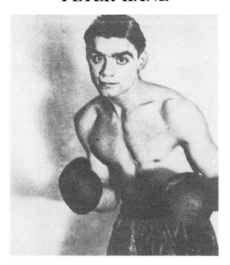

Peter Kane, flyweight boxing champion of the world from 1938 to 1943, died on July 23 aged 73. He was born on February 28, 1918.

THOUGH Peter Kane held the world flyweight title for five years, and after the war became European bantamweight champion, he never held a British title. He is as memorable for a stirring fight he lost as he is for his victories. His defeat over 13 rounds by the great Benny Lynch, then at the height of his powers, is part of boxing lore. Kane was renowned for his explosive punching; the flyweight division has seen few harder hitters. His power, combined with his Eddie Cantor eyes, earned him the nick-name, "the wide-eyed killer". Had the war not interrupted his career his strength and aggression would undoubtedly have reaped him greater rewards.

He was born Peter Cain in Golbourne, Lancashire, where apprenticeship to a blacksmith developed the strength which made such an impression when he turned boxer. He had his first pro fight in Liverpool at the age of 16 and over the next three years reeled off a string of 41 successive victories. In the mid-1930s he was the idol of boxing followers on Merseyside where he was managed by that wily guru of the ring, Nel Tarleton. He overwhelmed the tough and fiery Phil Milligan to win the Northern area flyweight title and then announced his arrival at international level when he destroyed the Irish champion, Jim Warnock, in four rounds.

This prowess was acknowledged when he was given his chance against Benny Lynch at Glasgow in 1937. Kane was a raw 19-year-old and Lynch then at his peak as world champion. None of this over-awed Kane who tore into his man from the opening bell. For a moment he looked like throwing him completely out of his stride. But the world champion's craft was not, in the event, to succumb to naked power. As the fight wore on Lynch's counter-punching began to take its toll and in the 13th round, after being floored for a count of seven, Kane was knocked out. But the crowd rose to such a display of youthful courage against skill, and in the following year Kane was given a re-match; Lynch was overweight and Kane held his own to box a draw. The vicious punches with which he had floored Jurich had also damaged his hands and after the fight he had to have a little finger amputated. War service as a physical training instructor in the RAF now claimed him, during the course of which he sustained an eye injury. When, therefore, he defended his title against the Scot Jackie Paterson in 1943 it was hardly the pristine Kane who had won it five years before. By now he was also having difficulty making the weight and Paterson knocked him out in 61 seconds.

This might have signalled the end of most careers but when the war was over and boxing in Britain got back into its stride, his fans were soon delighted to hear that the Golbourne blacksmith was campaigning as a bantamweight. In his first year back in action he had eight straight wins and in 1947 he took the European title from the Frenchman Theo Medina. He defended it against Joe Cornelis of Belgium before losing to the Italian Guido Ferracin. Beaten a second time by Ferracin, Kane, at 30, decided to call it a day.

ROBERT MOTHERWELL

Robert Motherwell, American painter, died in Provincetown, Massachusetts, on July 16 aged 76. He was born in Aberdeen, Washington state, on January 24, 1915.

ROBERT Motherwell wove himself into the history of contemporary art in America over its most adventurous half-century. He was one of the dozen painters regarded as the first generation of Abstract Expressionists; but he also functioned as philosopher, theoretician, teacher, lecturer and commentator in relation to this group. On a broader front, his editorship of the *Documents of Modern Art* series of publications brought these influential writings to America (and to Britain) in English translation, often for the first time, to inspire new generations of artists.

In his own art he remained open to new influences in each decade of his life. The wide scope of his imagery, from primitivism to cool abstraction, maintained the interest of other and younger artists in his work. The large number of articles by other writers about his art is equalled by the long list of his own writing, in prefaces, statements and interviews.

Robert Motherwell was born in the state of Washington but spent his childhood in San Francisco. At the precociously young age of 11 he was awarded a fellowship at the Otis Art Institute, Los Angeles, where he studied from 1926 to 1929. After a short period at the California School of Fine Arts in San Francisco he entered Stanford University in 1932, taking a degree in philosophy and writing his undergraduate thesis on psychoanalytic theory — a subject which remained an interest throughout his life.

In 1935 he toured Europe, became

interested in French literature and wrote on Andre Gide. In 1937 he enrolled in the department of philosophy at Harvard University, taking courses in aesthetics and working on a thesis on the aesthetic ideas in Delacroix's *Journals*. After another visit to Europe, including the universities of Oxford and Grenoble, he began to teach art at the University of Oregon; but in 1940 he moved to New York and enrolled as a graduate student at Columbia University, under Professor Meyer Schapiro.

That year Motherwell made wider contacts among artists, including the international Surrealists from Europe who had taken refuge in America. Although his own work was more abstract he was interested in surrealist theory and in automatism and collage in particular. In 1941 he visited Mexico with the Chilean surrealist painter Matta, staying there to paint with Wolfgang Paalen. Painting began to take a major role in his activities. In 1943 Motherwell was invited by Peggy Guggenheim to make collages for an exhibition at her "Art of This Century" gallery in New York, along with Pollock and Baziotes. His first one-man show followed there in 1944.

Also in this year Motherwell became director of the series *The Documents of Modern Art*, published by Wittenborn and Schultz, which introduced the writings of leading 20th-century artists and critics to the wider English-speaking art world. He himself edited *The Dada Painters and Poets: An Anthology* of 1951. In 1947 he had also edited the single issue of *Possibilities*, along with John Cage and Harold Rosenberg.

In 1948 Motherwell set out on another venture, founding the "Subject of the Artist" school, in collaboration with the artists Rothko, Baziotes, Newman and Hare. Its prime purpose was to emphasise that abstract art has its own subject matter and the idea was to have artists address students on this theme. Though the school lasted less than a year as an institution, it led to the more informal "The Club", where artists and writers met weekly for discussions throughout the 1950s. Meanwhile in 1951 Motherwell was appointed associate professor at Hunter College in the University of New York, a post which he held until 1959. From 1962 he was art director of Partisan Review and from 1969 to 1975 advisory editor to *American Scholar*. In 1971 he moved from New York to Greenwich, Connecticut, spending most summers – as he had since 1956 – at Provincetown, Massachusetts.

Motherwell's own art culminated in retrospectives mounted by the Museum of Modern Art, New York, of his works on paper, which toured North and South America from 1965, and a large retrospective in 1966 which subsequently toured Europe. His work was always open to new influences. But certain abstract images and tendencies continued through his career: on the one hand, the calligraphic, questing line; on the other, the ovoid forms, set against vertical lines, which in stark black and white form the mural-scale theme of his most famous series, *Elegy to the Spanish Republic*, which he began in 1949 and continued in nearly 150 canvases until 1976.

Brilliant colour he reserved for his collages, until in the late 1960s – inspired by leaning one coloured canvas against another in the studio – he launched into a series entitled *Open* (of which the Tate Gallery has two examples) which are simple, geometrical, colour-field paintings in saturated colour, with minimal rectangular markings, carrying a spatial sense of wall and window, or wall and door. In the 1970s – a time of some personal turbulence, physical, emotional, and aesthetic after a "cool" decade for Motherwell in the 1960s – his output became more varied, more energetic and more free, sometimes harking back to the early days of Abstract Expressionism. The Royal Academy mounted a retrospective of his work in 1978.

He was four times married and had four daughters. His third wife was the painter Helen Frankenthaler.

CYRIL MILLS

Cyril Bertram Mills, former chairman of the Bertram Mills circus, died on July 20 aged 89. He was born on February 27, 1902.

During the lifetime of the famous Bertram Mills circus Cyril Mills was regarded as one of the most successful circus managers. Going into the business with his father Bertram in the 1920s, he made its name virtually a synonym for the word circus and ran it with his brother Bernard until the economics of circus management in a climate of escalating travel costs forced it to stop touring in the 1960s.

Cyril Bertram Mills began professional life as an engineer. He was educated at Harrow and Cambridge where he took an MA in enineering and then worked in the oil industry. But after a couple of years he accepted an invitation from his father to take over the running of the recently founded Bertram Mills circus, jointly with his younger brother Bernard. His first task in this new and daunting role was to arrange the transport to the London Olympia from Paris of Alfred Schneider's act of 70 lions. From 1928 onwards for a considerable part of every year he travelled world-wide in search of exceptional circus acts which he could

190

book for the Christmas show at Olympia and for the tenting circus which visited virtually every major British town over a three-year tour.

For 20 years from 1931 (the war years excepted) he flew his own plane on these talent-scouting missions. His arrival on a continental circus site was signalled round every caravan within minutes and artistes changed into their Sunday-best costumes and resolved to attempt the latest death-defying addition to their acts in the hoping of catching his eye and winning a contract for Olympia.

Under the brothers' management the circus in Britain became revitalised. Whether at Olympia or in the big tent on some muddy ground, every piece of equipment, every act, every animal had to be immaculate. Thus, from being a somewhat down-at-heel and frankly down-market entertainment, largely for children, British circus within a decade became transformed into an adult entertainment of quality.

Of both Cyril Mills and his father it was said at different times that they were "the men who put the circus into Debrett". Certainly their circus enjoyed a unique position in the British establishment, with the inaugural lunch at Olympia each Christmas attended by leading figures from society and business. At Olympia and on tour the Bertram Mills circus became a milieu for writers, artists and circus fans. When, on December 18, 1952, the circus gave a royal charity performance before the Queen it was the first occasion on which a British monarch had made an official visit to a public circus performance. On the highly sentimental occasion of the Mills circus's last show at Olympia one member of the royal family told Mills: "We *had* to bring the children to the last peformance. We wanted them to be able to say in later years that they had actually seen the Bertram Mills circus."

Bertram Mills had been a showman whose genius was to communicate his own belief in what he had to sell to the public he wanted to sell it to. None of this, of course, would have worked without the sheer quality of what he had to offer. Following in the footsteps of this daunting personality, Cyril Mills maintained a far-sighted and flexible stewardship of the circus, which is after all a type of commercial activity whose attendant hazards and vicissitudes might well make the more orthodox business head shudder with apprehension. In the end, the influence perhaps of television and other more facile forms of modern entertainment and, more tangibly, the escalating costs of rail transport were to prove too much for the circus. In 1966 the Bertram Mills circus ceased touring and Cyril Mills retired.

An underwriting member of Lloyds, he nevertheless continued to indulge his lifelong passion for circus by touring Europe each summer and visiting as many circuses as possible. Everywhere he was received not only as an expert but as a friend.

Of his war service he was in the habit of saying simply that he was attached to the general staff at the War Office for special duties. However in June 1984 the British double-agent condenamed Garbo – officially reported dead some thirty years earlier – was found by an investigative writer alive and well in South America. Brought to London, he was pictured in the press being re-united with some of the surviving intelligence personnel who had directed his wartime exploits, in particular the man who recruited him and was his first case-officer. Friends felt sure they recognised the features of Cyril Bertram Mills and in this they were perfectly correct.

Cyril Mills leaves a widow, Mimi, two sons and two daughters.

ISAAC BASHEVIS SINGER

Isaac Bashevis Singer, Jewish novelist and short story writer, died on July 24 in Miami aged 87. He was born in Poland on July 14, 1904.

ISAAC Bashevis Singer was the greatest of writers in Yiddish and all his works were originally written in that language. He chose Yiddish before Hebrew because it seemed to him that, although it was in many ways becoming moribund, it best preserved the vital energy of Jewry. One of the miracles of his writings is that, as the American critic Irving Howe has observed, they have the power to evoke a vanished past as if it still existed. In the moving speech with which Singer accepted his Nobel prize of 1978 he spoke a single sentence in Yiddish: "The high honour bestowed on me by the Swedish academy is also a recognition of the Yiddish language."

Isaac Bashevis Singer was born in Radzymin, a small town near Warsaw. His father, Pinchas Menachem Singer, was a rabbi (Singer wrote of him extensively in his memoirs, *In My Father's Court*, 1966), as were his maternal and paternal grandfathers. His brother, Yisroel Joseph Singer (1893-1944), wrote several novels, including the famous *The Brothers Ashkenazi* (1936), and was much better

known than Isaac until about 1960. Isaac Bashevis Singer went to live with Yisroel in Warsaw in 1921, took work as a proof-reader and began to write stories in Yiddish (and sometimes in Hebrew). In 1932, as co-editor of a literary magazine called *Globus*, he published parts of his novel *Satan in Goray* as well as some of his stories.

In 1934 his brother emigrated to New York. Singer had by this time married and had a son. But he followed his brother in 1935, parting from his wife, Rachel, and child. She had become a communist and went to live in Moscow. She was later expelled from Soviet Russia and brought up their son in a kibbutz. In that year the whole of *Satan in Goray*, an historical novel of great power, was published in Warsaw.

Once in New York, Singer began to work for the Yiddish newspaper the *Jewish Daily Forward*; he published most of his fiction in it, though in its English form his work appeared regularly in *The New Yorker*. In 1940 he married a German refugee, Alma Haimann.

For some years Singer remained a relatively obscure writer. All his work had to be translated and this sometimes presented problems – until, with his vastly improved English, he was himself able to mastermind the difficult process. But his work early attracted the attention of another Jewish Nobel prize-winner-to-be, Saul Bellow, who translated some stories and publicised him as a great writer. He also owed a great debt to the early translations of Jacob Sloan and Isaac Rosenfeld. Singer's first two novels to be published in America were *The Family Moskat* (1950) and *Satan in Goray* (1958), possibly his finest essay in this form.

However, the majority of critics saw Singer at his inimitable best – at once reminiscent of Kafka and of Martin Buber's gloriously colourful re-tellings of the Hasidim – in the short story. By 1962, with the publication of his second collection, *The Spinoza of Market Street*, Singer was recognised as a master. The Nobel Prize for Literature was from then onwards almost an inevitability, as his stories were translated into more than fifteen languages, including Japanese, and became treasured by both general readers and critics alike. Few writers enjoyed so great a universal esteem and love. This love, unique in its time, was in spite of the violence, cruelty and near-obsession with the slaughter of animals in his earlier books. It was felt that, though he never mentioned the holocaust, or wrote directly of it, he chose the finest imaginative manner of indicating his awareness of its existence — and that he was always, despite this awareness, an affirmer of the best in man. A volume of *Collected Stories*, in reality a selection of his best, was published in 1982, with a useful introduction by the author.

Singer's varied background provided his imagination with the material for his extraordinarily versatile work: his childhood; what he learned from his brother's experiences as a leader of the "moderns" amongst Yiddish writers; his own rabbinical studies in Warsaw; the years spent (1917-21) in the Jewish village (*shetl*) of Bilgoray, where the traditions of hundreds of years ago still survived; and his life as a New York journalist in an alien culture, but one inhabited by thousands of fellow-Jews in exile.

The magic which pervades so many of the tales — the dybbuks and ghosts — seems real because it is a part of the Jewish culture which he has (against odds which must lengthen against it) kept alive almost single-handed. Singer always said that within himself he knew all about this world long before he read the standard studies of the subject — nor is this surprising when one considers that he read no secular literature at all before he was 12. His use of the Kabbala and other Jewish lore was never intellectual or forced: he had lived among people whose way of life this actually was. Nor had he any use for writing which set out to "teach, explain or improve". Wisely, he refused to interpret his own work. The polarity, early recognised by him, of his parents' orthodoxy and his brother's rationality, characterises his work throughout. Yet no philosophical infer-

ences may be drawn from it. Singer was, like an exuberant anthropologist, content simply to describe the part-superstitious, part-religious belief-system of a people whom he had studied; yet he was never — as a contemporary man — committed to it. Still, unlike an anthropologist, he was one of the people he studied. All that can be inferred from his fiction is that he believed in God, though in no dogmatic manner ("belief in God is as necessary as sex", he once wrote).

As he assimilated the realities of American life (he became an American citizen in 1943), Singer began to write about it, enterin urban Jewish territory similar to that most fruitfully explored by his friend Saul Bellow. He became one of the finest — as well as being among the most good-humoured — poets of the apocalypse of the twentieth century in which he saw people and literature "gone berserk and ready for suicide".

He began to write for children in the mid-1960s, and won great popularity in this role. He saw in children a last refuge. *The Fools of Chelm and Their History* (1973) was one of his most highly prized.

Yiddish writers did not admire Singer as much as the rest of the world did. They felt that he pandered to non-Jewish tastes. But the fact is that Singer was the last great Yiddish writer. He was, it is true, fortunate in avoiding the misfortune which befell his two great predecessors, Sholem Aleichem and Sholem Asch, who often saw the beauty and power of their original language mutilated in translation. Nevertheless in the ultimate analysis his work transcends theirs in artistry as well as in organisation, range and profundity. He received acclaim of a more popular sort when his short story "Yentl the Yeshiva Boy" was translated to the screen as the movie *Yentl*, starring Barbra Streisand, while his 1972 novel, *Enemies, Love Story*, was made into a film of the same name.

Singer was a genial, small, blue-eyed, lively man, a vegetarian and an animal-lover.

He leaves his widow, Alma, and the son of his first marriage.

LAZAR KAGANOVICH

Lazar Kaganovich, a devoted henchman of Josef Stalin, died on July 25 aged 98. He was born on November 22, 1893.

LAZAR Kaganovich was an old Bolshevik of working-class Jewish origins who became one of the most efficient and most ruthless of Stalin's lieutenants. He presided over the dictator's forced collectivisation in the 1930s that killed millions. Kaganovich was also the political patron of Nikita Khrushchev, though their relations soured in the post-war era and he was a member of the so-called "anti-party" group which tried to depose Khrushchev from office in 1957. This led to Kaganovich's own political demise and during the last 34 years of his long life he lived in relative obscurity.

Lazar Moisevich Kaganovich was born into a poor Jewish family in the village of Kabana (which for a time was renamed Kaganovich) in the Kiev region. At the age of 14 he found employment as a tannery worker in nearby Kiev factories and at the age of 18 he joined the Bolshevik party and soon became an active organiser and agitator among the industrial workers.

During the next two years Kaganovich engaged in Bolshevik party work in different towns and under different pseudnyms. Most of his political activities were directed against the continuation of the war, but, despite being dismissed from employment on a number of occasions, he extended his influence among the Bolsheviks, becoming a leading member of the Yuzovka committee of the party.

During the civil war he was for a time an active commander in the Red Army on the Voronezh sector of the southern front, but he soon returned to political work, first in the Voronezh region and then in Central Asia where his task was to carry through the Bolshevik policy of centralisation against the opposition of local nationalists. In 1921 he returned to Moscow where he held the post of political organiser in the All-Union Council of Trade Unions. After further service in the Turkestan bureau of the party Central Committee, he was elected to candidate membership of the Central Committee in Moscow in 1923 and to full membership in 1924. From 1925 until 1928 Kaganovich headed the Ukrainian Communist Party where his tasks were to deal with Ukrainian nationalist and Trotskyist opponents of the Stalin line and to raise the industrial and agricultural level of the Ukraine. In 1926 he became a candidate member of the Politburo, in 1928 (on his return from the Ukraine to Moscow) a secretary of the Central Committee, and in 1930 he achieved full membership of the Politburo. Kaganovich's prodigious energy, organisational abilities and loyalty to Stalin meant that many tasks were thrust upon him concurrently.

From 1930 to 1935 he headed the Moscow party organisation and was the originator of a general plan of reconstruction for the Moscow region. It was also under his leadership that the construction of the Moscow underground railway system (which, for a time, bore his name) was begun. He was simultaneously head of the agricultural section of the party and, as such, in charge of the collectivisation of agriculture which was carried out brutally between 1929 and 1934.

Kaganovich conducted the party purge of 1933-34 and in 1934 became chairman of the Commission of Party Control which carried with it disciplinary responsibilities. In the second half of the 1930s he was successively People's Commissar for Communications (in which post he greatly improved the performance of the Soviet railway system), Commissar for Heavy Industry and Commissar for the Fuel Industry and Oil Industry.

Stalin used Kaganovich as a "trouble shooter". Whenever things were going wrong, and required vigorous action to put them right, Kaganovich was the person Stalin most often turned to. One such assignment led to friction between Kaganovich and Nikita Khrushchev which ten years later was to play its part in ending Kaganovich's political career. Khrushchev had been a protege of Kaganovich when the latter was in charge, first, of the Ukrainian party organisation and then the Moscow party organisation during the first 20 years of Communist rule of the Soviet Union, but by the wartime and post-war period Khrushchev had become an important party leader in his own right – a member of the Politburo and from 1938 first secretary of the Ukrainia party organisation. In the immediate post-war period the Ukraine was in a devastated condition; there was severe famine and, even, as Khrushchev reported in his memoirs, cannibalism.

Khrushchev was not only party first secretary but also the chairman of the Council of Ministers in the Ukraine. In March 1947 Stalin decided that he needed "help" to sort out the problems of the Ukraine and that Kaganovich should be sent to assist him. Khrushchev had to relinquish the more important of his two posts and hand over the Ukrainian party first secretaryship to Kaganovich who had last held that office in the late 1920s. Khrushchev was at this time fighting for his political life and relations between him and his former mentor rapidly soured.

When Khrushchev fell ill with pneumonia, Kaganovich seized the opportunity to undermine the position of Khrushchev's supporters. After resumption of his duties, Khrushchev later recalled, his relations with Kaganovich went "from bad to worse".

By the end of 1947, Stalin had apparently recovered his faith in Khrushchev and Kaganovich was recalled to Moscow. He remained a member of the Politburo and a deputy prime minister, but his standing in Stalin's eyes declined during the last years of the latter's life. When Stalin abolished the Politburo in 1952 and replaced it with an enlarged presidium of the Central Committee and, within that presidium, a bureau of nine people, Kaganovich was one of the nine. But, according to Khrushchev, within the bureau there was an inner circle of five from which Kaganovich was excluded.

Stalin's last years were marked by an increase in his anti-semitism and though Kaganovich, who had always been exceptionally fulsome in his praise of Stalin, was rewarded by being the only Jew to remain within the top party leadership, even he was probably more suspect by this stage in Stalin's eyes because of his Jewish origins.

After Stalin's death, Kaganovich's authority recovered, and he was awarded the Order of Lenin. He remained, indeed – as he had been from the early 1920s – a Stalinist. When a coalition of Khrushchev's opponents in the presidium of the party Central Committee was formed in 1957, Kaganovich took a prominent part in it, and in the aftermath of this failure of the "anti-Party group" to remove Khrushchev, he was himself expelled from the presidium, from the Central Committee and from his post as deputy prime minister.

He was appointed manager of a cement works in Sverdlovsk and then allowed to live peacefully in retirement in Moscow where he shunned foreign correspondents, but was sometimes to be seen in libraries, at the theatre, or talking to young people on park benches.

FREDDIE BROWN

Freddie Brown, CBE, England and Northamptonshire cricketer, died on July 24 aged 80. He was born on December 16, 1910.

EXCEPT during the second world war, Freddie Brown was active in the cricket world from the time he emerged as a player of the highest promise in 1930 until his retirement as chairman of the Cricket Council nearly 50 years later. Only 21 when he toured Australia for the first time, with D. R. Jardine's MCC side in 1932-33, he went there as captain 18 years later by which time he was the very embodiment of John Bull.

Born at Lima, Peru, Frederick Richard Brown was 11 before he came to England and learnt to bowl leg breaks and googlies. He was taught by the great South African cricketer, Aubrey Faulkner, who was on the staff at St Piran's, Maidenhead, Brown's preparatory school. From the Leys, where he had great success as a schoolboy cricketer, Brown went to Cambridge where he was two years in the side, in the second of which he won the first of his 22 England caps.

Although he played only a minor role on the Bodyline tour of 1932-33 – this was only three years after he had left school — he was to become a formidable all-round cricketer. He was a strong attacking batsman and a good enough natural bowler, even at the age of 40, to take 18 Test wickets in Australia when he was captain, not with the wrist spin which he had bowled for most of his life, but at medium pace.

For Surrey in the 1930s he played often but not regularly. Then came the war, in which he was captured at Tobruk. Returning 4½ stone lighter and with little thought of playing Test cricket again, his career was given a new lease when, in 1949, he took up a business appointment in Northamptonshire and was offered the captaincy of the county. According to *Wisden*, the Northamptonshire players, so long accustomed to struggle, "seemed to reflect Brown's own character, keenness and determination". They finished sixth in the county championship, Northamptonshire's best position for 36 years.

Attracted by this, the England selectors gave Brown the captaincy for the last two Test matches against New Zealand in 1949 and, although he was not the first choice, they asked him to take the MCC side to Australia in 1950-51. Aware that Norman Yardley and George Mann had both been approached ahead of him, he went in to bat for the Gentlemen against the Players at Lord's at the end of July 1950 with something to prove — and prove it he did. His 122 on the first day of the match, scored in only 110 minutes and rounded off with a six into the pavilion, led to his being asked into the Lord's committee room on the second evening and offered the captaincy to Australia.

Once there he became a very popular figure, striding out at the head of his team

with a high colour and a 'kerchief round his neck. At evening drinks, had he had a hard day in the field, he would sometimes ask the 12th man to bring him out a whisky. He had a good tour on the field, and in the last Test match led England to their first victory over Australia for 13 years. It was an emotional occasion — and in the Sydney market they advertised cabbages with "hearts as big as Freddie Brown's".

On returning to England he captained in the four Tests against South Africa in 1951 and played once more, against Australia in 1953. He was chairman of the selectors by the time of this last Test and 42 years old, but someone was needed to bowl leg breaks at Lord's and in Australia's second innings Brown had figures of 4-82 in 27 overs. He played very little first class cricket after that, though he remained close to the heart of affairs as manager of the MCC sides to South Africa in 1956-57 and to Australia in 1958-59. He was president of MCC in 1971-72, chairman of the Cricket Council from 1974-79, and was appointed CBE in 1980.

In many ways Freddie Brown was a figure larger than life. A very large man, he was always forthright and although he did not suffer fools gladly there was a very kind side to him. He was great fun, an amateur of the old school who led by example. All told he scored 13,327 runs (average 27.37), scored 22 hundreds and took 1,221 wickets at 26.21 apiece. He was also an excellent golfer, often playing for his old school in the Halford Hewitt, and got a hockey blue, as well as his cricket blue, at Cambridge.

He married Marjorie Palmer; they had three sons and a daughter.

MAX JAFFA

*Max Jaffa, OBE, violinist who special-
ised in light classical music, died on July
30 aged 79. He was born in London on
December 28, 1911.*

MAX Jaffa was a popular performer with
his own ensemble on radio and television
as well as in concert and, for close on
three decades, he appeared at summer
seasons every year in the Yorkshire resort
of Scarborough. There he and his Spa
Orchestra became almost as permanent as
Peasholm Park.

Max Jaffa was born not far from
Broadcasting House, where he was later
to make his name, the son of an
immigrant Russian Jewish tailor. His
father encouraged him musically by
giving him a half-sized violin when he was
six and arranging music lessons for him.

When he was eight he was taken to the
Queen's Hall for the London debut of
Jascha Heifetz, for whom he developed
a lifelong admiration, acquiring every
recording that Heifetz ever made.

Jaffa won a scholarship to Marylebone
Grammar School and later became a
student at the Guildhall School of Music.
He received much encouragement from
its distinguished principal, Sir Landon
Ronald, and went on to win a succession
of prizes. To support his musical
education as a youth he played in cinema,
restaurant and hotel orchestras: at 16
when he completed his musical studies he
succeeded the violinist De Groot in the
Piccadilly Hotel Orchestra, London, and
had a spell as leader of the Scottish
Symphony Orchestra. When his contract
at the Piccadilly Hotel ended, Jaffa

became a freelance musician. He made his first broadcast in August 1929 during a period when live music broadcasts were regularly made from West End hotels.

During the second world war he abandoned music. After a brief period as a Royal Artillery gunner, Jaffa volunteered for aircrew training and subsequently joined the Air Transport Auxiliary ferrying aircraft between squadrons. Throughout the war he never touched his violin and on his demobilisation had to re-learn the instrument almost as though he were a beginner. He spent an entire year determinedly winning back his skill as a professional performer.

When he began to re-establish his musical career he met up again with former friends such as Reginald Kilbey, the cellist, and Jack Byfield, the pianist, when all three were engaged by the BBC for the London Studio Players. They later formed the Max Jaffa Trio, making countless radio broadcasts and developing the palm court style which was to bring them immense popularity. They made their first television appearance in 1952. Four years later Jaffa succeeded Jean Pougnet in the *Grand Hotel* programme. At the same time the trio appeared in another popular television series called *Music at Ten*. Their television appearances had a visual simplicity: the absence of props, script or music gave their programmes spontaneity and an appealing informality.

The illness and death of Byfield in 1976 brought about the demise of the Trio. Jaffa also led his own orchestra and made solo appearances. For several years he and his wife, the contralto Jean Grayston, gave concerts on world cruise liners.

In 1959 Jaffa had been appointed musical director for Scarborough Corporation: it was the beginning of a remarkably long association with the resort which, with its history as a spa and holiday centre, was an ideal location for Jaffa's musical style. Every summer he and his Spa Orchestra performed over a 17-week season, with a complete change of programme every night for a minimum of three weeks without repeating any piece of music in deference to regulars in the audience and those who spent every night of their holiday listening to his nostalgic performances.

His association with Scarborough ended in 1986 on a rather discordant note when his comments in a radio interview about possible retirement were apparently misunderstood and his contract was not renewed. He did not retire and his sudden availability brought further demands for his services elsewhere.

Jaffa's favourie instrument was a superb Guarnerius, dated 1704, which he acquired in 1948. As a musician he was punctilious at practice and had a vast repertoire but maintained a dislike of rehearsals. ''The people I have the good fortune to work with are players of distinction themselves — they don't need me to tell them how to play the pieces they have been brought up with,'' he once said, quoting with approval Beecham's view that his orchestra had probably played most of the works more often than he had conducted them, so why insult them by insisting upon hours of rehearsal.

Small in stature but of athletic physique and an immaculate dresser, Jaffa was a modest and unassuming man. He was the object of great affection from his colleagues and enjoyed a happy family life in his elegant home near Lord's cricket ground.

Max Jaffa gave his last concert in Cambridge in November and then retired from professional playing. His autobiography, *Max Jaffa: A Life on the Fiddle*, was published earlier this year.

He is survived by his second wife Jean and their three daughters.

LIEUT-COLONEL DOUGLAS STEWART

Lieut-Colonel Douglas Stewart, DSO, MC and Bar, equestrian gold medallist at the 1952 Olympic Games, died on July 25 aged 78. He was born on June 24, 1913.

DUGGIE Stewart uniquely achieved excellence in two totally disparate disciplines. In war he was the bravest and best of regimental officers and in peace a brilliant performer in equestrian sports.

Educated at Rugby, he joined the Royal Scots Greys from Sandhurst in 1933 and was serving with the regiment in Palestine when the Greys, the last mounted cavalry regiment of the line, were mechanised in 1941. Welcoming this change of role Stewart, with his habitual determination and attention to detail, soon became an expert in his new trade and during the campaigns that followed

won the highest renown as a most skilled armoured fighting soldier.

He fought with the Greys in Syria, at Alamein and in the Western Desert, in Italy, at the Normandy landings and then on through north-west Europe to the shores of the Baltic Sea where the regiment finally met the Russians near the town of Wiesmar.

He was a small man and seemingly not strong physically, but no-one showed a greater sense of purpose or more resolution than he; none mastered fear better and none endured suffering with greater patience or prevailed longer against exhaustion. He always set an example of excellence. His feats of arms became legendary; in the desert he once fought a duel with a German tank. After much coming and going they finally found themselves on either side of a steep ridge able to see only each other's heads and wireless aerials. In this stale-mate and each having the other at his mercy should either move first, Stewart waved in greeting to his opponent and saluted him. The German officer raised himself in his turret, bowed and returned his salute. Both then reversed slowly out of each other's sight and went safely on their separate ways.

During the assault landings at Salerno, Stewart's landing-craft was hit and sunk a few yards from the beach. Though badly burnt in the face and hands he swam ashore, mounted another tank and reassumed command of his squadron. No officer or soldier in the Royal Scots Greys throughout the war inflicted greater damage on the enemy or showed sterner fighting qualities than he.

He began his wartime career as a subaltern and by the age of 30 was a lieutenant-colonel commanding his regiment, revered and respected by all. He was three times decorated: in the Western Desert with a Military Cross, to which he gained a bar in Italy; and in north-west Europe he received the Distinguished Service Order.

With the coming of peace and now stationed in Germany he returned to his first love − horses. The British Army took with enthusiasm to equestrian sports and he entered into eventing and into show jumping with all the determination and thoroughness that he had previously shown in his profession. His eminence in these sports culminated in his representing Great Britain both in the 1948 and the 1952 Olympic Games. At the former he was in the team of four for the Three Day Event at Aldershot riding Dark Seal. Riding Aherlow at the 1952 Olympic Games in Helsinki he was a member of the show jumping team of three, with Harry Llewellyn and Wilf White, which won the team gold medal. This was the only gold to be won by Britain in the Helsinki games and all the more nationally treasured for that reason. Two years later Stewart was captain of the British team in Dublin that won the Aga Khan Cup.

He retired from the army in 1954 to take up farming, firstly in England and later in the Scottish Borders. He learnt to fly and became an enthusiastic pilot. Even in this field he achieved uniqueness. Over the Home Counties one Saturday on his way to visit his Lloyds underwriter he circled round an isolated farm house trying to place it on his map and to find his bearings. By chance the Great Train Robbers were hiding in that farmhouse, and, thinking themselves to be discovered and to be observed, panicked and fled after dark. In their hasty retreat they left behind much that was later to be used in evidence at their trial. Meanwhile Stewart landed in the adjoining field, was picked up by his host in a large black car, returned three hours later after his meeting and took off again, blissfully unaware of the commotion.

Stewart was twice married. His first wife Jill Hollick, with whom he had a daughter, Clare, and a son, Bobby, died in childbirth in October 1950. In 1952 he married Phoebe Gosling, with whom he had two sons, Ian and James. She and his four children survive him.

JOHN FIELD

John Field, CBE, dancer and later director of The Royal Ballet, London Festival Ballet and the RAD, died on August 3 aged 69, after long fight against cancer. He was born in Doncaster on October 22, 1921.

FOR A decade after the post-war reopening of Covent Garden, John Field was one of the leading dancers there, proving a pillar of strength for a series of ballerinas in the classics and creating two big roles opposite Margot Fonteyn. Then, still at the height of his ability, he gave up dancing to undertake the task of directing, enlarging and developing the sister company which until then had been based at Sadlers Wells.

This he did so successfully that its standards in the difficult circumstances of almost continual touring complemented, and in some respects surpassed, those of the resident London company. He revealed a great gift for developing young talent and a whole generation of the Royal Ballet's finest dancers grew up inspired by his leadership.

Field's ability was recognised by his appointment, jointly with Kenneth Mac-Millan, to direct the combined Royal Ballet companies on Sir Frederick Ashton's retirement in 1970. But the arrangements were badly mishandled and Field was put in a position where he felt obliged to resign. Out of loyalty to the company he refused to comment publicly on the way he had been treated and set about starting his career elsewhere at the age of 49. He became in turn director of ballet at La Scala, Milan, director of the Royal Academy of Dancing in London, and artistic director of London Festival Ballet.

All of these he handled with his accustomed skill, resource and cheerfulness, but with hindsight it seems clear that not only Field's career but probably that of MacMillan too and indeed the whole well-being of the Royal Ballet would have benefited if matters had been differently managed in 1970.

Field (he shortened the family name of Greenfield for the stage) began dancing at Shelagh Elliott-Clark's School in Liverpool and made his first appearances at 17 with the Liverpool Ballet Club. He soon made his way to London and at just 18 joined the Sadlers Wells Ballet for its first wartime tour starting in December 1939. Before being called up for the forces in 1942, he had several roles, the most important being as the solitary male dancer in *Les Sylphides* and the Lover in Ashton's *The Wanderer*.

After war service in Europe, Field rejoined the company in time for its move to Covent Garden. Among his wide range of roles there Florestan in *The Sleeping Beauty* and the Caricaturist in Massine's *Mam'zelle Angot* were early successes and he will be remembered also in Balanchine's *Ballet Imperial* and de Valois's *Checkmate*. He was especially suited to

Ashton's ballets, creating small parts in *Scènes de Ballet* and *Cinderella*, dancing both the hero and the villain in *Sylvia*, and being in the premieres of *Daphnis and Chloe*, as Dorkon, and in *Tiresias* as the lover of the female Tiresias, both with Fonteyn in the lead. Chiefly, he was invaluable in the classics as a partner for Beryl Grey, Violetta Elvin and Svetlana Beriosova: tall, slender, an excellent partner with a direct, manly presence, and displaying both brilliance and elegance in his solos. *Swan Lake* was the first and best of these assignments and he danced part of it with Grey in an experimental stereoscopic film, *Black Swan*.

By 1956 it was decided that the small Sadlers Wells Theatre Ballet must enlarge its classical repertoire and take on an increased share of touring in place of the Sadlers Wells Ballet at Covent Garden. Ninette de Valois chose Field to become its resident director, sensing in this shrewd, confident, intelligent and outgoing Yorkshireman a capacity for leadership and administration.

Within a few months, Sadlers Wells Theatre decided it could no longer take responsiblity for the company (which was costing it £6,000 a year) and the Royal Opera House became its official base. Later that year, a Royal Charter officially cemented the relationship between the two companies of what became the Royal Ballet with Field as assistant director.

Between 1956 and 1970 the Royal Ballet's touring company with Field in charge, mounted for the first time *Giselle*, *Swan Lake*, *The Sleeping Beauty* and *Raymonda* in very sound versions. It also presented new works by Cranko, MacMillan, Ashton, Tudor and Morrice and tried (although with disappointing results) to develop new choreographers. Field produced a constant stream of new dancers to take the leads. The most notable from a very long list were Doreen Wells, Lynn Seymour, Brenda Last, Lucette Aldos and Margaret Barbieri, Donald MacLeary, Christopher Gable, David Wall, Paul Clarke and Stephen Jefferies.

Equally important, Field inculcated throughout the company a strong sense of drama and a determination to entertain and fire the imaginations of audiences the length and breadth of Britain – and on long overseas tours – who might otherwise see and know little of ballet. Every performance ("even on Thursday night in Hull", one of his ballerinas said) had to be the best possible.

In 1968, Field was asked whether he would take over as director of London Festival Ballet where Donald Albery was about to withdraw after conducting a successful salvage operation following a financial crisis. Field told Sir David Webster, then general administrator at Covent Garden, who asked him to stay and announced that Field and MacMillan would become joint directors on Ashton's retirement in 1970.

However, when they took office, Field found that he was listed as administrative director with MacMillan taking precedence as artistic director. This apparent relegation and an increasingly obvious incompatibility of their views led to his resignation. Although he soon found similar employment in Milan, the Scala proved, as often before and since, unwilling to put itself out for ballet.

Field was glad to return to Britain to take charge of the Royal Academy of Dancing and later to succeed his old partner Beryl Grey as director of Festival Ballet (she had taken the job when he refused it). He tried to implement his old policies of developing talent within the company, with some success in respect of dancers but little luck in finding new choreographers. When he retired in 1984 his chief legacy to his successors was the acquisition of Cranko's *Onegin* for the repertoire. Field married the dancer Anne Heaton in 1958; they had no children. He was appointed CBE for his services to ballet in 1967. His lively personality made him widely liked and he retained the intense loyalty of his dancers from the old touring Royal Ballet. Many of them assembled with Field for a party last year to mark the 20th anniversary of their work together which achieved so much for British ballet.

SOICHIRO HONDA

Soichiro Honda, founder of the Honda Motor Company, died on August 5 aged 84. He was born in Tenryu, a village in Shizuoka Prefecture in central Japan, on November 17, 1906.

SOICHIRO Honda created a company which became the world's largest manufacturer of motor cycles and Japan's third largest passenger car maker. He was considered a genius by his contemporaries and had a glowing reputation for his exemplary devotion to his company employees. Honda was one of a handful of individuals who played a definitive role in re-building the wretched and war-torn Japan of 1945 into the most powerful economy in the world. He built a company which became noted internationally for its imaginative management, highly motivated work-force and its almost obsessive attention to detail. Beginning with 20 employees in 1948, Honda Motor Company became the largest Japanese business launched after the second world war. After producing its first small sports car, the S500, in 1963 it overtook five competitors, Daihatsu, Fuji, Mazda, Mitsubishi and Suzuki to become Japan's third most successful car manufacturer behind Toyota and Nissan. It enhanced

its international reputation by establishing assembly plants in more than 30 foreign countries.

Early in his career Soichiro Honda began to concentrate on building lightweight engines that were both powerful and efficient. When the energy crisis of the early 1970s occurred he was well positioned to exploit the demand of American consumers for smaller cars using less fuel. Between 1972 and 1977 imports of Japanese cars by the United States rose from half a million to one and a half million with Honda second only to Toyota in supplying them.

Unlike most of his Japanese contemporaries Honda was an extrovert and an individualist. He was inclined to wear colourful clothes including, on occasions, red or pink suits. This trait of dressing to please himself apparently stemmed from his experiences as a child. He had often been unwelcome at other children's homes because he had got himself dirty by pottering about his father's shop; and on one occasion he was jeered by his classmates for wearing his mother's blue sash in honour of the Emperor's birthday. The jeers reinforced his determination to dress to suit himself. Nonconformity, he said, was essential to an artist or inventor.

It was from modest beginnings as the son of a poor blacksmith and bicycle repairer in a remote village in central Japan that the young Honda began to develop a passion for engines that lasted until his death. He was the eldest son of nine children five of whom died before reaching adulthood. As a small boy he is said to have been particularly partial to the smell of oil in his father's workshop, but it was at the age of five that he began his serious research. Every morning he used to trot purposefully down the road to the local rice refinery, two miles from his home, stake out a position and watch the threshing machine at work all day long.

He caught sight of his first car, a Model-T Ford, at the age of eight, and from then on was determined to manufacture his own car one day. He began work in 1922 aged 16 as an apprentice at a car repair shop in Tokyo and soon began experimenting with racing cars using an old aircraft engine to build his first sports car. Six years later he opened his own car repair shop in Hamamatsu, a city near Komyo.

He also began building and driving racing cars. In 1936 while competing in the All-Japanese Rally he set a new Japanese average speed record of 78 miles per hour before crashing and injuring himself at the finish. He spent the war years making piston rings and in October 1945 he set up the Honda Technical Research Institute to conduct research and development into internal combustion engines. It became Honda Motor Company two years later. Originally the company built motor cycles by fitting small engines on to bicycles. These were immensely popular and became known as "bata-bata" − the Japanese equivalent of "phut-phut". Within a few years Honda was producing his "My Dream" range of fully-fledged motor cycles.

In 1961 Honda Motor won the first five positions in both the 250cc and the 125cc motorcycle categories at the Tourist Trophy race on the Isle of Man. The following year the first Honda motor bikes began rolling off container ships on to foreign roads to be followed a year later by the first sports car.

In 1957 Honda had entered the four-wheel vehicle market − 30 years behind Toyota and Nissan. Fifteen years later Honda produced its Civic model which together with the CVCC engine was the first to meet American anti-pollution standards without a catalytic converter. Following the success of the Honda Civic, Honda Motor became one of Japan's Big Three car makers, along with Toyota and Nissan. Today the company has assets of more than one trillion yen (£4.3 billion) and sells more cars in the US than any other Japanese manufacturer apart from Toyota. It established its own production plants in the US in 1982 and now ranks fourth behind General Motors, Ford and Chrysler. A British assembly plant is due to start operations in Swindon in late 1992.

Motor racing was always central to Honda's interests and in 1986 his dream was fulfilled when Honda become top in Formula One racing. Honda's engine division teamed up with the British chassis-maker, Williams, to win the annual Formula One constructors' title with cars driven by Britain's Nigel Mansell and the Brazilian Nelson Piquet. This was the first time the title had been won by a Japanese car maker. Since then, latterly with Britain's McLaren, Hondas have won the championship every year.

In labour relations Honda earned himself a reputation for his efforts to promote close relations between management and workers. Unlike the typical Japanese company, Honda Motors is a meritocracy. He told his biographers that the prosperity of his company relied on its trust in youth and leaving the responsibility of company operations to those with new and creative ideas.

Honda insisted, however, on personally testing new models himself until the age of 65. He was also known to work personally on the specifications for new models, sometimes without sleep for three nights in a row. Unlike his contemporaries at the top of other Japanese industrial empires, he did not groom his son to take over his position in the company, and went as far as barring relatives from assuming senior roles at Honda Motor.

Honda retired from the company presidency in 1973 at the age of 65 and again bucked the trend among Japanese corporate tycoons by completely withdrawing his influence from management affairs. A company prospers, he said, when its former head turns up as infrequently as possible. He served as vice-president of the Tokyo Chamber of Commerce and Industry and of the Japan Automobile Manufacturers' Association. He also devoted himself to the Honda Foundation which he created to promote the harmonising of technical advancement with ecological concerns.

Honda married in 1935. He leaves a wife, Sachi, one son and two daughters.

SHAPOUR BAKHTIAR

Dr Shapour Bakhtiar, the last prime minister under the Shah of Iran, was found dead from stab wounds on August 8 aged 77 at his home outside Paris. He was born on June 26, 1914.

SHAPOUR Bakhtiar was a politician of liberal persuasion who opposed both the Shah of Iran's regime and the fundamentalist rule introduced by Ayatollah Khomeini. He was a deputy minister during the National Front government of Dr Mohammad Mossadiq from 1951 to 1953 and, although he was imprisoned several times during the Shah's reign, it was to him that the Shah turned in January 1979 in a last desperate bid to save the monarchy from the fundmen-

talist revolutionaries. He agreed to become prime minister on condition that the Shah went into exile but after five stormy weeks in office during which he strove to introduce radical reforms Bakhtiar was forced to resign in despair as Khomeini was swept to power on a tide of fundamentalist fervour. Five months later Bakhtiar established himself in Paris from where he headed the National Movement of the Iranian Resistance. He favoured the institution of a constitutional monarchy under the Shah's son, Reza Pahlavi.

Shapour Bakhtiar's life-long stance on the centre-left of his country's politics was largely determined by the circumstances of his birth. His father, a scholar and a chieftain of the ancient Bakhtiary tribe in

206

south-western Iran, was hanged by Reza Shah after a dispute with the central government, and his grandfather, who was prime minister twice under the previous dynasty of the Qajar shahs, had been one of the main leaders of the civil war that earned for the country a parliamentary mode of government at the beginning of the century.

After the death of his mother when he was seven, Bakhtiar was educated in Iran, the Lebanon and France, where he obtained degrees in law and philosophy from the Sorbonne. Before returning to Iran, he spent eleven years in France, with the result that he became involved in the turbulent politics of pre-war Europe. Showing some interest early on in the rise of German nationalism, he was alienated by the Nazi occupation of Czechoslovakia and the Nuremberg rallies, at one of which he sat a short distance from Hitler at the invitation of German friends. Subsequently he supported the cause of Republican Spain and voluntarily joined the French Army on the outbreak of the second world war. The previous year he had married a French woman.

According to his autobiography *Ma Fidélité* (Edition Albin Michel, Paris, 1982) his artillery unit saw very little action, though at one time it was surrounded by the Germans, and Bakhtiar soon found himself posted to the Spanish border region after the signing of the French armistice treaty. However, he never lost confidence in the ultimate victory of the allies and spent 15 days in a military jail for fighting a fellow officer who saw little hope for France and Britain.

For the remainder of the war, he transferred his wife and two children to the small town of Saint-Nicolas-du-Pelem and acted as a courier in the resistance between Paris and Brittany. He also permitted the resistance to use his apartment in Paris and helped to hide an American airman, coming close to capture by the Gestapo several times. Towards the end of the war, Bakhtiar returned to the Sorbonne to obtain a doctorate in law, his prophetic thesis

being on the relationship between church and state in the classical world. For the rest of his life he would remain committed to secularism in politics.

On his return to Iran in 1946, he was received kindly by the young Mohammad-Reza Shah, whose pro-German father, Reza Shah, had died the previous year in exile in Johannesburg. Bakhtiar joined the new Ministry of Labour, rising to its top position of permanent secretary within four years before being sacked for displeasing the Anglo-Iranian Oil Company (later BP) and the Shah for advocating radical reforms in the area of labour relations.

According to his own account his main aim had been to reduce the influence of the pro-Soviet Tudeh (communist) Party among oil workers, but the real reason for earning the displeasure of the palace may have been his growing links with Dr Mohammad Mossadiq, the nationalist aristocrat and member of the Majlis (parliament) who advocated the nationalisation of the oil industry and the curbing of the power of the monarch. Bakhtiar had joined Mossadiq's Iran Party immediately after his return from France.

He became minister of state for labour in Mossadiq's second cabinet in 1951 and played an active part in guiding Iran's defence of its nationalisation of British oil assets at the International Court of Justice at The Hague and at the United Nations. However, he found himself in prison following the coup that toppled the nationalist government in August, 1953. Having turned down the offer of a full seat in the new cabinet of General Zahidi, he spent nearly six years in jail over the next 25 years, the first term for "insulting the Monarch and co-operating with the Tudeh Party", despite his well-known anti-communism. His continued opposition to the new regime was especially intolerable on account of his being related to Queen Soraya.

His underground activities at this period included the setting up (with, among other Mossadiquites, Mehdi Bazargan, the future first prime minister of the Islamic republic) of printing units for anti-government publications and the direction of efforts to get opposition supporters elected to parliament, a largely futile pursuit. But he did play an important part in 1962 in preventing the Mossadiquite National Front coalition of parties and societies aligning itself with Islamic fundamentalist rioters led by Ayatollah Khomeini.

Sixteen years later in 1978, by which time he had become the Front's deputy leader, he would be defeated on this same point by three votes to two. When rioters had taken over the streets all over the country, he broke away from his colleagues on the council of the National Front and was turned to by the Shah to come to the rescue of his tottering dynasty by forming a government.

So weak was the Shah's position by then that he accepted Bakhtiar's condition (and apparently the United States' recommendation) that he leave the country, so that Bakhtiar's claim that liberals were at last in charge of Iran would sound credible. Knowing that time was not on his side, Bakhtiar and his cabinet of former National Front figures set out on a programme of radical changes: press freedom was restored; all political detainees were freed; the hated SAVAK secret police agency was disbanded; and the enormous assets of the palace in the Pahlavi Foundation were transferred to the government.

Bakhtiar later wrote that his request to the Shah to leave the country was not a heartfelt desire but the consequence of hard-headed deliberation: if the Government succeeded in restoring stability to Iran, the Shah would resume his plotting: "After all, I would never be as strong as Mossadiq."

But Iran's first liberal government for 25 years lasted only 37 days. The vast majority of the country's mosques were now controlled by supporters of Ayatollah Khomeini who, after his return from exile on February 1, 1979, appointed Mehdi Bazargan, Bakhtiar's former fellow inmate and colleague in the National Front, as provisional prime minister with the mission to seize the reins

of government from its "present usurpers" as soon as possible.

Nine days later, fighting broke out all over Tehran after the rebellion of a unit of the air force. Army barracks and police stations were attacked by mobs of fundamentalists and armed left-wing partisans, resulting in "a declaration of neutrality" by the chiefs of staff of the armed forces, who were all appointees of the Shah. Bakhtiar went underground and surfaced in Paris in July. His premiership had come too late to have a chance of success. For this he blamed the Shah and the US "which did not contact the Iranian opposition for 20 years".

In Paris Bakhtiar formed a party out of his supporters in exile, the National Movement of the Iranian Resistance. He was sentenced to death in absentia by the Tehran authorities and was heavily guarded by the French police following two assassination attempts on his life by men pledged to the Ayatollah. In one of these incidents in July 1980, four Arabs attacked his flat, shooting dead a policeman and a neighbour. He lived under permanent guard, mounted by four French policemen and his own security men. He expressed disquiet last year when the French government, which was seeking to improve relations with Iran, freed Anis Naccache, the Lebanese who had been jailed for the assassination attempt.

During Iran's war with Iraq Bakhtiar criticised the west for supplying the Khomeini regime with military spare-parts and called for a boycott of Iran's oil. He formed an alliance with another liberal former prime minister, Dr Ali Amini, who shared his aim of restoring a constitutional monarchy in Iran but was scathing in his attacks on his left wing rivals, the National Resistance Council headed by ex-president Abolhassan Bani-Sadr and the Mujahedin leader, Mussad Rajavi, both of whom also lived in Paris.

Bakhtiar was twice married. He had two sons and two daughters from his first marriage to a Frenchwoman. His second wife was Iranian. Away from politics, he was a keen mountain climber and loved Persian and French poetry.

COL. JAMES B. IRWIN

Colonel James B. Irwin, lunar astronaut, died in Glenwood Springs, Colorado, on August 8 aged 61. He was born in Pittsburgh on March 17, 1930.

WHEN James Irwin went to the moon on July 26, 1971 on the Apollo 15 mission, he participated in the first use of a vehicle on the lunar surface. It was the fourth of the Apollo programme's flights to the moon following the Apollo 11 mission commanded by Neil Armstrong in July 1969 which made the first lunar landing by human beings.

Irwin together with Colonel David Scott, his fellow astronaut, used the specially designed vehicle the "Lunar Rover" to travel several miles from their landing craft. The Apollo 15's 295 hour flight to the moon and back was the longest and most ambitious lunar mission undertaken. It lasted 12 days with Scott and Irwin spending 67 hours on the moon's surface.

The mission had a profound spiritual effect on Irwin. He claimed on his return to earth that he had experienced an overwhelming awareness of God and later became a Baptist minister. "Some people make light of it and ask how can a technical person, an astronaut, believe in the Bible," Irwin told an interviewer. "I've come to believe what the Bible says as being true."

Recalling his feelings on first stepping on to the lunar surface, he said: "When I climbed down the ladder of Apollo 15's lunar module, I was really taken back by those mountains, the Apennines, that almost encircled Hadley Base. They seemed so close and so tall. "But the surprise was that [they] were not grey or brown as I had expected. They were golden.

"Running through my reflections, like the refrain from an old hymn, were the words from my favourite biblical passage, from Psalms: 'I will lift up mine eyes to the hills from whence cometh my help. My help cometh from the Lord'."

James Irwin was brought up in the southern Bible belt by a deeply religious family, and professed to a Salvationist conversion at the age of 11. He was a 1951 graduate of the US Naval Academy. Irwin transferred to the Air Force to become a test pilot. He accumulated more than 7,000 hours of flying time and rose to the rank of colonel. He earned a master's degree in aeronautical engineering from the University of Michigan in 1957. In 1966 he was selected for the Apollo space programme.

The Apollo 15 mission was hailed as a scientific success. Among the 171 lbs of moon rock brought back was the 4,000-million-year-old so-called "Genesis Rock." It was the first and only specimen of its kind: a pure white rock from the mountains of the moon. Irwin said it was because of that discovery that "I thought the Lord wanted me involved in finding artefacts from the Genesis time that would be more important than the Genesis Rock we found on the moon."

After the mission, Irwin and Scott both developed abnormal heart rhythms, thought to be a side effect of weightlessness, and Irwin suffered several heart attacks, the first at the age of 43. "I wouldn't like to say it was due to my moon trip," he said, "but I suppose the stress of that occasion might have played a part."

Some time after the return to Earth of

the Apollo 15 mission it became known that Irwin and Scott had hand-cancelled stamped envelopes while they were on the moon and the envelopes were sold to a European stamp dealer. NASA issued a reprimand and amended its policy on what astronauts could take with them into space.

After becoming a Baptist Irwin travelled the world with a piece of moon rock in his pocket to spread the Christian message. He founded a religious retreat for Vietnam war veterans, a venture which proved to be financially disastrous, costing him and his Colorado-based inter-denominational organisation, High Flight Foundation, $250,000.

His love of the mountains and his love of God took him to Mount Ararat in search of Noah's Ark. The search for the lost Ark had obsessed Irwin since his moon mission, and the former astronaut broke a leg on one climb, injuring himself again on another. But it was a repeatedly futile search, and, after the fourth ascent of the 15,800ft mountain in 1985, he declared: "I don't think I will come back."

Irwin is survived by his wife, Mary Ellen, and five children. He is the first of the 12 men who have walked on the moon to die.

DOUGLAS TOVEY

Douglas Arnold Robert Tovey, property entrepreneur, died at the age of 83. He was born on March 21, 1908.

SIR Charles Clore once sent Douglas Tovey to New York to buy him the biggest skyscraper he could find. Tovey obliged by purchasing Wall Street's tallest building — all 71 storeys and one million square feet. In the same year, 1960, he was commissioned by Clore's property firm City and Central to find £6 million to build London's Hilton Hotel. It had taken eight years to acquire the site and get planning permission. He raised the cash (from the Prudential) in less than 24 hours.

Property was Douglas Tovey's business and no one knew that business better than he did. Not only Clore but Sir Montague Burton and Lord Fraser relied on his knowledge and entrepreneurial skills. He was one of the instruments who forged the links as they built up their retail chains after the war. He would see the opportunity for a purchase, sell the idea to his powerful client, then raise the money needed for the deal. The technique he perfected was that of leaseback. An expert on London's soaring rental values, he would buy for his client a string of High Street shops, sell the freeholds (worth more than their business) then lease them back at five per cent a year.

A close friend of Hugh Fraser, he helped to engineer many House of Fraser acquisitions, including Derry and Toms, Barkers, D. H. Evans and Harrods. But his most fruitful relationship was with Clore. Tovey it was who put up to Clore in 1953 the idea of taking over the Sears Trueform Boot Company which included the Trueform and Freeman Hardy & Willis shoe shops — establishing Clore as a major figure in retailing. He was there again at Clore's side for future purchases, including Lilley & Skinner and Saxone; and brokered the "marriage" between the Clore and Jack Cotton property concerns — a scheme he had thought of while crossing the Atlantic.

Yet this ironmonger's son from Portishead, Somerset, started work as a £1-a-week clerk at Paddington station. A chorister at Wells cathedral, he left the cathedral school to join the Great Western Railway's survey office and became the assistant chief surveyor's right-hand man before leaving in 1938 for Greater London Properties. GLP had led the way in the development of suburban shopping parades and Tovey was put in charge of all shop letting. This brought him into contact with the West End estate agents Healey & Baker who, on the outbreak of war, recruited him. Although his brother, a fighter pilot, was killed in action Douglas himself was to spend the war as a civilian. He was occupied during the first two years with his new company leasing hundreds of small shops for Kemsley newspapers in which to shelter their reserves of newsprint from the Luftwaffe. But the market burgeoned during the last part of the war as businesses and speculators, scenting victory, began trying to accumulate new real estate. When peace came Tovey was invited to join the Healey & Baker partnership, building up his own portfolio of clients. Among these were Burton, Fraser and Charles Clore.

Tovey, known to colleagues as "Dart" (an acronym of his initials) acquired a reputation for forthrightness, especially in his letters, which he sometimes dictated at the rate of 100 a day. But his business style could also be spectacular. He would deal with Hugh Fraser at St Moritz or with Clore in the gaming rooms of Monte Carlo. There were meetings in Tel Aviv, Paris or Barbados and the fashionable bars at Ascot or the Derby.

He amassed a considerable fortune of his own, with a house in The Bishop's Avenue, Hampstead, and a 110-acre estate at Henley-on-Thames where he employed three gardeners full-time. He retired to the country, aged 60, in 1968, but continued to lunch at Claridge's once a week, transported in his huge chauffeur-driven Rolls-Royce.

For a man who relied on his wits and business judgement, Douglas Tovey was surprisingly superstitious. His favourite talisman was a spotted dalmatian dog which accompanied him at all times. When one dog died another was swiftly procured.

He is survived by his wife Norah to whom he was happily married for more than 60 years.

JAMES ROOSEVELT

James Roosevelt, eldest son of President Franklin Roosevelt, died on August 13 in Newport Beach, California aged 83. He was born in New York on December 23, 1907.

JAMES Roosevelt had to cope throughout his life with being the son of Franklin and Eleanor Roosevelt. He was at times closely associated with his father's presidential administration and had a varied career as a marine officer and as a businessman dealing in insurance and films. He went on to build his own political career but his life was marred by allegations that he used his famous name for personal financial advantage.

Roosevelt's first foray into elective politics was as Democratic party candi-

date for governor of California in 1950 but he lost to the Republican incumbent Earl Warren who went on to become a liberal chief justice. Five years later the former president's son won a California seat in Congress remaining there for 11 years before being appointed ambassador to the United Nations Economic and Social Council by President Lyndon Johnson. In later years Roosevelt formed a lobbying group, the National Committee to Preserve Social Security and Medicare with the aim of protecting the social services which were his father's greatest legacy but he was also associated with a Democrats for Nixon group which had aims which might be regarded as the antithesis of those of his father.

Much of Roosevelt's life was lived in

the glare of publicity as a result of being the son of FDR and he was alleged on several occasions to be involved in questionable business activities. In the 1930s he gave up his job as vice-president of a yeast company in New Jersey because of fears held by his father that it might be involved in bootlegging. And in 1938, when FDR was at the White House, Roosevelt junior resigned his post as secretary to the president after being there for just a year following unsubstantiated press criticism that he had used his position to enhance his business dealings. To refute the charges he later released his tax returns to a magazine. Years later Roosevelt gave up his Unesco post to become a director of Investors Overseas Services, a Swiss-based investment company run by Bernie Cornfeld whose business dealings were to become notorious and to lead Mr Cornfeld to prison.

In 1975 Roosevelt brought a libel action against *The Sunday Telegraph* in the High Court claiming that an article in the newspaper falsely implied that he had lent his famous name and prestige to an illegal operation and played an important part in a continuing swindle of investors. He lost the action and was ordered to pay the total costs. Roosevelt's personal life, too, had some turbulent moments. In 1975 he was discovered lying in a pool of blood at a lakeside mansion in Geneva. He had been stabbed in the back by his third wife, Irene, during a quarrel. The couple were divorced later the same year.

In 1941 when the US began to take a more energetic part in the war by way of preparing national defence and supplying Britain with all the aid possible, Roosevelt junior, acting as an official aide to the president, undertook a long tour to the Far East, then to the Near East returning by way of Gibraltar.

He went as a captain in the US Marine Corps Reserves, a rank he had held for some years. In the Far East he met American officials in the Philippines and British authorities at Singapore. He then went on to Egypt, where he was received by King Farouk, and to Crete where he presented to King George of the Hellenes a letter from the president. He met other political and military chiefs in Cairo, Palestine, Iraq, Turkey and elsewhere. His mission was one of goodwill from America and certainly did much to provide encouragement.

Roosevelt was brought up chiefly in Washington while his father was assistant secretary for the Navy from 1913 until 1920. There he went to the Potomac School, and then to the National Cathedral School for boys. He went on to Croton school in Massachusetts, to which his father and brothers went as well as a number of other Roosevelts. He graduated from Harvard in 1930. He was a popular figure during his time there and was elected permanent treasurer of his class for its annual gatherings. He studied law at the Boston university law school in 1930 and 1931 but gave it up when he found that work as an insurance broker on, which he had started, was succeeding beyond his expectations. He was president of an insurance company until 1937 and was generally supposed to be a successful man of business who had accumulated a considerable fortune at an early age so there was some surprise when he joined his father in Washington that year though it was well known that he had a keen interest in politics.

His affable manner and his ready way of winning the confidence and support of others made him a suitable appointment for a president's secretary. But then he resigned to go into films, producing *Pot of Gold* starring James Stewart. He visited this country in connection with some of his films in the summer of 1939 and was received by the King and the Queen at Buckingham Palace. He again visited London and called on Sir Winston Churchill in 1956. Relations between Britain and the US were strained by the Suez crisis a that time and he ventured to suggest that what was lacking was the close degree of personal contact which had been forged between Churchill and his father.

Roosevelt was married four times and had three sons and four daughters.

XAN FIELDING

Xan Fielding (without shirt) with a group of resistance fighters in Crete

Xan Fielding, DSO, wartime secret agent and author, died in Paris on August 19 aged 72. He was born in India on November 26, 1918.

IN HIS temperament, talents and physical courage Xan Fielding was well equipped to have made a mark in many spheres of life. Crete in the aftermath of the German invasion in May 1941 provided a theatre in which his individuality was able to blossom. Guerrilla warfare was particularly congenial to one of his character. He cherished the amateur's view of war which saw it as a clash between the prowess of individuals and not as a contest between technologies backed by armaments industries and reserves of manpower. In addition to an innate romanticism, he possessed in abundance the classical Greek quality of *arete* (that excellence in thought and performance so often imperfectly translated as "virtue" in school texts) and revelled to the point of exultation in the exercise of his own initiative. Yet at the same time, through his mastery of the language and his psychological insight, he extended a discerning admiration to the often contrary and ferocious Cretan *andarte* groups which his efforts were designed, at least in part, to serve.

Regimental soldiering was anathema to him and the sharpest barbs of his wit were always reserved for the staff. But his exploits went far beyond being of mere nuisance value to the allied cause. In two remarkable years following the fall of Crete the efforts of Fielding and that other like-minded spirit, Patrick Leigh Fermor, built up a guerrilla network in the occupied island, facilitated the escape

214

of many Australian and New Zealand soldiers who had remained in hiding and, most important, built up an intelligence network which provided invaluable information to the allies in North Africa on the movement of Axis *matériel* through this most important staging post.

Alas for the hopes of these romantics, who would have loved to have fulfilled the dream of the guerrillas and to have led an avenging descent out of the mountains to drive the German invader into the sea, such a moment was never to come. After the allied decision to invade Sicily and pursue the Italian option Crete was left to wither on the vine as a fruit to be plucked when a convenient moment should arrive. Guerrilla operations there were relegated to a sideshow and Fielding felt there was nothing more he could usefully do. More drama awaited him. Transferred to the Western European theatre, he was parachuted into France, captured by the Gestapo and escaped execution only thanks to the courage and resourcefulness of the ill-starred Christine Granville, to whom he later dedicated his book *Hide and Seek* (1954).

Alexander Wallace Fielding was born at Ootcamund, India, into a military family which had given long service in the subcontinent. His father was a major in the 50th Sikhs. After the death of his mother he was brought up in the South of France where her family had property and thus acquired fluent French. Sent to school in England at Charterhouse, he added the classics to his linguistic and cultural arsenal and acquired a profound knowledge of German through later studies at Bonn, Munich and Freiburg universities. This German sojourn gave him a thorough understanding of the nature of the Nazi threat to civilised values at a time when the British government under Chamberlain was temporising on the road to disaster. In a spirit of more than mild disillusionment Fielding wandered about Europe eventually gravitating to Cyprus. There after a short and unsuccessful flirtation with journalism on the *Cyprus Times* he ran a bar — with not appreciably greater success. He simply

could not comprehend the inability and unwillingness of his colonial compatriots to understand the island they administered while the automatic disdain which was extended to the governed populace was utterly odious to him. None of these attitudes endeared him to his British contemporaries and consequently made him a less than popular mine host in a colonial ethos. His determination to master Greek also made him an object of suspicion to the authorities, most of whom had neither the wit nor inclination to come to terms with the language. When war broke out Fielding went briefly to Greece, dreading the thought of being drafted into the forces in Cyprus and being forced to live by the dictates of the mess and the parade ground. But after Dunkirk, when Britain stood alone, this course came to seem a somewhat dishonourable one and he returned to Cyprus where he found a not totally uncongenial berth in army intelligence. Even this provided a somewhat circumscribed field for the exercise of his talents and it was not until after the German invasion of Crete that he was able to come into his own when he volunteered for service with the Special Operations Executive (SOE).

Put ashore on Crete from a submarine with a load of explosives and weapons, Fielding quickly linked up with local resistance leaders and adopted the protective camouflage of a Greek peasant. Nowhere in occupied Europe was resistance organised so quickly and effectively as it was in Crete. Clandestine operations took shape almost in the very chaos of evacuation. Fielding was lucky to team up with that other great linguist, philhellene and guerrilla leader, Patrick Leigh Fermor, and the mental kinship between the two men, who complemented each other in spite of their different temperaments, was instrumental in putting Cretan resistance operations on a sane and sound footing. Fielding realised at the outset that the task must be limited to building up an intelligence network and developing his guerrilla force with an eye to its use in the future, rather than wasting it in futile heroics which would certainly have drawn down ferocious reprisals on the unprotected civilian population. With great boldness he established an HQ not far from Crete's northern coast from which he often sortied forth with impunity in his persona as a local to the town of Canea to visit the mayor who was astonished at the audacity with which the resistance leader virtually brushed shoulders with Wehrmacht officers on these calls.

With the battle for North Africa in full swing Crete had become a major staging post for the supply of Rommel's forces and the intelligence Fielding was able to pass to the allies was invaluable. One of his most resounding successes was to be able to signal the precise air movements at Maleme airfield, thus enabling the RAF to intercept German supply aircraft on their way to the North African littoral.

After a spell in Egypt to rest and recuperate Fielding returned to Crete in 1942. In this second period one of his most remarkable feats was to engineer, in November 1943, a pact between the two main groups of *andarte*, the communist-led EAM-ELAS and the EOK, the national organisation of Crete.

But as the dream of liberating Crete faded Fielding felt more and more frustrated and early in 1944 he volunteered to join the French operations of SOE. Soon after being parachuted into the south of France, however, he and a French officer and another agent were stopped at a road block at Digne where minor discrepancies in papers, which had otherwise been forged with scrupulous care, led to their arrest and imprisonment by the Gestapo. Totally resigned to being shot, they were in fact rescued by the nerve and feminine guile of the SOE courier "Pauline", Christine Granville, formerly a Polish countess. "Pauline" who had already been arrested herself but escaped after convincing her captors that she was a French peasant girl arrived at the prison at Digne and through a mixture of bribery and by telling the agents' captors that the Americans had already landed on the French riviera, secured their release three hours before they were due to have been shot. Indeed Fielding was convinced that he was being marched from the prison to have precisely that sentence carried out on him and was astonished when he was, instead, bundled into "Pauline's" car and driven off.

Fielding, who had already been awarded the DSO was given the Croix de Guerre by the French later in 1944 and did subsequently return briefly to Crete. But in the meantime Leigh Fermor had carried out his legendary abduction of the German general Kreipe — later filmed as *Ill Met By Moonlight*, starring Dirk Bogarde as Leigh Fermor — and with no decisive further action in prospect the atmosphere there was something of an anti-climax for Fielding. He was sent briefly to the Far East by SOE but here, too, the war was coming to an end. After witnessing the winding down of operations in Indo-China Fielding made a journey to Tibet on his own account.

After the war he wrote a number of books. Besides his account of SOE's Cretan operations he published *The Stronghold* which combined the experience of his days as a kapetan of the resistance with a scholarly knowledge and love of the island, its history and culture, all of which shone through in his account. Among his other books were *Corsair Country*, an account of a journey overland along the Barbary coast from Tangier to Tripoli, and *The Money Spinner*, an elegantly constructed history of the Monte Carlo casino. At one time Fielding's linguistic abilities gave him a useful income as a translator and he was also a technical adviser on *Ill Met By Moonlight*. He had, in spite of illness, been able, recently, to attend Greek celebrations of the 50th anniversary of the battle for Crete, and was among allied officers awarded the commemorative medal of the resistance on that occasion.

He was twice married, first, in 1953, to Daphne Bath, nee Vivian. The marriage was dissolved and he married, secondly, in 1978, Agnes ("Magouche") Phillips, daughter of Admiral John H. Magruder of the US navy.

DODO LEES

Dolores ("Dodo") Selby Bennett, née Lees, nurse with the wartime Maquis, politician and journalist, died on August 26 aged 71. She was born on April 20, 1920.

DODO Lees led an extraordinarily varied life. Born into two well-known Dorset land-owning families, the Leeses and the Welds, she was determined to see more of life than the county of her birth. As a girl journalist before the war she was taken by friends to meet Hitler, but when German troops marched into Czechoslovakia in March 1939 she lent her passport to Jews in Prague to enable them to escape.

During the war she worked as a Voluntary Aid Detachment (VAD) nurse in various hospitals but for D-Day she took advantage of her family connection with the Chief of the Imperial General Staff, Lord Alanbrooke, to persuade Ernest Bevin, the Minister of Labour, to allow her to join the French Red Cross as an ambulance driver.

She served with the 6th Colonial Infantry Regiment in the French First Army and saw service in the battle of the Colmar Gap and during the Rhine and Danube campaigns, subsequently taking part in the liberation of Dachau concentration camp and tending the inmates. In the winter of 1944-45, hearing that the Resistance fighters in the Vosges mountains were in need of medical assistance she crossed the German lines, disguised as a civilian, and lived with the Maquis in a cave. She was awarded the Croix de Guerre and Bar for rescuing wounded men under fire and in minefields.

After the war, by now a well-known figure in the French Army, she was, despite her British nationality, made an officer and appointed personal staff officer to Marshal Leclerc, the dashing French soldier who had commanded French armoured units on D-Day and accepted the surrender of German-occupied Paris in August 1944. Leclerc was at that point going to Indo-China as commander-in-chief, but when he was killed in an air crash in Algeria in November 1947 Dodo Lees was seconded to the French Foreign Office and sent to make a series of lecture tours in America, informing audiences in the United States of the French attitude to the Marshall Plan.

She and Hitler shared the same birthday, April 20; indeed he had had the impertinence to tell her that on that score she would make a fine public speaker. In the event — an event Hitler could not possibly have foreseen — she joined the Labour party, much to her family's dismay, and fought Brendan Bracken in Bournemouth East in 1949. She also nearly unseated her cousin, Sir Fitzroy Maclean, another wartime hero, in Lancaster in 1951. In 1953, a week before her marriage, she was offered a safe Labour seat. However she felt that a political career was incompatible with following her future sailor husband around the world. In 1955 following her husband's destroyer to Malta, where the influential Strickland family were her cousins, she was virtually co-opted into the government by Dom Mintoff, the prime minister.

He put her in charge of starting

217

tourism; thus she made a contribution to the extraordinary change in Malta's standard of living. She kept a house in Gozo and remained a confidant of Mintoff and of his English wife, and played a key role in restraining many of his anti-British excesses when he was elected prime minister again in 1971. Rear-Admiral John Templeton-Cothill, the commander of British forces in Malta, had been best man at her marriage and she was able to ensure a close, if discreet, liaison between these two men throughout the period when Mintoff was outwardly seeking to throw the British out of Malta.

Meanwhile, back in Dorset, in 1962 she played a key role in ensuring the election of the Labour candidate Guy Barnett to what had always hitherto been regarded as the safe Conservative seat of South Dorset.

In 1966 her husband, Commander "Chipps" Selby Bennett, was appointed defence attache in Venezuela, Colombia, Panama and the Dominican Republic. For the next three years she travelled extensively in Latin America, parts of which were then threatened with Cuban-based uprisings.

Dodo Lees was a highly intelligent, but also warm hearted and attractive, woman who took her own line such as fiercely defending foxhunting in Labour circles. She even canvassed against her husband in 1989 when he successfully stood for the Dorset county council − as a Conservative. She spoke many languages and regarded both France and Malta as her second countries.

She leaves her husband and two sons.

MARSHAL SERGEI AKHROMEYEV

Marshal Sergei Akhromeyev, chief of the general staff of the Soviet armed forces from 1984 to 1988 and a special adviser on military affairs to President Gorbachev, committed suicide on August 24 aged 68. He was born in 1923.

THOUGH the death of Sergei Akhromeyev followed in the wake of the abortive coup against President Gorbachev and the suicide on August 22 of Major-General Boris Pugo, one of the conspirators, Akhromeyev is not known to have been connected with the coup attempt himself. Indeed, only a few months ago he had publicly, in a video symposium connecting Moscow and Paris, given the lie in most robust terms, to any suggestion that the Soviet army would ever present a threat to the process of reform in the country. None of this could, however, disguise the deep disquiet that a professional soldier such as Akhromeyev clearly felt about the effects of the current political process in the Soviet Union on the strength of the armed forces and on their influence in Soviet life.

He had himself retired as armed forces chief of staff in 1988 for "health reasons" on the very day President Gorbachev announced huge reductions in the strength of the Soviet army. And though he continued as a "special adviser" to

Gorbachev thereafter, it was evident that he viewed the weakening of Soviet military might and the disorder within the USSR with profound anxiety. Ironically, the man chosen by Gorbachev to replace him as chief of staff at that time, General Mikhail Moiseyev, has himself been dismissed by Gorbachev in the aftermath of the failed coup.

Sergei Fyodorovich Akhromeyev was one of that now shrinking band of serving officers who had had direct experience in combat in the second world war. An ethnic Russian and the son of a peasant farmer, he had come up the hard way, joining the Red Army in the ranks at the age of 17 in 1940. With the launching of Operation Barbarossa, the German invasion of the Soviet Union, in the summer of the following year he soon got the chance to display his leadership qualities and, as a cadet, fought with the Soviet armies at Leningrad in 1941, in the first winter of the desperate 900-day siege.

In the post-war period Akhromeyev moved up the promotion ladder to field rank, and became increasingly identified as an authority on arms control. He was abruptly propelled to the top job in the Soviet armed forces when, to the surprise of outside commentators, the abrasive but immensely capable Marshal Nikolai Ogarkov was removed as chief of the general staff in September 1984. Although he always liked to portray himself as the "simple soldier" type — on a visit to the United States in July 1988, the first by such a senior Soviet military figure, he described himself as the "Last of the Mohicans" — Akhromeyev had a shrewd grasp of strategic matters and his views were always taken serious account of in Nato military circles, especially as the Gorbachev era

gathered momentum and the often conflicting signals from Soviet military circles became difficult to interpret. Thus, although progressive in terms of the most hidebound traditions of the Red Army and a powerful force for reform within its reactionary ranks, Akhromeyev made very clear to Nato's strategists what his interpretation of *glasnost* meant in terms of detailing the relative military strengths of the alliances when he gave the Olof Palme memorial lecture in Stockholm in September 1988. On that occasion he strongly attacked Nato, and in particular the United States, for trying to remove naval forces from the Nato/Warsaw pact equation of total military power. On that occasion western analysts wryly observed that no warship under 4,000 tons appeared in the Soviet vessel count of its own navy.

But Akhromeyev was not far from the end of his own tenure of the post of armed forces chief. Barely three months later, on December 7, on the eve of President Gorbachev's announcement of plans to cut the Soviet armed forces by half a million men, he resigned. President Gorbachev appointed him as his personal military adviser. In this post, though publicly remaining loyal to President Gorbachev's policy of troop cuts, he made it clear that the Soviet army should remain loyal to the Communist party, the instrument of the victory over Hitler in 1941-45, in spite of the revaluation of Stalin.

As recently as June 1991 year he had attacked radical generals of the younger school as "anti-communist". Though deprecating any idea that the army might rise against President Gorbachev he had warned the Soviet president on a number of occasions that he was in danger of losing its support.

INNES LLOYD

Innes Lloyd, BBC television drama producer, died on August 23 aged 65. He was born on December 24, 1925.

INNES Lloyd was a drama producer within the BBC from 1967, having first served in outside broadcasts. He hoped, he would jokingly tell his friends, that his new job might land him some nice lazy days filming on the French Riviera. His career was to prove his roguish sense of humour. He fought for studio-based drama and was fighting to the last. It is ironic that his final production was pure film. He had just seen the "rough cut" when he became ill, and was wheeled out of the viewing theatre and taken home where he later died.

Lloyd was a writer's producer first and foremost and preferred those with a story to tell which was truthful and not a reflection of any political or social prejudice. He was fascinated by real-life characters and his many television "biographies" include Orde Wingate, Amy Johnson, Dietrich Bonhoeffer, Captain Scott, Donald and Malcolm Campbell and Bomber Harris. A number of writers came to prominence through his auspices, among them Andrew Davies, Don Shaw, Robert Holles, Robert Chapman and Roger Milner. Alan Bennett was an early name on his list with work ranging from *Sunset Across The Bay* in 1974 to *A Question of Attribution* in 1991. Lloyd was starting work on this project when he was taken ill last Christmas. It was its companion piece, *An Englishman Abroad*, also by Alan Bennett, which earned Lloyd 17 awards including BAFTA prize for best play in 1983.

Born in North Wales, Innes Lloyd was educated at Ellesmere College, Shropshire, after which he volunteered for the Royal Navy towards the end of the second world war, serving in Londonderry and Norway. Afterwards he attended the Central School of Speech and Drama and became an actor, performing in Ipswich and at the Malvern Festival. In the early 1950s he worked in the presentation department at Lime Grove with Paul Fox, later moving into the outside broadcast department as a producer. He worked on the first Christmas television royal broadcast and then with Henry Longhurst in a memorable series of golf telecasts.

In 1967 he became a drama producer responsible for the newly-created 30 Minute Theatre in which he produced 200 plays. In 1982 he won the Royal Television Society's silver medal for creative contribution to television. Among his outstanding productions, earning that award, where *Orde Wingate* by Don Shaw, *An Englishman's Castle* by Phillip Mackie, *Speed King* by Roger Milner, *The Brensham Trilogy* by John Moore, *Sunset Across the Bay* by Alan Bennett and *Snow Goose* by Paul Gallico.

Lloyd brought to his work some of the sterling character one might expect from a watch-keeping officer in a North Atlantic gale. His success lay in his boldness, placing faith and trust in the writer first and foremost, and then gathering around him a loyal and dedicated team. He had an independence of spirit which marked him as a highly individualistic producer, eschewing trends and fashions for strong and robust entertainment. He was always anxious to pursue a good story and hated false sentiment and intrusive ideology. He was his own man, disliking the compromise and shilly-shallying which sometimes stems from co-productions. This was one reason why he preferred the calmness and controlled situation of the television studio to the less predictable milieu of a film location. He was eager to try new ideas in every aspect of television production and he provided a launch pad for David Myerscough Jones, the set designer, whom he encouraged to break through established convention. *Orde Wingate*, designed by Myerscough Jones and directed by Bill Hays, stands to this day as a remarkable example of how studio design can triumph over the more realistic effects of cinematic film.

Style and presentation, though, were merely secondary to content and served only to promote the truths, dramatic and otherwise, contained in each drama. In his last days he rang Don Shaw to offer him a suggestion that he research the battle of Orgreave, which took place during the miners' strike of 1984. He was eager to see where the real truth lay despite his strong aversion to Arthur Scargill as a political figure.

His personal attraction lay in his natural warmth. Anger was often transformed into a bear-like growl accompanied by a winning grin. He could be ruthless with scripts, employing a blue pencil to excellent effect, but somehow his tactfulness was all persuasive. His last production, *A Question of Attribution*, was directed by John Schlesinger.

He is survived by his wife, Sue, and a son and daughter.

ALICK BUCHANAN-SMITH

Alick Buchanan-Smith, PC, Conservative MP for Kincardine and Deeside, died on August 29 from cancer aged 59. He was born on April 8, 1932.

ALICK Buchanan-Smith was the voice of anti-Thatcherite Conservatism in Scotland. He was frequently accused of disloyalty by opponents inside the party but nobody disputed his ability, his honour or his integrity. He was a self-described left-wing conservative, never tempted to leave his party but never able to conceal an unhappiness at some aspects of its policy which caused him on occasions to vote with Labour. He resigned a shadow post in 1976, refused a chance of office in 1987 and is reliably believed to have declined a knighthood. His determined independence had kept him well outside the Cabinet but he might well have eventually obtained a major ministry in his party's new circumstances if he had not lost his long and brave battle against cancer.

Buchanan-Smith came from a politi-cally-minded family as the younger son of the late Baron Balerno, the life peer who was deputy chairman of the Conservative organisation in Scotland. He was educated at Edinburgh Academy; Trinity College, Glenalmond; and Pembroke College, Cambridge. He returned to Edinburgh to obtain a diploma in agriculture at the university and expected to spend the rest of his life running his family's farm and dairy business, with Territorial service in the Gordon Highlanders as his other main interest. He had been a youth leader in Edinburgh, however, and he began to think about politics, not as a result of passionate convictions, certainly not as a vocation, but as a form of public service. He joined the Bow Group, fought Labour's West Fife in 1959, and in 1964 won the safe Tory seat of North Angus and Mearns, some of which contributed to the new Kincardine and Deeside constituency which he represented from 1983 until his death.

In the House he showed his principles early. He voted for the Silverman Bill to abolish hanging and protested against the suspension of the BBC's *Lift Up Your Hearts* programme. He consistently expressed liberal views inspired by his Christian beliefs. Under Heath he was parliamentary under-secretary at the Scottish Office, championing progressive causes, setting up the revolutionary special unit at Glasgow's Barlinnie prison and being responsible for the Clayton committee which brought about a relaxation of his country's licensing laws. After the Labour victories in 1974 he became Scottish spokesman but he resigned from the front bench when Mrs Thatcher abandoned the party's devolution commitment. As a long term devolutionist he described it as "a betrayal of all I have stood for".

Although this heralded his long term opposition to Mrs Thatcher he became Minister of State for Agriculture, Fisheries and Food under Peter Walker, a leader of the wet faction of the party, in 1979. When Walker moved to energy after the 1983 election Buchanan-Smith went with him as minister of state again. By 1987, however, he had become even more disenchanted with the direction of Conservative policies and he refused an invitation to be Malcolm Rifkind's deputy at the Scottish Office. He made his disaffection plain. With his party on the defensive in Scotland after election losses he described ministerial speeches north of the border as "at best inappropriate and at worst unsuitable". In the House he repeatedly showed his disapproval of government measures.

In 1989 he attacked Mrs Thatcher personally. He said: "She has got to listen, not to impose. We must avoid arrogance." If she did not heed Scottish pride she would put at risk the United Kingdom as a whole and he listed poll tax anomalies, opt-out plans for Scottish schools and student loans as instances where Mrs Thatcher's government was not heeding Scottish opinion. He left no doubt about his target when he added: "Arrogance in anybody, in public life or in private life, is someting to be deplored. I believe we want to see some changes in attitude."

Although a man of uncompromising principles, Buchanan-Smith was a genial figure, popular at Westminster, respected even by his opponents. He enjoyed walking the hills of Scotland, climbing its rocks and playing the bagpipes. He was particularly happy in his family life. He was married in 1956 to Janet Lawrie and she survives him with their son and three daughters.

LAURA RIDING

Laura Riding, American poet, critic and philosophical writer, died on September 2 in Wabasso, Florida, aged 90. She was born in New York on January 16, 1901.

A SMALL but on the whole highly articulate minority saw Laura Riding – styled latterly by her own wish as Laura (Riding) Jackson – as the outstanding woman poet in any language of our century. The most notable member of this minority was Robert Graves with whom she lived for a number of years. To his eternal credit he never changed his mind about her in spite of her vituperative treatment of him after their relationship had soured. But the vast majority of readers could not respond to her poetry or prose and understood neither. Of her many books, only *Lives of Wives* (1939) ever sold even reasonably well. But there is no doubt that litrary criticism and biography will have to come to terms with her unique achievement.

After 1939, when she ceased to write poetry, she proceeded to condemn it altogether as an activity, although (somewhat paradoxically) she allowed her own poetry to be printed, if only as a demonstration of how far poetry could be taken. She herself described it as "of the first water". In later years she became something of a guru (largely on the strength of her book *The Telling*, 1972), although without the usual wide audience. Nonetheless, she gathered some private disciples, whom she would "lesson" (as she put it) in the deficiencies of their characters as well as in the workings of the universe. A few of those apparently dedicated to her were too evidently compensating themselves for feelings of inferiority. Understanding of her work was not always advanced by the presence of this latter type of follower, since some (not all) of them parodied her own inimitably lofty manner; they would also feed her, even in her old age, with everything derogatory that had been said about her; plenty was, although little of it was more than gossip. But in the long and unhappy period following the death of her second husband in 1968 she herself showed tenacity and courage.

Laura Riding was born Laura Reichenthal in New York City. Her Austrian father was a tailor and a prominent socialist. He hoped to make a socialist of her. But she resisted this fiercely and was seldom overtly political. After attending Brooklyn Girls' High School, she went to Cornell university to take a general arts course. She did not stay to take a degree because she met and married, in 1920, a Cornell history instructor, later a distinguished historian, called Louis Gottschalk. This marriage was dissolved in 1925 on the grounds of what the astonished Gottschalk later called "sheer incompatibility". She changed her surname to Riding when she arrived in England in early 1926.

Meanwhile she attracted the attention of the very important group of Southern poets — including John Crowe Ransom and Allen Tate — who called themselves the Fugitives. She enthusiastically supported their cause, but, in the words of one of the historians of the movement, "tried to assume leaderhip in the project and ended by causing some little dissension . . ." This established a pattern in her life which was often to be repeated.

However, Ransom had sent her poems to his friend Robert Graves; and Graves, together with his wife Nancy Nicholson,

admired them so much that they invited her to join them in England. She accompanied them to Egypt, where Graves had a university appointment, and she returned to England with them a few months later.

By 1927 she was living with Graves, with whom she also formed a famous literary partnership. They wrote books together, including *Pamphlet Against Anthologies*, and they founded the Seizin Press, which published work by themselves, Gertrude Stein and others. They took this press with them when they emigrated to the island of Majorca in 1929. Their departure was caused by events which became a much-relished scandal — an indigent Irish poet called Geoffrey Phibbs, with whom Riding had also been having a relationship, then went off, instead, with Graves's wife. This prompted Riding to attempt suicide.

Riding at this time published several books of prose. Some of this was simply Steinesque; but the essays in *Anarchism is Not Enough* (1928) and some of the tales in *Progress of Stories* (1936) were remarkable. She also published much poetry, culminating in the *Collected Poems* of 1938, which has since been reprinted. But in spite of a strong publicity effort on her behalf the public for poetry could never be persuaded to take a real interest in her work. Auden, Larkin and many other poets were deeply affected by it in addition to Graves himself.

Riding and Graves (whom she had repudiated as a lover in 1929) were driven from Majorca by the outbreak of the Spanish Civil War. It has been stated that they were sympathisers with Franco's cause: but, although they were critical of the Republicans, the opposite is the case. While in London, where they went to live, Riding made an effort to stop the impending war. *The World and Ourselves* (1938) consists of letters from notables, on this subject, with commentary by her. Her attempts seemed naive and grandiose, but the means that she proposed — that people should change themselves from within rather than try for political change — were far from stupid. She acted too late, and her shocking innocence ("bodies have had their day"), combined with her dogmatism and pronouncements of her own rectitude, alienated almost all her supporters. Although she later admitted to having wasted much of her time in "lessoning" various recalcitrant people, she was never able to see the force of objections to her desire to take over and run things, which included people's lives and the nature of their relationships.

After a brief interlude in Brittany, Riding and Graves went to America. Here they parted company. Riding met and eventually married Schuyler B. Jackson — then himself the married father of a family — a literary farmer who had written unsuccessful poetry. She immediately renounced poetry (for reasons that are not quite clear but which certainly involved Jackson's objections to her poetry) and for many years publishing nothing. For a long period she and her husband tried to make a living by shipping citrus fruit (their shipper was called R. Graves — no kin to the poet) but they were not very successful. They also worked on a project which she had started in association with Graves: originally described as a "dictionary of related meanings", she eventually called it a work which would "help to dissipate the confusion existing in the knowledge of word-meanings". After her husband's death in 1968 she completed it but only a fragment has been published privately.

In 1967 she published *The Telling* in a magazine; in 1972 it appeared in book form. Its themes, of the universe becoming aware of itself, and of the necessity for man to renounce materialism, are not new; but her statement of them is unusual.

After this she published a number of lengthy "corrections", in more or less obscure periodicals, of various accounts of her given by literary historians and biographers. She expressed a fierce hostility towards Graves (a characteristic attitude to all who crossed her) but this was not reciprocated. One biographer, who had access to more facts than most, and who admired her, stated that she was sometimes guilty of "retrospective falsification". The re-publication of some earlier books did not gain her much new attention. Recognition may well come more easily without her abrasive presence. When she had a point to refute, she generally accompanied it with a sarcastic assassination of its holder's character.

Laura Riding, in certain respects a tragic figure, was among the most gifted women of this century. She influenced a few major and many minor poets. She did not get the public recognition for her poetry that she deserved; had she done so, she might have been more kindly disposed towards others.

FRANK CAPRA

Frank Capra, Hollywood film director, died at his home in La Quinta, California, on September 3 aged 94. He was born in Sicily, near Palermo, on May 18, 1897.

FRANK Capra's greatest successes came in the mid-1930s. He caught the mood of an America emerging from the Depression and had a sure touch for the public's appetite for comedy reinforced with large doses of sentimentality.

His heroes at this time were almost always little men, fighting and winning against the bosses. These heroes were honest, good- natured and patriotic. But the champion of the common man was quite enough of a showman to make sure that he had men of stature to play them: Clark Gable, Gary Cooper and James Stewart were among them.

Technically Capra is credited with having speeded up the pace of films by cutting instead of dissolving the picture between scenes, overlapping and speeding up dialogue and eliminating long walking sequences.

The two films by which he may be chiefly remembered are: *It Happened One Night* (1934) and *Mr Deeds Goes to Town*

(1936). Both were to have a considerable influence on Hollywood's comic style in the late 1930s. Those who prefer Capra in rather zanier and less mawkish mood may also point to *You Can't Take It With You* (1938) which deservedly won him Oscars for best picture and best director.

Capra, at times, came perilously near to bathos, but he was never afraid of sentiment, and his aim was always to create an atmosphere of warmth and friendliness. He was never very concerned with plot. Mood and characterisation were all-important to him; and the right player in the right part was his first consideration. He was helped greatly by the fact that he directed many of the finest light comedians of his era: Claudette Colbert, Barbara Stanwyck, and Jean Arthur were among those engaged by Capra to play with his major male stars. He was also helped by his association with Robert Riskin, one of the best comedy script writers of his day.

When the plot became important, and the need was for an imaginative and creative approach, Capra was less successful, as he showed in his direction of James Hilton's *Lost Horizon*. Yet he was not locked into the Thirties. He had the ability to adapt himself to a more modern style and still retain an easy-going warmth and humanity, as he proved in his handling of Frank Sinatra in *A Hole In The Head* (1959), which Capra made when he was nearly 60. He was never a pretentious director. He did not concern himself with any unduly elaborate technical devices but his skill was never in question.

Frank Capra was brought from Sicily to Los Angeles at the age of six in 1903, one of a family of 14 children, seven of whom died before the age of one. He was educated at the California Institute of Technology where he had ambitions to be an engineer. This led him to become an instructor in the American army during the first world war. He began his film career as an assistant director in short comedies, and later became a "gag" writer for Hal Roach and Mack Sennett. Many of the great comedians of the screen served a similar apprenticeship in short, slapstick comedies, learning the art of timing, and of thinking visually, before moving on to bigger films and marginally more sophisticated comedy.

Capra's first silent short film was *Fultah Fisher's Boarding House* in 1922 and his first feature film was *Tramp, Tramp, Tramp*, in 1926, in association with Harry Langdon. After this he forsook slapstick and made *For The Love Of Mike* for First National, with a young Broadway starlet called Claudette Colbert as his leading lady. It was not a success, but it taught him the necessity of having a carefully prepared script. Soon afterwards he began his long association with Columbia Pictures, which started with a film called *The Certain Thing*, in 1928. There followed numerous films of style and quality, including *Ladies Of Leisure* (1930), *Dirigible* (1931), *Platinum Blonde*, with Jean Harlow, and *The Miracle Woman*, with Barbara Stanwyck, both in 1931. *American Madness*, a topical film in 1932 about bank failure, marked his first collaboration with Robert Riskin who subsequently wrote the scripts for all his most famous films. Then came *The Bitter Tea of General Yen*, which had a certain cult following, and the first really typical piece of Capra warmth and sentimentality, *Lady For A Day* (1933). The last named had May Robson as Apple Annie, the Broadway apple seller, a story which he re-made nearly 30 years later under the title of *A Pocketful Of Miracles*, with Bette Davis playing Apple Annie.

During his peak period in the 1930s *You Can't Take it With You*, an inspired piece of lunacy, propounded Capra's favourite theme that wealth has little affinity with happiness. The best of his films were concerned with a background which he thoroughly understood – that of commonplace everyday American life. This he could invest with a homeliness and reality which was his great strength, for he believed deeply in the simple goodness to be found in ordinary people.

It Happened One Night was the first film to win Oscars for direction, screenplay and the two leading roles and Capra also won Academy awards for *Mr Deeds Goes to Town*, and *You Can't Take it With You* (1938) both of which he produced as well as directed.

The three films which effectively form his trilogy of American life are *Mr Deeds Goes to Town*, *You Can't Take it With You* and *Mr Smith Goes to Washington* (1939). All deal with honesty and simplicity, in the person of the hero, finding a response in the people around him and ultimately winning out over the forces of evil and deceit. The last film of this series, *Meet John Doe* followed in 1941. In the same year, with the rank of major, Capra was appointed head of film production for the US War Department. He also found time to direct a film version of the Kesselring comedy-thriller, *Arsenic and Old Lace*, with a star cast led by Cary Grant. It was a little blacker than most of Capra, but the pandemonium was characteristically well controlled.

During the war Capra supervised, and partly directed, a series of films under the title *Why We Fight*, putting the case for America's involvement in the conflict. These documentaries included the feature-length *Tunisian Victory*. In 1943 he took charge of all army pictorial relations and, when he left the service in 1945 he held the rank of colonel and had been awarded the Distinguished Service Medal and the Legion of Merit.

Capra eventually returned to feature film-making forming an independent production company, Liberty Films, with William Wyler and George Stevens. But his later work – which included *It's A Wonderful Life* (1947), *State Of The Union* starring Spencer Tracy and Katharine Hepburn (1948), *Here Comes the Groom* starring Bing Crosby (1951) and *A Hole In The Head* starring Frank Sinatra in 1959 – was possibly too sentimental for post-war tastes. Critics dismissed his optimistic style as "Capracorn". His last film, *A Pocketful Of Miracles*, was made in 1960 and slammed by the critics. Capra said he had been persuaded by others to make changes "for fear of losing a few bucks". By that choice, he said, he had sold out the integrity that had been his trademark for 40 years. He never directed another film.

Twenty years later Capra's work enjoyed a critical revival; Steven Spielberg credited him as a major influence, he received the Life Achievement Award from the American Film Institute and President Reagan, who presented the trophy, said Capra had captured in his movies "all that is wonderful about the American character". During his active career, Capra had frequent disputes with Harry Cohn, the dictatorial head of Columbia Pictures, and became a strong campaigner for the rights of film-makers to have artistic control over their pictures. He took a leading part in the establishment of the Directors' Guild and was its first president. His autobiography, *The Name Above The Title*, was first published in 1971. Capra was married for 52 years to his second wife, Lucille, who died in 1984; he is survived by three children.

JEAN ROOK

Jean Rook, newspaper columnist, died of cancer in Tunbridge Wells on September 5 aged 59. She was born in Hull on November 13, 1931

"BRITAIN'S bitchiest woman" was a soubriquet which Jean Rook wore with pride. She clawed away with ebullient viciousness at film and pop stars, celebrities of the moment and virtually every member of the royal family including the Queen. She was an early member of a band of Fleet Street women journalists who developed a style of catty comment and opinion which relied on down-to-earth homilies, seasoned with assessments of their victims' failings which were most notable for their venom. "Thoroughly unpleasant, style-less, vain and a self-orbiting woman" was how one female film star was described by Rook while Prince Philip was condemned as a "hawk-nosed, slit-mouthed tetchy old devil" and Prince Edward as "unready, unsteady, unemployed Eddie".

Rook was the longest-serving and most renowned member of this band of acid-tongued women hacks. She gained the loyalty of millions of readers for her particular style. It was peppered with alliteration and colourful metaphors and deliberately combative but it also featured studied warm-heartedness, which owed much to the ethos of her native Yorkshire. Others deplored her type of journalism for what they saw as contrived abrasiveness, which came to be parodied in the satirical magazine *Private Eye* where she provided the inspiration for the imaginary columnist Glenda Slagg. Rook was at various times described as the First Lady of Fleet Street and the First Bitch of Fleet Street. The title of First Lady was invented by a *Daily Express* sub-editor anxious to promote her before she ever joined the paper. It was always said the description of First Bitch had been originated by either Russell Harty, Terry Wogan or Michael Parkinson but she herself believed it was coined by Derek Nimmo. She claimed to be the highest-paid woman in newspapers and enjoyed both her status and her income, driving her Jaguar with style, sending her son to Eton and living in what she decribed as her yuppie flat in town and a house in Kent.

A tall, striking woman with a huge mane of blonde hair, usually a suntan and boldly adorned with jewellery, Rook had the presence to meet on equal terms even the most grand of Hollywood stars.

She ascribed her success at least in part to her ability to identify with her readers' likes and dislikes and maintained that she was "the most ordinary person living". She was not universally loved but she was universally admired for the courage which

went into her column and, above all, into her sustained fight against cancer.

Jean Rook was born in Hull, the daughter of a self-made consultant engineer. She was educated at Malet Lambert Grammar School in Hull but despite outstanding examination results she failed to gain an Oxbridge place. She always attributed this to coming from a little-known school and having the wrong accent. She went instead to London university where she narrowly missed gaining a First at Bedford College. Tempted to stay on by her father who bribed her with a second-hand car, she took her Master of Arts degree, where her study of T. S. Eliot's impact on English drama showed nothing of the tabloid style which made her name.

She came late to journalism, waiting until her mid-twenties before talking her way into the graduate training scheme run by the *Sheffield Telegraph*. She suffered at the hands of her news editor, known as the Barnsley Bull, but admitted afterwards that she owed almost everything to the professionalism he forced into her. She emerged from this period of terror to engage the interest of the *Yorkshire Post* where she became woman's editor. This was a considerable post in her county and in Leeds they thought she had come down very much in the world when she became fashion editor of *Flair* – again talking herself into a job for which she admitted she had few qualifications. *Flair* was based in the Strand, near Fleet Street, but was certainly not of it though she soon made a name for herself and Hugh Cudlipp hired her to become fashion editor of the pre-Murdoch *Sun*, the doomed IPC paper which succeeded the previously doomed *Daily Herald*.

Now began the provocative style which was to make her famous. She attacked the revival of Captain Molyneaux's fashion house where every other writer praised his collection – and was later proved right. A *Sun* article jeering at Princess Margaret's old-fashioned, diamond-patterned black stockings produced uproar as did a later comment that the Queen's eyebrows needed plucking. "Mine was the first foot on the road to realistic writing about royalty," she claimed. On she went to ask if people were not sick of "that ineffectual bleater, the Archbishop of Canterbury" and in order to provoke those whose interests were in show business rather than church business she reminded them that Elizabeth Taylor was once "squat-bottomed and broad-beamed as an overpainted Russian doll". As for the Duchess of York, who became a frequent target, she proclaimed: "Fergie is a frump."

Rook was not always abrasive however. Margaret Thatcher was her heroine and this was reflected in her copy and her access to Downing Street – ten interviews in 15 years. From the *Sun* she went to the old *Daily Sketch*, edited by David English, who took her with him when the paper merged with the *Daily Mail*. It was on the *Mail* that she became really well-known. She was believed to be that rare creature, a genuine circulation puller in her own right, who would take readers if she ever transferred to another paper — and transfer she did. She was lured to the *Mail*'s greatest rival, the *Express*, despite frantic efforts to keep her, led by Lord Rothermere as well as English. They offered more money, more fringe benefits, more everything, but she decided not to break her word which she had given to the *Daily Express*.

She always believed that her defection was responsible for personal attacks on her in *Private Eye*, inspired by former colleagues. She took Glenda Slagg seriously enough not to read the column, saying with typical honesty: "it was too near the mark". Slagg was not her only imitator. Rook's consolation was that despite all rivals she remained supreme in her field. Women were appointed editors of national newspapers but Rook continued to be the most famous woman journalist of all. She would do almost anything for a story, from taking part in outrageous, bold stunts such as appearing in cages with live lions to equally outrageous flattery of the famous. She became as successful a figure on television as she was in newspapers, while on radio she was awarded the great prize of being a substitute for Derek Jameson on his breakfast programme. In her 19 years on the *Express* there were eight editors but only one Rook. They made her an assistant editor. Then everything started going wrong.

In 1985 there was a vicious robbery at her Kent home. Masked men broke in and dragged her down the stairs by her hair. She and her husband, Geoffrey Nash, were assaulted and tied up and her jewellery was stolen. But worse was the effect the robbery had on her husband. They had been colleagues in Sheffield and he had been the great influence in her life despite the fact that his journalistic career had been in a much lower key. She was convinced that the assault on the two of them contributed to his breakdown and final illness. He died in 1988 on their 25th wedding anniversary and she wrote of her feelings in her column later that week. Not long after the robbery Rook developed breast cancer. She wrote a moving account of the ordeal. On the day of her discovery she spent hours rushing round London to see consultants and seek X-rays. It was the day she was due to write her column. She duly wrote it and apologised for the fact that, unusually, the copy was a little late. She wrote her last piece for the *Express* two weeks before she died. Her old news editor in Sheffield would have had to admit that she was a true professional.

She is survived by her son, Gresby.

GEORGE EARDLEY, VC

Sergeant George Harold Eardley, VC, MM, who won the Victoria Cross in North West Europe in October 1944, died on September 11 aged 79. He was born on May 6, 1912.

PRIVATE (acting sergeant) George Eardley was a platoon sergeant in the 4th (TA) Battalion, the King's Shropshire Light Infantry, in 11th Armoured Division, when he won his Victoria Cross during the bitter fighting in the Rhineland during the autumn of 1944. He was already the holder of the Military Medal, won two-and-a-half months earlier during the battles leading to the break-out from the Normandy beach head.

Eardley enlisted originally in the Queen's Royal Regiment in April 1940 and was transferred to the KSLI in July 1944. He was one of those men with an acute tactical instinct, which made him invaluable as a patrol commander. When he won his MM, he was part of a reconnaissance patrol near Le Beny Bocage on August 1, 1944 which unexpectedly bumped into a German machine-gun position. Pretending that he had been hit as he dived for cover, he managed to stalk and destroy the gun and its crew with two grenades.

After the collapse of the Arnhem bridgehead in September, 11th Armoured Division was sent to help drive those German forces still west of the Maas back over the river in the Venlo sector. On information provided by a patrol led by Eardley, a highly successful daylight raid on strongly held German positions east of Overloon was mounted on October 13, in which he played a prominent part. Three days later a battalion attack was mounted during which his platoon was ordered to clear some orchards to restore the momentum of the advance, but it was stopped by machine gun fire.

The citation for his VC says the fire was so heavy that it seemed impossible for any man to expose himself and remain unscathed. But Sergeant Eardley, who had spotted one machine-gun post, moved forward, firing his Sten gun, and killed the occupants with grenades. A second machine gun post beyond the first immediately opened up, spraying the area with fire. Eardley, who was in the most exposed position, at once charged over 30 yards of open ground and silenced both enemy gunners.

The attack was continued by the platoon but was again held up by a third machine-gun post, and a section sent to dispose of it was beaten back, losing four casualties. Eardley, ordering the section he was with to lie down, then crawled forward alone and silenced the occupants of the post with a grenade.

His destruction of the three machine-gun posts single-handed, carried out under fire so heavy that it daunted those who were with him, enabled his platoon to achieve its objective, and in so doing, ensured the success of the whole attack.

When the war ended, Eardley decided to join the regular army and served in a number of training establishments, including Sandhurst. He retired in 1950 and subsequently worked for Rolls-Royce at Crewe. In 1964 he was on his way to Shrewsbury with his wife to witness the presentation of new Colours to the 4th Battalion when his car was hit by a train on a level- crossing near Nantwich. His wife died of her injuries and he lost a leg.

In more recent years he and his second wife lived in retirement at Southbourne.

TOM BEAUMONT

Tom Beaumont, Lawrence of Arabia's number one Vickers gunner during the campaign against the Turks in Palestine in 1917-18, died on August 29 aged 93. He was born on January 10, 1898.

AS T. E. Lawrence remarks in his introduction to *Seven Pillars of Wisdom*: ". . . there were many other leaders or lonely fighters to whom this self-regardant picture is unfair. It is still less fair of course, like all war stories, to the unnamed rank and file, who miss their share of credit, as they must do until they can write the dispatches". Though a non-commissioned officer at the time, Tom Beaumont did, in fact get his chance to "write the dispatches" (in the form of an article in the *Journal of the Society for Army Historical Research* in 1981) of his experiences of the Arab revolt against the Turks, specifically of the remarkable role played by Lawrence's Arabs in 1917 and 1918, when they virtually formed the right wing of Allenby's army in its advance on Damascus. In this campaign Beaumont played a notable role, not only as a machine gunner in the small force of armoured cars Lawrence had at his disposal, but also as an Arab interpreter.

Thomas William Beaumont was born at Dewsbury, Yorkshire, and went to school and technical college there. Having failed to get into the army because he was too young, he found out about the Motor Machine Gun Service (later the Machine Gun Corps) through an article in *Motor Cycle Weekly*. This time, lying about his age, he was accepted as a recruit. He soon became an expert on Vickers, Hotchkiss and Lewis guns and was already a sergeant at 18. Drafted to Egypt, he was on the verge of succumbing to the boredom of endless lecturing in bug-infested huts roofed with mats of dried palm leaves and camel dung, when a chance came to join Lawrence's campaign in Arabia.

At that point, mid-1917, the capture of Aqaba by Lawrence had given the Arab revolt its first firm base in the Palestine theatre, at the same time removing all danger to British communications in Sinai. From this base it was possible to menace the vital Hejaz railway between Aqaba and Damascus, thereby acting as an Arab "lever" on the right of Allenby's army which had its eyes on the invasion of Syria. Landing at Aqaba with a reinforcement of armoured cars, Beaumont and his handful of fellow volunteers first had the task of blasting and digging a roadway 60 miles into the interior capable of carrying their vehicles. In shade temperatures which often topped 120°F at midday this was a frightful ordeal during the course of which many Arabs perished. In his article "Rank and File", first written in 1935-36 and revised and extended in 1978, Beaumont recalled his first meeting with Lawrence as he stood on sentry-go one dark night. Confronted with a berobed figure coming up silently out of the desert who refused to answer his challenge, Beaumont had the safety catch off his rifle and was about to fire when the figure said calmly "It's quite all right, I'm Lawrence." Beaumont, like so many others was soon impressed by Lawrence's magnetic personality. As he later recalled: "A prince of Mecca was in our midst."

Beaumont subsequently took part in railway bridge demolition operations, as well as in the many hard-fought battles which took place as Lawrence's Arab forces and their stiffening of British armoured cars, captured Turkish forts on their push northwards on the right flank of Allenby's army. In a matter of months they had blown up more than 80 miles of the railway, rendering it virtually useless for Turkish troop movements. Beaumont entered Damascus on the same day as Lawrence and Allenby, October 1, 1918. Triumphal though the occasion was, he confesses in his memoir that first thoughts were of a bath after weeks in the sweat of the desert. But triumph was to be short lived for Beaumont. He almost immediately contracted malaria and this was to keep him in hospital until March 1919.

After the war Beaumont worked in a textile firm and during the second world war trained Air Training Corps cadets in armaments at Dewsbury. He retired from the textile firm in 1965.

He remained under the spell of Lawrence for the rest of his life, keeping in touch with him through correspondence. The last letter he had from Lawrence (by then living in obscurity as Aircraftsman Shaw) was only a week before Lawrence's death in a motorcycle accident on May 13, 1935. On that occasion Lawrence said he hoped to visit him, begging him at the same time to keep his visit a secret as he much wanted to avoid publicity. These letters from Lawrence are now held in the Humanities Research Center of the University of Texas.

Beaumont attended Lawrence's funeral and was present at the unveiling of Lawrence's bust in St Paul's cathedral in 1936. On May 13, 1983, at a full military ceremony, Beaumont planted a commemorative oak tree near the spot at which Lawrence had died in Dorset. He was in constant demand as an adviser on T. E. Lawrence projects, including articles, books (he met his second wife at a *Sunday Times* party for the launch of Philip Knightley's and Colin Simpson's book) and the David Lean film *Lawrence of Arabia*. However he declined to go to America to appear on cinema stages before showings of the film because he felt it was not an accurate portrayal of Lawrence.

His first wife, Louisa, whom he married in 1919, died in 1964. He married secondly in 1971, and leaves his widow, Helen, and a son of his first marriage.

SIR RAYMOND BROWN

Sir Raymond Frederick Brown, OBE, founder of Racal Electronics, has died aged 71. He was born on July 19, 1920.

SIR Raymond Brown was one of the most influential figures in the development of the British electronics industry after the second world war. He founded Racal Electronics, which has been among the most successful companies in this country, chaired Muirhead, another leading electronics company, and was an executive director of STC, formerly Standard Telephones and Cables.

In between these appointments Brown found time to modernise the dealings of Whitehall departments with private industry. He was head of defence sales for the Ministry of Defence between 1966 and 1969, during which time he injected that department with a far more commercial attitude than had hitherto prevailed. He then applied similar disciplines to the Department of Health and Social Security, as it then was.

Raymond Frederick Brown was born in London. His father was a small shopkeeper and he was educated modestly, at Morden Terrace London County Council School. He left at the age of 14 and joined Broadcast and Relay Services, a precursor of Rediffusion, as little more than a teaboy. During the pre-war years he attended evening classes at South East London Technical College and Morley College, where he obtained a doctorate of science.

Instead of joining the armed forces on the outbreak of war, Brown was seconded by Rediffusion to the government. He installed radio navigation beacons for the RAF around the coastline and as far away as Iceland. These skills were transferred at the war's end to the establishment of mobile transmitters in Germany so that the British Army of the Rhine could receive broadcasts from the British Forces Broadcasting Service.

In 1949 Brown had a brief spell with Plessey, where he added sales and marketing expertise to his technical knowledge. A year later he became an entrepreneur. He founded Racal jointly with Wing Cdr George Calder Cunningham. The name was a combination of Ray and Calder, and the company was launched with £100 capital to make electronic equipment.

Cunningham died a few years later, but Brown's war-time contacts helped the new business to obtain work, mainly in the radio and related fields. When Racal shares were floated on the London stock market in 1961, the company was known internationally for high-frequency single-side band two-way radio equipment. Among its innovations was a device to lock into the timing of the BBC time signal. Its reputation was such that two-thirds of its sales were exported.

The obvious applications of Racal's output for the police, military and health services brought Brown to the attention of the 1960s generation of politicians and civil servants. He fitted well the silhouette of the technical-minded businessman from humble origins envisaged by Harold Wilson when he was elected prime minister in 1964. Wilson was determined to shake up Whitehall by installing such business leaders in positions of power. In 1966 Brown was appointed OBE and made head of a newly created department of defence sales, with a brief to reverse the heavy trade deficit in defence equipment.

He soon established a good rapport with Denis Healey, the defence minister, and pushed hard through the open door into the US defence market developed by Britain's decision to buy the American F-111 aircraft, counterbalancing US purchases from the UK.

Brown was knighted for his services in 1969 and became a consultant to the DHSS, advising on commercial and export policy. Results here were less dramatic. The change of government in 1970 meant that his proselytising zeal was less in demand in Whitehall. Although Brown became export adviser to the National Economic Development Office under the next Labour government, he increasingly devoted his energies to the private sector.

It would have been invidious to have returned to Racal, which by then was being managed by Ernest Harrison. So in 1970 he became chief executive of Muirhead, another electronics company, where his enthusiasm was fired by the development of the facsimile machine. Like the telephone, this invention was remarkably slow to catch on, even with the business community, largely because of doubts as to its advantages compared with telex. But he ran the company for 12 years and became chairman for another three, when he reached 65.

In 1970 he became chairman of Racecourse Technical Services, which gave vent to his passion for horse racing. Brown farmed his Surrey estate, where he had a prize-winning herd of Hereford cattle.

In 1942 Brown married Evelyn Jennings, but the marriage was dissolved in 1949. Four years later he married Carol Sprinks, who survives him together with two sons and a daughter.

SIR Y. K. PAO

Sir Yue-Kong Pao, CBE, shipping and property magnate, known universally as Sir Y. K. Pao, died in Hong Kong on September 23 aged 72. He was born on November 10, 1918.

SIR Y. K. Pao made his fortune and his name in shipping, buying his first vessel in 1955 and becoming by the early 1980s one of the three giants among the Hong Kong merchant fleet owners and one of the richest men in the world. Yet by the time Margaret Thatcher launched one of his ships in 1984 he had already shifted two-thirds of his funds out of shipping and into property. In a single year he had cut his fleet by almost a third, anticipating the bad times which were soon to cripple so much of the rest of the shipping industry.

It was the kind of unsentimental well-thought out business decision for which he was famous. A man who abhorred gambling and preferred to get a small return on a sure investment than play for high stakes on a hunch, Pao always liked to attribute his success to his thorough financial homework.

Pao was not always in shipping. Born in Ningpo, China into a wealthy family – his father Pao Sui-loong inherited a shoe-making factory in Hankow, and later moved to Shanghai where he bought a paper-mill and opened up a gold and silver shop – the young Pao originally went into banking. It was the career his father had mapped out for him. With the Communist takeover in 1949, however, the Pao family joined the stream of refugees for Hong Kong. He spoke no Cantonese – the British colony's native Chinese dialect – and only faltering English.

But together father and son began a trading business, bringing Taiwan sugar in for the mainland China market and importing Chinese goods for onward export. But inspired by the ships in Hong Kong harbour, and finding banking and trading too tame, he was soon looking for backers to turn a dream into a sound financial enterprise. Despite his father's warnings he went to the Hongkong Bank, the colony's oldest and largest, and asked for a loan. With that he bought his first ship. More than 30 years later, he was thought to have amassed a fortune of around US$3.5 billions. His main quoted companies, World International and Wharf Holdings, through which his empire is run are supplemented by an investment arm, World-Wide Investment. The most glamorous element of his business is the upmarket department store Lane Crawford, often described as the Harrods of Hong Kong.

Like other Hong Kong tycoons he gave enormous sums to charities and foundations, endowing a university and other projects in his native Ningpo. He was a member of the Peking-appointed committee that oversaw the drafting of Hong Kong's post-1997 mini-constitution – the Basic Law – and liked to maintain good relations with the Peking government, Hong Kong's future rulers.

Jovial and charming as well as ruthless and pugnacious, he liked nothing better than hobnobbing with statesmen and royalty, often arranging to meet them as if by chance. He spent his latter years in a round of meetings with Mrs Thatcher, President Bush, the Chinese patriarch Deng Xiaoping and many others.

Rumours of a terminal illness that had been circulating for more than a year before his death were countered with jokes about his good health and passion for exercise. He was a keen swimmer and enjoyed playing golf. Having no male heirs, he was faced with the problem, on his retirement a few years ago, of how to ensure that the family business should be maintained. He decided the best way was to divide the empire and have it managed by his four sons-in-law – a Chinese banker, an Austrian lawyer, a Japanese architect and a Chinese cancer-specialist. He encouraged his daughters to take an active role in their husbands' businesses. It is thought the task of holding the Pao businesses together will now fall to the daughters.

Sir Y. K. Pao, who was knighted in 1978, is survived by his wife, Lady Pao, and his daughters.

OLGA SPESSIVTSEVA

Olga Spessivtseva, Russian ballet dancer who was also known occasionally as Olga Spessiva, died on September 16 in the United States aged 96. She was born in Rostov-on-Don on July 18, 1895.

OLGA Spessivtseva was one of the few truly great classical ballet dancers of this century. Diaghilev was given to saying that she and Pavlova were "like two halves of an apple". Certainly it was she and Pavlova who best succeeded in realising that essential duality in the performance of Giselle which is the test – and was so often the graveyard of reputations – of prima ballerinas.

A *danseuse classique* in the grand style, she was noted for her cool reserve of technique but it was also the ethereal dreamlike quality of her performances which particularly struck both those who saw her and those who danced with her. Giselle, a taxing role, was perhaps her greatest and left an indelible impression on many spectators. And when, on one occasion with the Ballets Russes in 1927 she danced her celebrated variation in *Le Lac des cygnes* at half the prescribed tempo, owing to a mistake on the conductor's part, the sense of infinity imparted to her necessarily extended movements only enthralled the eye.

Olga Alexandrovna Spessivtseva's father, an opera singer, died when she was young, so she was sent to an orphanage in St Petersburg which had theatrical connections. She studied ballet at the Imperial Theatre School and joined the Russian Imperial Ballet at the Maryinsky Theatre in 1913. She soon attracted attention and became a soloist after three years.

Sergei Diaghilev invited her to join his company for their wartime tour of America, when she danced with Nijinsky. On returning to Russia she was promoted to be a ballerina and enjoyed great success in the old classic repertory including such ballets as *La Bayadère*, *The Corsair*, *Esmeralda* and *Giselle*.

She came to London in 1921 to dance Aurora in Diaghilev's production of *The Sleeping Beauty*, visited Buenos Aires as a guest star in 1923 and the next year she left Russia for good, becoming a star of the Paris Opera Ballet and making appearances also with other companies, including Diaghilev's. Among the roles created for her at this time were the title part in Balanchine's *La Chatte*, for Diaghilev; and at the Paris Opera the ballerina roles in *Soir de Fête* by Leo Staats, *Les Rencontres* by Nijinska and Serge Lifar's *Creatures of Prometheus* and *Bacchus and Ariadne*.

In 1932 she danced *Giselle* for the Camargo Society in London, partnered by Anton Dolin and with a cast including Ninette de Valois and Frederick Ashton. It led the way to the adoption of a classic repertory as the basis for what became the Royal Ballet.

Afterwards, when touring in Australia with the Classical Russian Ballet formed by Victor Dandré after Pavlova's death, Spessivtseva became ill with depression and thereafter made only a few appearances in Paris and Buenos Aires. She gave her last performance in 1937 and settled in New York the next year. The first sign of illness had become apparent early in her Russian career, and in 1943 she entered a mental hospital in America. She remained there for the next 20 years until a group of friends, including Dolin and Felia Dubrovska, arranged for her to move to a free but sheltered environment at the Tolstoy Farm in New York State where she spent the rest of her life visited occasionally by members of the dance world. Spessivtseva has no immediate survivors.

YEROCHAM COHEN

Yerocham Cohen, secret agent of Britain and, later, of Israel, has died aged 75. He was born in Tel Aviv on May 20, 1916.

YEROCHAM Cohen served the British as an undercover agent and saboteur with Orde Wingate's forces in mandatory Palestine before the second world war. He then became one of the most outstanding spies and saboteurs for Israel before it became a state — in the process becoming a personal friend to one of the Jewish state's most bitter foes, Gamal Abdel Nasser of Egypt.

Yerocham Cohen was a Yemenite Jew. His parents had trekked to the Promised Land from Yemen and the family lived in a small house in the grounds of a school in Herzlia where his father worked as caretaker. As a youth Cohen first joined the *Haganah*, the semi-secret Jewish self-defence movement, and then its military arm, the *Palmah*. On leaving school he went to Galilee to serve in the British-administered police force, protecting main roads, settlements and villages from attack by armed gangs.

From these police duties Cohen was recruited by Captain Orde Wingate. The British officer had created and trained a Jewish commando force initially to meet the danger of a German and Italian invasion. It later initiated raids and night

238

ambushes against Arab marauders who constantly sabotaged the oil pipe line from Iraq to Haifa as it passed through Galilee.

In 1940 Cohen was one of four Jews chosen to work on intelligence and sabotage missions with the British behind French-controlled lines in Lebanon and Syria which had declared loyalty to the Vichy government collaborating with the Germans. The Jewish agents, who were known as the Syrian Unit, were trained by British officers in sabotage and the use of various weapons and explosives. Cohen travelled to Beirut and Damascus posing as a merchant or labourer, which allowed him to move around seeking new business or itinerant work as he gathered military and political information and supervised other agents. Arrested on one occasion by Syrian police he was freed only after his British liaison officer discovered his prison location and engineered his release by saying he was a wanted Arab deserter from a British base.

As the Jews' campaign for their own state in Palestine intensified Cohen took command of the Mistaravim a unit of the *Palmah* which consisted of men and women trained to penetrate the Arab communities in Palestine and surrounding Arab countries for intelligence, sabotage and psychological warfare missions. Later the unit helped smuggle Jews from Arab lands into Israel.

Cohen continued to cross the borders on various undercover missions and twice managed to escape after being arrested and imprisoned. In the summer of 1946 he was appointed staff intelligence chief of the *Palmah*.

Towards the end of 1948, as the newly-declared Jewish state found itself at war with invading Arab armies, Cohen served as a captain at the southern front where some 4,000 Egyptian troops were besieged by the Israelis in what was known as the Faluja pocket, a sandy stretch of the northern Negev not far from Gaza. The Egyptians were in a desperate situation but refused to surrender unconditionally. In an effort to prevent further bloodshed for both sides, Yigal Allon, the commander of the *Palmah* sought a volunteer to try and reach Egyptian lines and arrange a meeting between the commanders of the two sides. Yerochem Cohen volunteered, driving through a minefield and calling through a loud hailer for an Egyptian officer to approach him.

Three officers eventually appeared, led by a major who introduced himself as Gamal Abdel Nasser. Over the next few weeks, as the two sides met to try and resolve the stalemate, Nasser and Cohen found themselves engaging in lengthy discussions.

In his autobiography, *By Light and in Darkness*, Cohen writes that he found Nasser "charming, open and full of strong patriotic feelings, who talked with anger and emotion of the miserable condition of his people and his country. He asked many questions about how we had organised popular rebellion and the *Haganah* underground army in our struggle against the British and he wanted to know all about our kibbutz cooperative farms and about our social and political systems and philosphy." The two men maintained intermittent contact through intermediaries after the Egyptians pulled out from the Faluja pocket and Nasser was later to write about their meetings in his own book, *The Philosophy of the Revolution*.

In 1951 Cohen ended his military service and studied for a BA in political science and Middle East studies at the Hebrew University of Jerusalem. He won a scholarship to St Anthony's College, Oxford, in 1956 gaining a Bachelor of Letters for a thesis on "The Rebellion of Urabi Pasha in Egypt". Then he joined Israel's foreign service and was posted to Nigeria, meeting and marrying his wife, Denorah, in a whirlwind courtship as he passed through London where she was studying medicine. In 1960 he became ambassador to Liberia. From 1965 until retirement in 1986 he was in charge of Tel-Aviv University's programmes for overseas students and disadvantaged youth. He is survived by his wife, son and daughter.

JOHN LEESE

*John Leese, Editor-in-Chief of the Lon-
don* Evening Standard *from 1986 to
March this year, died on September 23
aged 61. He was born on January 4, 1930.*

UNDER the editorship of John Leese, the
Evening Standard successfully beat off a
challenge to its monopoly status as
London's only evening paper. In the
process the *Standard* increased its
circulation by more than 12 per cent,
enlarged its size, often by as many as 20
pages a day, and improved its readership
profile to the extent that 72 per cent of
its readers were from the most affluent
ABC1 categories.

Earlier Leese had designed and edited
the *Mail on Sunday*'s colour magazine,
You, with such distinction that his efforts
were credited with contributing to the
immediate and continued growth of the
paper's circulation.

Leese's editorial philosophy at the
Standard was that London should be
reported as a state of mind rather than
simply a physical place. It is a concept
which prevails widely among New
Yorkers and Leese encountered this when
he spent 18 months as editor and publisher of *SoHo News*, a lifestyle weekly
newspaper with a magazine format
published in Manhattan in the early

1980s. Back in Fleet Street he developed his own notions in this respect, urging his staff to move away from merely providing "local" news coverage. His New York experience also served to strengthen his belief in the value of his reporters living the kind of life they were writing about and he sought this kind of informed expertise from his London staff.

John Arthur Leese was educated at Bishop Vesey's School, Warwickshire, and began his journalistic career on local papers in the Midlands. He was appointed editor of the *Coventry Evening Telegraph* at the age of 34 and remained in that post for six years. In 1970 he moved to Fleet Street to become deputy editor of the London *Evening News*. He moved into a management post with Associated Newspapers in 1976 from where he was seconded in 1980 to supervise the editorial department of the *Evening News* in the sensitive period leading to the paper's demise. He edited the last 15 editions of the *News* before its closure in November that year. The efficiency, not to mention the compassion, he displayed in this task led Associated Newspapers to dispatch him to New York to take charge of *SoHo News* which was the flagship of its American operations. Leese demonstrated a flair for magazine journalism which equalled his newspaper expertise. He doubled the weekly's circulation and increased the cover price by a quarter. The paper continued to make a net loss, however, and Associated decided to close it. Leese was brought back to London by Associated Newspapers to play a crucial role in the struggle to keep its newest and most ambitious publishing venture, the *Mail on Sunday*, from foundering. The paper had been launched in the spring of 1982 but was finding the going rough. In a desperate attempt to revive circulation, the launch of a colour supplement was brought forward six months to October 1982. Leese was given the task of designing and editing the magazine. The impact of *You* was such that it restored the flagging fortunes of the *Mail on Sunday*.

Leese became editor of the *Standard* at a moment when the paper was widely regarded as requiring a revamp and when Robert Maxwell was about to launch the *London Daily News* in an attempt to break the *Standard*'s monopoly in the capital. Leese entered the fray with relish, redesigning the paper, recruiting new writers and generally revitalising the editorial content. He targeted the affluent young people working in the West End and the City, striving to give the paper a sense of urgency and excitement. He bolstered the listings and entertainment sections and strengthened the financial analysis and comment columns. He said at the time: "An editorial staff needs to believe it's the cavalry. All great newspapers have had that. The *Express* used to have it; the *Mirror* used to have it. More than anything I'd like to restore that feeling at the *Standard*."

His editorial efforts were re-enforced by Associated Newspapers' tactical move in relaunching the old *Evening News* as a "spoiler" and the Maxwell challenge proved to be an ignominious failure.

In victory Leese displayed characteristic modesty saying: "It's no good asking an editor how he does it. The truth is that elements that make for a profitable and successful newspaper simply cannot be reduced to a formula, not even a secret one. A good newspaper is not like a bottle of Coke."

Leese was a cheerful, tough, chain-smoking newspaperman well respected by his colleagues. He retired because of ill-health. He is survived by his wife, a son and a daughter.

CYRIL RAY

Cyril Ray, journalist and wine writer, died on September 24 aged 83. He was born in Lancashire on May 16, 1908.

"MY FRIENDS call me Ray, acquaintances call me Cyril." On the matter of correct address, as on many others, Cyril Ray was dogmatic and, as so often, right. To some extent he was a Cyril, stout in middle and old age, short and with a well-cut three piece suit covering his comfortable paunch and a rose often in his buttonhole. He was certainly a Ray. His presence illumined and enlivened any gathering, whether it was a wine tasting, a formal dinner or a simple party. He was witty, sometimes acerbic, and a master of the anecdote.

On the outside he fitted the public's image of a wine connoisseur very well. He had his set in Albany, was a liveryman (the Fan-Makers) and delighted that his son was educated at Eton. When he was 70 he took up horse riding again with some skill — at one time in his life he had been an ostler. But Ray relished contradictions. He enjoyed declaring himself a lifelong socialist, albeit a champagne socialist, to what was a distinctly conservative wine trade. And the "English gentleman" claimed with some pride that

there was "not a drop of British blood in his veins."

His father was born Rotenberg and his mother Caminetsky. They were Jews from eastern Poland who anglicised their name after they had arrived in Britain and settled in Bury. The Ray family struggled to make a living: Albert Ray was an optician who eventually became a travelling eye-tester for the Co-op. They were not especially orthodox: Cyril Ray began his education at a Wesleyan school (where doubtless he was warned against the evils of drink) before moving on to Manchester Grammar and winning a history scholarship to Jesus, Oxford. There was alcohol at home, sweet wine kept for honoured guests. Ray was always apt to say in a gathering of claret connoisseurs that he found sweet wines much more interesting to write about than dry ones.

When he left Oxford the depression was at its worst and after a succession of jobs, including teaching and working in a riding school, Ray took a short service commission in the RAF. It soon became clear that he was never going to be an ace pilot, and he found himself posted to the only surviving balloon squadron, of which he was made adjutant. Here his daily programme was not exacting. With his dog and a good selection of books he would be winched up into the heavens. The balloon protected the basket from the elements and there were no duties to distract him. He read widely. From the point of view of Ray's comfort and education it was a pity that the obsolescence of the observation balloon was at last recognised by the authorities and the squadron disbanded.

After a spell as a shop assistant in Liverpool Ray returned to Manchester, becoming manager of a news and feature cinema. It was this which brought him into contact with the *Manchester Guardian*, for which he did bits of special reporting. In 1936 he was taken on to the staff.

The outbreak of war found him in the London office, where James Bone directed with urbane professionalism a team which included Evelyn Montague, A. G. Macdonell, Henry Boardman and F. A. Voigt. Ray was neither abashed nor outshone by this galaxy. He became a war correspondent, first with the Fifth Destroyer Flotilla in the Channel, and then covering the North Africa landings in 1942 and the Eighth Army's campaign in Italy. In 1944 he switched to the BBC and was their correspondent with the American airborne assault on Nijmegen and with General Patton's Third Army thrust into Germany.

Ray never made any bones about having thoroughly enjoyed a war in which he had often shown conspicuous courage. On one occasion he even – quite improperly – took temporary command of a platoon on the Italian front when its officer and senior NCOs had been put out of action. He was mentioned in dispatches.

After the war Ray was for a time *Daily Express* correspondent in Rome. This was followed by a period of freelancing, in which he consolidated the reputation he had made as a broadcaster, particularly in talks to North America, during the war.

In 1950 Ian Fleming asked him if he would like to go to Moscow for *The Sunday Times*, which he had joined as a general purposes reporter the previous year. There followed two years of almost total frustration. "General reporting" was never a concept easily understood by the Soviets, and at the height of the cold war the authorities could see no reason why an Englishman, who must of course be a spy, should be allowed to practise it. Bureaucrats and censors blocked every path. Even so, it was remarkable what bricks Ray made without any straw at all. His dispatches (the only ones at that time from a staff man to the national press) were witty and, as far as circumstances permitted, informative. But it was with enormous relief that he shook the snow of Moscow off his boots and returned to London.

The Sunday Times then sensibly gave Ray's real talents free rein. He produced a weekly notice of any event that took his

fancy – social, political sporting, and so on. This was the sort of descriptive reporting in which Ray excelled and which the preoccupations and paper shortages of wartime had almost killed. Its revival gave much pleasure, and some of the articles were published in 1960 in a book called *Merry England* illustrated by Edward Ardizzone. Ray moved from *The Sunday Times* to *The Spectator* in 1958, and thence to *The Observer*, where he stayed until he retired in 1973.

By that time Ray's position as one of Britain's foremost wine writers was well established. His connection with the trade had begun quite modestly in the early 1950s when he was asked to contribute to an in-house magazine (in those days the phrase was yet to be invented) called *The Compleat Imbiber* sent out to the customers of the old family firm of W. and A. Gilbey. When the company's centenary arrived in 1956 Ray was asked to edit a selection of Gilbey articles and the first hardback *Imbiber* emerged with some very distinguished contributors: Betjeman, Postgate, A. P. Herbert and Margery Allingham were among them. The *Imbiber* became an annual event, kept alive by Ray's enthusiasm as it passed from publisher to publisher and sponsor to sponsor. Contributors tended to be paid in liquid form.

Ray quickly developed his own style of wine writing, which was practical and factual with a lively spicing of anecdote. He contributed regularly on the subject to *Punch* and *The Director* and dealt ferociously with editorial assistants who dared tamper with his copy. His was a new voice in an area where flowery phrases had proliferated. He was perfectly happy to leave the realms of first growths and discuss everyday wines and he was among the first to spot that the supermarkets were going to make life hard for family wine merchants.

He was ready to write about Drink – in another word, spirits – as well as wine and some of the best pieces in his collection *In a Glass Lightly* are about strong liquors. But the memory of his days as one of journalism's foot-soldiers, albeit a first class one, remained: when it came to books Ray favoured writing about the top of the market, where the pastures of research were likely to be the lushest.

He produced monographs on Mouton-Rothschild, Chateau Lafite and Bollinger as well as a study of what in later years was his own favourite tipple, cognac. He did not claim to have especially sensitive taste buds but his powers as a listener and researcher were considerable. At the end of a dinner attended by many of Britain's most distinguished wine writers − Eddie Penning-Rowsell, Hugh Johnson and Harry Waugh among them − during which many fine bottles had been finished Ray stood up and began his speech:

"Many of those here have a much better palate than I, but I'm the best bloody journalist in the room by a long chalk." No one demurred.

His wife, Liz, whom he married in 1953 and who survives him, is an expert cook and has written a number of books on the subject as well providing the food to back up Ray's cellar. He was decorated by both France and Italy for his services to wine. He remained dapper and as he grew older his clothes took on a slightly sporting appearance. Not for nothing was his first published book *Scenes and Characters* from R. S. Surtees and when he was featured on *Desert Island Discs* his choice of reading was *Mr Sponge's Sporting Tour.*

GORDON BASHFORD

Gordon Dennis Bashford, motor design engineer, died on September 21 aged 75. He was born on August 27, 1916.

GORDON Bashford led the design and development of the original Land Rover, one of the most successful vehicles made in Britain. The versatility of the American-built Willys Jeep during the second world war underlined the need for British forces to have a similar vehicle capable of crossing rough terrain under any conditions. The Wilks brothers, Maurice and Spencer, who were then running the Rover company, called in Bashford, who had joined the company as a 14-year-old apprentice and tea boy in 1930.

Designing such a vehicle was a tricky task but Bashford and his colleagues started with technology already available. He went out to a US Army barracks in the Cotswolds and bought two old Willys Jeeps which he stripped down to their component parts to discover the strengths and weaknesses of the vehicle. There were two stories about the origin of "Jeep": one is that the name is derived from the description "general purpose" (GP); The other that it stood for "Just every essential part."

Both became aims for the design of the new vehicle. The post-war shortage of steel forced the development team to use aluminium for the body structure. The choice was to prove a master stroke giving the Land Rover the strength and the longevity demanded by farmers and other customers the world over. Being lighter than would otherwise have been the case, the Land Rover was able to carry a greater pay-load, it did not corrode like steel, there was a low centre of gravity, and the coming of peace meant plenty of aluminium was available as aircraft production fell.

The vehicle was shown for the first time at the Amsterdam Motor Show of 1948 and was an immediate success with orders pouring in from around the world. King George VI tested one at Sandringham and Balmoral and ordered the first vehicle for his royal estates. Its four-wheel drive and rigid construction gave the Land Rover ability to cover rough ground. At the height of business Land Rovers were assembled from kits supplied from Rover's factory at Solihull, Warwickshire, in 30 countries and a million had been built by 1976.

Bashford, however, had to turn his attention back to saloon cars and, in charge of chassis design, was responsible for developing a series of cars for the company in the 1950s and 1960s, notably the staid Rover P4s — which included the 90 and 95 range; aiming at luxury and refinement they rivalled the Rolls-Royce as being Britain's quietest car. Bashford was chief designer of chassis and body for the P6 Rover 2000, which recaptured in modern guise the dashing image of pre-war Rovers and proved a lively work-horse for the police. He went on to design the SD1 model in 1976 which was voted European Car of the Year and also became popular for police use.

A need to provide cross-country performance with the comfort of saloon vehicle travel led to his involvement in the development of the Range Rover. First introduced in 1970 it is still breaking sales records for the the Land Rover company. The Range Rover was the only motor vehicle ever exhibited at the Louvre in Paris as a work of art.

While Bashford played a major part in the development of most of the post-war cars from Rover, he was also involved in research work on vehicles, such as the energy conservation car which was to be capable of 100 mph and 100 mpg; but its development was shelved. He later worked at Rover's research and development centre at Gaydon, Warwickshire, until his retirement in 1981.

He had gained his experience working at the drawing board which was later to be translated into direction of a team of up to 30 people working under him. They found him fun to work for. Quietly spoken, he was patient in reaching his objectives. He would go round and ask people if they had any problems; if one emerged he would draw up a chair and say: "Let's find a solution," leaving colleagues with the impression they had found it themselves. He was a brilliant design engineer, putting into practice fundamentals, embodying good design as the most elegant solution to a particular set of circumstances. He had a grasp of detail and of the overall concept. It was in marrying the two that he showed his originality. While he would never put up with incompetence he was never known to lose his temper with a colleague.

The motor industry was his life. Even in his retirement he helped with the design of vehicle adaptations for the disabled. A silver candle-stick on his dining table has on it: "Midlander of the Year 1976. Rover 3500 design team. Gordon Bashford." He leaves a considerable reputation: it is estimated that 70 per cent of the more than 1.6 million Land Rovers which have been built are still in regular use.

He is survived by his widow, Gladys.

DOUGAL ROBERTSON

Dougal Robertson, author of the best-seller Survive the Savage Sea, *died on September 22 aged 67. He was born in Edinburgh on February 12, 1924.*

THE shipwreck and survival of the Scots family Robertson equals in drama and surpasses, in its graphic exposition of a daily confrontation with death by exposure, the fictional *Swiss Family Robinson* on which generations of children were formerly nurtured. In the book he wrote about this remarkable episode, *Survive the Savage Sea* (1973), Dougal Robertson told the story of the 37-day ordeal experienced by him and his family, set adrift in the vast expanses of the Pacific Ocean after their sailing vessel was holed and sunk by killer whales.

Few men can have been better equipped to cope with such an experience than Dougal Robertson. He had served in the merchant navy and as a young cadet had been torpedoed by the Japanese off Ceylon in 1942. Within ten years he had his master's ticket and after marrying his wife, Linda, whom he had met when she was a Hong Kong nurse, he left the sea and they settled down to farm at Leek, Staffordshire.

After 15 years, by now with a daughter aged 19, a son of 17 and two more twin boys of 12, the Robertsons sold up their farm and set out to give their family the experience of a lifetime by circumnavigating the globe in their 43-ft ketch *Lucette*. Putting out from Falmouth on January 31, 1971, they made untroubled progress across the Atlantic, reaching Miami in good order and staying there for some months. There, the daughter, Anne, fell in love and left them to be with her boyfriend.

Continuing through the Panama Canal they acquired a passenger, a Welsh student named Robin Williams who wanted a ride to New Zealand. They had passed through the canal and were bowling along before a fresh breeze in the open Pacific when Robertson, who had just taken a sunsight and was working out his sextant reading at the chart table below decks, heard a loud thump and felt a shock run right through the vessel. A school of killer whales had attacked the hull vertically from below, stoving a large hole in the bottom. Pulling up a duckboard to assess the damage Robertson found himself looking into the unfathomable depths of the ocean and immediately realised that *Lucette* was doomed. Pursued up the companion way to the deck by a torrent of water he had just time to cut loose the dinghy and the life raft, while his wife threw life jackets to the children, before the vessel foundered leaving the family struggling in the water. The whole process had taken little more than a minute.

The disaster was the beginning of an ordeal which would certainly have been the death of a family of less resolution and resourcefulness. They were 200 miles downwind and down current of the Galapagos archipelago, the nearest land. Their closest practical landfall therefore was Costa Rica, 1,000 nautical miles distant. They had only a few emergency rations, no navigational aids and practically nothing else, apart from a 9ft 6in fibreglass dinghy and an inflatable raft, to sustain them.

The resulting triumph over adversity is as much morality play as adventure story. Robertson's iron will − which tolerated no display of weakness from either the members of his family or their passenger − was the decisive factor. He instilled into all of them that castaways must never become embittered, that what Dr Johnson called "that deferred hope which makes the heart sick" must be utterly banished from the mental horizon. On the eighth day a coaster came within three miles of them and rescue seemed certain, only for the chance to be cruelly wrested from them as the ship glided by on radar watch and autopilot. Robertson utterly forbade any lapse into self pity. By sheer force of character he managed to bring about in his party a mental adjustment

from the hope of rescue to a steely resolve to survive unaided. The agonies of thirst in the long intervals between rain they allayed by drinking the blood and spinal fluid of turtles they caught. They ate the flesh of sharks and dorado either raw or dried after being hung up in the rigging.

After reaching a nadir of strength and morale on about the eighth day they began to improve in physical health. Yet the threat of death by capsizing was ever present, especially after the 17th day when their raft finally sank and four adults and two children had then to coexist in a ninefoot boat. Excretion suddenly became a highly difficult matter, threatening to upset the trim of the boat, besides being agonising in itself because of dehydrated tissue. Sleep had to be carefully organised, with each member of the family maintaining a meticulously pre-arranged position in the tightly-packed boat, in spite of raw and suppurating body sores.

There were frayed tempers among the family and anger was reserved for their passenger who alone was unable to reconcile himself to the administration of the enemas with which Mrs Robertson sought to ease the miseries of defecation. Yet, astonishingly, rescue on the 38th day by a Japanese fishing boat found *Lucette*'s survivors almost attuned to their extraordinary environment and certainly capable of making the remaining 200 miles to land.

When they returned to England the family were much in demand for television and radio interviews and went on lecture tours here and abroad. Robertson's account of the ordeal became a bestseller and a film of the same title is about to be screened in America. It was not the only book he wrote: *Sea Survival* (1975) encapsulated the experiences of the voyage in a manual which has won worldwide acclaim among mariners.

Robertson's marriage was dissolved in 1988. He is survived by his three sons and a daughter.

KLAUS BARBIE

Klaus Barbie, Gestapo chief in Lyons, who in 1987 was jailed for life for his "crimes against humanity", died on September 25 aged 77. He was born in Bad Godesberg, Germany, on October 25, 1913.

KLAUS Barbie, notorious as the "Butcher of Lyons" was never a very senior Nazi, merely a middle-rank executive. But he displayed a cold, zealous ruthlessness, an apparent delight in inflicting torture and watching his victims suffer, that marked him out as bestial even by Nazi standards. He played a key role in the fight against the Resistance in Lyons, where he is believed to have tortured with his own hands the Resistance leader Jean Moulin.

After the war he managed to escape justice. He then spent over 30 years pursuing his vicious career in Bolivia in the service of dictators and cocaine-dealers before he was finally arrested and taken back to Lyons to face one of the most elaborate and highly-publicised trials of post-war Europe. Unrepentant, he still remained obstinately loyal to the oath that he had sworn to the Fuhrer.

Klaus Barbie's parents were primary schoolteachers; he grew up in a village in the Eifel hills and attended a *Gymnasium* in Trier. His father, who had been wounded at Verdun, was a violent drunkard who later died of his war injuries. These traumas affected Barbie and may help to explain, but not excuse, his adult hatred of the French. He also developed a sense of frustrated ambition, for his mother was too poor to send him to university. Instead, he turned to the Nazis for a career and for security. He trained in the SS, and was soon noted for his efficiency and zeal. In 1940 he began Gestapo work in Holland, then in 1941-2 was on the Russian front where he is thought to have taken part in the SS mass murders of Jews.

In November 1942, aged 29, he was transferred to Lyons where in effect he ran the Gestapo operation for the region under the orders of two senior SS officers. As was later proved at this trial he was diligent in rounding up Jews and deporting them to the death camps – most notably, in April 1944, he seized 44 Jewish orphan children in a home at Izieux in the Ain. He also harassed the Resistance and in June 1943 arrested Jean Moulin who later died of the tortures he had received, from Barbie and others.

According to all the evidence, Barbie relished torture as a kind of contest between himself and his victim, and he later spoke of his "respect" for Moulin and others whom he had failed to get to talk. His sadistic armoury included electric shocks, beatings with spiked chains, even the torture of small children in front of their parents. And right to the end he did not relent: in August 1944, as Lyons was about to be liberated, he sent his infamous "last convoy" of 650 prisoners ahead of him – to the death camps. For his work in Lyons he received a congratulatory telegram from Himmler.

After the war, back in Germany, Barbie went into hiding and lived by his wits as a petty thief. Then in 1947 the Americans spotted him and decided that his anti-communist expertise and fanaticism could be useful to them: so for four years he worked for the US Counter Intelligence Corps. They refused French demands to hand him over to justice, fearing that some of their own secrets might thus get back to Moscow. When the French insisted, the CIC in 1951 arranged for Barbie and his wife and two children to be shipped safely to South America under aliases – with Red Cross protection. In 1952 and 1954 French courts condemned him to death in absentia, for the murder of Moulin and other war crimes.

In Peru and then mainly in fascist Bolivia his old tendencies found new outlets. He began to take part in illicit arms dealing and in helping the cocaine trade. He formed friendly links with senior rightist Bolivian officers, who put him in charge of their repressive apparatus, including torture. He joined the furtive network of nostalgic Nazi exiles in South America, for whom anti-Bolshevism and love of Hitler were still the creeds; he even used young neo-Nazi German thugs to form a terror group, "the Fiances of Death", in the service of the cocaine traders and the Bolivian right. In 1980 he helped to organise the coup that brought the dictator General Garcia Meza to power in La Paz.

Barbie's true identity and whereabouts were known to the French from at least 1971; Serge and Beate Klarfeld, those intrepid Nazi-hunters, spent years trying to winkle him out, but he was too heavily entrenched. Then in September 1982 the Garcia Meza regime fell and democracy came to Bolivia. The French saw their chance. But there was no extradition treaty between the two countries, and Barbie was now a Bolivian citizen. Nevertheless, with a justification more moral than legal, the two governments did a deal that led to Barbie's return to Lyons under arrest. He was put in the same Montluc prison where thousands had perished under his auspices. His wife

had just died of cancer, and his son earlier in an accident: the fight had by now gone out of him, and he seemed a frail, bewildered old man – but still unrepentant.

After many delays, his trial finally took place in May-July 1987, in the Lyons Assize Court. Under the French "20-year limitation" law he could no longer be retried for his war crimes so a new charge was prepared, "crimes against humanity", which covered his deportation of Jews but not his anti-Resistance actions. Even so, there was no shortage of prosecution witnesses. His flamboyant extreme-left defence lawyer, Jacques Verges, made a bid to turn the trial into an indictment of French rightist "collaborators" and "colonialists"; but this failed. He did, however, advise his client to boycott much of the trial proceedings, which took place with Barbie back in his cell. But he was finally found guilty on all 177 counts and sentenced to life imprisonment.

Neither at his trial or at other times did Barbie show any sign of remorse or guilt. He told the court that the Nazis' cause had been just and their only fault was to have been defeated. And he told a friend that he was proud to have remained faithful to the oath that he had sworn to the Führer in 1935. His personal love for Hitler seemed to have a mystical, even psychotic quality, transcending reason. Yet in some other respects he seemed commonplace. Some witnesses of his tortures recalled his bitter, tight lips, frightening face and mocking laugh; others remembered him as courteous and well-dressed. Clearly he was something of a chameleon – and a womaniser. His wife, also a devoted Nazi, stayed in Germany during his Gestapo years in Lyons, where he was often seen in night clubs.

He is survived by his daughter, Ute.

ROY FULLER

Roy Fuller, CBE, poet, novelist and critic, died on September 27 aged 79. He was born on February 11, 1912.

ROY Fuller established his primary reputation as a poet during the last war, in which he served in the Royal Navy. Though this reputation grew slowly rather than spectacularly, by the publication of his *Collected Poems* in 1962 he had emerged as one of the most serious of the poets that succeeded the generation of Auden and Spender.

But Fuller's fame was built as much on his breadth of writing. He produced excellent crime fiction. He was a critic of authority and controversy as professor of poetry at Oxford. He carried cultural influence through his governorship of the BBC and through a no less controversial period at the Arts Council. Nor should literary achievement outshine his professional success as a solicitor with the Woolwich Equitable Building Society, on whose board he eventually sat. He was one of a rare breed of poets who were also businessmen.

Roy Broadbent Fuller was the eldest son of Leopold Fuller. He was educated at Blackpool High School and was admitted solicitor in 1934. From 1938 to 1958 he was assistant solicitor to the Woolwich Building Society, was its solicitor from 1958 to 1969 and on retirement became a director. In 1941 he was called up into the Royal Navy where he was becomingly modest about his good looks, which remained striking in spite of the moustache he is said to have grown in the hope of diguising them. His first volume of verse, *Poems*, had already appeared in 1939. This had an Audenesque air about it, reflecting the Marxism to which Fuller was to remain faithful long after other fellow travellers had fallen away but which he finally renounced at the end of his life. His second and third books, *The Middle of a War* (1942) and *A Lost Season* (1944) established him as a highly individual war poet. They were marked by an honesty of response to experience which remained his hallmark even when − as in perhaps some of his later verse − he toyed with modes or fell under influences to which his own poetic impulses were alien.

The civilian world did not provide the same stimulus. Fuller regretted he did not at this time go to university and he found it hard to make poetry from the changed circumstances of peace. The post-war period saw him turning to the novel. *Savage Gold*, a book for children, had appeared in 1946, followed by his three crime stories, *With My Little Eye* (1946), *The Second Curtain* (1953), and *Fantasy and Fugue* (1954). These were all well-crafted thrillers. Their successor, *Image of a Society* (1956), was set in his own professional milieu, describing office life and its business and emotional conflicts with sympathetic irony. Fuller's subsequent novels, including *The Ruined Boys* (1959) and *The Father's Comedy* (1961), displayed the same qualities of observation which mark his poetry, but none of them was as successful as his first four. After a pause of five years Fuller found a second wind as a poet. Critics felt that *Counterparts* (1954) lacked the assurance of his earlier verse but his new direction was clearly seen in *Brutus's Orchard* (1957).

These later poems demonstrate an increased allusiveness, a turning away from the admirable clarity of the war poems towards the play of a sophisticated intelligence on the poet's surroundings. Some saw this as a loss. The sensuous directness of the earlier volumes is missing and the detachment of the poet sometimes seems close to mere distance from emotion.

However, Fuller embraced this new course wholeheartedly and produced prolific verse, including *Buff* (1965), *New Poems* (1968) which won the Duff Cooper Memorial prize of that year, *Tiny Tears* (1973) and *The Reign of Sparrows* (1980), as well as poems for children *Poor Roy* (1977) and *Fellow Mortals – An Anthology of Animal Verse* (1981). *Collected Poems* appeared in 1962, conveying a rounded view of his best verse to that date.

In 1968 Fuller was elected professor of poetry at Oxford. Though the appointment was not controversial, his stewardship of it was more so. Though politically left-wing, Fuller proved determinedly and, to his young audiences, infuriatingly conservative as a critic. They sought an endorsement of "exciting" new developments in artistic form and content and were discontented with his exposition of the virtues of traditional craftsmanship.

Fuller made it clear that he had little sympathy with theories and practices which posited a disruption of form and sense as a criteria of modernity. His excellent lectures published as *Owls and Artificers* (1971) and *Professors and Gods* (1973) underpin his concern for discipline and an educated appreciation of the English language and its centuries-old literature.

Fuller's tenure of the chair came to an end in 1973 but he carried his strong opinion on all matters of art and culture forward to the Arts Council (1976-1977), where he was chairman of the literature panel. Fuller was not there long. As a man with a deep love of the arts as a force for bettering men's minds, he detested the fashionable dogmatism then prevailing on the Council. He took particular exception to its obsession with funding "community arts projects" of limited, indeed often non-existent, artistic worth. He found such spending a foolish and extravagant use of public money and resigned from the council in 1977. His other public post was that of governor of the BBC, from 1972 to 1979.

Fuller produced three volumes of autobiography, *Souvenirs* (1980), *Vamp Till Ready* (1982) and *Home and Dry* (1984). Critics expecting confessions were disappointed in these memoirs which, like his later verse, were detached to the point of inscrutability. Emotion remained, with Fuller, deeply controlled. What was described as complete memoirs, in one volume, involving a conflation of the previous three, appeared as *The Strange and the Good* in 1989.

This was not the end of Fuller's autobiographical activity. *Spanner and Pen* appeared earlier this year. Again would-be biographers sought in vain for anything meaty from Fuller. *Spanner and Pen* revealed a solitary man, from an early age never robust in health and, as a near octogenarian, stoically accepting the limits of his life and achievement. His final renunciation of communism was dispatched in a paragraph. Fuller recorded that this enthusiasm had been replaced by an admiration for the Queen and a respect for the solid achievements of the Woolwich Building Society.

He had been appointed CBE in 1979 and in the same year was awarded the Queen's Gold Medal for Poetry. Meanwhile the professional side of his dual life led him to write *Questions and Answers in Building Society Law and Practice* as well as *The Building Societies Acts*. He was a former vice-president of the Building Societies Association and chairman of its legal advisory panel from 1958 to 1969.

He married in 1939 Kathleen Smith. Their only son John is also a distinguished poet.

OONA CHAPLIN

Lady Chaplin, widow of Charlie Chaplin, died in the night of September 26/27 aged 65. She was born on May 13, 1926.

PERHAPS Oona Chaplin herself never completely understood whether it was in the radiance of great men or in their shadow that she passed her life. Her father was the brilliant but erratic American playwright Eugene O'Neill; her grandfather the Irish-American actor James O'Neill. The turbulence of that heritage is chronicled in O'Neill's play *Long Day's Journey into Night*.

Oona was born at Spithead, Bermuda, where her parents were then living. Her mother, Agnes Boulton, was O'Neill's second wife, by whom he also had a son, Shane. Another son, Eugene O'Neill, Junior, was the offspring of O'Neill's previous short-lived marriage to Kathleen Jenkins.

When Oona was two years old her father fell in love with an actress, Carlotta Monterey. After the resulting divorce, Oona moved with her mother to New Jersey and was sent to school in New York. (By an odd coincidence, Charles Chaplin was at that time trying to console Ralph Barton, the man Carlotta had abandoned. Despite Chaplin's efforts, Barton committed suicide.)

From childhood Oona O'Neill was an astonishing beauty, with her serene, classical features, dark hair and large luminous eyes. Although she never overcame her acute shyness, she was named debutante of her year, and voted in New York the "Most Beautiful Woman in the World". Her closest school-friends were Gloria Vanderbilt and Carole Marcus, later to become successively the wife of William Saroyan and Walter Matthau. The three were to remain in close contact for many years — in Carole Matthau's case to the end of Oona Chaplin's life.

She took the Vassar entrance examinations, but decided instead that she wanted to act. A screen test she made for *The Girl from Leningrad* survives, and suggests that she would have been an extraordinary and vivid personality in the cinema: even in this fragment of film the mixture of hesitance and eager vitality is fascinating.

An agent, Minna Wallace, engineered a meeting with Charles Chaplin, hoping that he might see in Oona O'Neill a likely leading lady for a film he was then planning, based on Paul Vincent Carroll's play *Sunshine and Shadow*. She did not get the part and the film was never to be made. Instead the meeting sparked an instant romance that was to last to the end of their lives.

Chaplin was 54 and Oona 17 when they met in 1943. Chaplin's friends were gravely alarmed, remembering the disasters and notorious divorces that resulted from two earlier marriages with teenage brides, Mildred Harris and Lita Grey. The prospects were not made brighter by a series of pending legal actions, eventually including a paternity suit, nominally brought by a young actress Joan Barry – though ultimately engineered by the FBI and J. Edgar Hoover who had a long-standing vendetta against Chaplin.

Eugene O'Neill was violently opposed to the match between his daughter and a man less than one year younger than himself. Oona was never again to meet her father, who excluded her and her brother Shane from his will. The couple were married by a Justice of the Peace at Santa Barbara, with two studio employees as witnesses. The Justice, looking at Oona, asked: "And where is the young man?"

Despite the difference in ages, the marriage was to prove idyllic. They were inseparable. Oona supported Chaplin through the anguish of the Barry affair, as well as in the creation of his subsequent films. In his last American film, *Limelight*, she even doubled for Claire Bloom in a retake made after Miss Bloom had returned to England.

Chaplin's final years in America were clouded by the McCarthyist climate. Although a subpoena to appear before the Un-American Activities Committee was withdrawn, he became a target for the witchhunters, as a foreigner (he never gave up his British nationality) and an instinctive liberal and humanist. The Chaplins found many of their Hollywood circle had been fair-weather friends.

Chaplin had long wished to show Oona England; and he decided to take her to London for the premiere of *Limelight*. On September 17, 1952, they embarked from New York on the *Queen Elizabeth*, with their children Geraldine, Michael, Josephine and Victoria. When the ship was two days at sea, the American Attorney General announced that the re-entry permit, which Chaplin required as an alien, was rescinded. Chaplin refused to fight the decision, and instead settled in a handsome 19th century mansion at Vevey sur Corsier in Vaud, Switzerland. The Chaplins lived there in evident contentment, with a growing family: the eight children of the marriage were completed by Eugene, Jane, Annette and Christopher. Oona very publicly adopted British nationality. Chaplin's last two films, *A King in New York* and *A Countess from Hong Kong*, were made in British studios, always with Oona by his side.

The marriage was an extraordinary, self-sufficient companionship which became only closer as Chaplin grew older. In his last years he could not bear to be separated from Oona for even the briefest period. She insisted on nursing him herself during his final illness.

After his death on Christmas Day, 1977, Oona found it impossible to replace the presence that had dominated her entire adult life. For a while she tried to embark on a social life and to form new friendships, and established an apartment in New York; but her natural shyness and the persistent influence of Chaplin's memory made it difficult. She retired more and more to Vevey and the exquisite suite she had created for herself in the Manoir. In her later years she saw few people outside her family. She retained a passionate interest, however, in the cinema, and was a voracious reader and dedicated video-watcher.

Sadly her devotion to Chaplin's career probably inhibited her own creative abilities. Highly intelligent, indefatigably curious (she adored gossip), she was a writer of natural skill and style. Though she was always amused and delighted at the large offers she sometimes received for her memoirs, her talent was to be restricted to letters and diaries.

She died, after a long and solitary period of deteriorating health, at the Manoir de Ban.

MILES DAVIS

Miles Davis, jazz trumpeter, bandleader and composer, died of pneumonia and a stroke in Santa Monica, California, on September 28 aged 65. He was born on May 25, 1926.

MILES Davis was an enigmatic and restless artist who continually re-shaped his style and his career − if not his individual sound − over four decades. Most of the greatest jazz musicians have developed one distinctive approach; Davis fashioned three or four including a controversial blend of jazz-rock. Along the way he cultivated a brooding persona which earned him the sobriquet "Prince of Darkness". The image was compounded by the sound of his voice, an eerie whisper which he acquired in the late 1950s after trying to shout while recovering from an operation on his vocal cords. Whether or not his rock-influenced recordings will endure, he secured his place in history with a series of hugely influential albums in the 1950s and early 1960s.

Miles Dewey Davis III was born in Alton, Illinois, and raised in East St Louis, about 25 miles south along the Mississippi. Unlike most black musicians of his generation, Davis came from a well-to-do family. His grandfather had been a book-keeper and land-owner in Arkansas, his father an affluent dentist who, after moving to Illinois, purchased a 200-acre ranch. Given his first trumpet for his 13th birthday, Davis received private tuition and played in his high school band. In 1944 he enrolled at the Juilliard School in New York. Studying by day, he spent the evenings in the jazz venues of 52nd Street, where Charlie Parker and his circle were setting out the rudiments of bebop.

Within months Davis had abandoned his studies and entered the studios as a member of Parker's quintet. The results show that he was no virtuoso. The rapid-fire trumpet cadenza which opens "Koko", for instance, had to be played by Dizzy Gillespie, who had been "sitting in" on the piano. However Davis was later to turn his technical limitations to his own advantage; in contrast to the ultimately self-defeating pyrotechnics of the beboppers, he evolved a smoother, burnished sound rooted in the middle register.

The first real blossoming of his own talents took place in 1948, after he had set out to form his own band. Mixing with a circle of musicians who met in the flat of the arranger Gil Evans, Davis led a nonet which featured the saxophonists Gerry Mulligan and Lee Konitz. With its unorthodox instrumentation, including French horn and tuba, the group was too sophisticated for most audiences, and was a commercial flop. However Capitol Records were persuaded to stage recording sessions in 1949 and 1950. Years later the tracks were released on an album with the apt title *The Birth of the Cool*.

Davis was in no position to capitalise on his achievement. Once exceptionally clean-living he had fallen into heroin addiction. At one point he scraped together money for drugs by pimping. It was not until 1954 that he returned to full health. The following year saw a string of outstanding tracks for the Prestige label − among them "Walkin'" and "Blue 'n' Boogie". Perhaps the best of all came on a Christmas Eve session with a line-up featuring the eccentric pianist Thelonious Monk and the vibraphonist Milt Jackson. Davis's languid improvisations on "Bag's Groove" and "Bemsha Swing" made telling use of space and silence. During this period he also introduced the metallic harmon mute which, placed close to the microphone, produced the wistful tone that was to become his trademark.

In 1955 he formed his first great quintet, with John Coltrane (tenor saxophone), Red Garland (piano), Paul Chambers (bass) and Philly Joe Jones (drums). The group's finest recordings were made in unusual circumstances. Though Davis had been offered a lucrative contract with Columbia, he was under an obligation to make four more albums for Prestige. He solved the problem by recording all the required material in the space of just two sessions. A mixture of Broadway tunes and bop and blues themes, the music was released on four exceptional albums: *Cookin'*, *Relaxin'*, *Workin'* and *Steamin'*. His relationship with CBS was to last for 30 years. Highlights included the three ambitious orchestral collaborations with Gil Evans – *Miles Ahead*, *Porgy and Bess* and *Sketches of Spain*.

In 1959 came his masterpiece, *Kind of Blue*, a set based partly on modal patterns which freed the musicians from the constraints of the conventional song structure. Davis's terse solos were balanced against the effusive tenor saxophone of Coltrane, the bluesier alto of Julian "Cannonball" Adderley and the impressionistic chords of the pianist Bill Evans. While not the first album to explore modes, it did much to popularise the concept.

By this time magazine features were portraying Davis as a high-earning, debonair man-about-town, complete with expensively appointed home and Ferrari sports car. For all his wealth, he was not free from racial pressures. In the summer of 1959 he was savagely beaten by two New York policemen following an altercation outside the Birdland jazz club.

After a night in jail, he was later cleared of all charges against him. The experience left a residue of bitterness.

Another blow came with Coltrane's departure from the quintet. Davis, however, was in scintillating form on his first ever live album, taped in 1961 in the unglamorous setting of the Blackhawk club in San Francisco. Often overlooked in favour of later recordings at Carnegie Hall and the Lincoln Center, the Blackhawk double album contains Davis's most expressive live work.

The rest of the Sixties found him searching for a new direction. With the advent of Free Form jazz and, above all, the rise of the rock superstars he was being edged out of the limelight. Though he had recruited promising young players such as Herbie Hancock, his concerts were locked into ever more complex chromatic forms, with the old standards being played over and over at a frenetic tempo. The studio albums also seemed to lose the balance between abstraction and emotion. Though these were performances of enormous technical assurance, they seemed almost a private dialogue between the musicians.

By 1968 Davis's audience was beginning to dwindle. His response was to tackle the rock movement head on. There were already hints of the change on *Miles In The Sky*, *Filles de Kilimanjaro* and the ethereal *In A Silent Way* (arguably his last classic album).

With the release of *Bitches Brew* in 1970, Davis went all the way in an extravagant cocktail of jazz psychedelia. The venture had the desired effect: Davis was back in fashion and attracting a huge new audience and increased royalties. Soon he was appearing at rock stadia on the same bill as the likes of Neil Young and Steve Miller. The move ultimately proved a creative dead-end, apart from isolated flashes of excitement on *Live-Evil* and the soundtrack to the boxing documentary *Jack Johnson*. While Davis had acquired cult status amongst the young – and a suitably flamboyant wardrobe – the distinctive sound of his trumpet was soon submerged by the heavy rock ostinati of his musicians, who stayed rooted to one chord for minutes on end. With the release of the would-be street music of "On The Corner" in 1973 (perhaps the most monotonous album ever to bear his name), he was filtering his solos through an electronic "wah-wah" pedal. The world's greatest trumpeter now sounded like a middling guitarist playing on an inadequate PA system. On stage he began to appear increasingly remote and apathetic. His health had been poor, and in 1972 he had suffered fractures after crashing his Lamborghini.

In 1975, after further bouts of serious illness he withdrew into what turned out to be a five-year retirement. Speculation about his activities intensified: the truth, as later depicted in his autobiography, was that he descended into a squalid, semi-reclusive existence dominated by cocaine, heroin and alcohol.

After repeated rumours of a comeback, he finally returned, in 1981, with *The Man With The Horn*, a moderate amalgam of jazz and pop. Still looking extremely frail, Davis resumed touring, winning a well-deserved standing ovation in London in 1983. There were hopes that he was about to embark on a new phase of creativity. *Decoy*, released in 1984, contained some of his strongest playing for 20 years. But the next album *You're Under Arrest* set the pattern for the rest of the decade, with Davis content to mark time by playing brief phrases on undemanding pop themes. The Cindi Lauper hit "Time After Time" hardly stood comparison with "My Funny Valentine". The standard of his sidemen also declined; musicians of the calibre of the guitarist John Scofield were replaced by anonymous apprentices.

Davis, meanwhile, masked his fluctuations in tone and pitch by making ever-increasing use of his mute.

By the time he released *Tutu* in 1986 he had left Columbia for WEA. Assiduously crafted by the producer and multi-instrumentalist Marcus Miller, the synthesiser-based tunes required the mimimum of involvement by Davis, who had only to add his trumpet solos over the pre-recorded tracks. A similar process was used on the subsequent albums *Siesta* and *Amandla*.

Uninterested in celebrating the past, Davis preferred to discuss his enthusiasm for Prince and Michael Jackson. When not touring he devoted much of his time to drawing and painting; his abstract sketches adorned the sleeves of a number of his records. In 1986 he made an appearance on the TV detective series *Miami Vice*, playing a pimp.

1989 saw the appearance of his long-awaited memoirs, *Miles: The Autobiography*. It was marked by a monotonous flow of profanities and a tendency to settle scores with old enemies including former wives but it was also an unflinching self portrait which emphasized Davis's single-minded pursuit of his craft.

"To be a great musician," he wrote, "you've got to always be open to what's new, what's happening at the moment. You have to be able to absorb it if you're going to continue to grow and comunicate your music." In his continual search for something new, Davis was always alive to young talent in jazz, hiring Herbie Hancock when the keyboard player was 23 and the drummer Tony Williams as an 18-year-old. Among the experimentalist musicians he used were Chick Corea, Joe Zawinul, Dave Holland, John McLaughlin, Keith Jarrett, Airto Moreira, Billy Cobham and Jack De Johnette.

His irascible temper and seeming indifference to audiences in the early years made Miles Davis a controversial figure while his refusal to rest upon his laurels won him new admirers as it alienated others. More importantly, his elegant and lyrical musicality added anger, pain and deep sadness to the emotional lexicon of jazz, ensuring that his stature as an innovative influence on jazz trumpet playing – alongside Louis Armstrong, Bix Beiderbecke and Dizzie Gillespie – is unquestioned.

He was married at least three times – to dancer Frances Taylor, singer Betty Mabry and actress Cicely Tyson. He is survived by a daughter and three sons.

NATALIA GINZBURG

Natalia Ginzburg, Italian novelist and essayist, died on October 8 at her home in Rome, aged 75. She was born in Sicily on July 5, 1916.

NATALIA Ginzburg won Italy's most prestigious literary award, the Strega Prize, in 1964 for her autobiographical novel *Lessico famigliare* (1963) translated into English as *Family Sayings* (1963). She had been her country's most popular woman writer since the death of Elsa Morante. Many critics would put her achievements well ahead of those of Morante and indeed, of Grazia Deledda, the only woman from Italy to have won the Nobel Prize (1926).

She became increasingly celebrated as the skilful, quiet, almost withdrawn depictor of women trapped in boredom and routine. She was as much a mistress of understatement as of feminine psychology. In recent years the enterprising Carcanet Press has published some of her work in translation and has thus introduced her to a new generation of English readers.

She was born Natalia Levi in Palermo, the daughter of a Jewish professor of biology from Trieste and a Catholic mother from Milan. She herself observed that her lifelong sense of isolation – the state which she was so adept at describing in her novels and stories – might well have been caused by the fact that she was raised without religious training or affiliation.

She told the story of her parents, who were both socialists, in *Lessico famigliare*. When she was three her father moved to the university of Turin and she grew up in that city. Her house became a centre of anti-fascist activity. She began to write while still in her teens and made her debut in the Florentine magazine *Solaria* in 1934, with a story she wrote at the age of 17 called "Un'assenza" ("An Absence"). She herself regarded this as her first piece of writing and it does, indeed, almost uncannily, embody many of the unique qualities of her later work: a tragically bored protagonist, tormented and stifled by her family. But this was not avowedly autobiographical and it was only 30 years later as a mature writer that Ginzburg realised that she had been writing subjectively from the very beginning.

She was married in 1938 to an anti-fascist professor of Russian literature, Leone Ginzburg. Between then and 1943, when Ginzburg was arrested in Rome for working on a clandestine press, they had three children. On February 5, 1944, he died, almost certainly by poison at the hands of the Germans, into whose keeping he had been passed, in the infirmary at Regina Coeli Prison.

Meanwhile Natalia had published her first novel, *La strada che va in città*, translated as *The Road to the City*, with the Turin firm of Einaudi, under the pseudonym of Alessandra Tornimparte. It was quite successful and after the war she went to work for Einaudi as a consultant. Here she became a close friend of Cesare Pavese. In 1947 she published what was, according to a sizeable number of her admirers her finest novel, *É stato cosi*, translated as *The Dry Heart* in 1949.

Her first novel had told of a girl who drifted into a marriage with a man to whom she was barely attracted and whom she did not much like. In *É stato cosi* she told a more violent story: "Giovanna can neither draw her husband from his mistress nor (and worse) achieve any meaningful communication with him. She kills him, hardly because she wants to, but simply because she feels that it had to happen that way." This was generally recognised as a powerful and subtle novel: deceptively written in an everyday idiom, it creates its characters by means of the revealing phrases they use. Ginzburg's economy was often compared to Chekhov.

Later important works included her longest novel, *Tutti i nostri ieri* (1952), translated as *A Light for Fools* in 1956, which deals with the life of the family throughout the second world war, and *Lessico famigliare*, her own favourite. Here she perfected her device of revealing people by what they say and, in particular, by what they keep on saying. This bitter novel was also much praised by its

picture of inter-war Italy. Other translated fiction includes *Le voci della sera* (1961) and *L'inserzione* (1965).

In the latter half of her career Ginzburg became a cultural essayist, discussing whatever her astute mind found interesting – whether it was movies, books or current mores. She was a pessimistic writer, but never bitter and always engaging, unassuming, intelligent and sincere.

Some of her essays are collected in *Never Must You Ask Me* (1973). With her death, a quiet voice is silenced, one which conveyed density and wisdom in a deceptively chatty manner. She achieved a compressed poetry by using the plain prose that is so difficult to compose.

In 1950 she made a second marriage to an Italian professor of English Literature, Gabriele Baldini. She lived in London from 1959 to 1962, while he was head of the Italian Institute of Culture here. He died in 1969.

DR SEUSS

Theodor Seuss Geisel, the American author/illustrator, better known as "Dr Seuss", died on September 24 aged 87. He was born on March 2, 1904, in Springfield, Massachusetts.

EXASPERATED by the "Pallid Primers" that were designed to teach children to read, John Hersey, in an article in *Life* magazine in 1954, called for a conversion to jauntiness. He had in mind some best-selling picture books of the day like *Yertle The Turtle* and *If I Ran the Zoo* from the crazily inventive pen of "Dr Seuss."

Inspired by this article, Dr Seuss and an educational publisher got together and jauntily created for young children a new-style reading book *The Cat in The Hat*, the appearance of which in 1957 dismayed (but never finally routed) the pallid primer mongers. With a controlled

vocabulary of only 175 words the text took off into uncontrolled hilarity – using the principles of the reading scheme to send up the whole genre. Good little, bored children in the book find themselves at the mercy of an anarchic creature in a stove-pipe hat who is determined that they shall bouncily enjoy themselves to the consternation of a prim, admonitory goldfish.

> *I know it it wet*
> *And the sun is not sunny*
> *But we can have lots*
> *Of good fun that is funny.*

The Cat in The Hat was an immediate hit and brought its author the presidency of Beginner Books, a division of Random House, where he persuaded like-minded colleagues to help him pioneer easy reading through farce. His own final tally of 47 books sold more than 100 million copies in 18 languages. His best-selling title was the very simple *Green Eggs and Ham* of 1960.

Theodor Seuss Geisel (who also wrote as Theo Le Sieg) was the son of a Massachusetts brewer who at one time, significantly, ran a zoo. The boy had a conventional enough schooling, graduating from Dartmouth College, New Hampshire, in 1925 and then going to Lincoln College, Oxford, to read English. Philological studies had little attraction for him, however, and he left to travel in Europe and to develop a growing talent for cartooning. This had surfaced while he was editor of the Dartmouth College journal, *Jack O' Lantern*, and it was through a need to disguise his identity in that paper that he hit on the notion of calling himself by his middle name.

On his return to America in 1927, his comic skills were noticed by the wife of a Standard Oil Accounts Executive. He was engaged to devise an advertising campaign based on his slogan of "Quick Henry! the Flit", and as a result he gained a degree of security which enabled him to marry Helen Palmer, an English girl whom he had first met while doodling his way through the Oxford lectures on Old English.

During the 1930s Ted Geisel freelanced on several advertising campaigns and on cartooning for magazines such as *Judge* and *Life*. In 1936, however, during a stormy sea-passage, he found himself composing some thudding verses which turned themselves into his first picture book, *And To Think That I saw It on Mulberry Street* (1937). He claimed that his manuscript was rejected by 28 publishers before Vanguard accepted it, but as soon as it was published it was widely praised for its nonsensical verve. (Beatrix Potter, a severe reader, called it: "The cleverest book that I have met with for many years").

Mulberry Street set a pattern that Geisel was to follow through to *The Cat in The Hat* and beyond. Essentially this consisted of the marrying of a variety of nonsense texts, almost always in a compulsively rhythmic doggerel, to an equally nonsensical series of pictures, using a bestiary which included Sneetches and Grinches and a gazeteer that stretched from the Valley of Vung to the inaccessible Solla Sollew. The nonsense, however, was frequently tempered by moral considerations, which sometimes concerned the need for personal integrity, and sometimes concerned global issues. *The Lorax* (1971), for instance, hinges on the dangers of pollution, *The Butter Battle Book* (1984) on nuclear destruction, while one of his last books, *You're Only Old Once* (1986), was primarily intended as a text-book for the aged: "You buy a copy for your child now and you give it to him on his 70th birthday."

During the war Geisel worked on projects related to the making of information films and this interest continued afterwards, when he made his home at La Jolla in Southern California. Several documentary films of his won academy awards and he was especially proud of the award for the animated cartoon *Gerald McBoing-Boing* in 1951. In 1968 he received the first of several honorary doctorates – which gave some credence to the title that he had bestowed upon himself so long before. He also received awards for his children's books.

Helen Palmer Seuss died in 1967; a year later Geisel married Audrey Stone Diamond who survives him. There were no children.

LEONARD SAINER

Leonard Sainer, former chairman of Sears and senior partner of Titmuss Sainer & Webb, died on September 30 aged 81. He was born on October 12, 1909.

ALTHOUGH he will always be known as Sir Charles Clore's right-hand man, Leonard Sainer was a shrewd businessman in his own right, combining a commercial brain with legal training to become one of London's leading corporate lawyers in the 40 years or so after the second world war. The son of a tailor, Sainer was brought up in the East End of London. He was educated at the Central Foundation, near Old Street, before qualifying for University College and the London School of Economics.

He graduated in law in 1929 and his father paid 500 guineas for him to be articled to Bullcraig & Davis, a firm of solicitors just off the Strand. In 1931 he was asked to handle the purchase of a lease on the Prince of Wales theatre for £700. The client was Charles Clore.

They struck up a relationship which was to last until Clore's death in 1979. Sainer acted for Clore in several more property transactions in the 1930s, including the stock market flotation of the company which owned the Prince of Wales. Gradually, Clore transferred all his legal requirements to Sainer.

The volume of work for Clore enabled Sainer to leave Bullcraig & Davis and buy a share in a new partnership, Titmuss Sainer & Webb. Its London office was at 3 Fleet Street, above Weingott's the tobacconist.

Webb was in the Royal Air Force during the war, while Titmuss died in 1941. That left Sainer to run the practice as he was a lifelong diabetic and unfit for military service. After the war Webb left to farm. So Sainer was in charge, and took a large space in Serjeant's Inn near Fleet Street, when it was rebuilt after being bombed. He rapidly filled it with lawyers to cope with the work which flowed in over the years because of Sainer's connection with Clore.

Sainer's commercial experience expanded. He joined the board of other client companies such as Beautility, the furniture maker. Clore, meanwhile, became much more active. He exploited the opportunity to make money out of retail property by selling the freehold and buying back a long lease, or sale and leaseback. In 1952 he was advised by an estate agent that a footwear company, J. Sears & Co (True-Form) Boot Company, was worth much more than its value on the stock market. Clore bought Sears with the idea of breaking it up but he met a specialist shoe retailer, Harry Levison, who persuaded him that he could make more money by keeping the businesses. Sainer joined the board, and his time was increasingly taken up with helping to organise a series of takeovers for the company.

Sainer's contemporaries viewed him as a workaholic. He would go out on the town with Clore and then go home and work from 11pm until 3am. They went to parties together and frequented Annabel's club in Berkeley Square. Their other shared passion was horse racing.

They both owned horses and that was a major reason for Clore's decision that Sears should buy William Hill, the bookmaker, in 1972. But as a rule Sainer was the restraining influence, talking Clore out of some of his wilder schemes.

Although Sainer went into the offices of his legal practice each day, he had a direct line from there to Clore's office in Park Street, Mayfair. Sainer lived nearby, in South Audley Street, so they were constantly in touch. Lawyers cannot normally acquire substantial wealth because of the impact of the tax system on partnership income. But Clore helped Sainer to build a fortune by judiciously guiding him to create an extensive investment portfolio.

Despite his devotion to Clore, Sainer still became embroiled in other companies. He became a director of First National Finance Corporation, another TSW client, and advised London & County Securities. Both the latter companies were major sufferers from the secondary banking crisis of 1973-4 and Sainer spent a considerable time assisting in their rescue.

By the mid-1970s Clore was spending a rising proportion of his time overseas. In 1977 he finally decided to emigrate. On January 1, 1978, Sainer became chairman of Sears and resigned as a partner of TSW. But he continued to bring clients to the law firm until 1988.

After Clore died Sainer reshaped Sears, selling those businesses that he felt did not fit, such as engineering, knitwear, carpet making and a laundry. Sainer also enjoyed visiting America and wanted to make Sears a force over there. One of his greatest skills was his negotiating ability. He could judge accurately what was in the mind of his adversary and employed acute powers of persuasion and bluff. He was an opportunist who could assess the value of the possibilities that came his way.

Sainer was a gentle person, without being very emotional. Dedicated to his profession, he generated respect rather than affection and, by long years of training himself to be utterly discreet, had difficulty in forming deep relationships. Although he could be very tough, he was always ready to help others.

Like Clore, Sainer was a generous donor to charities. He set up the Clore Foundation in 1964 and was a trustee until 1989. He had his own substantial foundation, the Leonard Sainer Charitable Trust, which gave large sums to Jewish and racing charities. He was also closely involved in Mind, the mental health charity.

Apart from racing, Sainer's great love was soccer. Like his father, he went to Tottenham and Arsenal on alternate Saturdays. But he rose to his feet only when Spurs scored. In November 1989 he married his long-standing companion, Wendy, who survives him. They had no children.

HIS HOLINESS
DEMETRIOS I

His Holiness Demetrios I, Ecumenical Patriarch of Constantinople and spiritual leader of the world's Eastern Orthodox Christians since 1972, died of a heart attack in an Istanbul hospital on October 2 aged 77. He was born in Istanbul in 1914.

IN THE last four years of his life His Holiness Demetrios I assumed a much more positive stance than that which he had maintained during his first 15 years as spiritual leader of the world's 300 million Eastern Orthodox Christians. He became the first Ecumenical Patriarch to visit the western hemisphere when he undertook ceremonial visits to Rome, Washington, and London. He also made a lengthy tour of the most important Orthodox churches, visiting the patriarchates of Alexandria, Jerusalem, Serbia, Romania and Moscow. During

these visits he promoted discussion within the Orthodox community of liturgical and doctrinal questions that had not been formally aired since the last ecumenical council recognised by the Orthodox church in the ninth century.

The primary purpose of his visits to the West were to promote the dialogue of Christian unity — a cause which much exercised him — but these trips, and his action in stimulating doctrinal debate, also reflected his concern that any future resurgence of Orthodox Christianity in Eastern Europe might lead to the Soviet Union posing a threat to the Constantinople patriarchate's primacy in the Orthodox communion. Fears that the centuries-old rivalry between Constantinople and Moscow for the spiritual leadership of orthodoxy might be reactivated were also believed to be behind his decision to boycott the ceremonies in Moscow in 1988 marking the 1,000th anniversary of Russian Christianity. In April, however, the Russian Patriarch Alexei II visited the Constantinople Patriarchate — the first high-level contact in more than 400 years — and acknowledged it as the mother church.

Demetrios I was the 365th Ecumenical Patriarch — *primus inter pares* of the five Eastern Christian leaders. He was a modest and unassuming man who found himself on Orthodoxy's first patriarchal throne after the death of Athenagoras I, more by dint of Turkey's objections to the main contenders, than because of any personal ambition. The patriarchate had been based in Phanar, the Greek quarter of Istanbul and the seat of the Orthodox Church, for 1,500 years, first under the Byzantine empire and then under the Ottomans. But, like the Byzantine emperors of old, the Turkish authorities retained the power to disqualify undesirable candidates for patriarchal succession. Their power stems from the 1923 Treaty of Lausanne governing the status of the Greek Orthodox minority in Turkey and the Muslim Turkish minority in Greece. The patriarch and his team of 20 clerics and staff must be Turkish citizens, limiting the choice to a dwindling community of some 5,000 Orthodox in the country — mostly ethnic Greeks who trace their roots to the Byzantine Empire. Under the treaty the patriarch is defined as a religious leader only of the Greek Orthodox people in Turkey. The Ankara government does not recognise his ecumenical role.

A year before Demetrios was enthroned the Turkish authorities emphasised their power by closing the seminary at Halki, which for generations had been a training ground for Orthodox clerics and patriarchs, and forbade the wearing of Orthodox attire in public places. When Athenagoras died in 1972 they barred the most likely candidates to succeed him, then accepted the election of Demetrios as a compromise. It was generally assumed at the time that in so doing the Turkish authorities had sought to lower the prestige of the patriachate and relegate it to the role of a local church. Many Turks had resented the survival of the Ecumenical Patriarchate in the Phanar district of old Istanbul as the last vestige of a Greek presence.

Succeeding the charismatic Athenagoras was already a formidable task, especially after this powerful ecclesiastical personality set in motion, after 1967, the process for a dramatic reunion between Rome and Constantinople, after a rift lasting over 1,000 years. In pursuing this inherited mission Demetrios was fortunate to be served by the advice of his senior bishop, Metropolitan Meliton of Chalcedon, an indefatigable and inspired worker for the cause of Christian unity. Metropolitan Meliton died in 1989.

Patriarch Demetrios was born Demetrios Papadopoulos. He graduated from the theological school of Halki in 1937 and was ordained deacon. For two years he served as secretary and preacher of the diocese of Edessa, in northern Greece. Between 1939 and 1964 he served in Orthodox parishes of Istanbul except for five years after 1945 when he became chaplain of the Orthodox community in Tehran and taught ancient Greek at Tehran University for one year.

Elected titular bishop of Elaia in 1964,

he was assigned to the bishopric of Kurtulus in Istanbul. In 1972 he was elected Metropolitan of Imbros and Tenedos, but five months later he was called by the Patriarchal Holy Synod, with the blessing of the Turkish authorities, to serve as "Bishop of Constantinople and New Rome, and Ecumenical Patriarch."

It was, perhaps, the uninhibited intervention of the Turkish government in his election that for the first 15 years inhibited the patriarchate's contacts with the West under Demetrios. Two years after his enthronement the outbreak of the Cyprus crisis in 1974 increased the patriarchate's difficulties, involving travel restrictions and other encroachments by the Turkish officials. During his tenure, the patriarchate encouraged contacts among Orthodox churches. These initiatives culminated in preparatory meetings near Geneva for the Pan-Orthodox "Great Council" which has yet to take place.

It was on November 30, 1980, the feast of St Andrew, patron saint of the patriarchate, that Demetrios received, in the Phanar, the visit of Pope John Paul II, which was more in the nature of a gesture of support for the patriarchate's international role. During this visit the Pope and the Ecumenical Patriarch announced the opening of a theological dialogue on doctrinal differences between the Eastern Orthodox and the Roman Catholic churches.

In 1987 Demetrios undertook a series of overseas visits which were to become the climax of his patriarchate. His visit to the Soviet Union was the first by an ecumenical patriarch to the Russian Orthodox churches since 1589; his visit to Athens was the first by the spiritual head of Orthodoxy in 24 years. He also became the first Orthodox patriarch to visit the United States, where the Orthodox community is estimated at three million, meeting President Bush at the White House. His final stop was London, as the guest of Dr Robert Runcie, then Archbishop of Canterbury; he was also received by the Queen.

MARTIN ENNALS

Martin Ennals, general secretary, National Council for Civil Liberties, 1960-66, and secretary-general, Amnesty International, 1968-80, died of cancer in hospital in Saskatoon, Saskatchewan, Canada, on October 5 aged 64. He was born in Walsall, West Midlands, on July 27, 1927.

AN INDEFATIGABLE fighter in the cause of justice for the individual, Martin Ennals had careers with Unesco, at the head of the National Council for Civil Liberties and more recently as secretary-general of International Alert and as Professor of Human Rights at the University of Saskatchewan. But he will be principally remembered for his remarkable stewardship of Amnesty International from 1966 to 1980, a period which saw the independent organisation grow in a manner which could not have been dreamed of at its inception in 1961. This period culminated in the award of the Nobel Peace Prize to Amnesty International in 1977.

Martin Ennals was born into a family which was to be noted for its political activity in radical causes. He was the youngest of three brothers, the eldest of whom, John Ennals, who died in 1988, had fought with Yugoslav partisans during the war and was a former director-general of the United Nations Association. David (now Lord) Ennals was Secretary of State for Social Services in the Labour administration of 1976-79. Martin Ennals was educated at Queen Mary's School, Walsall, and the London School of Economics where he took a degree in international relations.

He spent the next eight years, 1951-59, at Unesco in Paris in its early days. In addition to his duties for the agency he was also noted for his work for its staff association when Unesco's American staff came under scrutiny from Senator Joseph McCarthy's House un-American Activities Committee. In 1960 he returned to London to become general secretary of the National Council for Civil Liberties (NCCL). From its offices in New King's

Road (which were to have their windows smashed with some regularity by disappoving groups) Ennals, with his small but devoted staff of only five, conducted a campaign of great energy, taking up cases of alleged injustice to individuals of every conceivable kind, including over-zealous or wrongful behaviour by the police and decisions on the cases of aliens wishing to live and work in Britain. Ennals's zeal was not always appreciated by either the inhabitants of Chelsea, who had to put up with the rowdy and often even violent opposition of NCCL's opponents, or by the police. Ennals was several times threatened with arrest, and on at least one occasion was charged with obstruction.

His concern for the situation of immigrants and would-be immigrants led naturally, in 1966, to a move for Ennals to the National Committee for Commonwealth Immigrants where he became information officer. But his stay there was neither a happy nor a long one. In March 1968 he resigned as chief information officer in protest at the passing of the recent Immigration Act which he saw as "racialist in nature".

A more effective opportunity to give outlet to his beliefs and energies presented itself in the secretary-generalship of Amnesty International, an independent organisation which had been founded by a British barrister, Peter Benenson, in 1961. In the following ten or so years Ennals's vigorous approach transformed the scale and scope of Amnesty's activities on the international stage in a way which would have previously been thought inconceivable. In the period 1970-1980 its staff increased eight-fold to 150, its budget grew from £28,741 to £1,666,280 and it had members, subscribers and supporters in 134 countries. Fighting against the gamut of violations of human rights, whether these were alleged or proven against South American dictators or against the conduct of the security forces in Northern Ireland, Amnesty's reports came to have unique credibility in the international community for the meticulously researched evidence they

presented and from the dispassionate manner in which they recorded the facts.

In consequence, among organisations with cognate aims and principles, Amnesty came to have unmatched authority throughout the world and developed the power to sow seeds of hope in individuals or communities who had come to accept unredressed oppression as their lot. The 1977 Nobel Peace Prize (often much less judiciously awarded than it was on that occasion) was a wholly merited recognitition of Amnesty's remarkable achievement and moral standing. Characteristically, when Ennals went to receive the prize on the organisation's behalf from the Nobel committee he insisted that it was a released "prisoner of conscience" who actually accepted the award.

After leaving Amnesty Ennals was head of the Greater London Council's police committee support unit from 1982 to 1985, subsequently becoming secretary-general of International Alert, which he founded in 1985, and spending two years, 1987-89, as chairman of Defence for Children International, based in Geneva. He knew he was already ill with lung cancer when, more recently, he took up his professorship of human rights at the University of Saskatchewan, and he died after a year-long struggle against the disease.

Although he never avoided the publicity his conscience-goading (and therefore very often far from popular) activities all too frequently brought him and his fellow human rights workers, Ennals was in essence a modest man. In a world where cruel oppression has so often appeared to be the order of the day, and where La Fontaine's cynical dictum: "La raison du plus fort est toujours la meilleure" has found no ready reply, he managed in a most practical and heartening manner, to erect a standard for the contrary notion: namely that the truth and decency, not brute force, will have the final victory.

Martin Ennals leaves his widow, Jacqueline, from whom he was separated, and a son and a daughter.

BARONESS BURTON
OF COVENTRY

Baroness Burton of Coventry, who as Elaine Burton was Labour MP for Coventry South from 1950 to 1959, died on October 6 aged 87. She was born at Scarborough on March 2, 1904.

BARONESS Burton of Coventry was a vivacious Yorkshirewoman who was well-liked in the House of Lords as she had been in the Commons. In both houses she enlivened the view to be seen from the benches opposite where she sat by a taste for exotic hats which became the cause for much innocent mirth among her fellow members.

As a girl and young woman she had been an outstanding athlete – she was the world girls' sprint champion at the age of 16 – and the encouragement of amateur sport, athletics and physical fitness was a life-long interest. When the Government

set up the Sports Council in 1965 to advise on the development of amateur sport and physical recreation services, Baroness Burton was appointed one of its first members. It was very largely due to her that in the preceding year the Government accepted what was then the novel obligation of helping – in selected cases – amateur teams to participate in international sporting events abroad. She was also active in other spheres of public work. In 1967 she was appointed chairman of the Council of Tribunals, in succession to Lord Tenby, and from 1962 to 1965 she was chairman of the Domestic Coal Consumers' Council. She was a member of the Independent Television Authority and had served for three years as a member of the Council of Industrial Design.

Without being aggressive she was an

266

ardent feminist and one of her minor victories after being made a life peer was to secure a change in the standing orders of the House of Lords to the advantage of her sex. When she sat in the Commons Miss Burton was noted for her recherché taste in hats, which considerably enlivened the drab back benches.

On her transfer to the House of Lords she found that the rules forbade a peeress to speak while wearing her hat. The ancient man-made standing order laid it down that any peer speaking in the House must be "standing and uncovered." This she felt to be unfair discrimination when applied to peeresses. For a peeress suddenly to dash off her hat before rising to speak would probably leave her hair awry, thus causing her embarrassment. She brought this matter to the notice of the House and the Lords obligingly accepted a subsequent recommendation from their committee on procedure that the standing order should be amended to provide that a peeress who wished to wear her hat when speaking might do so.

Elaine Frances Burton was the daughter of Leslie and Frances Burton. She was educated at Leeds Girls' Modern School and at the City of Leeds Training College for teachers. She won the girls' world sprint championship at school and from 1924 to 1932 she played hockey for the Yorkshire first eleven. She taught in Leeds schools and evening institutes for 11 years and afterwards spent two years with the South Wales Council of Social Service and teaching in educational settlements. She was later associated as an organizer with the National Fitness Council and worked as a writer, lecturer, broadcaster and public relations consultant. She was a founder-member of the National Federation of Business and Professional Women.

At the general election that followed the second world war Miss Burton stood as Labour candidate for Hendon South but was beaten. When the next general election came, in 1950, she stood again as a Labour candidate for Coventry South and scored a notable success by defeating the Conservative, Leslie Hore-Belisha, by over 6,000 votes in a three-cornered fight. This was no mean feat over an opponent who had had a distinguished parliamentary and cabinet career, even if much of it had been as a Liberal; Hore-Belisha had been Secretary of State for War from 1937 to 1940 and had previously earned himself a permanent place in the vocabulary of the language when, as Minister of Transport from 1934 to 1937, he introduced the still-familiar Belisha Beacon to mark pedestrian crossings.

As a back-bencher in the House of Commons Elaine Burton served as a delegate to the Council of Europe and accompanied parliamentary delegations to Russia and several other countries. She was appointed a member of the select committee on estimates and became the first woman chairman of one of the select committee's sub-committees. In the House she championed the feminist cause and kept an alert watch on the interests of housewife consumers. In 1955 she did a party political broadcast for the Labour party.

After having represented Coventry South for nine years she decided in 1959 not to seek re-election. Three years later she was created a life peeress on the nomination of Hugh Gaitskell, then Leader of the Opposition. On her taking her seat in the House of Lords she created another little piece of history by being introduced by two other peeresses, the first time that had taken place.

In the House of Lords she was a vigorous speaker on a wide variety of topics ranging from women's rights and representation in public life and sport to the iniquity of high air fares. She was also an indefatigable letter writer to newspapers on these and cognate subjects. During the Labour party crisis of the late 1970s and early 1980s she frequently urged moderation and vigilance against the encroachment of the extreme left. Outside Parliament she was chairman of the Mail Order Publishers' Authority and president of the Association of Mail Order Publishers from 1980 to 1984.

She was unmarried.

DONALD HOUSTON

Donald Houston, Welsh screen and stage actor, died on October 13 at his home in Coimbra, Portugal, aged 67. He was born in Tonypandy on November 6, 1923.

DONALD Houston and his loin cloth achieved instant fame in the film of H. de Vere Stacpoole's lachrymose romance *The Blue Lagoon* in 1949. He was chosen by the casting director, Dennis Van Thal, to play opposite Jean Simmons, the fastest rising British female star of the day, as the pair of adolescents shipwrecked on a desert island. Frank Launder's film reached a large audience, helped by the technicolor photography of South Seas locations, a good enough antidote to the gloom of postwar Britain. *The Blue Lagoon* may look a little naive now, but at least it was considerably better than the disastrous remake with Brooke Shields in 1980.

Houston's celtic good looks – blue eyes, blond hair, broad shoulders – certainly aided him in winning the part. But he was immediately dubbed as "beefcake", yesterday's parlance for hunk. It was an image he tried to throw off, not altogether successfully, pointing out that he had trained for the stage and was not one of Rank's starlets. For the next ten years he was to be tugged between screen and stage, often hungering after the one while performing for the other.

The other tag attached to Donald Houston in the early days was that of the "Bevin Boy Star". It is true that he spent a period in the mines after being invalided out of the RAF, where he was an air-gunner and wireless operator. But soccer rather than coal was in the family. His father played for Swansea and Dundee and the young Donald at one time had an ambition to be a professional too. But the stage called and he made his debut with the Pilgrim Players in Penzance in 1940 before joining the Oxford Repertory Company. His younger brother Glyn was to follow in his footsteps, taking a small role in *The Blue Lamp* a couple of years after the *Lagoon* of the same colour.

Houston also ran the risk of being cast as the British cinema's resident Taffy. In *A Run For Your Money*, which followed immediately after *Lagoon*, he teamed with Alec Guinness to play the Welsh rugby fan up in London for the big day. Charles Frend's warm film was in the vanguard of the Ealing comedies. The stage claimed him back immediately as Peter Quilpe in T. S. Eliot's *The Cocktail Party*, seen first at the Edinburgh Festival and later at the New Theatre (now the Albery) in the West End. Houston held his own in a cast which was led by Alec Guinness (Rex Harrison in London) and Irene Worth (Margaret Leighton in London).

There was a chance to make a Broadway debut when Eliot's verse drama transferred to New York. But Houston did not sail on the *Queen Mary* with Guinness, Worth and the rest of the cast, preferring to star opposite Natasha Parry in *Dance Hall*, a minor Charles Crichton film which gave the bands of Geraldo and

Ted Heath an opportunity to appear on screen. Broadway had to wait until *Under Milk Wood* for its first sight of Houston and then it was a brief one. Dylan Thomas's play which, like *The Cocktail Party*, began at the Edinburgh Festival before coming to the New in 1956, provided Donald Houston with the stage part by which he will be best remembered. As the Onlooker he captured the cadences of Thomas's chosen mouthpiece and *alter ego*. They delighted British audiences but proved too foreign for New York, where the play closed within a month.

Possibly encouraged by the example of his contemporary and fellow Welshman, Richard Burton, Houston joined the Old Vic Company for the 1959-60 season, playing in Shakespeare and Shaw. His performances were solid, with integrity to the fore, but they did not light up the house. Houston remained better known for film comedies such as *Doctor in the House* and an occasional appearance in grittier new wave films including *Room at the Top*.

Some of the allure began to fade. During the Sixties much of his work was in Hollywood wartime epics, where he could be relied on for a good cameo portrait and, when required, more than that. Britain gave him a decent part as Dr Watson to John Neville's Holmes in *A Study in Terror* (1965) in which the good sleuth comes up against Jack the Ripper.

The early Seventies brought television series such as *Now, Take My Wife* and *Moonbase 3* in addition to a number of appearances on other stars' comedy shows. The hair was still bushy, the face still handsomely craggy, but the loin-cloth days of *The Blue Lagoon* were well over.

VISCOUNTESS
STANSGATE

Viscountess Stansgate, religious cam-paigner and member of the distinguished political family, died on October 21, aged 94. She was born on June 7, 1897.

VISCOUNTESS Stansgate was a feminist long before the word became popular. She supported the suffragette cause from her schooldays and she was a lifelong campaigner for the ordination of women. She was in the forefront of the ecumenical movement and she was honoured in Israel for her work to improve relations between Christians and Jews. She was also deeply supportive of her husband and son who both became government ministers.

Religion and politics were the two themes running through her life. From her father, Daniel Holmes, Liberal MP for Govan from 1911 to 1918, she acquired her original interest in politics but not her Christianity, for her father was an atheist. She paid her initial visit to the House of Commons in 1910 and it was from a seat in the Ladies' Gallery that she later had the first sight of her future husband, William Wedgwood Benn, the then Liberal MP for Leith. They married in 1920. He had recently been demobilised as Captain Wedgwood Benn, having been awarded the DSO and DFC as an airman on the western front.

They joined the Labour party together in 1927 and he proceeded to become MP for North Aberdeen, Secretary of State for India under Ramsay MacDonald, and Secretary of State for Air under Attlee. In 1942 he had accepted a peerage, a move which meant little to his wife at the time in terms of the title, but was to mean a great deal to her son, Tony Benn, when he inherited it, to his great discomfort, in 1960.

She might have become another political wife – a very useful one, of course, and a role which she did actually fulfil – but this would never have been enough for her. She could have been described as formidable, if the words would not have obscured the notable kindness and charm which accompanied her commitments to all her causes.

As a young mother she managed to attend London University as a theological student and in 1948 she went to the World Council of Churches Assembly in Am-

sterdam as an Anglican. But she moved increasingly towards Congregationalism which was her husband's background. After the establishment of the United Reformed Church she remained outside it in a group of independent Congregational churches. Thereafter she was involved in the establishment of the Congregational Federation, of which she became first president. There, and in the movement for the ordination of women, she was associated closely with the Rev Elsie Chamberlain, who died earlier this year, and whose appointment as the first woman chaplain to the forces, by Lord Stansgate when he was air secretary, caused much opposition at the time. After her husband's death in 1960 Lady Stansgate seriously considered entering the ministry herself.

Instead, she continued her work for the causes in which she believed, particularly for Christian-Jewish understanding. She was a member of the Council for Christians and Jews, and a memorial library was dedicated to her in the Hebrew University in Jerusalem. Few people have known so many world leaders. She was a considerable figure in her own right and she also travelled widely with her husband. Among those she knew were Eisenhower, Nehru, Nasser, Ben Gurion, Makarios, Ho Chi Minh and Chou En-lai. In 1990 she paid her last visit to the House of Commons. She had tea on the terrace just 80 years after she had first taken her seat as a young girl in the Ladies' Gallery.

Her eldest son, William, was an RAF pilot who was killed on operations in 1944. She is survived by two sons – Tony Benn, former minister in Labour governments, whose published diaries reveal the central role she played in the life of her family, and David Wedgwood Benn, a sovietologist and former head of the BBC's Yugoslav programmes.

EUGENE RODDENBERRY

Eugene Wesley Roddenberry, better known as "Gene", creator of the Star Trek *television series, died of a heart attack in Los Angeles on October 24, aged 70. He was born in El Paso, Texas, on August 19, 1921.*

GENE Roddenberry was a leading member of the American Humanist Association and his unshakeable confidence in the capacity and future of humanity was the bedrock of his film and television work. He once wrote: "To be different is not necessarily to be ugly; to have a different idea is not necessarily to be wrong. The worst possible thing that can happen to humanity is for all of us to begin to look and talk and act and think alike. The best measure of maturity and wisdom in a human is the recognition of value received in hearing another say: 'I disagree with you for the following reasons . . .'"

But Roddenberry found that the importance of being different and tolerating differences among others, was not a major priority in American society. Nor did television executives much appreciate his humanism, deploring the lack of a Christian message in *Star Trek* and opposing Roddenberry's wish to portray sexual and racial equality in his programme. When *Star Trek* made its NBC debut on September 8, 1966, chronicling the missions of the Starship Enterprise 200 years in the future, the response was lukewarm. The show ran for only three seasons and was considered a failure in terms of a mass audience, having achieved no better than 52nd place in the ratings. Critics parodied his slogan, "To boldly go where no man has gone before" as "To split infinitives where no infinitives have been split before". In 1969 studio executives decided to cancel *Star Trek*.

They failed. A massive protest campaign by legions of fans from all over the world, calling themselves Trekkies, forced the studio to reconsider. In all, *Star Trek* ran for 79 episodes, made for a bargain price of $186,000 each. They are still being shown on television stations around the globe and a new series, *Star Trek: The Next Generation*, is currently running.

The series became an industry of its own, spawning five successful movies; a sixth is to be released later this year. Devoted fans hold annual *Star Trek* conventions and models of the Enterprise are still big sellers in the toy stores.

Gene Roddenberry grew up in a family of regular churchgoers but in his formative years was very much an agnostic. He went to the University of Miami but his studies there were interrupted by the outbreak of the second world war for America on December 7, 1941. He joined the US Army Air Force and became a pilot, flying 89 bombing missions in the South Pacific. He was awarded the Distinguished Flying Cross and the Air Medal.

After the war, Roddenberry flew for Pan American World Airways, once surviving a crash in the Syrian desert when his engines caught fire on a flight from Calcutta. He gave up flying in 1949 to become a patrolman with the Los Angeles Police Department, rising to the rank of sergeant while he began to work on film and television scripts in his spare time.

By 1953 Roddenberry was selling scripts to such television series as *Naked City*, *Dragnet* and *Jane Wyman Theatre*. He left the police force and free-lanced for the next nine years, becoming head writer for *Have Gun Will Travel* and creating the television series *The Lieutenant*, which he also produced. But it was his work on *Star Trek* which finally made his name.

The secret of the show's success was something of a mystery, even to its stars. William Shatner, who played the lead role of Captain James Kirk, once said: "The funny part of it is, none of us know. We know the ingredients and we hope they work."

Roddenberry, who was on the editorial board of the American Humanist Association's periodical, *The Humanist*, described the programme as his political, social and racial philosophy, his "overview on life and the human condition". But he never persuaded television executives completely to share his views and, although he made considerable strides towards a racial and sexual mix in the programme, he never succeeded in getting a 50-50 gender- or race-ratio on the bridge of his starship. In May this year he was presented with the 1991 Humanist Arts Award.

Gene Roddenberry is survived by his wife, one son and two daughters.

SIR GILBERT INGLEFIELD

Sir Gilbert Inglefield, GBE, former Lord Mayor of London, died November 14 aged 82. He was born on March 13, 1909.

GILBERT Inglefield survived great hardships as a prisoner of war in the Far East during the second world war to become an outstanding Lord Mayor of London, well known also in Church, musical and architectural circles.

Gilbert Samuel Inglefield, born the second son of Admiral Sir F. S. Inglefield was a delicate child and did not go to school until he was eleven. But afterwards he was educated at Eton and Trinity College, Cambridge. The third class in Part I of the Classical Tripos in which he was placed in 1930 was atoned for by his proficiency in Latin verse composition. On coming down from Cambridge he qualified as an architect, registering with the Royal Institute in 1935 and taking his AA Dipl in 1939. By then the shadow of war was looming and he had joined the Territorial Army.

On the outbreak of war he was called up into the Sherwood Foresters and served in France before being sent out to the Far East with the rank of captain. He was with the 18th Division in Malaya when Singapore fell and was taken prisoner by the Japanese. After a spell in Changi he worked on the infamous Burma-Thailand railway in sweltering heat that reduced him to little more than a skeleton, some seven stones in weight. His ordeal lasted three-and-a-half years, but his indomitable will not only saw him through his experience but helped others to survive as well. At one point he organised a performance of Handel's *Messiah*. It was characteristic of his kindly nature and Christian faith that he could later say: "I don't bear the Japanese any ill-will, but I wouldn't care to go through it again."

When peace brought release he worked with the British Council, first as assistant representative in Egypt and then in London until 1956. He became a director of the family group of light engineering companies, of which his brother, Sir John, was chairman. One bore the name Tubal Cain, which must have puzzled customers who did not know the Bible as well as he did. But his mind was turning to the government of the City of London, in which his greatest achievements were to lie. He became alderman for the Aldersgate ward in 1959 and held that office for 20 years.

He was made a sheriff in 1963 and as chairman of the Barbican committee from 1963 to 1966 he had a major share in that effort to bring a residential population back to the City. His architectural training stood him in good stead in this venture. He was especially keen on the arts centre. He played the flute himself and sang for many years with the London Choral Society and other choirs. He regarded the Barbican as the most exciting thing in the City since the Tower of London and St Paul's were built.

In 1967 he became Lord Mayor. For his Lord Mayor's Show he chose as his theme "The return of the arts to the City". He had a stereo radio installed in his official car — a novelty in those days — so that he could listen to short Bach pieces in the City and Beethoven symphonies on longer journeys. Even as Lord Mayor he sang in Bach's *St Matthew's Passion* at the Royal Festival Hall on Good Friday. At his Guildhall banquet, mindful of his own wartime experiences, he inaugurated the practice of a chair for the "absent guest", the equivalent of whose cost would be given to help the world's hungry. It was a practice widely copied. Another innovation was a prize for artists, musicians and writers who had contributed to British culture without receiving adequate recompense.

Among his overseas journeys was a visit to Rome in which he attended ceremonies commemorating the foundation of that city. The most memorable of his overseas visits was that to Lake Havasu City to lay the foundation stone for the reconstruction of London Bridge,

which had been bought by a developer and transported across the Atlantic. He did so in his full regalia in a temperature of over 90 deg F. He was thereafter made an honorary chief of the Chemehuevi Indian tribe who had been displaced from the area. When his time as Lord Mayor came to an end it was universally acknowledged to have been a memorable year.

In the following year he was again in the public eye when he protested against the siting of a third London airport at Cublington on the ground that it would mean the destruction of the Norman church at Stewkley in Buckinghamshire. He did so not only on behalf of the St Michael's Church Preservation Committee but as a member of the Royal Fine Art Commission. He had a strong religious faith without ostentation and was a devoted son of the Church of England. He served from 1962 to 1976 as a member of the Redundant Churches Fund. The cultural bodies which he served included the Royal Shakespeare Theatre, the London Festival Ballet Trust, the Federation of British Artists, the London Symphony Orchestra and the City Arts Trust.

Inglefield had been made a knight bachelor in 1965 and on retiring as Lord Mayor was made GBE. His overseas honours included Icelandic and Sudanese decorations. He was given an honorary doctorate of science by the City University. He was master of the Haberdasher's Company in 1972 and of the Musicians' Company in 1974, and was also on the court of the Painter Stainers' Company. He was chancellor of the Order of St John of Jerusalem from 1969 to 1978. He served as a governor of the Thomas Coram Foundation and was Deputy Knight Principal of the Imperial Society of Knights Bachelor. He was a member of the Athenaeum and of the City Livery Club.

His exacting work was made easier by a happy family life. He married in 1933 Barbara, daughter of Captain Gilbert Thompson, Connaught Rangers. She survives her husband with two sons and a daughter.

SIR KENNETH CORK

Sir Kenneth Cork, GBE, former Lord Mayor of London, died on October 13 aged 78. He was born on August 21, 1913.

KENNETH Cork was the doyen of insolvency accounting, a former Lord Mayor of London and chairman of the board of governors of the Royal Shakespeare Company. He was influential in making the Barbican the RSC's London home.

Kenneth Russell Cork was the son of William Henry Cork, a chartered accountant with his own practice in the City. It was expected that he would follow his father into the family firm although, he later said, he would have preferred to have skippered a rum-running schooner in the South Seas. On completing his education at Berkhamsted, however, he complied with his father's wishes and began his accountancy studies – and thereby in later life became the owner of a number of vessels, one of which, a 26-ft cruising catamaran, he called *Rum Runner*.

He took his ACA in 1937, and the next year embarked upon a long career of service in and to the City of London by enlisting in the Honourable Artillery Company. After war service in Italy and

North Africa he was demobilised with the rank of lieutenant-colonel and completed his accountancy studies, becoming FCA in 1946. In that year he also became a senior partner in the family firm, W. H. Cork Gully.

Sir Kenneth's father in his early days had worked with Oscar Berry, the father of insolvency accounting. By the 1930s W. H. Cork Gully had developed a substantial practice in this area. Kenneth Cork, however, was at first considered too quiet and plodding for the knock-about world of receivership and liquidation, a judgment which amused where it did not amaze. For the moment, and to his chagrin, he was put to work in the more decorous audit side of the business.

After the war, however, his moment was at hand. Business after business foundered as the post-war boom in company flotations broke upon the rocks of difficult trading conditions. He began by unscrambling a failed grocery business in Cambridge and at the same time as he was finding his feet in accountancy his love of tradition and of service quickened. In 1951 he became a Common Councilman of the Corporation of the City of London, and so with that active diligence which was his hallmark embarked upon a career in City public life which reached its apogee when in 1978-9 he became Lord Mayor.

During the 1960s and early 1970s insolvency accounting flourished as never before. The increasing size of the company crashes, the mushrooming costs attendant upon legislation such as the Redundancy Payments Act and developing concern over job losses all conspired to make practitioners of insolvency accounting figures of some consequence. Sir Kenneth and his partners were now acting as receivers or liquidators in some very big crashes indeed, among them Emil Savundra's Fire, Auto and Marine Insurance, John Bloom's Rolls Razor and that of the Lyon property group.

Sir Kenneth's mastery of, and advocacy for, correct insolvency practice brought him into the public eye perhaps as no accountant before or since. Although urbane, he nonetheless was more forceful and outspoken than many in his profession. He disputed the idea of receivers and liquidators as a species of commercial knacker or undertaker, seeing off firms and depriving the employees of their livelihood. A good insolvency practice, he maintained, was as strong on assistance to avert a crash as upon clearing up afterwards. The damage done, he saw it as his duty to preserve the business that otherwise might be extinguished. Insolvency, he said, was merely a means of transferring ownership of the business.

Throughout the 1970s and 1980s Cork was constantly at the service of the City and of Whitehall. He was consulted over the "City Lifeboat", the means whereby during the secondary banking crash of the mid-1970s the Bank of England and the main clearing banks staved off a panic. He became chairman of the Department of Trade's EEC bankruptcy convention advisory committee, then of the Northern Ireland Finance Corporation. His greatest service, however, was as chairman of the Insolvency Law and Practice Review Committee which reported in 1982. At the time of his death he was a vice-chairman of the Ladbroke Group.

In public life as in business Sir Kenneth was as indefatigable as he was ubiquitous. He was a formidable fund-raiser for charity. He took great satisfaction in having persuaded the Royal Shakespeare Company to make its London home at the Barbican. Although a man of robust rather than refined tastes in the theatre and music, he himself was a natural performer and liked the society of actors and musicians. As chairman of the board of governors of the RSC he was aware that it could never be economic to stage the number and scale of productions demanded of the company but strove to make the RSC as economical and efficient as it could be.

In private life, Sir Kenneth was scarcely less active. He was a painter and a photographer and even into his seventies he ran two large power boats from the Hamble. He is survived by his wife, Nina, and their son and daughter.

GENERAL SIR NIGEL POETT

General Sir Nigel Poett, KCB, DSO and bar, General Officer Commanding-in-Chief Far East Land Forces from 1961 to 1963, died on October 29 aged 84. He was born on August 20, 1907.

NIGEL Poett will be remembered, first, as the commander of the 5th Parachute Brigade, which took the famous "Pegasus" bridge in Normandy during the early hours of D-Day; secondly, as the director of military operations in the War Office during the Suez crisis in 1956; and thirdly, as the army commander in the

Far East during the Azahari rebellion in Brunei and the subsequent confrontation with Indonesia in the early 1960s.

Joseph Howard Nigel Poett was the son of Major-General J. H. Poett, CB, CMG, CBE of Filleigh House, Bath, and Julia Baldwin, *née* Caswell, of Rhode Island, USA. He was educated at Downside and Sandhurst before being commissioned into the Durham Light Infantry in 1927.

He spent the first 10 years of his long army career with his battalion in Egypt, on the North-West Frontier of India and in the Sudan. He went to France in 1939 as GSO 2 of the 2nd Division, and after Dunkirk was promoted lieutenant-colonel as a GSO 1 in the War Office. He commanded the 11th Battalion of his regiment in 1942-43, before volunteering to join the recently formed parachute force, in which he was given command of the 5th Parachute Brigade for the invasion of Normandy.

Poett was ideally cast in this role: a tall, physically strong and immensely fit man with a dominating personality, he always led from the front. He was painstaking in his planning and convinced of his own invincibility, but he could be stubborn and dogmatic at times. Nevertheless, he had the invaluable knack of being at the right place at the right time to "read" the battle correctly at first hand.

He was intensely interested in the wellbeing and survival of his men, which endeared him to them but sometimes infuriated them when he would appear among their slit trenches oblivious to his own safety and to the occupants' urgent wish not to draw fire unnecessarily. Throughout his military career and afterwards, he never lost the innate courtesy and consideration with which he treated all ranks. His brigade's glider and parachute landings astride the Orne and Caen Canal bridges to protect the left flank of the Allied beachhead in Normandy were some of the most successful operations on D-Day. He himself jumped with the advanced elements of the brigade. By dawn he was able to report to his divisional commander, Major-

278

General Richard Gale (later General Sir Richard), GOC 6th Airborne Division, that his men had captured the bridges intact and all his other objectives were secure.

For the next two months his brigade doggedly held on to their sector of the 6th Airborne Division's perimeter in severe fighting and suffered many casualties. Subsequently he led it in the breakout to the Seine and in the advance into Belgium and Holland. Withdrawn to England with his division for retraining for further airborne operations that autumn, he dropped again with his brigade during the crossing of the Rhine in the spring of 1945 and led it on across north-west Germany to the Baltic coast. When the war ended in Europe, he and his brigade were sent out to the Far East where they took part in the reoccupation of the Dutch East Indies. For his stalwart leadership in these highly successful operations, he was awarded the DSO and bar and the American Silver Star.

As one of the stronger, more experienced personalities of the post-war army, Poett was soon developing military policy as director of plans at the War Office (1946-48); as deputy commander of the British Military Mission to Greece (1949); as chief of staff, Far East at the height of the Malayan campaign (1950-52); and as commander 3rd Division in the Suez Canal Zone when Nasser seized power in Egypt (1952-54). He was promoted major-general in 1951.

In 1954 he became director of military operations at the War Office where he had to bear the cross of the political misjudgments and vacillations of the Eden government during the Suez crisis of 1956. In his later years he admitted that the military were not entirely without blame for the mistaken assumption that the Egyptian tanks and aircraft would be manned by Eastern Bloc "volunteers". This over-estimate of Nasser's military capability resulted in the cumbersome Normandy-style landing at Port Said. He accepted in retrospect that only quick, decisive military action, using parachute and air mobile forces, could have neutralised world opinion and inhibited American financial sanctions.

The military lessons of Suez had been learned by the time Poett became C-in-C Far East Land Forces in 1961 after being the commandant of the Staff College, Camberley (1957-58), and GOC-in-C Southern Command (1958-61). Azahari's revolt in Brunei was crushed by rapid airborne intervention which he directed from Singapore, but the subsequent "confrontation" with Indonesia in the jungles of Borneo was still far from resolved when Poett retired from the army at the end of his tenure as GOC-in-C in 1963.

When he left the army he joined the British Productivity Council and served as its director until 1971. He also gave generously of his time, working with his wife, in helping the Sailors', Soldiers' and Airmen's Families Association in the south west of England.

In 1978 he accepted the chairmanship of the newly created Airborne Assault Normandy Trust, set up to record and tell the history, in France, of the 6th Airborne Division. It was an ideal task for him: he loved France, spoke fluent French and had a great respect for the French way of life, as well as possessing first hand knowledge of the operations and boundless enthusiasm for the project. He never lost interest in perfecting the telling of the story, nor in the welfare of the division's veterans.

On General Gale's death in 1981 he donned the mantle of doyen of the Airborne community, and each year led the Airborne Forces Security Fund Pilgrimages to Normandy. Shortly before he died he was appointed a chevalier of the Legion d'honneur in recognition of his work in cementing Anglo-French relations.

He married Julia, daughter of E. J. Herrick of Hawkes Bay, New Zealand, in 1937. Their marriage was a great partnership, in which she "followed the drum", giving him unstinting support throughout his career. They had two sons and one daughter. His family survive him.

MARIO SCELBA

Mario Scelba, prime minister of Italy 1954-5, died on October 29 aged 90. He was born on September 5, 1901.

MARIO Scelba, one of the founders of the Christian Democratic party, served as Italy's prime minister from 1954 to 1955 but was best known for his tough anti-communist stand as interior minister in the difficult period from 1947 to 1953. He was that strange combination of a politician wedded to parliamentary democracy who is willing, eager even, to apply authoritarian measures in its defence. He had seen democracy succumb to tyranny and that was why he was such a vigorous defender of it. The communists, who were influential in the partisan movement during the war, wanted to keep their political and military positions. They also controlled the trade unions. Scelba, as minister of the interior, was confronted by political strikes, riots and demonstrations. And he dealt firmly with them. The police, purged of partisans associated with the communists, came to be called *Scelbieri*.

More than any other Christian Democratic politician Scelba stood for the traditional centre coalition of all democratic parties based on a strong anti-Communist appeal. To a greater extent than almost any other of his colleagues he stood by his opinions, whether leading a government or virtually leading the opposition to change within the ranks of the Christian Democratic party. By the time of his death Scelba's views had long been overtaken by events.

Son of a peasant farmer, Mario Scelba was born at Caltagirone in eastern Sicily. This was also the birthplace of Don Luigi Sturzo, founder of the Popular Party which was the precursor of Christian Democracy as the official Catholic political party. Impressed by his attitude and ability, Don Sturzo is said to have paid for his university fees; he then made him his secretary and assistant. With a law degree, Scelba began an active career as a journalist. Don Sturzo's influence and example determined his political outlook. During the Fascist period, when Don Sturzo was forced into exile, Scelba retired from political life and concentrated on his legal practice in Rome.

As the war drew to an end he was close to De Gasperi in the organisation of the Christian Democratic party. He was given the Ministry of Posts and Telegraphs under Parri and in De Gasperi's first two administrations. In the next five governments led by De Gasperi Scelba held the Ministry of the Interior.

During this period he established his public character as a firm opponent of communism, using all means available and, where necessary, manufacturing new ones, to defeat extremism. Though most of what he did was aimed against the Communists there should be no doubt of Scelba's genuine dislike of Fascism. His detractors say that by nature he would have moved towards Fascism if it had not been for the accident of his friendship with Don Sturzo. Given that accidents, particularly in Italian politics, count for a lot he should be given the credit due to a man who remained faithful to the principles which he adopted.

As prime minister from 1954 to 1955 he maintained the traditional centre coalition and there can be no question that his administration was far from reactionary. In fact, one of his objections to the centre-left was that its advocates were proposing scarcely anything that he had not himself favoured when in office, and with more reliable allies. He refused office in centre-left administrations though later, as the formula became to be accepted as without any reasonable alternative, he allowed his followers to take places in coalition governments shared with the Socialists.

He came back to his old post at the Ministry of the Interior in the government which Signor Fanfani formed after the riots of the summer of 1960 but that was not a coalition which included the Socialists. He made himself the spokesman of the conservative wing of his party, constantly warning his colleagues against taking the Socialists at their word in the matter of breaking with the Communists. He wanted action from them in the form of breaking with their former allies of the extreme left at all levels. This they were gradually to undertake though whether they would have done so in the natural course of events − which seems likely − or only because Scelba and his friends pressed so insistently for it is a matter largely of conjecture.

When the Christian Democratic party itself moved more to the right in order to recuperate votes in that direction Scelba naturally could have expected to have a part to play. Early in 1965 he took over the chairmanship of the party.

Scelba was minister of the interior for the last time under Fanfani between 1960 and 1962, but refused a ministry in the subsequent government led by Fanfani which admitted for the first time the Socialists to the cabinet. He was elected to the Chamber of Deputies in 1963, and to the senate in 1968. He was a senator from then until he retired from active politics in 1983.

Between 1969 and 1971 Mario Scelba was president of the European parliament, and while a senator he was for a time also president of the senate's foreign affairs commission.

In what was probably his last interview, almost exactly a year ago, Scelba denied being responsible in the 1950s for crushing riots and demonstrations by peasants and factory workers with unnecessary violence. Contemporary reports spoke of jeeps with screaming tyres and sirens, bearing their helmeted occupants with automatic rifles towards trouble. He was reported to be ready to use armoured cars and tanks. But Scelba reflected: "People died because the police and the Carabinieri had the habit of shooting during strikes and demonstrations . . . It was the legacy of the 19th-century. I built a police force that used the baton instead of the pistol, the water-hose instead of the machine-gun. In my life I never gave the police the order to open fire."

Mario Scelba is survived by a daughter, Maria Luisa.

JOSEPH PAPP

Joseph Papp, American producer, died of cancer on October 31 aged 70. He was born Joseph Papirofsky in Brooklyn, New York, on June 22, 1921.

THAT New York City in the 1990s still has claims to be a theatre capital of the world owes much to the director and impresario Joseph Papp. From 1954 on, with his founding of a theatre workshop which was to become the New York Shakespeare Festival, it was his tremendous energy and vision which made Shakespeare a part of the fabric of New York life. Performances in churches with unpaid actors gave way over the years to annual free performances of Shakespeare's plays in Central Park with American actors of the calibre of James Earl Jones, Meryl Streep, Robert de Niro and Kevin Kline. At the time of his death he was more than halfway through presenting a six-season marathon of all 36 of Shakespeare's plays – a venture notable and controversial for its insistence on American voices and a rejection of English theatrical tradition. But Papp was not only an American rival to the Shakespearian evangelism of Lilian Baylis. With his entrepreneurial flair and passionate dedication to new writing, theatrical innovation and musical theatre he was also its Michael Codron, its ICA and its Cameron Mackintosh.

Papp was brought up in the tough Williamsburg section of Brooklyn, New York. His family were Jewish, immigrants from Poland, and Yiddish not English was the prevailing language at home. His interest in drama developed when he was in high school. There, an early stage appearance was as one of "three little maids from school" in *The Mikado*. Later he was to say: "What the hell was a trio of rough ghetto kids like us doing singing about ladies' seminaries?" With or without the help of Gilbert and Sullivan he developed his belief in a politically and socially active theatre. The crucial influence on him in the 1930s was the government-funded Federal Theatre Project which brought drama into 40 states, into rural communities, schools and on to Broadway. Earlier this year, while rejecting grants worth more than $750,000 from the National Endowment for the Arts because of new congressional restrictions on "obscenity", Papp was still battling for proper government investment in the arts.

Papp's entry into his chosen profession was delayed by the second world war, but on his discharge in 1946 he used his GI Bill education provisions to study at the Actors Laboratory Theater in Hollywood. After touring nationally as an

282

assistant stage manager in Arthur Miller's play *Death of a Salesman*, he worked his way back to New York to become a director and begin the Shakespeare Festival, a career that he paid for by his work as a stage manager for CBS-TV. Typically, even that bread and butter job was not without controversy. In 1958 he lost the job for invoking the Fifth Amendment before the House Committee on un-American Activities. Reinstated in 1959, he was soon back in court to fight for the principle of free Shakespeare in the Park.

He won that fight as well and in 1962 the Delacorte Theater, his last Central Park home, opened by the site where his previous stage, a flat-bed truck, had broken down in 1957. With productions playing in the Park and touring schools, Papp looked for a permanent indoor theatre and found the monumental Astor Library by the site of the notorious Astor Place riot, where followers of the rival Shakespearean actors Macready and Forrest had killed each other in 1849.

That new home, the Public Theater, opened in 1967 with the musical *Hair*, a show that moved quickly to Broadway where it ran, with fewer clothes in some cases, for years and was exported around the world. The Public became a powerhouse of theatre with six stages under its own roof and a web of associated productions in schools, on Broadway, on national and international tours. It spread into the cinema and television. Writers such as David Rabe and directors such as JoAnne Alkalaitis and George C. Wolfe, whose adaptation of Zora Neale Nurston's *Spunk* recently visited the Royal Court, became associated with the theatre.

The Public went on to spawn other hits: one was *A Chorus Line* (which became the longest running Broadway show in history on September 29, 1983, and went on to run for years after); another, the spirited modern production of *Pirates of Penzance*, was ironically the result of a year of crisis at the Shakespeare Festival. It brought Linda Ronstadt to Broadway and drew a marvellous performance from the veteran George Rose. At Drury Lane George Cole took over from Rose, and Pamela Stephenson from Ronstadt. Papp's other successes included *That Championship Season*, which picked up a number of Broadway prizes, and a musical of *Two Gentlemen of Verona*, which many found a good deal more entertaining than Shakespeare's original.

But with all the success, crisis was also a constant part of Papp's empire. While he indeed sponsored generations of significant writers and directors, many of those relationships began in glory and ended in animosity. Papp's consummate involvement in theatre made his interest in productions more than proprietorial. Involvement sometimes became interference, and major writers such as Sam Shepard had notable separations. His sometimes triumphant residency at New York's Lincoln Center ended in financial chaos after four years; a failure which he blamed in an interview with a *Times* critic in 1977 on his temporary seduction by the idea of an American National Theatre in a United States which had become many different nations.

Yet no other American producer had brought more of the United States theatre under one roof than Papp. In dividing up responsibility for the Public Theater earlier this year, he brought in directors 30 and 40 years younger than himself and also initiated the first black theatre in a white organisation. He was intent on expanding the theatre beyond national boundaries and here commercial rewards were of little concern. He set up an exchange between the Public and London's Royal Court Theatre in 1983, brought plays such as Larry Kramer's AIDS drama *The Normal Heart* to London and Caryl Churchill's *Serious Money* to New York, contributing much-needed cash to the Royal Court in the process.

In 1976 Papp married for the fourth time, Gail Bovard Merrifield. He is survived by three daughters and two sons from previous marriages.

SIR RONALD SWAYNE

Sir Ronald Swayne, MC, former chairman of Overseas Containers Ltd (OCL), died on October 29 aged 73. He was born on May 11, 1918.

AS A driving force in Overseas Containers Ltd (OCL) from 1965 and its chairman from 1973 to 1982, Ronald Swayne played an influential role in the introduction of containerisation. An ex-commando and survivor of the St Nazaire raid, he brought tenacity and skill to this task which, once early traumas had been overcome, made OCL one of the most visible names in the field. But the first years were tough; much inevitably went wrong, and many of the more conservative spirits in shipping had a vested interest in seeing OCL, and the revolution it represented, fail. It was then that Swayne's staunchness and instinctive comradeship regularly rallied the spirits of his hard-pressed colleagues.

Ronald Oliver Carless Swayne was educated at Bromsgrove School and University College, Oxford, which he attended before, and for a year after, the war, finally taking his MA in 1946. At Oxford, as the third of the three formidable rugby-playing Swayne brothers, his chances of a blue were curtailed when he concussed himself crash-landing a University Air Squadron plane. When war came in 1939 he broke off his studies to join the Herefordshire Regiment before transferring to the commandos in 1940.

Serving as a lieutenant with No 1 Commando, Swayne took part, on the night of March 27-28, 1942, in the raid on St Nazaire whose aim was to smash its U-boat pens and deny the use of its dry dock facilities to the German battleship *Tirpitz*, thus preventing her from operating against allied shipping in the Atlantic. With him were a dozen soldiers, mostly from south Wales and his native West Country. Their flimsy motor launch was at the rear of the two assaulting columns which, led by the destroyer *Campbeltown*, sailed into the mouth of the Loire just before midnight on March 27. Reaching the port a few critical minutes after *Campbeltown* had rammed the dry dock, they thus met the full fire of the German defences.

His naval commander, Lieutenant Ian Henderson, made two attempts to get alongside, but decided that a third would be suicidal and gave the order to turn for home. Evading the coastal guns, the launch reached the open sea but just before dawn, 45 miles out, the launch was intercepted by the German destroyer *Jaguar*, which came on it out of the morning mists. A fight of a most unequal character now ensued. Henderson was soon killed; Sergeant Thomas Durrant, though hit many times, continued to fire his Lewis gun in answer to German demands to surrender. As dawn broke, Swayne, coming up from below with fresh ammunition, found 20 of the 28 naval and commando personnel either drowned, or dead or wounded on board, and the deck awash with blood. The only officer unhurt, he called out to the German captain in a seemingly casual voice: "I'm afraid we can't go on."

The destroyer captain took the dead and wounded aboard, and returned to St Nazaire. As the British survivors were lifted ashore, he called his ship's company to attention and saluted. Later a German officer visited the prisoners' commanding officer, Colonel Newman, in their PoW camp at Rennes to bring to his attention Durrant's gallant conduct. Swayne made his own eye-witness recommendation and Sergeant Durrant was posthumously awarded one of the five VCs given for the raid. Swayne was himself decorated with the MC in 1945.

Following a brief return to Oxford to collect his degree, Swayne joined the Liverpool-based Ocean steamship company of which he became managing director in 1955, at the same time becoming partner of Alfred Holt. His principal responsibility was the Ocean group's important Australian trade and this experience, and the good relations he established with Australians (to whom a Pom could not always guarantee to recommend himself) was to stand him in good stead when the container revolution got under way.

Cargo liners had dominated their field of sea transport for 100 years before the needs of traders made a radical change necessary. The US armed forces had already experimented with transporting cargo in large boxes during the Korean war; in the aftermath of that conflict it became abundantly obvious that the container, and door-to-door, as opposed to quay-to-quay, transport would sweep away the old cargo liner.

But the concept required specially designed vessels and dockside facilities – a revolution in handling cargo afloat and ashore. As a founder director of OCL and full-time member of the initially small executive team charged with the task of applying the new technology of container shipping, Swayne's task was formidable. The trade between Europe and Australia was chosen as the first to be fully containerised, and Australia was already his second home. Much of the burden of making the operational and political choices in Australia therefore fell to Swayne.

Once the early traumas were overcome, and the skills which Swayne had deployed to bring suspicious and often ill-assorted shipowners of many nationalities to associate together in shipping consortia began to bear fruit, the new concept became accepted and profitable. In 1973, Swayne took over from the first chairman of OCL, Sir Andrew Crichton, and led the company with his own brand of humanity, good humour and common-sense for nine years. During this period he became president of the General Council of British Shipping and president of the association of EC shipowners. He retired in 1982, having by then presided over a period of years during which his company became one of the two or three consistently most profitable container shipping companies in the world. Swayne was knighted in 1979 for his pioneering achievements at Overseas Containers Ltd. He was also a director of the National Freight Company from 1973 to 1985.

As those who heard him in his PoW camp might testify, Ronnie Swayne was an excellent flute player, far above the amateur standard which was all he claimed. In Liverpool after the war, it was not long before he had joined the board of the city's Philharmonic Orchestra and instituted a fund for bringing otherwise unaffordable soloists to its programmes.

When he moved to London, he was quickly recruited (by the Earl of Harewood, whom he had met when they were both prisoners of war) for the New Philharmonia Trust and he worked for it for a number of years, before joining the board of English National Opera. He may not have been a natural fund-raiser, although he used to bring influential people to performances, but he was judiciously enthusiastic, full of well-based comment and keen to get things done. Music was a great love and he had a quiet pride in the success of his composer son, Giles Swayne.

He married, in 1941, Charmian, daughter of Major W. E. P. Cairnes. She died in 1984. He leaves his son and daughter.

RAYMOND BLACKBURN

Albert Raymond Blackburn, Labour MP and campaigner against pornography and gaming abuses, died on November 3 aged 76. He was born on March 11, 1915.

RAYMOND Blackburn's life encompassed Parliament, prison, periods of wild drunkenness, soberly conducted campaigns of great tenacity, seemingly incessant litigation, and an unlimited capacity for self-destruction together with talents which fleetingly caused him to be spoken of as a possible future prime minister. Churchill, who went out of his way to praise his maiden speech, was aware of his potential and described him as "a man of perfect independence and a law unto himself." This judgment was delivered in 1951 and it remained true of

Blackburn until he died.

He was the son of Dr Albert Edward Blackburn, of Bournemouth, and was educated at Rugby and London University, where he gained the Newton prize of the Law Society. He was admitted a solicitor in 1937 but had only a short time to practise as he volunteered for the army on the day war was declared. He served from 1939 to 1945, taking time off from his military duties in 1943 for an unsuccessful fight as the Commonwealth candidate at the Watford by-election.

Captain Blackburn – he retained his military title for years afterwards – joined the Labour party while still in uniform and he succeeded in obtaining the nomination for the Birmingham Northfield constituency. This was a previously solid Tory seat but he defeated the sitting MP by more than 12,000 in the

286

Labour landslide of 1945. This election, like the 1918 khaki election, swept many young officers into Parliament, but on this occasion a fair number came to sit on the Labour benches. None made a better impression with his maiden speech than Blackburn.

In the Commons he concentrated on foreign affairs and the then novel subject of atomic energy. He was informed, energetic and a striking figure with his shock of prematurely grey hair, soon to turn completely white. His party leaders smiled on him – but not for long. An early rebellion against the American loan was followed by a more serious deviation when he voted against the government on an important bill which he considered would involve direction of labour. He became increasingly critical of Labour policy and there were clashes with his constituency association though he managed to fight off criticism and retain his seat in 1950. Almost immediately, however, he resigned from the Labour party and sat as an Independent MP before deciding not to fight the 1951 election. He said he believed more socialism would be a disaster and urged his supporters at Northfield to vote for Churchill.

But his seat stayed with Labour and he was never to have political influence again. He had been drinking heavily while he was an MP and he did so in his new life outside politics. His business affairs, his first two marriages and his whole life turned sour. There were frequent appearances in court – for drunkenness, for domestic troubles, and for failing to attend his examination at the Bankruptcy Court. In 1955 came worse. He was sent to prison for two years on charges of conspiracy concerning property company shares. He represented himself at the Central Criminal Court and his concluding speech lasted seven hours but failed to convince the jury.

After he was released from prison he married for the third time in 1959 and his wife, Tessa, a 19-year-old actress, brought some stability into his life. His marriage helped give him a new sense of direction in which he fought to regain his reputation, by campaigning against what he saw as failure by authorities to uphold the law – something for which, in spite of his record and because of his legal training, he professed respect. He wrote a book, *I am an Alcoholic*, frankly admitting his problem and giving advice to others. It did not prevent other court appearances for drink offences over the years though for long periods he managed to avoid alcohol.

It was in the 1960s that he began challenging the legality of the "pool" system of roulette being played at many of the big gaming clubs. At one point he took the Metropolitan Police Commissioner to court and secured an undertaking from him to withdraw a policy directive not to apply the law on games of unusual chance. In one fortnight three of London's major gambling clubs were convicted of unlawful gaming as a result of his private summonses. He was never a serious gambler and he said his actions were based on his belief that if there were laws they must be enforced. He turned his attention to what he believed was pornography in the 1970s. He had a famous victory over the GLC on the way in which it was exercising its powers of film censorship and he had other successes against cinemas showing films which he maintained were indecent.

He was a persistent litigant. At different times he mounted actions of one kind or another against the BBC, the Press Council, successive Metropolitan Police Commissioners, Lord Hailsham and the publishers of the Channon diaries, with varying degrees of success. He usually represented himself though he had long since been struck off as a solicitor.

He was married three times: to Barbara Mary Robinson in 1939 (marriage dissolved 1954); to Marianne Ferguson in 1956 (marriage dissolved 1959); and to Tessa Hume in 1959. There are a daughter and two sons of the first marriage, one of them Robin Blackburn, the left-wing academic and author. By his wife, Tessa, who survives him, he had three daughters and two sons.

ROBERT MAXWELL

Robert Maxwell, MC, newspaper proprietor, was found dead on November 5, after apparently falling overboard from his motor yacht in the Canaries, aged 68. He was born on June 10, 1923.

ROBERT Maxwell was one of the most turbulent and controversial entrepreneurs of his day. He never owned a pair of shoes until he was seven. When he died he owned newspapers, magazines, printing works, private jets, helicopters and the 190-ft yacht, *Lady Ghislaine*, from which he disappeared. He had owned two football clubs, Derby County and Oxford United, and just failed to own another, Tottenham Hotspur. Though there were emerging doubts about the fragility of his enterprises in view of the great debts he had accumulated, there was no doubt about the scale of his success. A socialist who publicly admired Mrs Thatcher, he was often a guest at Downing Street as well as being the host at the most expensive parties of Labour party conferences.

In eastern Europe, where he was born in extremely poor circumstances to an Orthodox Jewish family in what was once Czechoslovakia and then Hungary, he was regarded as one of the most powerful Englishmen of his time. The neo-Stalinist leaders, from Zhivkov to Honecker, welcomed him and he published their books at inordinate and flattering length. Later, as the new men took over, he claimed to be the trusted adviser of Gorbachev. A recent article in *Playboy* described him as one of the biggest "lords of the global village – that elite handful of individuals who control most of the world's media".

Maxwell always wanted to be a media baron. He failed to buy the *News of the World* and later the old *Sun*. In both cases he lost to Rupert Murdoch. Later he tried unsuccessfully for the London *Evening Standard*, *The Observer* and *The Times*. But his chance came at last in July 1984 when Reed International accepted his bid for the Mirror Group after saying that it would not be sold to a single bidder. On the night of the deal, Maxwell strode into the *Mirror* building after being warned that his arrival would start a strike by journalists or printers or both. "If one copy is lost tonight I shall close the paper", he announced. Not a copy was lost. And he went on as he began, dominating executives, interfering with specialists, rewriting copy. Joe Haines the former Wilson press secretary who had told a union meeting that he would lead a walk-out if Maxwell arrived, became his leader-writer and biographer. Editors were changed, numbers of journalists and print workers were slimmed down, colour was introduced with remarkable success. Maxwell became one of the leading public figures of the 1980s.

His latter years were consumed by his desire to maintain control of his business interests until two of his sons, Ian and Kevin, were old enough to succeed him. But his attempts to establish himself beyond the narrow but highly profitable sector of scientific publishing were dogged by controversy.

Ian Robert Maxwell was the last of several names acquired during his war-time career. The facts of his early life are obscure but it appears that when he was born, in Slatinske Doly, a village in the Carpathian mountains on the Czech-Romanian border, he was named Abraham Lajbi Hoch. Those forenames were unacceptable to the Czech authorities and he was renamed Jan Ludvik. As the Nazis advanced eastward in 1939 he was sent to Budapest to evade anti-semitic restrictions. He arrived in France as part of the Czech Legion early the following year, sailing to Liverpool a few months later.

Arriving there with, as he was later to say: "a rifle in my hand and a desire to fight the Germans", in 1941 he volunteered for the Pioneer Corps. He claimed to have learned English in six weeks, adding to the several other languages he had collected at the European crossroads where he grew up. Throughout his life he demonstrated a remarkable fluency in languages, and this was a considerable asset in his international business dealings.

After two years he was accepted as a private into the North Staffordshire Regiment and his command of languages earned him recruitment to the battalion's intelligence section. His Czech name was changed to Leslie du Maurier, after the cigarette brand. Once he landed in France after D-Day, du Maurier's name was rapidly changed to Jones and finally became Maxwell. Equally quickly, he was promoted to second lieutenant and met Elisabeth Meynard, his future wife, in Paris. Maxwell was transferred to the Queen's Royal Regiment (West Surrey), stationed in Brussels. On January 29, 1945, he led his platoon against a German defensive position, for which he was awarded the Military Cross. The medal was pinned on his chest by Montgomery and he married Elisabeth in Paris on March 15.

In the immediate aftermath of war, Maxwell was employed interrogating Germans. In what became a turning point in his career, he was then appointed to the Public Relations and Information Services Control in Berlin, the branch of the Allied Control Commission responsible for licensing films, plays, books and newspapers. Maxwell's duties, which covered arranging paper supplies, editing and distribution, gave him a taste for publishing which was the foundation of his subsequent business empire. He was by this time a captain and had admitted to colleagues an ambition to become a millionaire.

In August 1945 the US dropped atom bombs on Japan, events which Maxwell subsequently claimed demonstrated to him the power of scientific knowledge, which he realised he could tap by publishing that knowledge. The next month a fellow Czech, Arnos Lobl, went to London and formed a £100 company called Low-Bell, an import-export company in which Maxwell took a controlling interest shortly before he resigned from the Control Commission in March 1947. Once established in London, he began distributing German newspapers to German prisoners of war in Britain, as well as laying hands on any goods in short supply to resell them abroad.

In October 1947 Maxwell returned to Berlin to renew an acquaintance he had formed with Ferdinand Springer, a scientific publisher to whom he had supplied paper in his army days. He became Springer's foreign agent, making his own fortune and reviving that of the German. The bureaucratic controls applied by the Allies to exports of publications from Germany were tailor-made for Maxwell to exploit. Springer had a British company, jointly owned with Butterworth, the UK publisher. When the arrangements with Maxwell dissolved in acrimony in 1951, Maxwell borrowed from the banks to buy the company for £13,000. Renamed Pergamon Press, it was to become his master company.

At this stage he was keen to ingratiate himself with the British book publishing establishment. So he agreed to take a headache off their hands, a loss-making wholesaler called Simpkin Marshall. But within four years it failed, owing £556,000 and the Official Receiver criticised the directors – including Maxwell – for not closing it sooner. Maxwell was gaining a reputation as a brash, arrogant showman, the obverse of the typically restrained 1950s British publisher. But meanwhile he was developing a powerful strategy for Pergamon. He realised that he could create narrow but unshakable monopolies by launching scientific journals on precisely defined topics which would be the accepted medium for the experts in that discipline.

While academics would compete to write in the journals for no payment, or even pay for the privilege, universities and science-based companies would pay a high premium for the journals by advance subscription. Newcomers would have to buy back-numbers from Pergamon at updated prices.

By 1964 Pergamon was publishing 600 book titles a year and 70 journals. It was floated on the Stock Exchange with a value of over £4 million. That year Maxwell was also elected Labour MP for Buckingham. He presented himself as a bridge between business and socialism, a theme that fitted well with Harold Wilson's commitment to a "white-hot technological revolution".

But this was to be Maxwell's zenith for the next 17 years. In 1968 he was rebuffed by shareholders in the *News of the World* in a takeover bid where he was defeated, not for the last time, by Rupert Murdoch. The newspaper's editor, Stafford Somerfield, ran a notorious editorial comparing Maxwell's foreign origins unfavourably with the *News of the World* which, he wrote, "I know is as British as roast beef and Yorkshire pudding". But that defeat was a trifle set against the following year's disastrous attempt to merge Pergamon with Leasco, an American computer company headed by the equally sharp-witted and brash fellow Jew, Saul Steinberg. The idea was that Pergamon's scientific database could be loaded into Leasco's computers. But while Leasco's accountants were having difficulty obtaining information from Maxwell, it emerged that two of Maxwell's family trusts had been selling Pergamon shares bought by Leasco at inflated prices. Then Leasco discovered that a large proportion of Pergamon's recent profits were derived from dealings with private Maxwell companies, thus casting doubt on their true value. Leasco withdrew its £25 million bid, but by then the American firm held 38 per cent of Pergamon's shares. Leasco banded together with institutional investors to vote Maxwell off the board, which did not please the academics who wrote for Pergamon's journals. Profits suffered accordingly.

The Department of Trade and Industry ordered an investigation into Pergamon in which the inspectors stated: "We regret having to conclude that, notwithstanding Mr Maxwell's acknowledged abilities and energy, he is not in our opinion a person who can be relied on to exercise proper stewardship of a publicly quoted company."

It was a verdict which was to dog Maxwell for the rest of his life, and would have broken a lesser man. He attempted to have the DTI report set aside by the courts. Although Lord Denning decided that the inspectors had behaved fairly, the rules were modified to give those criticised in such reports the explicit right of reply.

In 1970 Maxwell lost his parliamentary seat. Although he contested Buckingham twice more in 1974, he never again became an MP. But 1974 was also the year when he regained control of Pergamon, taking it private through an offer of 12p a share against Leasco's 185p bid six years previously. By that time Leasco and the institutional investors were glad to be rid of what they regarded as a troublesome investment. For Maxwell, of course, it was the return of his commercial base. He kept out of the spotlight and cultivated relationships with the City of London.

In 1980 National Westminster Bank turned to Maxwell to rescue the country's leading printing concern, British Printing Corporation, from financial difficulties. Notwithstanding the fact that it was a publicly quoted company, he gained control and turned the business round in the teeth of union opposition. The DTI slur was set aside, although not forgotten. In 1984, during an unsuccessful takeover bid for John Waddington, it emerged that control of Maxwell's business interests had been vested in Pergamon Holding Foundation, a trust incorporated in Liechtenstein. Although Maxwell claimed that the trust gave substantial sums to charity, the device had tax advantages and was understood to cede ultimate ownership to members of his family resident overseas.

Under Maxwell, BPC was soon strong enough to buy the Odhams printing operation from Reed International. In 1984 Reed decided to float Mirror Group Newspapers on the stock market, but Maxwell pre-empted that with a private offer of £80 million which Reed accepted. The Holborn head office was believed to be worth that much alone. He had fulfilled his dream of owning a national newspaper. Indeed, in addition to the *Daily Mirror*, *Sunday Mirror* and *The People*, in 1987 he attempted to launch a 24-hour paper, *The London Daily News*, but had to close it within five months in the face of a relentless defensive campaign by Associated Newspapers, the owners of the *Evening Standard*.

Through BPC, renamed Maxwell Communication Corporation, he achieved the aim of the abortive merger with Leasco, to publish electronically on a global scale. But in 1987 he decided to abandon printing in favour of publishing, selling the BPC operations to their management. Two years later he tilted the balance of MCC firmly towards the United States by buying the Berlitz language-teaching business the American Macmillan book-publishers and Official

Airline Guides. In 1990, after several delays, Maxwell launched *The European*, a London-produced English-language weekly designed to appeal to a current affairs readership throughout Europe.

During the past year, he was beset by the double impact of the transatlantic recession and high interest rates. In an effort to generate cash he floated Mirror Group Newspapers on the London stock market. He also sold part of his beloved Pergamon to Elsevier of The Netherlands – but he shrewdly kept Pergamon's electronic publishing operations in America. Cash problems did not prevent him from buying the New York *Daily News*, which he did in characteristically dramatic manner, sailing up the East River in the *Lady Ghislaine* and announcing the deal just three days before the title would have closed forever. In remarkably trouble-free negotiations with the print unions he obtained savings equal to more than $80 million including the shedding of 800 jobs. But the *Daily News* and *The European* were kept within his private interests. He was unable to resist the temptation to return to the habit which had attracted criticism during the Pergamon-Leasco battle, his tendency to shuffle businesses between his public companies and his private empire.

One ambition which he never realised was the ownership of a glamorous British football club. His name was linked at different times with Manchester United and Tottenham Hotspur, but he had to content himself with Oxford United and Derby County. Maxwell created a substantial business empire which will live on in various forms after his death, although it will be run on very different lines by his sons. His success owed everything to his boundless energy, despite a continual fight against overweight. But his achievements were overshadowed by his bullying and arrogant style of management, which seemed to be driven by the insecurity of his impoverished beginnings.

Maxwell had nine children, seven of whom survive him and at least three of whom are employed in his businesses. He also leaves his widow, Elisabeth.

GENE TIERNEY

Gene Tierney, Hollywood film actress, died of emphysema at her home in Houston, Texas, on November 6 aged 70. She was born in New York on November 20, 1920.

WITH her sultry voice and fragile, high-cheekboned beauty, Gene Tierney was one of the leading box office draws of the Forties and early Fifties. She rose smoothly to stardom by the age of 20 and her poise and refinement always contrived to suggest a life of unruffled serenity. But she knew personal sorrow: a daughter was born mentally handicapped; she suffered a mental breakdown, and her love life was strewn with unhappy romances until she found happiness with her second husband, W. Howard Lee. Perhaps her best-remembered role was that of the beautiful, enigmatic murder victim in the Otto Preminger film *Laura*, though she came closest to winning an Oscar for her performance in *Leave Her to Heaven*.

Gene Tierney was born in Brooklyn, the daughter of a prosperous New York insurance broker, Howard S. Tierney. She attended the fashionable Miss Porter's School in Farmington, Connecticut, and finished her education in Switzerland, also travelling around Europe on the twentieth century American version of the Grand Tour. She returned to America, intended for the life of a wealthy socialite and marriage. When she told her family she wanted to be an actress, rather than issue a flat veto her father − though secretly disagreeing with her wishes − encouraged her, calculating that her chances of crashing Broadway were slim and that she would soon be discouraged. He was somewhat disconcerted when she was hired at her very first interview and began to act bit parts on Broadway in 1939.

She was appearing in a suppporting role in *The Male Animal* in 1940 when she was spotted by Darryl Zanuck who plucked her off to Hollywood to star, still aged only 19, with Henry Fonda in his *Jesse James* sequel, *The Return of Frank James*, in which the outlaw's brother comes back to avenge his murder. She followed this with *Hudson's Bay* (1940), *Tobacco Road* (1941) and *Belle Starr* (1941) in which her distracting beauty and amiable personality always threatened to make a mockery of a film purporting to tell the life story of America's most notorious, most vicious, female outlaw. Nevertheless at 21 she had thoroughly arrived at the top of Hollywood's greasy pole − a feat so often only achieved by years of toil.

After several more films came *Laura* in 1944, which made a star of Clifton Webb. She played a socialite who is apparently a murder victim, with Dana Andrews as the investigating police officer who has fallen in love with her through seeing pictures of her. It was a landmark in murder mysteries and set the tone for the *film noir* of the later Forties. *Leave Her to Heaven* (1945) took its title from the line in *Hamlet* in which the

ghost, having told his son to avenge his ''murder most foul'' orders him not to harm his mother. For her role as a self-centred, jealous woman who has the capacity to cause misery for all with whom she comes into contact, even after her own suicide, Gene Tierney was nominated for a best actress Oscar, though eventually beaten to the prize by Joan Crawford.

Among later films were *Dragonwyck* (1946); *The Razor's Edge* (1946) a none too successful attempt to catch Somerset Maugham's pretentious parable on celluloid; *The Ghost and Mrs Muir* (1947) *That Wonderful Urge* (1948), *Whirlpool* (1948) and *Night and the City* (1950). But her life was already clouded by unhappiness. In 1941 she had married the couturier Oleg Cassini. During her pregnancy with her first daughter she contracted German measles and the child, Daria, was born mentally handicapped in 1943. Her marriage was foundering and, although they had had another daughter, Christina, in 1948 in an attempt to hold it together, it eventually ended in divorce in 1952.

Unhappy romances with the young and handsome John F. Kennedy, with Aly Khan and Tyrone Power were widely publicised but did nothing for her peace of mind. Beneath the tranquilly beautiful surface she presented to the outside world inner torments were propelling her to the brink of insanity and in 1955 she suffered a severe mental breakdown, on one occasion attempting suicide. She spent the next five years, on and off, as a voluntary patient in private hospitals.

In 1960 she married a Texas oil magnate, W. Howard Lee (who had once been married to Hedy Lamarr); she moved to live with him in Houston and her life achieved a new stability. She made films from time to time among them *Toys in the Attic* (1963) and *The Pleasure Seekers* (1964) and did some work for television. But basically from the early Sixties on she liked to consider herself as retired. Her autobiography, *Self Portrait*, appeared in 1979.

Her husband died in 1981.

LORD SALMON

Lord Salmon, PC, Lord of Appeal in Ordinary 1972-80, died on November 7 aged 87. He was born on December 18, 1903.

CYRIL Salmon was one of the most distinguished judges of his generation and a man of outspokenly liberal views. He was a proponent of a bill of rights for Britain and a critic of legal measures which he felt intruded on the civil rights of individuals. His outstanding characteristic was his intellectual integrity. He had a profound concern for justice, but never permitted it to lead him to legal conclusions which he could not support from authority and logic. And when he felt that something required to be said, he was not restrained by considerations of popularity.

Ironically for someone with such undoubted liberal sensibilities, it was the passing of stiff deterrent sentences by Salmon which had perhaps the greatest impact of his legal career. These sentences were passed on white men responsible for attacking blacks in disturbances in Notting Hill in 1958 and they were credited with playing a considerable part in reducing the potentially explosive racial tension of that period.

Salmon's concern for civil rights led him to make a number of controversial judgments and statements. In 1968 he delivered a fierce condemnation of the "trial by television" which he thought David Frost had conducted against the cut-price insurance swindler Dr Emil Savundra. The interview had taken place and been transmitted live seven days before Savundra was charged with conspiracy to defraud. But after dismissing the financier's appeal Lord Justice Salmon sharply criticised the televised interview saying it was obvious to all that Savundra was about to be arrested. The safeguards of fairness that existed in a court of law might seem prosaic to those engaged in the entertainment business, he said, but they were the rocks on which freedom from oppression and tyranny had been established for centuries. Trial by television was not to be tolerated.

In another notable stand Lord Salmon made one of the first legal rulings in support of women's rights when he declared that a woman could be a race-horse trainer. He was the chairman of two important royal commissions: the first, in 1966, into the workings of the Tribunals of Enquiry (Evidence) Act, 1921, and the second, following a scandal involving corruption in local government, into standards of conduct in public life.

Cyril Barnet Salmon was educated at Mill Hill and Pembroke College, Cambridge. In 1925 he was called to the Bar by the Middle Temple, and after a pupillage with Walter (later Lord) Monckton, he practised at the Common Law Bar where he earned a reputation particularly in commercial matters. Even in his early days, he displayed the capacity for stinging comment for which he was reputed in later life. It is said that, appearing before a magistrate's court, he was asked by the clerk: "Are you trying to teach me my job?" "I haven't time", was the reply. "I am hoping to catch the afternoon train."

By 1940 he had acquired a busy junior practice, but this was interrupted by the war, and in 1940 he was commissioned in the Royal Artillery. In 1943 he was appointed in the capacity of judge-advocate to the headquarters staff of the 8th Army, where he served until he returned to the Bar in 1944. Although little remained of his junior practice, he took silk in 1945.

After a lean period, his ability became known and he became one of the busiest and most fashionable leaders with a varied practice. His cases were conducted from the scantiest of notes, and sometimes with no notes at all, the result partly of a retentive memory, capable without difficulty of retaining dates and page references, and partly of a preference for a fluid approach, varying with the situation. Anecdotes of his acidity abound during this period. It is said that his argument in the Court of Appeal was once interrupted by a member of the Bench with the complaint "I do not understand your point, Mr Salmon". "My Lord," he replied, "I apologize. I must take comfort from the fact that your Lordship's learned brethren grasped it twenty minutes ago."

In 1947 he became Recorder of Gravesend, and in 1955 was a Commissioner of Assize. His appointment to the Bench in 1957 occasioned no surprise. As a judge he disposed of cases expeditiously, grasping a point quickly and effectively discouraging unnecessary repetition.

To this stage, his career had followed a pattern normal to High Court judges, and he had attracted little public attention. His name first appeared widely in the press in 1958 when he presided at the Central Criminal Court over the trial of nine youths accused of beating up coloured men at Notting Hill. At the Bar he had been conscious of his Jewish origin as a source of possible discrimination and he seized the opportunity to denounce racialism. Passing sentence of four years' imprisonment on all the defendants, he said: "Everyone, irrespective of the colour of their skin, is entitled to walk through our streets in peace, with their heads erect and free from fear. That is a right which these courts will always unfailingly uphold." In 1964, he was appointed to the Court of Appeal, where his judgments were frequently outstanding for their liberal approach, provided that he felt that he could reconcile liberalism with the authorities by which he was bound.

When the Royal Commission on the working of Tribunals of Enquiry was appointed in 1966, Salmon was chairman. Set up in February, the commission reported in November, and was accorded "full marks for dispatch" by *The Times*, which also, in common with the press generally, commented favourably on the content of the report. It advocated the retention of the procedure established by the Tribunals of Enquiry (Evidence) Act,

1921, and regretted that the then government had not made use of that procedure in the Profumo enquiry, but recommended certain amendments to protect witnesses from injustice and financial loss, and to confer immunity on members and advocates for things said in the course of the enquiry, or in the report.

Salmon's views again attracted public attention when, in July 1967, he addressed a public meeting of Justice, an organisation favouring legal reform, on the subject of "The French as the last bulwark of individual liberty". He condemned the rule compelling the courts to accept, without question, an objection by a minister to the production of documents on grounds of crown privilege. His language, as ever, was forthright. "It seems to me," he said, "that it is an insult and injustice to civil servants to hold that they are so timid and supine that they would not write freely and candidly unless they knew they had a special privilege and that nothing could ever in any circumstances be revealed."

His blistering comments on trial by television after the Savundra trial followed rapidly upon his appointment to chair an inter-departmental committee on the law of contempt as it affects tribunals of enquiry and as a result he was the centre of a lively controversy. In fact, when the committee reported in June 1969, it was widely held to have maintained an acceptable balance between freedom to comment and the danger of prejudicing proceedings.

In December 1970 he delivered the Haldane lecture at Birkbeck College, London. He chose for his subject "The Law and Individual Liberty", and used the opportunity to formulate his philosophy on the judicial role. Liberty, he asserted, was in danger both from increasing governmental restrictions and from "a minute minority" who equated it with licentiousness, so that it degenerated into anarchy. And this inevitably led to dictatorship. Refusing to dismiss the possibility that freedom might at some future time be threatened in England as it had in some other countries, he declared

that judges were the last bulwark of individual freedom, and argued for a bill of rights, giving them power to declare certain kinds of legislation illegal, a proposal which subsequently became fashionable, but was then regarded as startling.

In January 1972, upon the death of Lord Donovan, he was appointed a Lord of Appeal in Ordinary, but shortly afterwards he fell victim to the ill health which marred his career as a Law Lord. In the supreme tribunal his speeches retained their clarity and logic, and he did not court publicity by any ringing declarations.

In 1974, following the Poulson affair which revealed corruption in local government, Salmon chaired a Royal Commission on Standards of Conduct in Public Life. The commission reported in 1976 and recommended numerous amendments to the Prevention of Corruption Acts to accord with modern needs. Its recommendations have not been followed, but it is arguable that the report itself did much to improve standards among public bodies.

Lord Salmon retired in 1980 at the age of 76 but continued to take a public stand on issues of civil liberties which concerned him. He argued forcefully against the Police and Criminal Evidence Act of 1984 expressing particular objection to the extension of the period in which a suspect could be held in detention. He also strongly advocated the tape-recording of police interrogations as a safeguard against the extraction of false confessions. He was not anti-police, he said, but the only reason they could have for wanting to keep someone in custody for four days was that if they had him in for less they might not be able to get him to confess.

Lord Salmon was widely liked and admired for the breadth of his knowledge, his courtesy, humour and patience and also for his strength of will. He was married twice: in 1929 to Rencie Vanderfelt who died in 1942, and in 1946 to Jean, Lady Morris, who died in 1989. He is survived by a son and daughter from his first marriage.

CYNTHIA FELGATE

Cynthia (Harris) Felgate, television producer, died of cancer aged 56. She was born in Birmingham on October 8, 1935.

LARGELY due to Cynthia Felgate's vision and determination, generations of under-fives have been entertained and informed by toy characters like Big Ted, Little Ted, Jemima and Humpty in television series that have become household names — *Play School, Playaway, Playdays, Camberwick Green* and *Postman Pat*. By chance *Play School* was the first programme broadcast on BBC2 when it was launched in 1964, and it continued to be transmitted five days a week, every week, for the next 25 years.

Cynthia Felgate, who had no children of her own, was a founder member of the production team and executive producer when *Play School* was dropped — in spite of vociferous protests — in 1988. After its demise she continued as an independent producer and launched its effective successor, *Playdays*. These programmes were in sharp contrast to the American cartoons and racier, noisier productions like *Sesame Street* which make up the staple diet of television fare for children. The *Play School* keynote was its slow pace, its quiet humour and its gentleness:

and more than 70 per cent of the nation's under-fives watched the afternoon programmes and 46 per cent the morning ones — an extraordinary viewership. Not only did the programme rivet the attention of its young audiences but it was trusted by millions of parents not to scare or indoctrinate their children. The concept was exported in kit-form and a dozen countries transmitted their own versions.

Cynthia Felgate's philosophy was simple: to create television programmes for pre-school children that reflected all aspects of their play, on the basis that play is a child's first school; and to show ways of developing playtime to make it more interesting or perhaps more stimulating. Her programmes were primarily entertainment and only incidentally educational, and they were made with the single child watching alone very much in mind. Some adult critics complained that they were old-fashioned and too middle class but the enduring appeal of *Play School* was indicated by the sale of videos of past programmes after live transmission ceased.

She first joined Brian Way's Children's Theatre, which taught at schools throughout the country, and then joined the BBC as an assistant floor manager and worked on *That Was The Week That Was* and *Steptoe and Son* before joining the children's programmes department.

In the earliest years of *Play School* Cynthia Felgate, as she had become, was not an ideas person, but she understood exactly how to make ideas work on television. She was the natural successor when Joy Whitby, the original producer, retired in 1969. From then on she made *Play School* her own.

When, in 1988, the powers that be decided that the programme was "dated", Felgate came up with a new format that retained *Play School's* original concept but broadened the scope, widening the young viewers' horizons by using a toy bus, different locations around the country and introducing regional accents.

Cynthia Felgate is survived by her husband Richard.

YVES MONTAND

Yves Montand, actor and music-hall singer, died of a heart attack while filming near Paris on November 9 aged 70. He was born in Monsumano, Italy on October 13, 1921.

YVES Montand regularly headed French opinion polls as the most popular living Frenchman (especially with women). He was a good actor more than a great one: but he had a special charisma, deriving maybe from his Italian peasant origins — a wiry physical magnetism, debonair charm, vulnerability, and an appealing integrity and honesty. This honesty informed all his best screen work (he made nearly 60 films), whether he was playing a truck-driver in *La Salaire de le peur* or a liberal Czech victim of Stalinism in *L'Aveu*. It also marked his ebullient political campaigning, alike during his pro-communist period of the 1950s and in his strongly anti-communist phase of the 1980s.

Ivo Livi (his real name) was born in Tuscany in 1921, into a peasant family of communist sympathies who in 1924 fled to Marseilles to escape Fascism. There Livi grew up in poverty: he left school at 11 and took odd jobs in a pasta factory, as a delivery boy and as metalworker and docker. From childhood he was keen to be a singer, and his talent was soon spotted: by 1939 he was singing in the Marseilles music-halls. After the war, he moved to Paris, where Edith Piaf helped launch his career and was for three years his mistress. By 1959 his one-man shows were a roaring success, and by 1955 he had taken New York too by storm. Among his most popular songs were "Les Feuilles Mortes," and "Les Gamins de Paris" and the ironic Western, "Dans les Plaines du Far West." He began also appearing in films, making his name as an actor in *Le Salaire de la peur* (1952), an action-suspense thriller in which he played a lorry-driver taking a consignment of nitro-glycerine into the jungle to put out an oil-fire. It earned him a prize at the Cannes Film Festival.

In 1951, Montand married the actress Simone Signoret. It was a tempestuous relationship but a true *mariage d'amour* that was to last until her death in 1985. The Montands became by far the most popular couple in France, symbols of happy stability in the rickety showbiz world. They acted together in the Paris stage production of Arthur Miller's *The Crucible*, and in its film version, *Les Sorcières de Salem* (1956). This was also their heyday of political activism: though never Communist Party members, they often took part in communist-led rallies and marches – against the bomb and the Rosenberg executions, etc. But the invasion of Hungary sapped their faith in the Soviet Union and the Soviet invasion of Czechoslovakia led to their final break with the movement. Although remaining a Leftish radical, Montand now took up an increasingly anti-communist stance.

In 1960, he moved into the Hollywood orbit, making some 'big' (but not very good) American films such as *Aimez-vous Brahms?*, with Ingrid Bergman, *My Geisha*, with Shirley Maclaine, and notably *Let's Make Love*, with Marilyn Monroe who called him "the most exciting man I've ever met" (his much-publicised love-affair with her was treated with remarkable forgiveness by Signoret). He made other Hollywood films including *On a Clear Day You Can See Forever* (1969) with Barbra Streisand but Montand was never at ease in Hollywood, much preferring his serious French roles such as the wearied anti-Franco agent in Resnais' *La Guerre est finie* (1966).

For Costa-Gavras in 1968-72 he starred in a remarkable trio of political films that castigated tyrannies both of Right and Left – *Z*, *L'Aveu* and *Etat de siège*. In the first two he played noble liberals (*L'Aveu* was probably his finest work), but in *Etat de siège* he had the courage to play an unsympathetic "villain" – a CIA agent in Latin America.

In his later years Montand returned with success to the stage. In 1981 he performed a one-man show at the Paris Olympia and then toured with it abroad, appearing in New York at the Metropolitan, a rare if not unique distinction for a singer of popular songs.

Montand did little notable screen work after *Etat de siège* until 1986 when he received renewed critical acclaim playing the scheming patriarch of a Provencal mountain village torn apart by a feud over a vital water supply in *Jean de Florette* and its sequel *Manon des Sources*.

Following the death of Simone Signoret, Montand married Carole Amiel, a woman much younger than himself, with whom in 1988, he had his only child, a son named Valentin.

As a singer Yves Montand was in the great French tradition of Piaf, Trénet and Chevalier. With his deep-timbred, rasping voice, he would often portray some garage-hand or dockworker, and his songs, in turn wistful, funny and erotic, would echo the dreams, desires and failures of the *petit peuple* of Marseilles, where he grew up. As a star, he was a true man-of-the-people, yet also a serious, committed actor in his choice of such works as *The Crucible*, *Z* and *La Guerre est finie*. He ranged easily between light-comedy and drama.

Someone said of him: "He has the mind of an intellectual and the physique of a truck-driver." Hence his massive popularity. Hence too the public's acceptance of his curious political evolution. On many issues he was always a radical: but by the early 1980s his frequent public utterances were devoted mainly to warnings of the communist menace. He criticised his good friend Mitterrand for including communists in his government. He spoke up in favour of Euro-missiles, even of Thatcherite economic policies. And, because he was Montand, his views carried weight. A French public grown cynical about career politicians turned eagerly to this persuasive amateur: one of his late-night TV broadcasts on economics held an audience of eight million till over midnight, a French record! Voices were even raised, "Montand for President!" and in a newspaper poll 29 per cent of those questioned said they would vote for him. But Montand declined. "No" he said "Reagan stood because he was a bad actor. Since I'm a good one, I won't."

HENRY HARPUR-CREWE

Henry Harpur-Crewe, squire of Calke Abbey, Derbyshire, died on November 8 at Warslow, Staffordshire, aged 70. He was born on February 25, 1921.

HENRY Harpur-Crewe was at the heart of a preservation battle which, in the early 1980s, propelled the previously little-known Calke Abbey, in south Derbyshire, to the centre of the nation's consciousness. The problems of Calke, an eighteenth century Palladian mansion, began on the death of Henry Harpur-Crewe's brother, Charles, in 1981. Inheriting the property, Henry Harpur-Crewe found himself faced with a capital transfer tax bill of £8 million and a government reluctant to accept Calke for the nation, in lieu of payment.

It was Calke's misfortune that it was virtually unknown except among cognoscenti (and even some of them denounced its allegedly priceless collection of artefacts as "junk"). At that time, too, the National Trust was planning to take over the much-publicised Adam gem, Kedlestone Hall, only a few miles from Calke. Fierce wrangles between reluctant government officials and the heritage lobby developed over Calke while interest on the unpaid tax mounted remorselessly by well over £1,000 daily. A reclusive bachelor, Harpur-Crewe threw off the retiring habits of a lifetime and flung himself energetically into the struggle which was eventually resolved when, in his budget speech of 1984, the Chancellor of the Exchequer, Nigel Lawson, announced a donation of £4.5 million to the National Heritage Memorial Fund, for the purpose of saving Calke.

Harpur-Crewe was born Henry Francis Jenney, grandson through his mother of the redoubtable Sir Vauncey Harpur-Crewe, tenth and last baronet. Sir Vauncey was a renowned eccentric who carried reclusiveness to such a pitch that he communicated with his servants only in writing and barred all motor vehicles from the grounds of Calke. He was also a whimsical tyrant who banished one of his daughters from the estate for life for

300

smoking and had a cousin's house in the grounds demolished after they had had an argument. Sir Vauncey was a rapacious collector, filling room after room with stuffed birds and animals, seashells, pictures (of mainly indifferent quality), geological specimens, snail shells, swords, butterflies and a host of assorted bric-a-brac. These were piled indiscriminately into rooms; when one became full it was simply shut up and the collector moved on to the next.

Of this ramshackle collection, the house and its 14,000 acres of land, Henry Jenney found himself master on the death of his brother. In the interim he had served in the RAFVR during the second world war, been a Derbyshire county councillor and was a lay member of the General Synod. At the time of his brother's death he was leading a quiet, bachelor existence in a house on the Calke estate.

Changing his name to Harpur-Crewe, the new owner emerged from his cocoon of reclusiveness and set about confronting the well-nigh intractable problems of his inheritance. He could of course have sold Calke, but it had been the family home since 1703 and he was reluctant to do this. Merely voicing this possibility, however, immediately woke up conservationist interests and, amid a flood of letters from various people to national newspapers, the parliamentary heritage group visited Calke to form some opinion of what might be lost to the nation if the abbey were to be demolished. They found, by and large, an impressive exterior, a largely undistinguished interior and, naturally, Sir Vauncey's illimitable, if intriguing, piles of junk. But it was felt that Calke was well inside the limits of what public money ought to be spent on.

The National Trust was keen to run it, but not without an endowment for repair and upkeep which would have to come from the government. Eventually the Department of the Environment declared itself willing to accept the house and its park in lieu of the due tax, but balked at taking over much of the farmland and providing an income to run the house.

This caveat effectively scotched a rescue from that source. Edwina Currie, who had become South Derbyshire's MP in 1983, entered the fray, declaring of the Harpur-Crewes: "They have been the most benevolent landlords imaginable – but have not noticed any tax change since Lloyd George."

Suddenly the name of Calke was on every lip. It and its collection of junk were to be cherished as a "time capsule". Its bracken-covered slopes were held up as examples of ancestral landscape which it would be sheer vandalism to send under the hammer. The National Trust's publicity rose to new heights of lyricism in its advocacy of Calke, while its director-general castigated the government's reluctance to provide the necessary money to save it for the nation as "inconceivably pusillanimous".

Meanwhile Harpur-Crewe threw himself into the campaign. Banishing his hereditary shyness he made himself available for the television crews, posing for endless footage against the backdrop of his home, his flocks and his fallow deer herds. Warming to his task, he went to Washington to accompany the great state bed at Calke on its journey to America where it featured in an exhibition entitled "Treasure Houses of Britain". Those few who knew Harpur-Crewe really well would scarcely have recognised their old friend in the man who even agreed to sleep in the great bed as a fund-raising idea, as it lay on display in Washington's National Gallery.

When Mr Lawson eventually made the House of Commons announcement that resolved the crisis, the National Trust, to whom Calke then passed, carried out a restoration whose fidelity to the spirit of the place satisfied the nicest of antiquarians. Harpur-Crewe latterly spent most of his time at his country seat at Warslow, Staffordshire, though he retained a room at Calke. Earlier this year he had become High Sheriff of Derbyshire, an office in which he dispensed sumptuous hospitality.

He leaves his sister, Miss Airmyne Harpur-Crewe.

TONY RICHARDSON

Tony Richardson, English stage and film director, died of Aids in Los Angeles on November 14 aged 63. He was born in Bradford on June 5, 1928.

IN THE decade that followed the first night of John Osborne's *Look Back in Anger* in May 1956 the Royal Court staked a substantial claim to be London's most exciting theatre. Tony Richardson directed that play and he was to direct most of Osborne's major work of the period. George Devine ran the English Stage Company, which occupied the Court.

On the surface the two men appeared an oddly contrasting pair. Almost twenty years separated their ages. By the time he took over the Court Devine was in his mid-forties, a gruff, pipe-puffing, almost avuncular, figure. He provided the stability and took the knocks from an often petulant board. Tony Richardson was the young whirlwind, bursting into the theatre with ideas and ideals, making snap decisions before rushing off to a fresh project. Both were determined that their theatre would put on plays with a bit of the intellectual muscle that was

missing in a frivolous West End. And in this they succeeded.

The two men first met when Devine was at Stratford and Richardson was trying to make his name as a television director. Richardson, with his quickfire delivery and highly persuasive manner, talked the actor into appearing before his cameras. Devine in turn recognised that here was a talent worth harnessing and when the ESC was set up he insisted that Tony Richardson was there as his assistant.

Richardson had already acquired a modest reputation. His schooldays in Yorkshire were unhappy, but one of his friends there, Bill Gaskill, was later to join him at the Court. When he went to Wadham, though, and Ken Tynan's Oxford, he flowered. He was flamboyant in a milieu where flamboyance was prized; his slightly gangling appearance sweeping around Wadham gave him the look of an animated wading bird.

His views were fashionably left-wing and he joined the Free Cinema movement, which had part of its roots in a short-lived but influential film magazine called *Sequence*. With Karel Reisz he made a documentary about a London jazz club, *Momma Don't Allow*, which had Richardson's great hallmark of energy. It also showed his determination to get out and shoot the film where the action was. The astute use of location was to characterise the best films made by Woodfall, the production company he founded with John Osborne.

Richardson remained true to his declared intention of bringing ideas — and authors of stature — back to the theatre. Sometimes he was successful: he acted as nursemaid and director to Nigel Dennis when *Cards of Idenitty* was turned from novel into play. Sometimes he flopped: nothing could save the adaptation of William Faulkner's *Requiem for a Nun*. Always his mind was on the next project or the next project but one. He was forever off "to a meeting with someone". Richardson rarely said where, with whom and least of all what the subject might be. But it was clear that he was always going to be seduced back to film.

In 1958 he had formed Woodfall Films, the name being taken from the house off the King's Road, which Osborne shared with Mary Ure, the Alison of *Look Back*. He directed the screen version (with Richard Burton) and also *The Entertainer*. Woodfall started to acquire a reputation for "gritty and honest" films, which put working class life, especially as experienced in the Midlands and North, on screen. Two Alan Sillitoe works provided a couple of Woodfall's greatest successes, *Saturday Night and Sunday Morning*, produced by Richardson and directed by his old partner Karel Reisz, and *The Loneliness of the Long Distance Runner* which he filmed himself.

But his greatest success of the Sixties was *Tom Jones*, script by John Osborne, a Rabelaisian romp which established Albert Finney as an international star. It proved that Richardson could be a straightforward entertainer and it won him an Oscar for best director. He managed to find a reasonable part in it for his partner at the Court, George Devine, and a little money rolled into the coffers of the perennially hard-up theatre in Sloane Square. Finney himself came to the Court in the title role of *Luther*, which some reckon to be Richardson's finest piece of direction and Osborne's best play.

In 1964 the English Stage Company felt strong enough to launch a season in the West End at the Queen's with a starrily cast *The Seagull*. The Nina, an outstanding one, was Vanessa Redgrave, whom Richardson had married in 1962 after a romance that had left, according to John Osborne in *Almost a Gentleman*, a whirlwind of destruction in its wake. Even the marital home in Hammersmith had "a ferocious toucan, South American parakeets, bush babies and an assortment of lizards" as well as their first daughter Natasha.

In the cinema his touch was becoming less sure. Two pretentious pieces with Jeanne Moreau, *Mademoiselle* and *The Sailor from Gibraltar*, won few friends

and even less money. At the end of the Sixties he moved to larger scale enterprises such as *The Charge of the Light Brigade*, which he declined to show to the critics who once had so revered him, and *Ned Kelly*, which scarcely made the most of the talents of Mick Jagger.

After an outstanding *Hamlet* at the Round House with Nicol Williamson, which was later filmed and went to Broadway, Richardson's work began to be seen less frequently in London. He, too, seemed to turn against contemporary England which he had once observed so acutely. Perhaps he felt that what, as a young man, he had tried to change simply remained unalterable. He even lost touch with John Osborne. The Richardson with the Thunderbird and the villa in the South of France from which Osborne had written his famous "Damn you, England" letter was changing.

He set up his new home in California, buying a house from Linda Lovelace who, in her day, had been as flamboyant as Richardson himself. He continued to make films, some of which were flops, like *Dead Cert* which certainly did not live up to its title, while others such as *Hotel New Hampshire* showed the old Richardson wit and delight in duplicity – his own and that of the characters he had to play with. But the man who once was so much in the public eye preferred now to keep a safe distance from it; perhaps that fearsome energy had diminished.

Tony Richardson was complex and restless, rarely at ease with himself. He had the ability to energise and inspire, but also to antagonise with thoughts darting ahead of those around him and a tongue that could wound. His greatest monument will be the Osborne partnership, so perhaps Osborne should have the final word:

"No one has inflamed my creative passions more tantalizingly than Tony, nor savaged my moral sensibilities so cruelly. Whatever wayward impulse of torment he inflicted, his gangling, whip-lash courage, struggling within that contorted figure, was awesomely moving and, at the last, unimpeachable."

FREDDIE MERCURY

Freddie Mercury, rock star and lead singer of Queen, died of Aids on November 24 aged 45. He was born Frederick Bulsara in Zanzibar on September 5, 1946.

TO MARK the occasion of his 41st birthday in 1987, Freddie Mercury hired a DC9 and flew 80 of his friends to Ibiza. There he took over Pikes, one of the island's most exclusive hotels, and threw an outrageously lavish party complete with flamenco dancers, a fireworks display flashing his name in lights across the sky and a 20-foot long birthday cake carried in by six Spaniards dressed in white and gold.

The affair was typical of a life lived, until the last two or three reclusive years, to the hilt in an unashamedly extrovert, over-the-top fashion. "I always knew I was a star," he declared after the first flush of success, "and now the rest of the world seems to agree with me."

Be that as it may, Mercury was also a remarkably private man when out of the limelight, granting few interviews and giving little away about his family background. The son of Bomi and Jer Bulsara, he was born in Africa; his father was of Persian descent. Part of his childhood was spent in comfortable surroundings in India, where he went to boarding school, before his family moved to Feltham, Middlesex, in 1959. There Mercury's early interest in music took him into the ranks of a local blues-based band called Wreckage.

For a while he studied design and ran a clothes stall in Kensington market. He was helped by a friend, Roger Taylor, who was a student at London University and the drummer in a group called Smile. Mercury would go along to see Smile perform on the local college circuit. "Why are you wasting your time doing this?" he would exclaim to Taylor and the group's guitarist, Brian May, also a London University student. "You should be more demonstrative."

When Smile split up in 1970, Mercury invited Taylor and May to start a new group featuring himself as lead vocalist. He also suggested the name Queen, a deliberately camp, attention-grabbing title which he was well equipped to embody. They recruited bassist John Deacon from the small ads, and played their debut performance at the London College of Estate Management in February 1971.

In the years that followed the group forged a unique combination of heavy metal thunder, complex vocal harmonies and a preposterous glamrock image, woven into a package of dramatic excess. Mercury made a pivotal contribution not only as singer, pianist and one of the group's principal songwriters, but also in defining the group's image thanks to his flamboyant persona and ambiguous sexual appeal.

It was Mercury who wrote the group's best known hit, "Bohemian Rhapsody", a long, elaborate piece which incorporated a cod-operatic sequence followed by a bludgeoning heavy metal finale. The single stayed at No 1 in Britain for nine weeks in 1975 and its host album, *A Night at the Opera*, also sailed to the top of the chart. Such was the group's popularity at the start of 1976 that all four of their albums released to that date appeared simultaneously in the Top 30.

In keeping with the grandiose splendour of their music, Queen's live shows became ever more spectacular events, employing vast sets and lighting rigs. Deacon and May were both naturally retiring types and Taylor was stuck behind his drums, so the group depended heavily on Mercury's commanding stage presence. Prancing down multi-layered catwalks in a sequinned, skin-tight jump suit and ballet slippers, preening his way through a myriad of costume changes, and singing in his majestic, slightly frayed tenor voice, Mercury always matched up to the demands of projecting the group's music and image to the four corners of the world's biggest stadiums.

The group's popularity continued unabated into the Eighties. *The Game* (1980), *Greatest Hits* (1981), *A Kind of Magic* (1986) and *The Miracle* (1989) all topped the UK chart. At the Live Aid concert in 1985 they turned in arguably the most resounding performance of that remarkable event, and their *Greatest Hits* album was rarely out of the UK chart for the following two years.

Mercury embarked on a sporadic solo career, which he slotted into breaks in Queen's schedule. His debut album, *Mr Bad Guy*, reached No 6 in 1985, while his greatest success with a single was his cover version of the Platters' 1956 hit "The Great Pretender", a typically overwrought performance which he took to No 4 in 1987.

Also in 1987 he teamed up with Montserrat Caballe to record "Barcelona", a mock-operatic folly composed by Mercury which was then mooted as the official anthem of the 1992 Olympics. It is still in contention for that accolade. In 1986 he contributed three songs, including the title track, to the cast recording of Dave Clark's stage musical *Time*, but despite his various outside activities his first commitment was always to Queen whose personnel remained unchanged to the end.

The group's last tour, which included two shows at Wembley Stadium and a pioneering appearance in front of 80,000 Hungarian fans at Budapest's Nepstadion, ended with a date at the Knebworth Festival on August 9, 1986.

Mercury's renowned bisexual proclivities made him the target of sustained speculation when the Aids epidemic began to take its toll. "Yes, I did have an Aids test and I'm fine," he told *Woman's Own* magazine in November 1987, but rumours persisted that he had tested HIV positive.

In February 1990, after Queen pulled out at the last minute from an appearance at the BRITS Awards, photographs of a very sick-looking Mercury were circulated. But by the autumn of 1990 he was back in the studio with Queen, recording what was to be the group's last new album. Entitled *Innuendo*, it entered the UK chart at No 1 earlier this year and was followed more recently by a compilation, *Greatest Hits II*, which also topped the UK chart.

The current single "The Show Must Go On", which has been in the chart for the last six weeks, has a decidedly valedictory flavour and is accompanied by a video stitched together from old footage of Queen. In a nostalgic sequence of vignettes, Mercury's enduring generosity of spirit and his arch sense of humour continue to shine through.

"I don't expect to make old bones," Mercury once said. "What's more I really don't care. I certainly don't have any aspirations to live to 70. It would be boring."

CAPTAIN JOHN STEVENS

Captain John Stevens, DSO and bar, DSC, submarine commander, died in Lisbon on November 12 aged 75. He was born on March 19, 1916.

IN 1942 when Winston Churchill ordered the Admiralty to give names rather than numbers to all new submarines, it was a happy coincidence that that the 550-ton U-Class submarine P46 should henceforth be known as HMS *Unruffled*. For it precisely matched the temperament of her 26-year-old commanding officer, Lieutenant John Stevens.

It would have been less appropriate if she had become *Unbroken* or *Untamed*, in spite of General Dwight D. Eisenhower's description of Stevens as "the maddest submarine captain in the Royal Navy". Stevens's many friends and the press latched on to that soubriquet with glee, not realising that Ike had used the word in the American sense to explain the anger Stevens must have felt after he had blown the bows off the Italian cruiser *Regolo* with his last salvo and thus did not have another torpedo to complete her destruction.

In fact Stevens was far from being prone to anger or even eccentricity, although he had a keen sense of the ridiculous and was quick to spot the offbeat side of any situation. His equable temperament and ability to make light of difficulties stamped him as the ideal submarine captain, much loved and respected by officers and ratings at all levels, including the ship's cat Timosheko which shared all his war patrols in the Mediterranean.

John Stevens was born in London into a family without any apparent military connections. At Newlands preparatory school in Seaford a master who happened to be an enthusiastic member of the RNVR persuaded him to try for Dartmouth, which he duly entered as a bewildered 13-year-old cadet in 1929. Service as a midshipman in big ships in the Home and Mediterranean Fleets prompted him to volunteer for the more

exciting life of a submariner in 1937.

At the outbreak of war he was torpedo officer in HMS *Triumph*, a sister-ship to the ill-fated *Thetis* which sank during acceptance trials in Liverpool Bay in July 1939. Patrolling on the surface in the approaches to the Skagerrak on Boxing

306

Day that year *Triumph* struck a mine which blew off the outboard ends of all eight forward torpedo tubes, luckily without any torpedoes exploding. Repairs took so long that Stevens was sent as liaison officer in the French submarine *Circe* patrolling in the North Sea, where his impressive ginger beard earned him the nickname "Henri Huit". When France was overrun *Circe* reverted to her national control, and Stevens left her with memories of their four-course fully-licensed lunches and a searing rocket he got from the British flotilla captain for not having persuaded the French to be more aggressive between the hours of noon and 1600, when the coxswain (known by the other matelots as "Le Patron") stood the periscope watch.

He was then appointed first lieutenant of *Thetis* after she had been salvaged and recommissioned as HMS *Thunderbolt*. Her first patrol off the Gironde in the Bay of Biscay exorcised her past when she sank the Italian submarine *Tarantini*, for which Stevens was awarded the DSC.

From June 1942 until October 1943 he commanded HMS *Unruffled* in the 10th Submarine flotilla based on Malta. He arrived there after a period of severe losses and an enforced temporary evacuation to Alexandria. In all he made 23 war patrols, declining all suggestions that a Spare CO might stand in for him as a break. *Unruffled* returned to the UK with 21 symbols of achievement stitched on to her Jolly Roger. Besides the cruiser *Regolo* and various small targets despatched by gunfire, Stevens sank 11 transports on Rommel's supply lines, totalling 40,000 tons. His submarine was also used for beach reconnaissance before the Sicily landings and to launch two-man chariots against shipping in Palermo. These operations earned him a bar to the DSO which had been gazetted in May 1943. When the Japanese war ended he was on the point of sailing on his first Far Eastern patrol in his new command, HMS *Turpin*.

Peace-time brought him promotion to commander in 1952 after a commission in the training squadron at Portland. He then was appointed as a Nato planner in Oslo. His modesty and self-effacement were largely responsible for his career tapering off, as he recalls in his aptly-named memoirs *Never Volunteer* (1971). Others sought or wangled appointments to keep them in the mainstream of those destined for flag rank. That was not his way, so he found himself in Halifax, Nova Scotia, in charge of the small division of British submarines operating for the benefit of the Canadians. Although this was widely recognised as a professional dead-end, he accepted the situation with characteristic equanimity, from which he was rescued by selection to captain.

Service as flag captain to the last C-in-C Home Fleet who flew his flag afloat (Admiral Sir William Davis), led to another Nato planning appointment, this time on General Norstad's staff at SHAPE in Versailles. His last job was in command at Fort Blockhouse (HMS *Dolphin*) and its operating squadron of 15 boats. Having been chairman of the Admiralty committee on the subject, he became keenly interested in the development of submarine escape by free ascent; first from the 100ft tank, where, after years of trouble-free training, two fatalities in a matter of days might have put a stop to further trials. But his instructors pushed the frontiers of submarine escape much further, down in fact to 600ft, achieved from a submarine off Malta.

After retirement in 1967 he became a schools liaison officer, encouraging teenagers to consider the Royal Navy as a career. He settled in Emsworth near the sea which he loved. He regularly sailed along the Brittany coast, usually in the company of some of his old brother officers from wartime days. His deserved popularity as a loyal friend and lively companion was in part attributable to his total lack of malice towards anyone.

He is survived by his devoted wife, Sybil, and their daughter.

COMMANDER HUGH HAGGARD

Commander Hugh Alfred Vernon Haggard, DSO, DSC, second world war submarine captain, died on November 17 aged 83. He was born on June 21, 1908.

THROUGHOUT the dark days of 1940-42 — years of the blitz, Dunkirk and the fall of Singapore — the exploits of Hughie Haggard and his boat *Truant* provided bright spots in the gloom for beleaguered Britain. Tall and good-looking, this great-nephew of Rider Haggard, author of *King Solomon's Mines*, captured the imagination of the press at a time when its readers were desperate for good news.

His two years at the periscope saw *Truant* become one of the most successful Royal Navy submarines of the war. Her "Jolly Roger" pennant (now in the RN submarine museum at Gosport) showed 17 "kills", representing a total of 77,206 tons of enemy shipping sunk.

The 1,325-ton *Truant* with her 59-man crew served off Norway, in the Atlantic, the Mediterranean, the Adriatic and the Far East, covering a total of some 80,000 miles. She attacked (and fortunately missed) a British-manned merchantman, was twice fired on by her own side (they missed too) and got stuck in the mud on the seabed off Yugoslavia — all penalties of the fog of war.

But when *Truant* left Europe in May 1941 for a brief refit in the United States, the commander-in-chief Mediterranean described Lieut-Commander Haggard's handling of his craft as "a model of daring and enterprise, tempered with just the right degree of caution".

He had been first mentioned in dispatches the previous January when *Truant* intercepted the SS *Tropic Sea* off the coast of Spain. The Norwegian freighter had been captured by the Germans and her cargo of wheat was being taken to Bordeaux by a prize crew when *Truant* surfaced and trained her 4-inch gun on her.

The Germans scuttled the merchantman and took to the lifeboats, while *Truant* picked up the imprisoned crew of the British freighter *Haxby* (sunk by the same Germans) together with the Norwegian skipper and his wife. She made history, according to Haggard, as the first female submarine passenger in a wartime operation.

That August Haggard was awarded the DSC after a series of attacks on supply ships destined for enemy forces in North Africa, then in October was mentioned in dispatches for the second time. In March 1942, by which time *Truant* was engaging the Japanese in the Pacific, he won the DSO after operations which included two more sinkngs and two "damagings".

His success owed much to his professional self-confidence. In November 1940 while patrolling east of Tripoli he deliberately flouted orders not to sail within 15 miles of the coast because of mines. Observing Italian minesweepers at work, he quietly followed them to within seven miles of the shore, thus charting a clear channel through the minefield, which was of immense value to the navy. His C-in-C later endorsed Haggard's initiative in turning a blind eye to his signal.

In April 1941 he again won praise for the part played by *Truant* as a navigational beacon during the fleet's bombardment of Tripoli. Haggard never forgot the experience of lying like a mini-roundabout at sea, a light shining on top of her periscope, as the towering British battleships glided past.

His confidence was partly inspired by his pedigree. The son of Admiral Sir Vernon Haggard, a former sea lord and chief of the submarine service, his entry to Dartmouth, aged 13, appeared predestined. As a midshipman he sailed in the battleship *Renown* on her voyage round the world with the then Duke and Duchess of York (later King George VI and the present Queen Mother). This produced a famous photograph of the future king being unceremoniously bathed by King Neptune on crossing the equator for the first time. Later Haggard served in the royal yacht and seemed set at one stage for a career in the upper social reaches of the navy. But in 1933 he made a conscious decision to follow his father into the submarine service, with its emphasis on technical expertise and judgment.

He was posted to Britain on leaving *Truant* before returning to Malta as commander (submarines). He was executive officer of the cruiser *Devonshire*, then used for cadet training, in the late 1940s. To his bitter disappointment, however, tuberculosis ended his naval career in 1954.

He entered industry after retirement and was at one time a local councillor for Barnes in west London. He also served as master of the Clothmakers' Company in 1973-4.

Commander Haggard's first marriage ended in divorce in 1954. He married again in 1957 but his second wife died seven years ago. He leaves one son by his first marriage.

GUSTÁV HUSÁK

Gustáv Husák, first, and subsequently general, secretary of the Czechoslovak Communist Party, 1969-1987, and President of the Republic of Czechoslovakia, 1975-89, died on November 18 in hospital in Bratislava aged 78. He was born at Dubravka near Bratislava on January 10, 1913.

IN HIS twenty-year stewardship of Czechoslovakia Gustáv Husák presided over his country's spiritual abasement and brought it to the brink of economic ruin. He came to power in the wake of the brutal crushing of the "Prague Spring"

by the Soviet Union and he thereafter remained the obedient creature of the Soviet leader, Leonid Brezhnev. After 1969 he orchestrated vengeance against all those who had been associated with the bright hopes of 1968 and in particular against Alexander Dubček, their source.

But even these, perhaps expected, reprisals were as nothing to the mental and moral misery he heaped upon the Czechoslovak people. Prague, one of the loveliest capital cities of Europe, with its gleaming facades and majestic palaces, came in its increasing drabness to symbolise the intellectual debasement of an oppressed people. After 1969 it was visibly a city in thrall to a conquering and ethically alien power and Czechoslovakia more firmly than at any time since 1948, a dependable province of the Russian empire. The Czechoslovak spirit was quenched or driven underground. All thought of political progress was suspended. Economic activity also atrophied by degrees. All this was in marked contrast with the developments which, in their very different ways, were taking place in other Soviet satellites, such as Poland and Hungary.

That the rage and shame of the Czechoslovak people did not express itself more violently against the person of Husák, when it became clear that his days were numbered after the liberalisation of the Soviet Union, is to their credit. In the event Husák was allowed to quit the scene with dignity intact, though mourned by none.

Gustáv Husák was the son of a Slovak worker. In 1933 he began to study law at Bratislava University and at the same time joined the Communist Party. For a time he worked as an articled clerk in the office of Vladimir Clementis, but after the break-up of Czechoslovakia in 1939 and the establishment of the so-called Slovak Autonomous Republic, when Clementis was forced to flee to France and Britain, Husák was able to remain in Bratislava and open his own lawyer's office there.

Husák's great chance came when those Slovak communist leaders who had not escaped abroad were rounded up and imprisoned for the duration of the war. A Czech, Smidke, was sent from Moscow in 1943 to take charge of the Communist Party in Slovakia, and he appointed Husák and Novomesky to join him in forming the fifth illegal central committee of the party, of which Husák became vice-chairman. Husák's role was resented by the other communist leaders, who were condemned to inactivity in prison. It was even alleged that he had deliberately sabotaged attempts to free them.

A visit by Eduard Benes, the exiled Czechoslovak president, to Moscow led to the signing of the so-called "Christmas agreement" of 1943, under which the communist and non-communist resistance leaders came together to form the Slovak National Council in preparation for a Slovak rising. Husák was later attacked for his collaboration with the Slovak Democrats during the rising and charged with "bourgeois nationalism". But in fact his true view was that Slovakia should become a Soviet republic and indeed he had sent a report to Moscow, claiming that this was what the Slovak workers really wanted. The collapse of the Slovak rising, which was due to a number of causes, including the postponed advance of the Soviet army, put paid to these hopes and Husák had to accept that Slovakia's future would continue to lie within the framework of the Czechoslovak Republic.

Nonetheless, when Slovakia was eventually "liberated" by the Soviet army in 1944, Husák was in a strong position, as the most active Slovak communist there. In discussions on the future structure of Czechoslovakia he became a leading spokesman for the views of the Slovak "home front" and spent some months in Moscow working on the Kosice programme. Determined to strengthen Slovakia's position within the republic, he eventually came into conflict with Siroky and those Slovak communist leaders who had posts in the government in Prague and were equally determined that he should not succeed.

Thanks to Soviet support Smidke was made chairman of the Slovak National Council and Husák himself one of the deputy chairmen and commissioner for the interior. But in the first state elections of 1946 the Slovak communists gained only 30 per cent of the poll as against the 62 per cent won by the Slovak Democrats. As a result the communists had to cede the chairmanship, but Husák remained a vice-chairman and concentrated his efforts on undermining and eventually destroying the Slovak Democratic Party.

He was probably responsible for fabricating the alleged "fascist" plot which enabled him to discredit its leaders and edge himself into the position of chairman of the Board of Commissioners – the equivalent of Slovak prime minister. Having achieved this, he made further government impossible by resigning and taking the other communist commissioners out with him. However, his attempts to secure a majority on the board were frustrated until February 1948, when, in the crisis preceding the *coup d'etat*, he used the resignation of the Slovak Democrat ministers in Prague as an excuse to force the resignation of all their counterparts in Bratislava. The reformed board was now communist dominated. Husák wielded supreme power in Bratislava and had become, as well, a member of the presidium of the Czechoslovak Communist Party in Prague.

Up to this point Husák had proved himself a shrewd and ruthless operator, but his many enemies in the Slovak Communist Party were already plotting his downfall. In May 1950, after having been subjected to severe party criticism, he was relieved of his post as chairman and at the immediately ensuing party congress stripped of all his high party functions on the charge of "bourgeois nationalism" and "anti-state activity". The following year he was arrested and, at his trial four years later, sentenced to life imprisonment. The sentence was passed when Siroky, his rival in Prague, was prime minister of Czechoslovakia.

After six years' imprisonment he was amnestied in 1960 but not officially rehabilitated until three years later. Up to this time he had spent three years as a building worker and was later allowed to work at the Institute of State Law in the Slovak Academy of Sciences, writing his "Testimony on the Slovak National Rising" and eventually obtaining a doctorate in law. It was only after Antonin Novotny's replacement as Czechoslovak leader by Dubček that he was able to resume his political activity and begin his rapid climb back to power. In April 1968 he was appointed deputy prime minister and in August succeeded Bil'ak as first secretary of the Slovak Communist Party.

At first he appeared to stand shoulder to shoulder with Dubček and the reformers, but there were soon indications that he had other plans and was putting his own ambitions and Slovak nationalist considerations before the interests of the reform of the state. He opposed general reformist movements in Slovakia, refused to sanction the reappearance of the liberal weekly *Cultural Life* and questioned the validity for the Slovaks of the clandestine 14th congress of the party, held during the invasion on August 20 and later to be annulled under the Czechoslovak-Soviet agreement of August 26. In a Christmas Day broadcast in 1968 he demanded that the chairman of the new federal assembly should be a Slovak, thus blackballing the candidature of the popular Czech reformer Smrkovsky. All these were moves in a power struggle aimed at discrediting Dubček and the reformers, removing him and them from office and seizing supreme power himself. He achieved his purpose in April 1969, when Dubček stepped down from the post of the first secretary of the Czechoslovak Communist Party and Husák succeeded him.

Once having established Husák in supreme power the Russians found in him the ideal *gubernator* of their Czechoslovak province. He proved himself a far more servile vassal of Brezhnev than Hacha had been of Hitler. Between 1969 and 1977 he was reported to have visited Brezhnev 26 times (more than three times more often than any other bloc leader), and his frequent meetings with the Soviet ambassador in Prague were prominently reported in the press in contrast to the more discreet handling of them by Novotny.

Husák's policy was "normalisation", a euphemistic term for a vindictive purge of party and government, the devastation of Czech literary life, *Gleichschaltung* of education, persecution of religion, the eradication of any form of dissent and the obsequious endorsement of Soviet policy in a fashion characteristic of Stalinist times.

In domestic affairs Husák had a fairly easy run. He at least created a semblance of making the economy work and meeting the material needs of the population to the extent of not provoking them to open revolt. Unlike Novotny he never allowed production to grind to a halt although state indebtedness greatly increased. His *bête noir* must have been the emergence of Charter 77 and its signatories.

Their exposure of the countless illegalities of his regime and his unrelenting attitude to them, culminating in their imprisonment, set an indelible black mark on his name and compromised him in the eyes of the world.

Popular Czechoslovak opinion of him was well summed up in the catchphrase *Husák-Rusak*. Under his grim-faced leadership morale in Czechoslovakia receded to its lowest ebb with increased alcoholism, more frequent suicides and an intensification of other symptoms of national despair. Corruption and bribery attained unprecedented proportions.

In 1975, when President Svoboda was unable to continue in his office, special legislation was introduced to enable Husák to succeed him. In doing so he combined the offices of general secretary and president – an accumulation of power which he had opposed in the case of Novotny. In 1980 at the age of 67 he was re-elected for a further five-year term.

The accession to power in the Soviet Union of Mikhail Gorbachev sent a frisson through Czechoslovakia as it did through other conservative Soviet satellites. Mr Gorbachev's increasingly outspoken criticism of Husák's patron, Leonid Brezhnev, opened a rift between Moscow and Prague which grew wider as

time went on. When the two men met it was clear that they were radically different types of communist, Husák of the "old guard" whose beliefs had been kept alight by the struggle against Nazism, Gorbachev, the reforming communist of a rising generation. In the political currents which began to flow around him Husák became increasingly isolated. Eventually, in December 1987, he stood down as general secretary of the Czechoslovak Communist Party, to be succeeded by Milos Jakes.

It was the beginning of the end for Husák. With popular opposition towards him growing and focusing itself on the figure of the imprisoned playwright Václav Havel, his position, as one of the last opponents of *perestroika*, became untenable. Released from prison early in 1989, Havel appeared on the political stage as the man with increasingly authoritative title to become his country's next president. On December 10, 1989, Czechoslovakia's first government without a communist majority since 1948 was sworn in by Husák who then resigned the presidency. Outside in Wenceslas Square the crowds roared: "Havel for president!".

After leaving office Husák played no further part in the politics of his country, and was expelled from the Czechoslovak Communist Party in February last year. He was permitted to live in seclusion, an increasingly sick man after undergoing surgery for stomach cancer. On November 8 he was given the last rights by a Roman Catholic priest and, at the request of his sister, a practising Catholic, was confessed by the Archbishop of Trnava.

His wife, Viera, died in 1977.

LORD MOYNIHAN

Lord Moynihan, former bongo-playing playboy who fled from Britain in 1969, died from a brain haemorrhage in Manila on November 24 aged 55. He was born on February 2, 1936.

ANTONY Patrick Andrew Cairnes Berkeley Moynihan, 3rd Baron, was a gossip column celebrity of some renown before leaving England suddenly 22 years ago rather than face fraud charges in court. At the subsequent trial of his associates he was described as "the evil genius" behind a series of frauds carried out through bogus companies including airline ticket swindles and the use of worthless cheques to pay for expensive dinner parties at luxury restaurants and the purchase of a Rolls-Royce.

After a spell in Spain, he settled in the Philippines where he ran a chain of massage parlours and strip-clubs using the family crest to publicise the services provided. He also wrote a weekly gossip column under a pen name for a weekly Manila magazine. An Australian Royal Commission into drug smuggling described him, in 1980, as being a "shadowy figure" involved with Sydney's so-called "Double Bay Mob" in the export of heroin from Manila to Australia. Although he denied this he was certainly involved in an extensive marijuana peddling ring, double-crossing his associates and becoming an informer for the United States Justice Department. In return for immunity from prosecution he gave evidence at the trial in the US in 1988 of the ringleader, Howard Marks, an Oxford graduate, who was sentenced to 25 years imprisonment.

Moynihan's grandfather, Sir Berkeley Moynihan, had been an eminent surgeon who introduced surgical rubber gloves to Britain and was created a baronet by Lloyd George and then a peer in 1929. His son, Patrick Moynihan, the second lord, was a barrister and stockbroker who served as chairman of the Liberal Party executive from 1949 to 1950. Moynihan, the third lord, was educated at Stowe and served as a second lieutenant in the Coldstream Guards during his national service. He first came to public attention when his father packed him off to Australia in 1956 to work on a sheep farm after police broke up what was described in the popular papers of the time as a "rock 'n' roll" party which culminated in bottles of champagne being thrown into a Mayfair street at 5 o'clock in the morning. It later emerged that, a year earlier, he had secretly married a blonde nude model who had taken out a summons against him for assault.

He fitted the popular 1950s perception of a "Champagne Charlie" and tales of his night-club exploits were regularly recycled in the popular papers of the period. Although his musical abilities were uncertain, he was usually described as a bongo-playing playboy and was for a time manager of a night club in Soho. The nude model divorced him in 1958 and in December that year, in Tangier, he married Shirin Berry, a Malayan-born belly-dancer and fire-eater.

After succeeding to the title in 1965 Moynihan earned a living as an agent for cabaret artists and was occasionally active in the House of Lords, making speeches in favour of the nationalisation of gambling casinos, greater aid for the British film industry, and giving Gibraltar to the Spanish. In 1968 he married Luthgarda dela Rosa, a niece of the Philippines ambassador to Cambodia, and after a brief spell attempting to run a nightclub in Ibiza, managed a coffee bar in Beckenham. He fled to Spain in 1969 as police began investigating his business activities. He had already appeared in the dock on charges of stealing bedsheets from the furnished flat he was renting but had been found not guilty. This time the charges were more serious and in a statement, issued once he was safely out of reach of the British law, he said he had no intention of returning to Britain because the allegations of fraud made against him were "a personal vendetta" by the police.

Taking advantages of his wife's connections and the fact that at that time there was no extradition treaty between Britain and the Philippines, Moynihan settled in Manila. He appeared to have good relations with President Marcos's administration and was soon involved in the city's night-life, running a girlie bar called The Yellow Brick Road in the Ermita district. After the ousting of Marcos however, Filipino newspapers and the authorities began investigating his underworld activities.

Giving evidence at the trial of Howard Marks in Miami in 1989, Moynihan claimed he had worked for the Aus-tralians in the Philippines since 1980, reporting regularly to a police contact at their embassy, supplying intelligence on a notorious drug-dealer named Joe Smith who once flung $50,000 in cash at him suggesting they go into business. Little credence was given to such claims. He admitted on another occasion: "I know I'm a cheat, liar, thief and scoundrel."

He maintained in the Miami court that he had played a dangerous double game inside Marks's $1 billion smuggling empire, gathering information while posing as a middle-man in various drug deals. He had certainly secretly tape-recorded his dealings with Marks, in return for promises from the US Drug Enforcement Agency of immunity from prosecution.

After Marks had been found guilty Moynihan nursed the hope that his efforts on behalf of the law might have improved his chances of returning to Britain and of reclaiming his seat in the House of Lords. His hopes were in vain, however.

Moynihan had one daughter by his second wife and three by his third wife. He married for a fourth time, in 1981, another Filipino, Editha Eduardo; the couple had a son, Andrew Antony Joseph Berkeley in March 1989 before divorcing later the same year. According to a death notice placed in *The Times* in June 1990, the child – Moynihan's heir – died at the age of 15 months but in June this year the boy was said by newspaper reporters to be alive and living with his mother who was running a massage parlour in the red-light district of Manila.

Moynihan married, for the fifth time, a third Filipino called Jinna by whom, in January this year, he had a second son, Daniel.

KLAUS KINSKI

Klaus Kinski, German film actor, was found dead at his California home on November 24 aged 65. He was born in Danzig in 1926.

POSSESSED of a gloomy intensity which riveted audiences through his large-eyed, often baleful, stare, Klaus Kinski had a screen presence which was memorable however poor the material he was acting in. His qualities were seen to best advantage in the films he made under the director Werner Herzog. But he had had a chequered career, acting in Berlin theatres in the hard, unheated months which followed the end of the war; playing small roles in films like *Dr Zhivago* and – bizarre as it seems in retrospect – featuring in spaghetti Westerns, before his partnership with Herzog enabled him to break out of a typecasting which came close to condemning him to a professional life of "mad", "monster" and "the creature . . ." type roles in shocker and B-movies.

The screen persona of Kinski fitted well into Herzog's scheme of things as a filmmaker. The director had no compunction in resorting to extreme measures to extract what he required in terms of emotional intensity from his players, and in Kinski he could always be sure of a response. The chemistry between the two was often explosive. Kinski frequently tore about the location threatening to kill his director, to trample him underfoot in the mud (a not infrequent attendant hazard of Herzog locations) or to hurl him into a river full of bloodthirsty piranhas. But in spite of the actor's incendiary personality, Herzog seldom failed to extract from Kinski what he wanted. In a Herzog film Kinski's intensity becomes subsumed in the whole. Thus, in what is perhaps their best collaboration, *Aguirre, der Zorn Gottes* (*Aguirre, Wrath of God*) Herzog is not interested in the character of the conquistador whom Kinski plays, for itself, but uses the power of Kinski's screen presence to convey his vision of a colonial impulse which has become completely unhinged and is descending into madness.

Klaus Kinski was born Nicolaus Günther Nakszynski, in Sopot, Danzig, then a free city leading a precarious life under the never-too convincing aegis of the League of Nations, now Gdansk, a Polish port. His father was a pharmacist and his mother the daughter of a local pastor. With the arrival of the Depression in Danzig the Nakszynskis found it impossible to make ends meet. In 1931 they moved to Berlin where they took German citizenship (had they remained in Danzig that step would have been delayed until no later than 1939, since the seizure of the city was among Hitler's first aggressive acts of the second world war).

During the latter part of the war Klaus Kinski was drafted into the Wehrmacht, but his military career was to be mercifully brief. During a training exercise which was being conducted in Holland during the winter of 1944 his unit was overrun by the advancing British and Kinski became a prisoner. His first stage experience was in a show put on in a British prisoner-of-war camp.

Following the war he drifted into stage work in Berlin before taking the first of the many minor film roles he was to plough through before his association with Herzog lifted him from obscurity. Among some 200 titles to which he made contributions, often as madman or thug, lurking in the shadows to spring out upon the unwary, were such offerings as *Die toten Augen von London* (*Dead Eyes of London*) and *Scotland Yard jagt Dr Mabuse* (*Scotland Yard hunts Dr Mabuse*) in the 1960s, before a small role in *Dr Zhivago* (1965) gave him a slightly more visible professional profile. This was reinforced by an appearance in the spaghetti Western *For a Few Dollars More* (1966), but there was still a long way to go and a welter of such fare as *Bang! Bang! You're Dead!* and *Circus of Fear* to be negotiated before *Aguirre* (1972) gained him (and — as important for his future — its director) proper recognition.

Herzog's remake of F. W. Murnau's 1921 *Nosferatu* — *Nosferatu, The Vampyre* (1979) — was not to everyone's taste. It was, visually speaking, too faithful a copy of its original, perhaps, with colour seeming to add nothing to Murnau's flickering monochrome. Yet at a distance it would appear to warrant a less dismissive judgement than those which were passed in the press at the time; certainly Kinski provided a riveting account of Dracula himself, imbuing the concept with hauntingly sympathetic qualities.

Fitzcarraldo, another Herzog film, provided another perfect role for Kinski, as an eccentric Irishman who in nineteenth century Peru strives to establish an opera house in the depths of the jungle. At the centre of a landscape of impenetrable forests and teeming rivers Kinski's performance as an indomitable, if possessed, struggler against circumstances communicated a profound sense of the strangeness of human existence.

In his personal life Kinski distanced himself from such sympathetic images in a robust, not to say monstrous, manner, delighting in verbal abuse of interviewers, acquaintances and in boasting about the priapic excess of his private life. His behaviour was more of a piece with the crazed roles he had acted in his early film career. Herzog was not the only director to feel his vituperative abuse. When offered the leading role in *Indiana Jones* Kinski demanded to see the script which, he then screamed, was "a yawn-making, boring, pile of shit!" His memoirs, entitled *Ich brauche Liebe* (tr. *Everything I Need is Love*), also got him into hot water for their frank "revelations" (many of which were subsequently contested as being merely vindictive, libellous fantasies) about the women he had been associated with. His daughter, the actress Nastassia Kinski, threatened him with a libel suit, while one German critic described the book as having no more literary or biographical value than a "well-used condom." Latterly Kinski had based himself in America, declaring, hotly, that he would "rather wash dishes in America than make films in Europe".

Kinski's daughter Nastassia is of his second marriage, to the German writer Ruth Brigitte. By his first wife, Gislint Kuhlbeck, he had a daughter, Pola, and by his third, Genevieve Minhoi, he had a son.

SIR TERENCE MORRISON-SCOTT

Sir Terence Morrison-Scott, DSC, director of the British Museum (Natural History), 1960-68, died on November 25 aged 83. He was born in Paris on October 24, 1908.

BEFORE taking over the running of the British Museum (Natural History) in 1960, Terence Morrison-Scott had been director of the Science Museum from 1956 to 1960. He thus had the rare distinction of heading two of the nation's most prestigious storehouses of knowledge, artefacts and specimens. He was a key figure in the drafting of the British Museum Act (1963) and in its passage through Parliament. In particular he participated in the establishment of a board of trustees related to natural history. He was also a prime mover in retaining – during his tenure – the title of British Museum (Natural History). Although the museum is now known simply as the Natural History Museum, he favoured retaining the old title because of the important part that the natural history collections (many dating back to 1753) played in the origi-

nal foundation of the national museum.

At a critical time in the museum's development he established an easy and efficient relationship with the trustees and cultivated a fruitful and happy partnership between their chairman, Professor C. F. A. Pantin, and himself as director.

Morrison-Scott recognised that the primary need was to develop the research side of the museum's work which utilised most of its funds. As a result, in 1966-67, the museum ceased to compete for funds with other museums and art galleries. Instead it was classed with research councils, receiving its financial allocation from the Civil Service budget on the recommendation of the Council for Scientific Policy. On Morrison-Scott's initiative the council considered and approved a long overdue programme of new buildings for the scientific departments. This enabled the bird section, whose large collections had for more than 30 years been "temporarily" accommodated in the entomology block, to be moved to a purpose-designed building in the museum's out-station at Tring, and for the large and important collections of insects at Tring to be transferred to London for incorporation in the national collections there. On the South Kensington site an east wing linked to the Geological Museum was built to accommodate the department of palaeontology and a tower block was built as an extension for the library and to accommodate other sections of the museum that were in desperate need of more space. With his background of experience of the needs of the departments Morrison-Scott gave effective support to their requirements for special cabinets for the systematic curation of the various departmental national collections, for the provision of optical and other equipment and, by no means least, for the increase of the scientific staff to provide cover for the main fields of natural history and a better balance between research and support staff. Certainly in Morrison-Scott the museum benefited by having as its director one who, in addition to having an innate administrative capacity, had

318

served his apprenticeship in the place where he ultimately took charge.

Terence Charles Stuart Morrison-Scott was the only son of Lieut-Col R. C. S. Morrison-Scott, DSO. The implications in his second two baptismal names were borne out in himself for, like his illustrious name-sake of the mid-seventeenth century he had the same distinguished bearing, stature, good looks, charm of manner, assurance and a self-admitted arrogance that was but a facade behind which lay a quite unwarranted intellectual modesty and a warmth of sympathy that endeared him to those privileged to be his friends.

He went to Eton and from there to Christ Church Oxford. He studied zoology at the Royal College of Science, London, and in 1935 graduated BSc, ARCS with first class honours. In 1952 he received his DSc from London University.

After a brief time as an assistant master at Eton, in 1935 he became a member of the scientific staff in the mammal section of the museum's zoology department. Even before the beginning of the war, 1939, he had started the flow of his original contributions to knowledge of the mammalia. Rodents from British Guiana, shrews and voles from Jersey and Guernsey, a supposedly extinct Cuban *Capromys*, the giant panda, mammals collected by St John Philby in Arabia, a key to British bats, and the teeth of elephants – all these had been subject to his illuminating exposition.

As an officer in the RNVR, Morrison-Scott was on active service throughout the second world war in motor torpedo boats on combined operations. As a lieutenant commander he won the Distinguished Service Cross.

With the war behind him Morrison-Scott returned to the British Museum where he, Sir John Ellerman and, in part, R. W. Hayman gave their attention to the great works that brought them distinction throughout the zoological world. *The Check-list of Palaearctic Mammals* (1952), *Southern African Mammals – a reclassification* (1953) and a *Handlist of Malaysian Mammals (Supplement to Chasen)* 1955, are working tools of all mammalogists. But while this work was going on Morrison-Scott was also engaged in the production of smaller contributions such as the specific status of Egyptian mummified cats, deer antler anomalies, the coat colour of the grey squirrel and a list of British mammals. During this period, too, he gave considerable attention to the use of plenary powers for the purpose of stabilising the names, by validation or rejection, of various mammals in taxonomic literature.

During his four years as director of the Science Museum from 1956, Morrison-Scott developed his administrative flair and was respected by the staff who appreciated that his objective was to help them to enhance the standing of the museum.

Morrison-Scott's experience was exploited by various committees and governing bodies. He was honorary treasurer of the Zoological Society of London from 1950 to 1976 and, in a similar capacity, contributed greatly to the success of the International Zoological Congress in 1953. He was a trustee of the Imperial War Museum (1956-60), a fellow (1963) and governor of the Imperial College of Science and Technology (1956-72), a council member of the National Trust (1968-83) and a member of the Standing Commission on Museums and Galleries (1973-76), a fellow of the Linnean Society and of the Institute of Biology.

Morrison-Scott indulged diverse interests in the time not absorbed by his professional duties. Real tennis, ski-ing, shooting, sailing, and – as he put it – an occasional interest in the relative speeds of equine perissodactyls. As a craftsman he excelled in the turning of wood, ivory and other media. The beauty of his lettering in stone expressed not only his calligraphic apprecation but the inscriptions, in Latin, his love also of the classical languages.

He married in 1935 Rita Layton who survives him.

FRANÇOIS BILLETDOUX

François Billetdoux, French playwright, actor and novelist, died in Paris from cancer on November 24 aged 64. He was born in the same city on September 7, 1927.

FRANÇOIS Billetdoux was a man of contradictions both physically and intellectually. Bushy, black eyebrows were perched precariously above the glistening, pink Pickwickian face. In his plays he delighted in taking a real-life situation and then introducing something quite unexpected which slowly unhinged reality so that audiences caught a glimpse of a more essential truth beyond.

Billetdoux disliked being pigeon-holed and he moved easily between a number of arts. He was a pupil at Charles Dullin's now legendary acting school and then enrolled, in 1946, at the Institut des Hautes Etudes Cinematographiques. Simultaneously he developed a career both as a journalist (most notably with the magazines *Opéra* and *Arts*) and as a radio dramatist, his first broadcast work being a detective series.

In 1957 his third novel, *Royal Garden Blues*, established him as a writer of note. Cinema scenarios and television series were quick to follow. But it was through the theatre that he reached his widest public, and it was the stage which gave freest rein to his singular imagination. Billetdoux instinctively knew what the stuff of dreams was made of and had the knack of fashioning it into a social allegory. Billetdoux's plays were to attract several of Europe's leading directors, including those of the avant-garde.

From adolescence Billetdoux had been an *habitué* of the cabarets, music halls and experimental theatres that proliferated in the Paris of the Forties and Fifties. He started writing and performing sketches and poems in the cafés and tiny theatres of the Latin Quarter before making his debut as a fully-fledged playwright in 1955, at the Théâtre de l'Oeuvre, with *A la nuit la nuit*. He later spoke of it, with characteristic irony and complete lack of bitterness, as: "My first respectable failure."

An embryonic "Billetdoux-ian" psycho-drama, liberally laced with black comedy, the play recounts a series of meetings between a prostitute and a mystery man. Revived recently in Paris at the Renaud-Barrault's small experimental studio theatre, its enigmatic 30-year-old dialogue remains socially relevant and its dramatic structure can now be judged to have a skin-prickling power akin to that of early Pinter.

True success came in 1959 with the premiere of *Tchin-Tchin* at the Poche-Montparnasse, which recounts the decline of an alcohol-doused love affair of a bricklayer and a doctor's wife. Subsequently translated into 19 languages – in English it lost the initial "Ts" – it played successfully in the West End and then on Broadway, with Anthony Quinn in the role of the bricklayer. Peter Brook mounted a highly successful revival in Paris in 1984, with a cast headed by Natasha Parry and Marcello Mastroianni.

Billetdoux's individual dramatic style reached its maturity with *Comment va le monde môssieur? Il tourne, môssieur* ("How goes the world, sire? It turns, sire"). Premiered in 1964, it recounts the meeting of two war heroes as they leave a concentration camp. That same year was the first performance of *Il faut passer par les nuages*, a dramatic composition in five movements, that takes its title from a Jean Joubert quote, the implication being that those who make it through life's clouds get to see the light. It came to London in the World Theatre Season with Madeleine Renaud.

The epic rise and fall of a middle class matriarch, the play is according to Billetdoux "total theatre". Like *Tchin-Tchin* it was considered worth reviving and in 1988 in a blockbuster production directed by Lucien Pintilie, its experimental label came up as good as new. So readily, and so well, did the work adapt to a stadium-sized video screen, an electronic storyboard system, flottilas of video cameras and banks of computers, that it was surprising how successful Jean-Louis Barrault was in directing the first performance in the silicon chipless Sixties.

In 1967 Billetdoux was on Jean Vilar's Avignon Festival programme with *Silence! L'Arbre remue encore*. In 1970, the avant-garde Billetdoux, gained "classical" status, with the entry of two of his plays into the repertory of the Comédie Française.

For the next 15 years Billetdoux wrote nothing for the stage but was far from idle. During this time he was busy with a series of television films and setting up a local radio station. He was also invited to join the Haut Conseil de l'Audiovisuel, one of France's top audiovisual authorities and was an active member of the Audiovisual Institute. From 1981 to 1986 he presided over the Societe des Gens de Lettres arts fellowship and in 1980 he was appointed to the Unesco national commission.

It was Jorge Lavelli, artistic director of the Colline, national theatre for contemporary works, that finally lured Billetdoux back to the stage in 1988. Lavelli directed Billetdoux's final play, *Reveille-toi, Philadelphie*. This adult fairytale describes the adventures of a young girl who, for love of a wolf, ages one year for every day she is apart from him and as a consequence gives her father the problem of how to handle a pubescent 84-year-old. For *Philadelphie* Billetdoux justly received a Moliere, France's top theatre award, as author of the year.

Until ten days before his death, Billetdoux was completing *Appel de personne à personne* (Call from no-one to nobody), a new film for La Sept, France's haute culture television channel. With his customary gentlemanly obstinacy, Billetdoux persuaded his family to allow him to finish the film explaining: "This is the last time I will do something experimental."

He leaves a wife and two daughters, Virginie and Raphaelle.

SIR ROY WELENSKY

Sir Roy Welensky, PC, KCMG, formerly prime minister óf the Federation of Rhodesia and Nyasaland, died December 5 in a Dorset hospital aged 84. He was born in Salisbury, Rhodesia on January 20, 1907.

SIR Roy Welensky, a former professional boxer and railwayman, was one of the main architects of events in southern Africa in the 1950s. He became prime minister of the Federation of Rhodesia and Nyasaland, which was forged in an attempt to produce a solution to the problems resulting from the end of colonialism. Although his policies ended in failure he will be regarded by many as one of the few really constructive leaders produced by the Europeans in southern Africa during this century. He made mistakes, but it was primarily the strong flow of racialism among both Africans and whites in Africa that defeated him. He was a fierce critic of both the Macmillan government, which he accused of failing to support the Federation, and of the unilateral declaration of independence of Ian Smith's Rhodesian Front government in 1965.

He believed that if the British had given greater backing to the Federation it might have been possible to have achieved majority rule by evolution rather than revolution.

After seven years at the centre of events as prime minister of the Federation from 1956 Welensky found himself a private citizen once again, at the end of 1963, when it was finally dissolved. His last years in office had been marked by a succession of stormy disagreements with the British Conservative government. He had battled strongly to keep the Federation in being, but he failed, as he was bound to do, given the growing intensity of African feelings.

In September 1964, with hints of UDI by the Rhodesian Front government being freely discussed, Sir Roy returned to politics as leader of the Rhodesia Party, and he contested a Salisbury by-election but was defeated. This action put paid to his political career but clarified his political stance to posterity.

Roland Welensky was the thirteenth child of Michael and Leah Welensky. Leah Welensky, who was of South African-Dutch origin, died in 1918. The 12-year-old Roy and is father, who was a Polish Jew, settled in two shabby rooms in the poor quarter of Salisbury. At the age of 14 Roy left school. When he was 17 he became a railway fireman and shortly afterwards took up professional boxing as a secondary source of income.

In 1938 he entered the Northern Rhodesia legislative council as member for Broken Hill (he was unopposed), and struck up a close friendship with Lieutenant-Colonel (later Sir) Stewart Gore-Browne, who was leader of the unofficial members as well as representative of native interests. By working as one under Welensky and Gore-Browne the unofficial members hastened constitutional development.

In 1946 Gore-Browne resigned. Welensky then emerged as a coming leader with a definite policy; self-government for Northern Rhodesia under white control, amalgamation with Southern Rhodesia, and the winning of the mineral rights from the British South Africa Company.

Welensky and Lord Malvern (then Sir

322

Godfrey Huggins), prime minister of Southern Rhodesia, were in full agreement on the need to amalgamate the two Rhodesias, but by 1948 Welensky realised that the British government would not ratify any such naked takeover and persuaded Huggins (who was never happy at the inclusion of Nyasaland) to back the idea of Federation between the two Rhodesias and the far poorer Protectorate of Nyasaland. The Labour government, with James Griffiths as Colonial Secetary, launched the scheme. After the 1951 election the Conservatives adopted it with enthusiasm.

Fiercely attacked in Britain in 1953, the final constitution, with safeguards for African interests in the form of an African Affairs Board, was published. Welensky was knighted in the coronation honours in 1953. He had become CMG in 1946.

Welensky became federal minister of transport and development and later leader of the house and deputy prime minister. From the first he fought strongly to widen the base of support for the federal idea, attacking South African ideas of apartheid and upholding the concept of "partnership" but insisting that the government must remain in civilized hands.

Welensky welcomed the Copperbelt agreement in 1955 under which jobs were reclassified to permit Africans to advance to skilled status. Welensky's other great theme was the necessity to put the economic development of the country ahead of political liberalization.

When Lord Malvern finally resigned on November 1, 1956, Welensky became prime minister. He gave no portfolio to an African, but he did so later. As prime minister he immediately girded himself for the battle to win independence for the Federation, and a sharp note in his references to Britain became noticeable.

Never an admirer of Colonial Office rule, he now found a ready response among his white party supporters for fierce attacks on the policy of handing over power to African nationalists. None the less, the Gold Coast became Ghana

in the following year and at his first Commonwealth prime ministers conference Sir Roy in the following year found himself inferior in status to Dr Kwame Nkrumah.

In March, 1957, he won, however, a considerable degree of independence in the conduct of foreign relations, subject only to overriding British obligations while the Federation was not an independent entity. He won an agreement from the British government not to initiate any legislation to amend or repeal any federal Act except at the specific request of the federal government and later contended itself.

The fall of Garfield Todd from power in Southern Rhodesia and his replacement by Sir Edgar Whitehead seemed to indicate a strong rightward swing by the electorate on which Sir Roy depended.

During 1958 and 1959, too, it was clear that African opinion was hardening against the federation far more than Sir Roy realized; his political antennae, so sensitive in other ways, malfunctioned when the views of the African on his doorstep came into his line of vision.

For a time, Sir Edgar Whitehead, who had introduced draconian legislation on law and order, was more unpopular with liberals then Welensky. Both were as discomfited as the British government by the strictures of the Devlin commission, which inquired into the troubles in Nyasaland in which federal troops had been sent to back up the Nyasaland government.

A new phase began when the new colonial secretary, Ian Macleod, determined to open the way to African rule in Nyasaland, to give Africans a strong if not preponderant voice in a new Northern Rhodesian constitution, and to set up an all-party commission to prepare a brief for the constitutional federal review.

The fierce wrangle over the formation of the Monckton Commission led to Labour's decision to boycott it because Sir Roy flatly refused to allow its terms of reference to envisage any break-up of the federation: he continued to insist that independence must come by "1961 at latest." The Commission, in a lather of reservations and minority statements, frankly declared that African suspicions of federation were paranoic.

Then came the Congo debacle — which Sir Roy had foretold. While Macleod won Dr Banda's confidence in Nyasaland and ultimately installed him in power, Sir Roy became involved simultaneously in the problems set for the federation by the United Nations actions in the Congo — and especially Katanga — and the inconclusive discussion of the first stage of the federal review during 1961. During that year Sir Roy was mainly interested in two things, closely related. The first was a Northern Rhodesian constitution which would leave power in "civilized" hands. His second objective was a friendly and orderly multi-racial Katanga.

When in March, 1962, Rab Butler took over central African affairs there was a brief period of euphoria when every section of opinion thought he would solve matters favourably to them. But his decision on the Northern Rhodesian constitution angered Sir Roy, and so did his obvious intention to ease Nyasaland out of the federation first; Sir Roy called a general election and won it easily, but at a fearful price; for the opposition led by Winston Field refused to stand at all on this occasion and the African vote was minimal. Field transferred his attentions to Southern Rhodesian politics.

In November, after the Northern Rhodesian elections, Kaunda's Unip party and Mr Nkumbula's African National Congress formed a government pledged to secession. In December, Field led his Rhodesian Front to victory against Sir Edgar Whitehead in Southern Rhodesia under its new constitution, granted in 1961 on independence. In November Butler announced that Nyasaland could secede and Sir Roy attacked him mainly for doing this without prior consultation or the necessary agreement of the federal government and for breaking "solemn undertakings" made in 1953. Butler's plans for a post-federal association to carry on the good work of the federation came to nothing when inconclusive talks were held in London in March, 1963.

Welensky's career had in it many of the elements of Greek tragedy. He came from a narrow background, that of the white working classes in Southern Africa. He had scanty formal education, and evolved in a background where self-education was hardly won. He overcame these handicaps by great spirit and a naturally inquiring mind. These qualities led him to develop his thought towards liberal ideas which were not innate to him. He came to see plainly that the European could not survive in central and southern Africa save in partnership with the African, but by the time he had arrived at his position and had achieved such constricted power as the leadership of the Federation brought him, the tides of history were already sweeping past both in South Africa and the Congo.

His health was never robust and the burden that he laid on himself was enough to kill far stronger men. He had immense tenacity and thoroughly enjoyed politics, fighting what many observers of the African revolution thought a losing battle with skill. His weakness was intolerance of opposition: and his cabinets were chosen (admittedly from a tiny pool) for compliance. He was a natural journalist, and was working on a definitive account of the Federation. In 1964 he published his book, *Welensky's 4000 Days, The Life and Death of the Federation of Rhodesia and Nyasaland*. He read much, and had few relaxations, of which gardening was one. His personal happiness lay in his family and in his great gift for long-lasting friendships. He was a fascinating talker and companion. He owed much to the resilient and cheerful personality of the first Lady Welensky, whom he married in 1928. She died in 1969 and in 1972 he married Valerie Scott. In 1981, the Welenskys left Zimbabwe — as Rhodesia had by now become — to live in Blandford Forum, Dorset, because of Sir Roy's health.

He is survived by Lady Welensky, their two daughters, and a son and daughter from his first marriage.

CLIFF BASTIN

Cliff Bastin, Arsenal and England footballer, died on December 4 aged 79. He was born on 14 March, 1912.

CLIFF Bastin was the finest left-winger of his generation and gained every honour in the game before he was 21. Known as "Boy" Bastin, he played league football for Exeter at 16, was a regular member of Arsenal's first team at 17, won an F.A. Cup medal at 18, a League championship medal at 19 and played for England at 20. He was capped for England 21 times and set up a new record for an outside-left in the 1932-33 season when he scored 33 goals in 42 league games.

Blessed with speed and an ice-cool temperament, a natural body-swerve and a deadly shot from both feet, Bastin gave the impression of having a mystical fore-knowledge of where any pass was going long before it started and was thus able to take up position in readiness to deal with it.

Only after his retirement in 1947 at the age of 34 did Bastin disclose that during the previous ten years he had been suffering from increasing deafness and in the end had been unable to hear the roar of the crowds. The affliction had resulted from a bout of influenza that affected his middle-ear and had, he admitted, a serious psychological affect on his playing in the latter days.

Arsenal discovered Bastin by accident towards the end of the 1928-29 season. Herbert Chapman, the Arsenal manager, had gone to watch a Watford player in a match against Exeter but it was the fair-haired inside-forward in the Exeter team that caught his eye. Bastin agreed to sign professional forms for Arsenal after his 17th birthday.

His mentor at Highbury was Alex James, the great Scottish inside-forward. The two men developed an almost tele-pathic understanding that often bewil-dered opponents and their partnership helped Arsenal to dominate English football in the 1930s.

Bastin thrived on the big occasion, scoring England's goal in the 1-1 draw with Italy in Rome in 1933; twice hitting crucial goals in semi-finals; and supplying the passes which enabled James and Ted Drake to score in Arsenal's cup final wins over Huddersfield in 1930 and Sheffield United in 1936.

Clifford Stanley Bastin grew up in Exeter. He initially turned down the Arsenal transfer when he discovered that, in the days of the maximum wage, London would pay him no more than Exeter. The Arsenal manager refused to take no for an answer. Bastin subse-quently claimed that he finally gave in and signed in order to get away for a game of tennis.

Bastin was then an inside-left, the position he preferred, and he subsequently earned several of his 21 England caps there. Chapman however quickly recognised that with James alongside to guide him, his pace and goal-scoring ability would be a formidable weapon on the wing and after early season appearances at inside-right and centre-forward he was picked at outside left at Christmas 1929.

Bastin stayed there for the third round FA Cup tie with Chelsea at the beginning of January, scoring his first goal for the club in Arsenal's 2-0 victory. The manner was significant, Bastin coming in to meet Joe Hulme's cross from the right wing, a move which was to bring countless goals in years to come. This one put Arsenal on the way to Wembley, Bastin becoming the youngest player to appear in a Cup Final until Howard Kendall supplanted him in 1964. It was the beginning of Arsenal's era. A year later they won the championship for the first time, with Bastin contributing 28 league goals and winning his first England cap, against Wales. That debut was not a success, his club colleague Bob John marking him closely and effectively, but his club performances ensured that he was to get another chance.

Following the 1931-2 season, a rare fallow one, Arsenal embarked upon a run of three successive championships in 1933, 1934 and 1935. Although their success was based primarily on defence, their quick counter-attacks, with James supplying their two flying wingers, were devastating. In 1932-3 the team scored 126 league goals, as Bastin set his record 33. He thus reclaimed his England place at the end of the season.

Club success was unabated as two more championships were followed by a Cup win over Sheffield United in 1936. The death in 1934 of Herbert Chapman affected Bastin deeply, but did not initially interrupt Arsenal's smooth running machine. Although the team was beginning to show signs of age, Bastin remained an integral part during the rebuilding process, contributing 15 goals as the championship was won in 1938. That was Arsenal's last major honour of the decade as war came and in the same year Bastin made his last international appearance.

His increasing deafness ruled him out of military service, and he played for Arsenal throughout the war, appearing more and more at inside forward as his pace declined, and sometimes dropping back to wing-half. He did not, however, win wartime international caps. Although he began the first post-war season with Arsenal, he made only six appearances, retiring on Boxing Day, 1946. He returned to Exeter, keeping a pub for a time.

RODNEY ACKLAND

Rodney Ackland, playwright and actor, died at his home in Richmond, Surrey, aged 83. He was born at Westcliff-on-Sea on May 18, 1908.

DISAPPOINTMENT ruled the last decades of Rodney Ackland's life, though at the very end there was some resurgence in his fortunes. During the 1930s and 1940s he had been accepted as one of the most valuable young writers of his period and had developed into what seemed to be permanent fulfilment. John Gielgud was happy to direct his plays and actresses of the stature of Flora Robson and Edith Evans equally happy to appear in them.

Then his career went into sad eclipse.

The once fashionable young man about London went out of favour. But certain critics, among them Hilary Spurling and Francis King, continued to speak up in his support and of late there had been some signs of a revival in his reputation, with a number of attempts to resurrect and update his plays; a version of *Absolute Hell*, reworked by Michael Hastings, was seen on BBC 2 recently. But, these small stirrings of a revival apart, it appeared for a long time that Rodney Ackland had been forgotten by the theatre-going public at large.

It was not a situation that he accepted with serenity. He had seen his personal circumstances change from having a set in Albany to living in a couple of rooms in Richmond. He felt that he had been ostracised by managements and deprived of his rightful audience. When, in 1980, it was decided to revive his play *Before the Party* he was quite vociferous on the subject and told an interviewer: "The theatre is my life and I've been excluded from it, through no fault of my own, for years." When it was suggested that he would be understood and loved after his death he replied tartly: "Screw posterity. I want it now when I am still alive."

Rodney Ackland had a Jewish father and a mother who sang on the London halls. He trained as an actor in various repertory companies and appeared on the halls himself, on some occasions getting both the bird and a fistful of rotten tomatoes. He played a number of juvenile leads, including Young Woodley in the play of the same name. His own first play, *Improper People*, was written when he was 21.

Within a few years critics were speaking of him, a little unwarily, as "the English Chekhov", too glib a label for a small-scale dramatist, and one that did him no good when the tide of fashion turned.

His quality had been generally acknowledged two or three plays after *Improper People* when he had a success with *Strange Orchestra* (1931), a comedy of paying guests at a Bloomsbury flat, with Laura Cowie as a generous and slatternly

Bohemian. *Birthday* (1934), in which he appeared himself, was a study in selfishness; in his stage version of *The White Guard* he subtly adapted Bulgakov's tragi-comedy of Russia in the early phases of the Revolution; and *The Old Ladies* (1935) was a powerful and atmospheric re-working of Hugh Walpole's macabre anecdote.

For a long time he wrote consistently and with an even flow. Within twenty years almost a score of his plays and adaptations were staged and there was another twenty or so film scripts. He may have been too prolific. But nothing seriously blurred his observation or impaired his progress until in the late Fifties an apparently established dramatist was to be completely silenced by shifting fashion.

In such pieces as *After October* and *Strange Orchestra*, Ackland made a firm landing on his favourite coast of London's Bohemia. Among his most important works were *The Old Ladies*, adapted from Walpole's story and *The Dark River*, which had too brief a run. If there is to be a successful attempt to resuscitate Ackland's reputation as a dramatist, then *The Dark River* looks a likely candidate. A number of supporters reckon it to be his best play.

In 1936 James Agate had enthused over *After October*, set in a Hampstead flat, and it had a long run. Rodney Ackland continued to be highly prolific, after that, turning out not only a quantity of plays but scripts for British films as well. He worked for Emeric Pressburger on *49th Parallel* and with Thorold Dickinson on *The Queen of Spades*. The latter led Ackland into an expensive court case when he sued the production company for giving him and his collaborator, Arthur Boys, smaller billing than Alexander Pushkin, on whose novella the film was based. Ackland and Boys won and received modest damages, but they claimed that to bring the matter to court had drained all their savings. It was not Ackland's only excursion into litigation: in 1975 he threatened action against *The Times* for a contentious item which had

appeared in the paper's diary and won a handsome retraction.

Ackland had been living with Boys, an Australian, for some years in a fairly stormy relationship. Boys offered considerable support, especially when first nights came around, but there were a number of quarrels between the two men. To general surprise, and perhaps even to his own, Rodney Ackland married Mab, the youngest daughter of another playwright, Sir Frederick Lonsdale. He was 44 at the time and Mab was probably the only woman he ever seriously looked at.

The flow of new plays was beginning to thin a little. But *A Dead Secret*, suggested by the Seddon poisoning case, ran for six months in 1957 and allowed Paul Scofield to triumph as an arrogant, brooding man driven by avarice. This was probably his last important original work. But the partnership of Margaret Rutherford and Peggy Mount ensured the life of *Farewell, Farewell Eugene*. In the Forties and early Fifties Ackland had little difficulty in attracting the major actors of the day: Edith Evans and John Gielgud had appeared in his adaptation of *Crime and Punishment* and Peggy Ashcroft in *The Dark River*, an impressive portrait of men and women betrayed and destroyed by remembrance of things past.

Mab Ackland died in 1972 after a serenely happy marriage and her husband cracked up. The will to write left him temporarily. When he was allowed to return to the theatre it was with past plays or past plays reworked. Tom Conti directed *Before the Party* at Oxford and later at the Queen's in London. In 1988 The Orange Tree theatre in Richmond, which had been supportive to a playwright on its own doorstep, put on *Absolute Hell*, a reworking of *The Pink Room*, a 1952 play set in a Soho drinking club peopled by the disaffected and the sleazy with whom Ackland had felt so much sympathy. *The Dark River* is to be done at the Orange Tree next year, while *A Dead Secret*, starring Edward Woodward and Michele Dotrice, is scheduled for the Theatre Royal, Plymouth, in March.

BARONESS HART
OF SOUTH LANARK

Baroness Hart of South Lanark, DBE, PC, former Labour cabinet minister and three times Minister for Overseas Development, died December 8 aged 67. She was born on September 18, 1924.

ALTHOUGH Judith Hart had a considerable career in government she nevertheless remained a prominent member of the hard-left group of Labour MPs who consistently opposed party policy and provided endless trouble for the leadership in the Commons and on the national executive committee. Her own left-wing credentials were near-perfect. Even before she entered parliament she attracted national notice when she delivered an emotional but highly effective ban-the-bomb speech at the 1957 Labour conference. She was on the first Aldermaston march in 1958. She was against the Vietnam war and the European Commission. She was for the Allende regime in Chile and the guerilla movements in southern Africa. The South African security service tried to smear her and British intelligence investigated her.

Above all, she maintained Labour's commitment to the Third World, fighting Whitehall for more money for overseas development with the same conviction with which she fought so many unpopular left-wing causes. The Lomé Convention of 1975, providing aid for developing countries from the European Commission, also owed much to her and remains as her memorial. She spent more than 200 hours in the negotiations which led to the signing of the convention covering trade, aid and co-operation between the Commission and 46 developing countries, mainly former colonies. It was an achievement characteristic of her toughness and determination.

Behind her left-wing orthodoxy were some inconsistencies. A grandness of manner and keen sene of position seemed at times inappropriate for the representative of Strathclyde industrial workers. In 1967, when Peggy Herbison, a right-winger, resigned as Minister of Social Security in response to spending cuts in her department, Judith Hart replaced her and had no difficulty in imposing the economies. In 1969, when she succeeded Reg Prentice — another right-winger who later became a Tory MP — it was the former minister who complained more loudly about cuts in aid. In 1979 she incurred criticism and some derision, even among her keenest supporters, when she became a Dame Commander of the Order of the British Empire. In 1988 she went to the Lords but failing health prevented her from becoming as visible a figure there as she had been in the Commons.

Judith Hart was the daughter of a Lancashire linotype operator. She began her education at a Burnley primary school before winning a place at Clitheroe Royal Grammar School where she became school captain and head prefect. The aura of head prefect in fact stayed with her for the rest of her life. She became a socialist in her early teens, joining the Labour party at 18. A scholarship took her to the London School of Economics, which was evacuated to Cambridge during the war. There she took a first in sociology, became secretary of Cambridge University Labour Club and chairman of Cambridge Labour party.

Marriage and her husband's career brought her first to Dorset, where she fought her first parliamentary seat at hopeless Bournemouth West in 1951, and then to Scotland, where she was defeated at Aberdeen South in 1955. She worked to ban corporal punishment in Scottish schools, and the eventual abolition of the tawse owed much to her efforts — which were the braver because they hardly helped her search for a winnable Scottish seat. She managed to get selected for Tory-held Lanark which she succeeded in winning in 1959. Her majority was only 540 but it was still a considerable victory in the year of Macmillan's sweeping success.

In the House she soon revealed her views. She abstained on Labour's amendment to the government's defence policy, opposed the establishment of the Polaris base and annoyed Gaitskell sufficiently for him to remove her from a party political broadcast. This did her no harm with Harold Wilson, however, and when he became prime minister in 1964 he made her joint Parliamentary Under Secretary for Scotland. After his second general election victory she was promoted to Minister of State at the Commonwealth Office where she would have stayed for some time but for the surprise resignation of Margaret Herbison as a result of spending cuts in her department.

Confronted with the spectacle of a right-winger resigning on a matter of socialist principle Harold Wilson reacted typically by looking for a left-winger who would take the job. He judged correctly that Judith Hart would accept the post. In little more than a year she progressed further to a seat in the cabinet as Paymaster-General. It was about this time, though, that she started to irritate Mr Wilson. She announced that she had overall responsibility for issuing government statements — something which he went out of his way to deny. In the summer of 1969 she came out against the Wilson-Castle "In Place of Strife" plans for trade union reform. He took revenge in his autumn reshuffle when he dropped her from the cabinet and made her Minister for Overseas Development. A few days before her demotion she had been elected to Labour's national executive where she became a key member of the left-wing element which continued to infuriate successive Labour leaders well into the 1980s.

In opposition after the 1970 election she shadowed her old department and began her long association with Chile, a country which at times dominated her public life. After meeting President Salvador Allende, the Marxist leader of its Popular Front government, she declared: "It is unique, this democratic revolution". Years later, when she was back in government and Allende had been killed, she was instrumental in cutting off aid to Chile. Besides Chile she concentrated on Africa and as chairman of Labour's Southern Africa Solidarity Fund she sent money to three African guerilla organisations – a move which drew a fair amount of criticism. In Labour's pre-election policy discussions she championed the plan to bring 25 leading British companies under state control.

When Harold Wilson was returned in the first 1974 election he sent her back to overseas development. She was soon in trouble with him again, receiving a well publicised rebuke – together with Tony Benn and Joan Lestor – for going too far in anti-South African activities. In the 1975 reshuffle, which saw Tony Benn demoted, she had her ministry taken from her. She rejected an offer to switch to transport and insisted in making a personal statement in the House about her sacking. This was attacked as a breach of Commons procedure. A minister who resigns is entitled to make a personal statement but her critics maintained that this practice did not extend to a minister who had been fired.

Her return to the back benches enabled her to attack government policies openly. She described one bout of Wilson-Healey spending cuts as "the greatest kick in the teeth for the welfare state since the war". She pleaded for import controls and more nationalisation; while on the national executive she voted for the Trotskyist Andy Bevan as the party's youth officer. In 1977, however, she was unexpectedly recalled to head overseas development for the third time. James Callaghan, who had become prime minister, was never one to sympathise with left-wingers but he may well have been influenced by her sway on the national executive. She faced one more big controversy – an interest-free loan to Mozambique – but the end of the Labour government in 1979 also meant the end of her ministerial career. When she was created DBE, in recognition of her work for the third world, she explained her acceptance by saying that there was a place in society for a non-hereditary honours system. Certainly her views did not change after she became Dame Judith. She favoured the candidacy of Peter Tatchell in Bermondsey, opposed the expulsion of Militant Tendency leaders and campaigned vigorously against the Falklands war. She decided not to fight the 1987 election and went to the Lords in the following year.

Judith Hart was an object of interest to the security services over a period of years with reports of her telephone being tapped. This interest was presumably prompted by her visits to eastern Europe and her work in helping refugees from post-Allende Chile which involved close association with communists. She was undoubtedly unwise to speak at a rally organised by the *Morning Star* early in 1974. It is reasonable to conclude that nothing damaging was ever discovered by British intelligence because otherwise it is inconceivable that she would have been retained in the governments of such cautious politicians as Harold Wilson and James Callaghan.

She leaves her scientist husband, Dr Tony Hart, and their two sons.

SIR RONALD GARDNER-THORPE

Colonel Sir Ronald Gardner-Thorpe, GBE, TD, Lord Mayor of London, 1980-1981, died on December 11 aged 74. He was born on May 13, 1917.

TO RONALD Gardner-Thorpe London was like a village even before he became Lord Mayor. In Knightsbridge and Kensington, where he was well known for his family business, people would often stop him in the street and chat. Then he deeply immersed himself in City life and was thought to be one of only three Roman Catholic Lord Mayors since the Reformation.

His ability to get on with people — though he could be forthright and was not one to go with the crowd — first brought him to national prominence in a by-election in West Derbyshire where he stood as a Liberal in 1962. He caused political shock waves with his near-victory in a strongly Conservative seat: Aidan Crawley defeated him by only 1,220 votes. This was part of what was perceived to be a developing Liberal trend, which included the famous Liberal victory at Orpington. He became a treasurer of the party.

Someone who very much "belonged" himself — in his life he collected many honours and served on many bodies — he could also recognise someone who did not belong: as a result he was to be responsible for capturing probably the first foreign spy to be detained on British soil in the second world war.

Ronald Laurence Gardner-Thorpe was born in Portsmouth and was educated by the de la Salle brothers at St John's College, Southsea. Before the war he became interested in architecture and planned a career in the family building business. The family had supplied steel for the construction of parts of Brunel's railway system including Paddington Station.

Gardner-Thorpe joined the Territorial Army in 1937 and was later commissioned into the Hants Heavy Regiment. In September 1939 he was stationed as a young officer on the south coast and through binoculars saw a woman sketching the seaside. When she appeared next day he took a boat across the water and she accepted his invitation to the army quarters but as he drove her past the gatehouse he called for her to be arrested. She turned out to be an enemy agent noting shipping entering the harbour: a German girl who had married a British soldier. After capture she was released under surveillance and led to a number of other spy contacts.

Soon after the United States entered the war Gardner-Thorpe undertook liaison duties with the Canadian and United States forces in Ottawa and Washington to help unify communications between the British forces and Allies. He took part in lecture tours and fund raising activities and appeared on stage with Shirley Temple, Rita Hayworth and Deanna Durbin. Many thousands of dollars were raised to help build Spitfires. In due course he became a Barker of the Variety Club of Great Britain and was particularly involved in providing Sunshine Coaches to transport underprivileged children. He became a director of the Miss World competition and vice-president in 1982.

After the war he continued in the Regular Army until 1947 when he moved to London and became interested in building development. Nevertheless he remained in the Territorial Army for most of his life. He commanded the 5th Battalion The Buffs from 1956 to 1960 when he was promoted colonel. He was installed as Knight Commander of The Royal Order of the Dannebrog in 1960 by King Frederik, honorary colonel of the regiment, during a parade which Gardner-Thorpe led in Canterbury. He was a member of the Court of the Honourable Artillery Company in 1972. He was awarded the Territorial Decoration in 1948 and subsequently three bars.

In 1964 Gardner-Thorpe became Justice of the Peace for the Inner London

Area and deputy chairman in 1968, then a JP for the City of London in 1969 and deputy chairman in 1970. Thus his interest developed in City affairs. He became a freeman of the City of London in 1971 and Sheriff in 1978-79. He served as Lord Mayor in 1980-81 and was created GBE. He made trips to Egypt and was received by President Sadat, to Rome for a private audience with Pope John Paul II and to Saudi Arabia at the personal invitation of the late King Khalid. Among other honours and appointments he became honorary colonel of the Kansas Cavalry in 1981.

His theme tune for the Lord Mayor's Show in 1980 was "Maybe it's because I'm a Londoner". The procession included Chelsea Pensioners and Pearly Kings and Queens. His special charity during the mayoral year was the Duke of Edinburgh's Award Scheme. He carried the Pearl Sword in advance of the Queen in St Paul's Cathedral on the occasion of the marriage of the Prince of Wales and Lady Diana Spencer. When he left mayoral office in 1981 he was honoured by an escort from the Light Cavalry Squadron of the Honourable Artillery Company, a rare event for a Lord Mayor.

He was a friend of The Royal College of Physicians and was awarded an honorary fellowship. Three of his grandchildren are training in medicine. He was interested in fine arts and in the City of London tradition. He published two books, *The City and The Buffs* in 1985 and *My Lord Mayor* in 1988.

Ronald Gardner-Thorpe leaves a widow, Hazel, and a son, Christopher, a neurologist in Exeter.

GORDON PIRIE

Gordon Pirie, who set five athletics world records between 1953 and 1956, died in a Bournemouth hospital on December 7 aged 60. He was born on February 10, 1931.

AS MUCH for his arrogance as his bravado on the track, Gordon Pirie was a magnetic sports figure of the 1950s, when his world record-breaking exploits put him at the head of Britain's resurgence in world distance running. Britain had not enjoyed a hero such as Pirie since the best days of Sydney Wooderson in the 1930s.

Like Wooderson and David Bedford in the 1970s, Pirie broke record after record but never won an Olympic gold medal. As he admitted later in life, he had probably trained too hard for his own good: when he needed to be at his best he was tired from his colossal running schedules and Christopher Chataway, one of his predecessors as 5,000 metres world record holder, used to say that track running would lose its appeal for him if he attempted only a fraction of what Pirie did. In March this year Pirie reckoned to have run 265,000 miles in 50 years, more than 100 miles a week.

His 22 British records, from 1952 to 1961, ranged in distance from 2,000 metres to 10,000 metres. In 1956 he defeated Vladimir Kuts over 5,000 metres in Bergen in world record time, but five months later the Soviet reversed the result at the Melbourne Olympics: Pirie's silver medal was the closest he came to gold in any of his three Olympics.

In the 1952 Helsinki Olympics he was fourth in the 5,000 metres and seventh in the 10,000 metres; in 1956 his Olympic silver medal was accompanied by eighth place in the 10,000 metres; in the 1960 Rome Olympics he was tenth in the 10,000 metres and failed to qualify for the final of the 5,000 metres.

Pirie and Kuts had been close rivals since the day that Pirie claimed he would eventually run 5,000 metres inside 13 min 40 sec, a seemingly outrageous prediction given that the record at the time was almost 20 seconds slower; the statement infuriated his detractors. But, in Bergen, Pirie fulfilled his promise, beating Kuts in the process.

The filiform Pirie stayed in the wake of the stocky ex-marine throughout and used his finishing kick to sprint away to the record. Three days later, in Trondheim, he equalled the 3,000 metres world record. But, come Melbourne, he found Kuts too strong and, after 21 laps of a classic 10,000 metres duel between them, the South London Harrier was broken and fell back down the field.

Douglas Alistair Gordon Pirie was born in Leeds. He came to be known as "puff-puff" Pirie. His exaggerated breathing technique was picked up on Farthing Downs, Coulsdon, where he found himself swallowing flies in training and worked on blowing while running so as to keep the insects away from his mouth.

Pirie's most successful years were 1953 and 1956. In 1953 he set a six miles world record, was a member of the British team which set a four by 1500 metres world record, won the first Emsley Carr Mile at White City and took the first of his three successive English cross country titles. In 1956 he followed his 5,000 metres world record and equalling of the 3,000 metres world record by taking single ownership of the 3,000 metres mark. Typical of his brashness, he had forecast 24 hours earlier that the record would go.

Pirie was voted BBC Sports Personality of the Year in 1955 but struck a discordant note on screen by using the occasion to accuse the written media of doing immeasurable damage to British sport. He was widely criticised for being ungracious to the occasion, but he was used to being at the centre of controversy.

In 1961 he was dropped from the British team for the match against West Germany for failing to report on time; then, when he declined to explain his lateness to officials, he was omitted from a subsequent fixture against Poland. His personality was as spikey as his haircut. "I am a ball of fire as a character and you have to have that to win," he said.

In 1962, while bound for Australia to commentate for television on the Empire Games, he accepted an official MCC invitation to put England's cricketers through a tough physical training course while sailing to Fremantle. In Australia he received money from a newspaper to describe the MCC cricketers as "an unfit, paunchy bunch of barflies," which prompted the Duke of Norfolk, the MCC tour manager, to say that his team would have no more dealings with him. The athletics team manager ostracised him, too, forbidding members of the squad to talk to him after he offered a young high-jumper money to appear on television, which was against the strictly enforced regulations to protect amateur status.

Bank clerk, paint salesman and lumberjack at various times in his life, Pirie emigrated to New Zealand in 1956 claiming that taxation in Britain was too high. He returned to spend the last few years of his life in Fordle, near Lymington, having found work in the New Forest, clearing up after the hurricane of 1987.

His marriage to the international sprinter Shirley Hampton ended in divorce. He leaves two daughters.

JOHN ARLOTT

John Arlott, OBE, cricket commentator and journalist, died in Alderney on December 14 aged 77. He was born in Basingstoke on February 25, 1914.

"AFTER a few comments from Trevor Bailey, it will be Christopher Martin-Jenkins." With these words, at the end of the Centenary Test against Australia at Lords in 1980, te distinctive voice of John Arlott ceased to be heard on BBC Radio's ball-by-ball cricket commentaries. Thus ended the career of a broadcaster who extended his presence beyond the bounds of the sport he described with such consummate style. With his rich Hampshire burr, rare gift of description and original turn of phrase, John Arlott delighted, for 35 seasons, not only cricket-lovers but others, including many housewives, who had neither a love nor knowledge of the game. The Arlott accent became one of the most familiar − and most mimicked − in Britain, evoking the essence of both cricket and those qualities of Englishness that surround it − sunny days on village greens and at country pubs and nostalgia for days gone by.

From 1946 until his retirement at the end of the 1980 season Arlott was a member of the BBC ball-by-ball commentary team, covering in that time more than 160 Test matches. In the summer of 1948 his meticulously accurate and colourful descriptions captured the excitement of the matches played in England by Don Bradman's all-conquering Australians and brought huge audiences to the day-long programmes on the BBC Light Programme. He developed a fine sense of timing with which to pace his commentaries. Arlott's broadcasting expertise, knowledge of the game and his audio-charisma were such that he was able to hold the attention of his audience for hours at a time, even when rain stopped play for lengthy periods.

If the rich Arlott accent became synonymous with cricket, Englishness and the BBC it was not immediately so. In the early post-war days, when Oxbridge English reigned supreme in Broadcasting House, there were those in the organisation who regarded his voice as not quite right for "the wireless". Said one BBC executive: "You have an interesting mind, but a vulgar voice." Arlott was apparently deterred, fortunately, from attempting to modify his burr by the actor Valentine Dyall who threatened: "If you change it, I shall personally cut out your tongue."

John Arlott was also the author of many books, the majority of them on cricket, and from 1968 until 1980 he was cricket correspondent of *The Guardian*.

If this conveys that cricket was Arlott's whole life, that was by no means so. He was a man of many interests and encyclopaedic knowledge. He lived through cricket, and loved it deeply; but the variety of subjects on which he was well-informed often amazed his companions, and he collected, with singular sagacity, acquatints (most of them published between 1775 and 1830) and engraved glass, as well as, inevitably, a well-informed assortment of cricketana. When, before moving to Alderney, which he did within a month of his retirement, he auctioned his wine at Christie's, it was reckoned to be among the best private collections in the country.

Leslie Thomas John Arlott was educated at Queen Mary's School, Basingstoke. His father was assistant registrar and keeper of the town cemetery, where the family lived in the lodge. On leaving school at 16, he became a clerk in a local mental hospital before, in 1934, joining the police force. By 1945, when he resigned from the police as a sergeant, he had spent more time as a detective than on the beat, and his affection for cricket had taken root. By the beginning of the war, through occasional duty at the Hampshire grounds, he had struck up his early friendships with the first-class players of the day.

Arlott entered the BBC in 1945, as a poetry producer, someone having told John Betjeman, who passed on the information, that the police had a poet in their ranks. From the following year, when he began to specilise in cricket (he was never much of a practitioner himself) until his retirement there was hardly a single county cricketer or member of a touring side to England with whom Arlott was not on christian name terms. As president of the Cricketers' Association fron 1968, an office which he valued greatly and continued to hold after moving to the Channel Islands, he had a considerable influence on the way in which the first-class game developed.

Arlott was very much closer to the aspirations and thoughts of the "average" player than to the game's administrators. He had a horror of being looked upon as an "establishment figure" and never was. He vehemently opposed apartheid and made clear that he would not commentate on the proposed 1970 South Africa Test series in England which subsequently was called off. But during the bitter split caused by the intrusion of Kerry Packer, the Australian entrepreneur, and the creation of World Series Cricket, Arlott' voice was one of moderation. If it had not been for his influence, the 200 or so first-class cricketers over whom he presided might well have acted belligerently enough to have made a settlement between the two sides even more difficult than it was.

The wisdom of his decision to emigrate to Alderney was doubted by many of his friends. He had lived most of his life in Hampshire, the 19 years before his retirement in an old pub in Alresford, and had never been happier than at his oak dining table, surrounded by an untiring audience and numerous bottles of wine. He had a remarkable capacity for work and was a fast worker. His four hymns were written in a single evening: one of them, *God Whose Farm Is All Creation*, is quite widely used. *Fred: A Portrait Of A Fast Bowler*, his book on Trueman, he wrote in a fortnight, during the postal strike of 1971.

Arlott travelled frequently to France, writing several books on wine and being for some years wine correspondent of *The Guardian*. It was more reluctantly that he undertook overseas cricket tours, the only two he made being to South Africa for the BBC in 1948-49 and to Australia as a contributor to the London *Evening News* in 1954-55. Until becoming disenchanted with football, he preferred to stay at home and write about that and to do his monthly article, on all kinds of subjects, for the *Hampshire Magazine*, of which he was a director.

The black tie which Arlott wore from the day the eldest of his three sons was killed in a motor accident in 1968 was the mark of his emotionalism. After his lst Test broadcast, the England and Australian players turned and saluted him, a unique tribute which moved him greatly. Soon afterwards, when he was made an honorary life member of MCC (to go with the OBE he was awarded in 1970) he was unsure whether to laugh or cry.

Urged by many friends for many years to write his autobiography he embarked on it without real enthusiasm, writing it in the third person and publishing the first volume, *Basingstoke Boy*, in 1990.

By his first marriage to Dawn Rees, which was dissolved, he had two sons; by the second to Valerie France, who died in 1976, he had one. He married Patricia Hoae a year later.

DAVID WADDILOVE

David Waddilove, former director of the prison service's borstal administration, has died aged 81 following a motor accident. He was born on August 6, 1910.

DAVID Waddilove, a passionate opponent of capital punishment, had managerial responsibility for two hangings when he was governor of Pentonville prison. He hated every moment of them but took the view that when he joined the prison service he might become a governor and might have to take part in an execution. He was a faithful public servant, and he reacted against such a role not by resigning but by campaigning against capital punishment.

The two Pentonville executions took place in rapid succession. Waddilove had come to Pentonville from a career in borstals and had never even been a deputy governor in a major prison. In April 1959 a man called Joseph Chrimes, a small time burglar with one previous conviction, was under sentence of death for murder in the course of furtherance of theft. Pentonville had not had an execution for five years. Chrimes did not get a reprieve and was hanged on April 28, 1959. It was a dreadful execution in more ways than one and was distressing for everybody who witnessed it. Somebody who was in the prison at the time saw Waddilove immediately afterwards. The look of horror lingered on his face.

He then received into the prison a local young man called Ronald Marwood, known to many inmates at Pentonville; he had been convicted of murdering a policemen in a fracas outside a local dance hall. The prison had barely recovered from the shock of Chrimes's execution when on May 8 Marwood had to be hanged. The tension built up in Pentonville to a high pitch. On the night before the execution there was a riot in the prison, which disturbed even more the atmosphere surrounding the death cell, its

338

inmate and guards. The hangman had arrived to sleep on a camp bed in Pentonville's boardroom. The next morning a crowd of 1,000 gathered outside the prison from daybreak and mounted police had to be called. Marwood was executed at 9 am.

Technically the task of arranging the execution was that of the High Sheriff: mainly he had to select and pay the executioner in guineas. The governor was responsible for the prisoner and for seeing the condemned man did not commit suicide. Waddilove had to arrange the death watch, a series of officers always with the condemned man and drawn from another prison. The governor was responsible ultimately though his foreman of works for seeing the trapdoor was kept properly lubricated and regularly tested. He had to ensure there was a bag to be filled with sand approximately to the weight of the prisoner so that three days before the execution tests of the apparatus could be made. He had to organise the digging of a grave in the burial ground which in those days in Pentonville was known as "Crippen's grass", Crippen having been buried there. The governor had to be present at the execution and through the period afterwards. The body had to be left hanging until the doctor had checked to see life was extinct.

Waddilove's time at Pentonville was an extraordinary break in service with borstals. He had been recruited by Sir Alexander Paterson, the penal reformer and prison commissioner. He completed his career by being appointed as the director of borstal administration.

David Granville Waddilove was educated at Marlborough College and on leaving school worked for the Royal Exchange insurance company. In 1936 he became an assistant house master at the original borstal institution at Rochester. He was to work at Rochester for some years, including wartime when the institution was largely taken over by the Navy but then quickly re-opened to cope with the rising number of young offenders.

He moved to Sherwood borstal in Nottingham (now Nottingham prison) as deputy governor towards the end of the war and then to Feltham borstal, again as deputy. In 1949 he was given his first command – at Gaynes Hall open borstal – a challenge he greatly enjoyed. He gained further promotion moving to Hollesley Bay Colony borstal and then in 1958 to Pentonville prison in the governors' most senior grade.

In 1960 he went back to the part of the service he loved, joining prison headquarters as an assistant commissioner responsible for borstal and detention centres. In 1965 he was promoted to director of borstal administration and was the last person to hold the post: it was abolished in a Home Office management review in 1969.

In 1970, with his prison service experience behind him, he became an active member of the Howard League for Penal Reform and remained on the council until the early 1980s. David Waddilove is remembered as an effective governor, a good delegator who was still able to know personally both his staff and his charges. He retained his great interest in the work of young offender establishments throughout his decade at headquarters, visiting governors regularly and encouraging staff. He always looked on the positive side of everyone he met and at the possibility of individuals improving, a reflection of his strong Christian faith and beliefs.

After retirement he continued to be active in public life as chairman of his local parish council and a district councillor. He was also a council member of the Howard League for Penal Reform and a member of his deanery and diocesan synod. He had a great interest in choral singing. Throughout his retirement he retained a keen interest in the prison service and its latest problems. Only a week before his death he was telephoning his former borstal service colleagues to ask them that something be done to halt suicides among young people in custody.

He leaves a widow, Elspeth, two sons and a daughter.

JOEY SMALLWOOD

Joseph Roberts Smallwood, who led Newfoundland into the Canadian federal union 43 years ago and became the east coast province's first premier, died at his home near St John's on December 17 aged 90. He was born on December 24, 1900.

JOEY Smallwood, a diminutive but dynamic figure with a puppy-dog look that belied a highly combative nature, was often fondly called the only living father of confederation. This was a tribute, if somewhat far-fetched, to the spearhead role he played in making Newfoundland the tenth Canadian province in 1949. ("Fathers of confederation" is the title long ago conferred on the men who forged the original union of Britain's North American colonies, under the name Canada, in 1867.)

Smallwood waged a bitterly-fought, two-year campaign to make Newfoundland a member of the Canadian family. At the time, immediately after the second world war, it was still a British colonial possession, as it had become in 1534 when Sir Humphrey Gilbert sailed into St John's harbour and claimed the territory for the crown.

Many of the fewer than 350,000 people living on the barren, craggy, triangular-shaped island at the mouth of the Gulf of St Lawrence in the North Atlantic wanted it to stay a British possession. Not a few others wanted it to apply for membership of the United States. Smallwood, the son of a small-town sawmill owner, had already become well known to New-foundlanders as a belligerent politician and also, at various times, as a journalist – both print and broadcast – and trade union organiser. Impressed by Canada's social-welfare structure and relatively high living standards, which he had witnessed as a travelling journalist, he led the pro-confederation forces in two bruising referendum campaigns.

The first vote ended in a stalemate, but the pro-confederation forces won the second by 7,000 votes, or less than two per cent. Despite the narrowness of the margin, negotiations with Canada were allowed to proceed and Newfoundland officially became a province on March 31, 1949.

The Liberals, led by Smallwood, won the subsequent election and he was premier for 22 straight years after that, becoming probably Canada's best-known provincial politician. For Newfoundland they were years of industrial growth as Smallwood – who was also minister for economic development from 1955 to 1971 – promoted development of the province's iron ore, logging and hydro-electric resources to balance its traditional dependence on fishing.

They were also years of turbulence, as when Smallwood persuaded the federal government in Ottawa to send in the Royal Canadian Mounted Police to smash a loggers' strike in 1959. On another occasion he ordered provincial government buildings to be draped in black mourning crepe to protest against a threatened cut in special, C$8 million-a-year federal payments to the province. The prime minister of the day, John Diefenbaker, backed down and the payments continued.

Some of the industries Smallwood attracted, with generous provincial incentives, went bankrupt or otherwise betrayed his expctations. In one case a provincially-chartered company, with his encouragement, locked itself into a long-term hydro-export agreement with Quebec that turned into a financial disaster for Newfoundland. Quebec is still getting electric power at bargain-basement rates under the accord.

In early 1954, Smallwood shocked Newfoundlanders by announcing that Alfred Valdmanis, a Latvian economist whom Smallwood had personally hired as director-general of economic development, was under arrest. Valdmanis later pleaded guilty to defrauding the government of C$200,000 and was sentenced to four years in imprisonment.

Despite such setbacks, Smallwood led a charmed life politically, largely because of his reputation as a doughty defender of Newfoundland's rights. This began to change when Pierre Trudeau came to power in Ottawa and federal grants were cut. Smallwood's winning streak finally came to an end in late 1971 when the Conservatives won 21 seats to the Liberals' 20 in the provincial election and were called upon to form a government.

Smallwood made a couple of abortive comeback attempts. After resigning the leadership of the Liberal party he became, for a short time, leader of a Liberal Reform party but then retired to his home to exercise his love of writing. His last years were largely taken up with writing an encyclopaedia of Newfoundland. Three volumes have already been published, and two others are awaited.

In 1984 Smallwood was laid low by a stroke which left him unable to speak – a cruel blow for someone who loved to chatter and whose oratorical talents had become almost legendary in Canada.

He probably composed his own best epitaph in 1976 when he told an interviewer: "No man should retire until he is buried. And when they bury me, they better put a few tons of rock on top or I'll be back."

He is survived by his wife, the former Clara Oates, and three children.

DR JAMES FLETCHER

James Chipman Fletcher, former administrator of America's National Aeronautics and Space Administration, died of lung cancer at Georgetown University Hospital in Washington, DC, on December 22 aged 72. He was born in Millburn, New Jersey, on June 5, 1919.

JAMES Fletcher was the father of America's space shuttle programme. He was also the only person to serve twice as administrator of the National Aeronautics and Space Administration (NASA), holding the post from April 1971 to May 1977, and from May 1986 to April 1989.

Both were critical periods in the history of NASA; the first coming as the agency struggled to redefine its mission after the Apollo flights to the moon, and the second following the disastrous explosion of the shuttle Challenger.

Fletcher, who was known for his thoughtful, low-key style of management, proved to be a calming influence on both occasions. During his first term he saw NASA's role as one of using space technology to solve problems on earth, and to this end he placed special emphasis on the construction and launching of weather and communications satellites. He also controlled the three Skylab missions in 1973 and 1974.

In the field of unmanned space exploration, Fletcher initiated the Voyager space probe, the Viking missions to Mars in 1976, and the space telescope programme. Over the past two decades he was responsible for virtually every major space project originating in the United States.

Perhaps his most remarkable achievement, however, was to sell the concept of the space shuttle to the Nixon administration and to Congress, assuring them that it would pay for itself in an era of shrinking budgets for space projects. The promise proved false. None the less, the shuttle programme flourished until January 28, 1986, when the Challenger exploded killing all seven astronauts on board.

At the request of President Reagan, Fletcher returned to NASA after the disaster, charged with putting back together an agency that was demoralised by the accident and suffering from severe managerial problems. He returned with some reluctance, having formed his own aerospace consulting company in the meantime and taken a teaching post at the University of Pittsburgh, and he soon had cause to regret his decision.

During the intense scrutiny that followed the tragedy, Fletcher became caught up in accusations that there had been waste during his first administration and that he had helped steer a contract for the shuttle's booster rockets — blamed for causing the disaster — to the Morton Thiokol company. He was also investigated for alleged conflict-of-interest violations but was subsquently cleared of the charge by a congressional committee. Over the next three years he reorganised the NASA bureaucracy, brought a sense of calm and purpose to the agency and returned the shuttle to flight in 1988 before retiring for a second time.

James Fletcher was initially a physicist, gaining his undergraduate degree from Columbia University and a doctorate from the California Institute of Technology. He held research and teaching positions at Harvard and Princeton universities before joining Hughes Aircraft in 1948.

From 1958 until 1964, when he returned to academe as president of the University of Utah, he occupied senior positions in California's aerospace industry.

Fletcher is survived by his wife, Fay, one son and three daughters.

WILLIAM BUCKLEY

William Buckley, whose death was confirmed on December 27, was CIA head of station in Beirut. Kidnapped on March 16, 1984, he is believed to have died, after being tortured, on June 3, 1985. He was aged 55 when he was kidnapped.

WILLIAM Buckley was a specialist in paramilitary logistics and had a reputation among his intelligence world peers of being a dedicated professional operative. But he was not an obvious choice to be made the agency's head of station in Beirut. His appointment appears to

have been a consequence of both the car-bombing of the American embassy in Beirut in 1983 and a "clear-out" of the agency's operatives conducted by Admiral Stansfield Turner, the director appointed by President Carter in 1977.

When a suicidal Lebanese Shia crashed a car, laden with explosives, into the US embassy gates in the Lebanese capital in April 1983, a regional conference of CIA operatives was under way there. At least 5 CIA officers died as a result of the blast, including Kenneth Hass, Buckley's predecessor as Beirut station chief. The problems caused to the CIA by this

344

catastrophic loss of Arab-region expertise were exacerbated by the blood-letting which had occurred at the agency six years earlier when 17 of its staff were sacked, 30 others transferred to new posts and 157 others provoked into taking early retirement. Had it not been for these two unrelated occurrences, it is unlikely that Buckley would have found himself elevated to a central role in America's middle-east espionage activities.

His abduction by the pro-Iranian Shia fundamentalist group, Islamic Jihad — jeopardising as it did all the agency secrets to which he had access — was a devastating blow to American intelligence-gathering activity in the region and to William Casey, the CIA's director at the time. This kidnapping was widely regarded as the incident which provoked the Reagan administration into negotiating the secret trading of arms with Tehran in the hope of gaining the release of the American hostages held in Lebanon.

William Buckley was of Irish-American origin and born in Medford, Massachusetts. After graduating from Boston University in 1955 with a degree in international relations, he served as a captain in the US Army at the time of the Korean war won a silver star for gallantry. He later worked as a school librarian in Concord, Massachusetts and as a building contractor. He is thought to have been recruited by the CIA in the early 1960s. During the Vietnam war he is reputed to have helped organise private anti-communist armies among the Meo hill tribes and the Montagnards in both Laos and Vietnam. His "deep cover" as an intelligence operative was blown in 1970 when a former CIA agent, Philip Agee, published a list of the agency's secret operatives. Later Buckley helped train bodyguards for President Anwar Sadat in Egypt and then moved to Zaire where he was involved in the funding and equipping of British, French and American mercenaries fighting the Marxist MPLA forces in Angola.

He arrived in Beirut as station chief in June 1983 under the cover of being a political officer. Nine months later gunmen stopped his car and seized him as he set out for work from the block of flats where he lived. He was one of the first Americans abducted from the streets of Beirut and nine months later a 56-second videotape was received by Visnews, a British television news-agency, which showed him saying he was well and asking the American government to take action to win his release. In October 1985 Islamic Jihad released blurred photographs of what it said was Buckley's body saying he had been killed in retaliation for an Israeli air-raid that month on the Palestine Liberation Organisation headquarters in Tunisia.

For relaxation William Buckley, who was divorced, enjoyed antiques, John Le Carre novels and the history of the American civil-war. He disliked socialising and having his photograph taken.

GENERAL
SIR DUDLEY WARD

General Sir Dudley Ward, GCB, KBE, DSO, former C-in-C Rhine Army and Governor of Gibraltar, died on December 28 aged 86. He was born on January 27, 1905.

DUDLEY Ward came to political prominence as Governor of Gibraltar in the mid-1960s, when Franco started demanding the return of the Rock to Spain. He was then at the end of a long and successful military career as Commander 4th Division during the Italian Campaign in 1944, and during the communist rebellion in Greece at Christmas-time that year; and post-war, as Commander 1st British Corps (1951), Deputy Chief of

Imperial General Staff (1953), C-in-C Northern Army Group and BAOR (1957), and C-in-C British Forces Near East (1960) before going out to Gibraltar in 1962.

He was educated at Wimborne Grammar School and joined the Cable and Wireless Company, for whom he worked for a short time in Gibraltar before enlisting in the Dorset Regiment in 1924. An outstanding, forceful personality and good games player, he was soon selected for Sandhurst from the ranks, and was first commissioned into the Dorset Regiment in 1927, transferring to the King's Regiment in 1937 on accelerated promotion.

By 1943 he was commanding the 17th Infantry Brigade in the 5th Division during Montgomery's crossing of the Straits of Messina and the advance northwards through southern Italy to the German Gustav Line, based on Cassino. His successful assault crossing at the mouth of the Garigliano River and defence of the Damiano sector of the 5th Division's bridgehead led to his promotion to command 4th Division, just in time for him to play a decisive role in Alexander's "Diadem" offensive at Cassino in May 1944.

Dudley Ward won his spurs as a divisional commander in that battle. He had the hazardous task of crossing the Rapido in its most strongly fortified sector, close under the ruins of the Monastery of Monte Cassino. On the first night of the battle, his infantry managed to secure shallow bridgeheads, but no bridges could be built for tanks to give them support by the time dawn broke next day. His determined leadership throughout that long, hard-fought first day of the battle led to the epic construction of Amazon bridge on the second night, and to the establishment of a firm bridgehead from which 13th Corps broke out, forcing Heidrich's German paratroopers to evacuate Monte Cassino by endangering their escape route up the Liri Valley.

Under Dudley Ward's command, 4th Division became a formation that the

Germany army grew to respect. It played crucial roles in the battles of Lake Trasimeno, Florence, the Gothic Line, the Rimini Line, and the Romagna rivers. He was taking his division back to Egypt for a well-earned rest in December 1944 when he was ordered to Greece to help crush the communist rebellion against the Allied-supported Greek government of Giorgios Papandreou.

At that time his division was scattered in troopships between Italy and Egypt and he, himself, was in Cairo with only a skeleton headquarters. Through superb feats of improvisation he secured the British base area around Faliron Bay with troops flown in to Kalamaki airfield. His foothold was initially so tenuous that he found himself having to play a personal part in the defence of his headquarters against ELAS attacks. As more troops arrived by sea and air he fought his way into the centre of Athens, where General Scobie's original occupation force, the British embassy and the Greek government were closely besieged. Fourth Division played a decisive part in the subsequent street fighting that cleared the city and forced the communists to seek an armistice.

After the war, his command of 1st British Corps coincided with the rapid build-up of Nato forces in Europe during the Korean war. As DCIGS he had the problems of Suez and the ending of National Service; as C-in-C Northern Army Group he was deeply involved in the development of Nato's original nuclear trip-wire strategy; and as C-in-C Near East he set up the Sovereign Base areas in Cyprus after the Zurich Agreement had brought temporary peace to the island.

He arrived in Gibraltar as Franco was beginning to build up his case for the return of the Rock under the United Nations' de-colonisation resolutions of 1960. He is perhaps remembered in Gibraltar more as C-in-C than as Governor. Indeed, he saw himself essentially as a military man, and tended to leave the civilian administration to the Colonial Secretary and the Chief Minister

while he concentrated upon making sure that the fortress could discharge its primary task of securing the Straits in global war, and that any military *coup de main* attempted by Spain would not succeed.

Nevertheless, he worked in close harmony with the Chief Minister, Sir Joshua Hassan, on the reforms inaugurated by the 1964 Constitutional Conference which gave Gibraltar a Westminster-style government and opposition. He gave the greatest encouragement to local ministers in the exercise of their new responsibilities, and made internal self-government a reality. Sir Joshua, who held political power in Gibraltar for over 40 years, has written: "Dudley Ward was a very civilised and courteous man with whom I had an excellent relationship and never had any problems. From the very beginning he seemed to have felt that he was a military man and that civilian administration was not his top priority . . . There was no lack of sympathy on his part but rather an attitude of mind as to what his functions really were . . . He managed the transfer to the 1964 Constitution in a very statesmanlike manner, accepting that it was proper to devolve more power to elected ministers, and he co-operated fully.''

In October 1964 Franco started imposing his restrictions at the frontier, which culminated in its closure in 1969. Dudley Ward retired at the end of his tenure as Governor in 1965; but, by then, he had laid the foundations for close co-operation between the expatriate officials and the local members of the Gibraltar government, which was to stand Gibraltar in good stead during the Rock's 15th and longest, though mercifully bloodless, siege.

In 1933 he married Beatrice, daughter of the Rev T. F. Griffith, and had one daughter. Beatrice died soon after they reached Gibraltar in 1962. His second marriage was in 1963 to Joan Elspeth de Pechell, daughter of Colonel D. C. Scott. She was head of the Red Cross in Gibraltar.

LOUIS ALLEN

Louis Allen, broadcaster, Japanese scholar and former reader in French at Durham University, died on December 22, his 69th birthday. He was born on December 22, 1922.

LOUIS Allen, co-chairman of radio's *Round Britain Quiz*, could claim with some justice that he shortened the second world war in Burma without even firing a shot. His armaments were an old army typewriter and his own brilliant linguistic mind. It happened in 1945 when, as a young Intelligence Corps captain attached to No 4 mobile translation and interrogation section, he was handed a set of Japanese operational orders which had been captured by forward-based British army units. He subsequently unveiled a plan by enemy troops in the Yomas mountains behind Pegu to break

out east across the Sittang river and regroup with formations in Rangoon or Thailand.

Thanks to Allen's speed and skill as a translator, the British were waiting for them when they moved and 6,000 Japanese perished in the ensuing battle, the last major engagement in Burma. His crucial role in the Allied success was recognised by his being mentioned in dispatches and led to his account *Sittang: The Last Battle*, one of five books he wrote about the war in the Far East.

Allen was one of eight students who had been sent by the War Office to the School of Oriental and African Studies in 1943-4 on an intensive 18-month course in Japanese before being drafted as intelligence officers to the Far East. He invariably attended their annual reunions, the last of which took place in London last April. After the war, however, he switched from trying to outwit the Japanese to befriending them and developing his interest in their history and culture. He turned himself into a formidable oriental scholar, lecturing on Japanese military history in the United States and becoming president of the British Association of Japanese Studies in 1980. At the same time he worked to strengthen Anglo-Japanese understanding and for many years helped to organise visits by British war veterans to Japan and exchange tours by the Japanese to this country.

Allen was best known to the wider public as a broadcaster, mainly through the cerebral and long-running *Round Britain Quiz* and its sibling, *Transatlantic Quiz*. He took part in the former for many years as a member of the North of England team, then succeeded Lord Quinton as co-chairman in the early 1980s. But he was also a frequent contributor to the Radio 4 arts programme *Kaleidoscope*, delivering theatre and literary reviews.

These multifarious activities, however, were pursued in addition to Allen's principal career which was that of a French don at Durham University. Born at Middlesbrough, he was educated locally at St Mary's College, then Manchester University and the Sorbonne. After the war he was attached briefly to the British mission in Saigon, then became a Kemsley research fellow at his old university before taking a post on the staff at Durham — where he remained for the rest of his academic life.

His French scholarship was never suitably rewarded, perhaps because his radical approach and free-range interests led him outside the more traditional areas of study. He completed his MA thesis, for example, on the 20th-century South American-born French poet Supervielle and, though he published a schools edition of Beaumarchais, he concentrated on contemporary French writing. He had to wait a long time for his promotion to reader, but never seemed too disappointed by his failure to advance further or more quickly.

He was a stimulating, humorous teacher and a naturally gifted linguist. In addition to his French and Japanese, he knew some Arabic and most of the major European languages, including Russian. He was latterly an honorary fellow of the Northumbrian universities' East Asian Centre.

Louis Allen was a devout Roman Catholic. He wrote for *The Tablet* and his published works included a volume of Cardinal Newman's correspondence, *John Henry Newman and the Abbé Jeger*. His other books were: *Japan, the Years of Triumph*; *The End of the War in Asia*; *Singapore 1941-42*; and *Burma, the Longest War*.

He was a member of the general advisory council of the BBC and chairman of the north-east advisory council, 1969-75. Indeed, his range of interests and omniscience so impressed the poet, the late Roy Fuller, that Fuller dedicated a poem to him, "Strange Revelations", which appeared in his anthology *Consolations*.

He is survived by four sons and a daughter.

Index by classification

Academics

John Bardeen American physicist, co-inventor of the transistor and double Nobel prizewinner 19
Martin Ennals Secretary-general Amnesty International 1968–80 264
Dr James Fletcher Administrator of America's National Aeronautics and Space Administration (NASA) 342
Edwin Land The inventor of instant photography and founder of the Polaroid Corporation 39
Cynthia Longfield Entomologist 169
Jack Meyer Founder and first headmaster of Millfield School 50
Sir Terence Morrison-Scott Director of the British Museum 1960–68 318
Sir David Piper Director of the Ashmolean Museum, Oxford 1973–85 6
Lord Penney Creator of the British atom bomb 41

Armed Services

Marshal Sergei Akhromeyev Soviet soldier 218
Tom Beaumont Lawrence of Arabia's number one Vickers gunner during the campaign against the Turks in Palestine in 1917–18 232
Brigadier Lorne Campbell of Airds VC Argyll and Sutherland Highlander who won the VC for gallantry in North Africa 132
Rear Admiral Dudley Davenport Captain of the aircraft carrier HMS *Victorious* then Flag Officer Malta 3
Viscount De L'Isle VC Soldier, businessman, former government minister and Governor-General of Australia 78
Rear Admiral Royer Dick Wartime naval action afloat from first battle of the Falklands (1914) to command of HMS *Belfast* in Far East (1944) 104
George Eardley VC Infantry sergeant 231

Brigadier Sebert Green Soldier's life that was filled with adventure 108
Commander Hugh Haggard British wartime submarine captain 308
Colonel James Irwin American lunar astronaut 209
Admiral Sir Frederick Parham Former commander of HMS *Belfast* during hunt for German battleship *Scharnhorst* 59
General Sir Nigel Poett General Officer Commanding-in-Chief Far East Land Forces from 1961–63 278
Rear Admiral Philip Powlett Wartime destroyer captain 8
Parkash Singh VC Punjabi soldier who won VC medal in Burma 64
Captain Sir Aubrey St Clair-Ford His ship rescued Lord Mountbatten and later commanded HMS *Belfast* 88
Captain John Stevens British submarine commander 306
Lieut-Colonel Douglas Stewart Soldier and Olympic horseman 200
Brigadier Peter Thwaites Soldier, sportsman and playwright 130
Colonel 'Monty' Westropp Colonel 8th King's Own Royal Regiment 16
General Sir Dudley Ward Commander-in-Chief Rhine Army 346

Special Operations

William Buckley CIA head of station, Beirut 344
Yerocham Cohen Secret agent of Britain and later of Israel 238
Lieut-Colonel John Codrington Soldier and spymaster 106
Miles Copeland CIA agent and novelist 4
Xan Fielding Secret agent 214
Dodo Lees Nurse with the wartime Maquis, politician and journalist 217
John McCone Director CIA from 1961 to 1965 28
Vladimir Petrov Soviet spy who defected 160

351

Michael Pertwee Actor, screenwriter 90
Bertice Reading Blues singer 148
Lee Remick American actress 174
Tony Richardson English stage and film director 302
Eugene Roddenberry American creator of the *Star Trek* television series 272
Rudolf Serkin American pianist of Austrian birth 116
Don Siegel American film and television director 94
Olga Spessivtseva Russian ballet dancer 237
Gene Tierney Hollywood film actress 292
Thorley Walters British character actor 183
Bernie Winters Comedian 110

Politicians and Diplomats

Shapour Bakhtiar Last prime minister under the Shah of Iran 206
Raymond Blackburn Former Labour MP and campaigner 286
Alick Buchanan-Smith Conservative MP for Kincardine and Deeside 222
Baroness Burton of Coventry Labour MP for Coventry South 1950–59, life peer from 1962 266
Rajiv Gandhi Prime Minister of India from 1984–89 122
Sir Ronald Gardner-Thorpe Lord Mayor of London 1980–81 332
Baroness Hart of South Lanark Labour cabinet minister 329
Eric Heffer Labour MP for Liverpool Walton division 126
Russell Hinze Australian politician 172
Gustáv Husák Former President of Czechoslovakia 1975–89 310
Sir Gilbert Inglefield Lord Mayor of London 1967–68 274
Sir John Kerr Governor-General of Australia 1974–77 who dismissed Premier 61
Paulo Muwanga Vice-president of Uganda 72

Sir Godfrey Nicholson Conservative MP for Farnham 1937 to 1966 178
Frank Rizzo Mayor of Philadelphia 186
Mario Scelba Prime Minister of Italy 1954–55 280
Joey Smallwood Premier Newfoundland 340
Robert Wagner Mayor of New York from 1954–65 25
Sir Bernard Waley-Cohen Lord Mayor of London 1960–61 176
Sir Roy Welensky Prime Minister of the Federation of Rhodesia and Nyasaland 322

Relatives

Oona Chaplin Widow of Charlie Chaplin 252
Jiang Qing Widow of Mao Tse-Tung 118
James Roosevelt Eldest son of President Roosevelt 212
Viscountess Stansgate Religious campaigner and member of the distinguished political family 270

Royalty

King Olav V King of Norway from 1957 to 1991 10

Sports

Cliff Bastin Arsenal and England footballer 325
Jack "Kid" Berg World welterweight boxing champion 98
Freddie Brown England cricket captain 196
Peter Kane World flyweight boxing champion 187
Farnham Maxwell Trainer who won the Ascot Gold Cup three times 139
Gordon Pirie Athlete who set five world records between 1953 and 1956 334

Tyrants

Index

356